Monographs in Visual Communication

David F. Rogers
Editor

Monographs in Visual Communication

Hall: Illumination and Color in Computer Generated Imagery
von Bechtolsheim : TEX in Practice, Volume I: Basics
von Bechtolsheim : TEX in Practice, Volume II: Paragraphs, Math, and Fonts
von Bechtolsheim : TEX in Practice, Volume III: Tokens, Macros
von Bechtolsheim : TEX in Practice, Volume IV: Output Routines, Tables

Stephan von Bechtolsheim

TEX in Practice

Volume I:
Basics

Springer-Verlag
New York Berlin Heidelberg London
Paris Tokyo Hong Kong Barcelona Budapest

Stephan von Bechtolsheim
c/o Springer-Verlag New York
175 Fifth Avenue
New York, NY 10010
USA

Library of Congress Cataloging-in-Publication Data
Bechtolsheim, Stephan von
TEX in practice / Stephan von Bechtolsheim
p. cm. (Monographs in visual communication)
On t.p. E is subscript
Includes bibliographical references and indices.
Contents: v. 1. Basics v. 2. Math and fonts v. 3. Tokens, macros v. 4. Output routines, tables.
ISBN 0-387-97595-0 (Springer-Verlag New York Berlin Heidelberg: v. 1). ISBN 3-540-97595-0 (Springer-Verlag Berlin New York Heidelberg: v. 1)
1. TeX (computer system) 2. Computerized typesetting 3. Mathematics printing. I. Title. II. Series.
Z253.4.T47B4 1992
686.2"2544 dc20 90-10034

Printed on acid-free paper.

Production supervised by Kenneth Dreyhaupt, manufacturing coordinated by Vincent Scelta.
Photocomposed copy prepared from the author's TEX files.
Printed and bound by R.R. Donnelley & Sons, Inc., Harrisonburg, Virginia.
Printed in the United States of America.

9 8 7 6 5 4 3 2

ISBN 0-387-97595-0 Springer-Verlag New York Berlin Heidelberg
ISBN 3-540-97595-0 Springer-Verlag Berlin Heidelberg New York
ISBN 0-387-97296-X (4-vol. set) Springer-Verlag New York Berlin Heidelberg
ISBN 3-540-97296-X (4-vol. set) Springer-Verlag Berlin Heidelberg New York

To my two grandmothers
who have always been there.

The present letter is a very long one, simply because I had no leisure to make it shorter.

Blaise Pascal

Preface

Although you only have one volume in front of you, writing four volumes and 1600 pages on a single subject needs some form of justification. And then on the other hand, why write even more?! Can't, at least, the preface of something that long be short?!

Very well, so let's keep it short. It is my sincere hope that the series "TeX in Practice" will be useful for your own TeX work. But *please*, before you get started, read the "Notes on 'TeX in Practice'," because it instructs you how to use this series. You will find these notes on pages xxxi–xl.

The first volume of this series discusses the very basics of TeX, that is, characters, registers, boxes, glue, rules and so forth. These are the *very basics* of TeX. It is useful to discuss these basic aspects of TeX because their understanding allows you to use TeX to its full potential.

Stephan von Bechtolsheim

Arlington Heights, Illinois
May 1993

Table of Contents

List of Figures

List of Tables

Acknowledgements

A long list of people is what a long book deserves. So let's get started.

My editors, Kim Miller (who did the bulk of the work) as well as Kris Schlenker and Judith Lewis, tried patiently to make this series sound like "real English." If it doesn't sound right always, blame me (a quote from one of my students: "by now you are probably *bilingually illiterate*"). Last minute corrections on my part may also have introduced errors.

At Purdue University Chris Hoffman and Bob Lynch (Computer Sciences Department), Mark Senn (Statistics Department; by the way he is the person who brought TeX to Purdue), and Steve Samuels (also Statistics Department) helped; there was also Ed Ramsey (National Pesticide Center of Purdue University) who let me use his SPARCStation to process this series. Clients of mine such as Siemens-Nixdorf Corporation (Jörg Heinemann, Joachim Haenel, Bernd Stümke), Jörg Steffenhagen, of Munich, West Germany, and Technical Typesetting, Inc. (Bill Taylor and Harry Kirk) located in Philadelphia allowed me to publish macros I had developed for them. Gerhard Rossbach, Mark Hall, and Rüdiger Gebauer of Springer-Verlag all waited patiently for me to finish my series. Dave Rogers (United States Naval Academy, Anapolis) gave some valuable hints. Chris Thompson (Cambridge University Computing Service) and Thomas Reid (Computing Services Center, Texas A&M University) provided some input too. A.C. Conrad of the Menil Foundation in Houston hired me as a consultant. Some of the TeX problems I solved for him found their way into this series. I used Oliver Schoett's idea (Institut für Informatik, TU München, München (or should I have written "Munich"), Federal Republic of Germany), designing macro `\PrintHyphens`. One of the tables in the table chapters was submitted to me by Cynthia Rodriguez, Computer Center, University of Illinois at Chicago. Michael Doob, University of Manitoba in Canada, helped with a problem in the output routine chapters. Kabelschacht's article (Kabelschacht (1987)) was used in a chapter in this series.

To thank Donald E. Knuth, the author of TeX and METAFONT, warrants a separate paragraph, in particular, because he replied to my mail instantaneously even after he had announced that he would not be involved in the further development of TeX. Not only that, *he* provided TeX to all of us! Thank you *very much.*

Leslie Lamport also deserves special mentioning. When I started to write this series, there were plenty of things I did not understand. For instance, verbatim mode was one of the things I initially simply ignored. What I did was rather straightforward: I started to write this series using LaTeX. As time proceeded I replaced one part of LaTeX after another by my own macros. You will probably also recognize some macro names in this series which remind you of LaTeX macro names such as `\Section` (written `\section` in LaTeX) and `\normalsize` (called the same in LaTeX). Even now some of the diagrams are done with LaTeX's picture environment. Other things I stole / borrowed / adopted include the definition of macro `\frac`, the idea of a font selection scheme which separates size and type face, etc.

Victor Eijkhout, Center for Supercomputing Research and Development, University of Illinois at Urbana-Champaign, also deserves his own paragraph: he actually went through the whole series. Maybe he did not read every page, but he certainly read *almost* every page. There were a lot of little things he pointed out to me.

Of course, what would be a series on TeX without mentioning Barbara Beeton of the American Mathematical Society in Providence, Rhode Island, who helped me with a lot of small details. Ray Goucher of the TeX Users Group, who was a good boss while I taught classes for the TeX Users Group, deserves acknowledgement too.

Addison-Wesley gave permission to reprint and distribute (in modified form) some macros of the TeXbook (see 16.8, p. II-297). Penguin Books gave permission to use Shakespeare (1605) for examples in Chapter 10 (this material is in the public domain, but I thought you might want to know where I got it from).

The Free Software Foundation must be mentioned too, because it provides the GNU Emacs to which I am addicted by now. GNU Emacs is the only editor you want to use after you have used it a couple of times. It certainly has done wonders for me. I designed my own "TeX-mode" and that made the tedious task of editing hundreds of pages much more tolerable.

Finally my current employer (Datalogics Incorporated in Chicago, a subsidiary of Frame Technology of San Jose, California) allowed me to use one of their printers for printing the last n revisions of this series ($n < 10$).

Trademarks

The following trademarks are used in this series.

TeX is a trademark of the American Mathematical Society; METAFONT is a trademark of Addison-Wesley Publishing Company; POSTSCRIPT is a trademark of Adobe Systems Incorporated; UNIX is a registered trademark of AT&T; DEC, VAX, and VMS are registered trademarks of Digital Equipment Cooperation; Apple LaserWriter, Macintosh are trademarks of Apple, Inc.; IBM is a registered trademark of International Business Machines Corporation; HP LaserJet is a trademark of Hewlett Packard; SUN is a trademark of Sun Micro Systems, Inc.; Mercedes is a registered trademark of Mercedes-Benz AG, Stuttgart, Federal Republic of Germany; SPARC is a registered trademark of SPARC International, Inc., licensed exclusively to Sun Microsystems, Inc.; SPARCStation is a registered trademark of Sun Microsystems, Inc.; Porsche is a registered trademark of Dr. Ing. h.c. F. Porsche AG.

Other brand or product names are the trademarks or registered trademarks of their respective holders.

A Note About the Dedication

I would like to explain briefly the dedication of my books to my grandmothers. My maternal grandmother was a fairly wealthy woman, but also a very generous woman (the first trait alone wouldn't have done me any good). Among many other things, before I left in June 1980 for the United States to become a student at Purdue University, she invited me to come home for the following Christmas. So she did, and it was not the last time that she paid for my trips back and forth between Germany and the United States. And with all her generosity, she was a very modest person when it came to herself. She died in October of 1989 after a very long illness, blind for many years, without ever complaining about her health.

My other grandmother is the type of person you can go to day and night and always find a friendly and warm reception. I spent many happy hours in my grandparent's house, and I always felt understood and appreciated without having to explain myself. More than anyone else she trusted my judgements and believed in me.

Stephan von Bechtolsheim

Arlington Heights, Illinois
May 1993

General Notes on "TEX in Practice"

This part of the book contains some general comments about the series "TEX in Practice." It is reprinted in the beginning of every volume of this series and provides kind of a "general introduction and series-wide table of contents." I urge you to read the following material carefully.

1 Some Friendly Advice Up Front Or What To Do If You Hate to Read Lots of Material

If you hate to read lots of material you are in trouble, obviously. But here are some hints anyway (who knows whether you even read this paragraph ...):

- Continue reading this part, "General Notes on 'TEX in Practice'," please, please.
- Quickly look through the tables of contents of all four volumes. I suggest limiting yourself to reading the title of all chapters and sections, but to ignore subsections and further subdivisions.
- Read the overview of all chapters on p. xxxiii.

Thank you!

2 Terminology, Conventions, Other General Remarks

Let me make some general comments about the terminology used in "TEX in Practice" and some conventions I followed.

1. The series "TEX in Practice" is subdivided into *four volumes.* Each volume is identified by a *capital Roman numeral.* Each volume is subdivided into *chapters.* Chapters are identified by *arabic numerals* and numbered across volumes. Each chapter is further subdivided into *sections* (the second section of chapter 12 would be numbered 12.2), and sections, in turn, are divided into *subsections* (the fourth subsection of section 12.2 would be numbered 12.2.4). There are also *subsubsections*, which are numbered accordingly.

   Note that in cross-references to sections, subsections, and subsubsections the words section, subsection or subsubsection respectively are dropped. So a reference to Section 12.3 might read "see 12.3, p. 23, for further details." References to other entities like chapters, figures or tables are "spelled out" that is a reference to a figure might read "Fig. 3.4."
2. Arabic page numbers are used with the exception of the preliminaries of each volume in which Roman page numbers are used. The page numbering starts at page 1 in every volume.

   In references to page numbers, the volume number precedes the page number; in references to the *current* volume the volume number is dropped. For instance, "p. 23" refers to page 23 in the current volume, and "p. I-12" refers to page 12 of the first volume (in any volume other than the first).
3. The table of contents of each volume lists all chapters, sections and subsections of the volume, but not the subsubsections.
4. "TEX in Practice" tries to give a comprehensive and detailed view of TEX, but it does *not* claim to be complete. For very tricky questions I suggest that you first consult this series, but then also look into the TEXbook. I hope that reading this series will make understanding the TEXbook much easier, but I skip over some of the more bizarre details (which the TEXbook does not).
5. In this series I need to occasionally refer to the series itself. I do so using the expression "this series."
6. In general in this series I refer to TEX 3.0. The extensions implemented in TEX 3.0 are described in Knuth (1990). Note that TEXbooks published prior to 1990 do not contain a description of these extensions. The 3.0 extensions are minor, but nevertheless important. In some instances I will identify those differences by a short phrase such as "a TEX 3.0 feature" to identify a TEX 3.0 extension (*not all* such extensions are identified as such).

3 The Intended Audience of "TEX in Practice"

Let me now discuss whom this series was written for. The more of the following statements apply to you, the better:

- You want to learn TEX thoroughly because you have to typeset complicated documents. Your text might include mathematical formulas and tables; both areas are very well covered by TEX.

- You are a curious person: when you use a tool (and TEX, of course, is a typesetting tool), then you wish to *understand* the tool. You do *not* only want to apply it.
- You believe that having lots of examples will allow you to understand something better. This series contains plenty of examples.
- You think that designing your own macros is something you may want to do, now or in future, because none of the existing macro packages fulfill your needs precisely. This series should come in handy, because it already contains the basics of a fairly sophisticated macro package plus it contains many basic utility type of macro definitions.
- You recognize that WYSIWYG (What-You-See-Is-What-You-get) systems, where your typeset output is immediately displayed on the screen, are limited in their power in that they cannot be easily adopted to specialized needs.

  Also note, that WYSIWYG systems cannot solve the real problem of writing, that is to present thoughts in an orderly and organized fashion, either. Owning a Porsche doesn't make you necessarily a good driver (though probably a happy one), if you know what I mean.

4 A Brief Overview of "TEX in Practice"

The series "TEX in Practice" is divided into four volumes. An overview of each volume follows.

1. Volume I:

   - Chapter 1 explains the existing relationship in the complexities of problems and tools to solve these problems. It explains that the complexity of TEX is a direct consequence of its power.
   - Chapter 2 provides a general introduction into TEX. It explains the basics of entering data into TEX and processing a document.
   - Chapter 3 begins the discusses of registers concentrating on counter registers primarily. Generic counter macros are discussed and an overview of all TEX's parameters is given.
   - Chapter 4 continues the register discussion looking at dimension registers and box registers. Also glue registers are discussed
   - Chapter 5 discusses glue (a very important concept of TEX), rules and leaders.
   - Chapter 6 discusses horizontal boxes. This is important in itself and also forms the basis of the discussion of the following two chapters. We also discuss how to do tables using hboxes.
   - Chapter 7 discusses vertical boxes, their dimensions, and different types line spacing and struts.
   - Chapter 8 discusses more advanced concepts relating to vertical boxes such as `\vsplit` and the shifting of reference points of vboxes.

- Chapter 9 discusses boxes and rules and introduces macros to draw rules around boxes. Boxes with rules are a very useful debugging feature of TeX.

2. Volume II:

- Chapter 10 discusses how paragraphs are built. You find the very basics of typesetting text in this chapter.
- Chapter 11 continues the discussion of the previous chapter and shows how more complex paragraph shapes are typeset.
- Chapter 12 concludes the discussion of the typesetting of paragraphs.
- Chapter 13 discusses the basics of typesetting mathematical formulas.
- Chapter 14 continues the discussion of typesetting mathematical formulas.
- Chapter 15 discusses fonts. This discussion includes an introduction to the Computer Modern fonts and how special fonts can be used in TeX.
- Chapter 16 continues the discussion of fonts. A major point in this chapter is the proper organization of fonts.
- Chapter 17 deals with the "environment" of TeX. This includes the discussion of METAFONT and the WEB system.

3. Volume III:

- Chapter 18 discusses tokens, grouping and category codes. You will also find an explanation of verbatim modes.
- Chapter 19 continues the discussion of the previous chapter explaining cross-referencing, list macros, and the use of token registers.
- Chapter 20 discusses token lists and arrays.
- Chapter 21 explains the basics of macro definitions, based on `\def` with delimited and undelimited parameters.
- Chapter 22 continues the discussion with macro definitions based on `\edef`, nested macro definitions and goes into more details about macro arguments.
- Chapter 23 discusses `\let`, `\futurelet` and `\afterassignment`.
- Chapter 24 discusses `\expandafter` and its applications as well as `\the`.
- Chapter 25 discusses conditionals.
- Chapter 26 discusses date and calendar related macros.
- Chapter 27 discusses more additional macro related issues such as recursion, environments and error handling.
- Chapter 28 discusses input and output. This includes a discussion of delayed and immediate writes, writing of table of contents files, and literal writing.
- Chapter 29 continues the preceding chapter discussing index file and verbatim file macros. It also discusses table of contents and endnotes generation.
- Chapter 30 discusses how the partial processing of a document can be administered (one document's text is stored in separate files which also

   should be processed separately).
   - Chapter 31 continues the discussion of the preceding macro. It in particular offers some rather sophisticated and interesting cross-reference macros.

4. Volume IV:

   - Chapter 32 begins the discussion of tables typeset with TEX's `\halign` instruction.
   - Chapter 33 also discusses tables, including vertical spacing, struts and rules in tables.
   - Chapter 34 discusses the centering of tables, tables and paragraphs and preamble related macros.
   - Chapter 35 discusses numerical computations in tables, splitting tables, `\valign` and double tables.
   - Chapter 36 discusses the determination of page breaks by TEX.
   - Chapter 37 discusses the basics of output routines, and introduces concepts like logical and physical pages.
   - Chapter 38 presents some simple output routines.
   - Chapter 39 discusses the output routine of the plain format and variations of it.
   - Chapter 40 discusses output routines with insertions.
   - Chapter 41 discusses double column output routines.

Each volume furthermore contains two prefaces, the first one is common to all volumes, the second one is a preface particular to the specific volume. The bibliography and the acknowledgements are identical in all volumes as is the "General Notes on 'TEX in Practice,'" the part you are currently reading.

One other brief point: I found it *extremely* difficult to present TEX in a linear order, without forward references. There is of course the possibility of making two or three passes over a subject such as TEX, each time with increasing difficulty. If I had done that, this series would have become even longer. At least in the approach I took I found it unavoidable and regrettable to have a fair number of forward references.

5 Using the Macros Presented in "TEX in Practice"

I hope that the macros presented in this series are useful, and that you will actually apply these macros. Here are some general comments about these macros, how they should be used, and so forth.

1. All macro source files presented in this series have the file extension `.tip` for "TEX in Practice." The file extension `.tex` is *not* used by any of the macro

source files. Some of the example source files use file extension `.tex`.

I *ask* everyone to *not* use the file extension `.tip` for any files other than the files of this series. I also ask you to *not* change any of the source code files of this series. If you need to change any of the published macro source code files (which you are encouraged to do, because one of the main purposes of this series is to use all the presented macros), then please *rename* the file you are using, and please also *change the file extension* at that point.

2. There are three classes of TeX source files presented in this series:

   - *Published* files. Those are those files, which are available to you in machine readable form. The published macro source files are identified by a $\mathcal{P}$ in the line preceding the beginning of the source code listing. The file names of these files are at most 8 characters long, a restriction which is probably useful for the PC environment.

     Here is an example of a published source code file.

     $\mathcal{P}$ • `publish.tip` •

```
\def\SampleMacro{%
    ... Sample of a macro which is published on a diskette.
}
```

     • End of `publish.tip` •

   - Most of the published files are pre-loaded as part of the `texip` format which is defined in 31.3, p. III-612. Those macros *need not* be loaded, *if* the format defined at the given reference is used. Those macros are marked by a $\mathcal{P}'$.

     See item 13, p. xxxix, for some additional information.
   - *Unpublished* files. In most cases unpublished files are example files, which apply one or more of the published files. These files are obviously *not* marked by $\mathcal{P}$.

3. The file names of those macro source files, which were designed particularly for the publication of this series, start with "`ts-`," which stands for "TeX in Practice Series."
4. To get your own copy of the published macro source files contact one of the following places:

   (a) The TeX Users Group (see further below for the address).
   (b) Your favorite TeX supplier.
   (c) The standard places for TeX source code on the networks, if you are hooked up to one of the national or international networks.

   If you acquire those macros commercially, you must *not* be charged any fee other than a nominal fee for media and shipping (the same way you do not have to pay extra for the plain format or LaTeX macro source files). One more request: if you modify a macro, you are required to rename it, even if the modification is minor. With the exception of the conditions laid down in this paragraph you can do anything reasonable with these macros you want.
5. The following additional information applies, in particular, if you retrieve

the macro source files using a network (I try to establish a convention here and I hope everyone will follow it).

(a) The macros will be stored in a separate subdirectory called **`texip`** (all lower case).

(b) With the macros comes a file **`readme.tip`** which you should read first. This file contains the following information:

   i. A release date of all macros.

   ii. A version number for all the macros together. This version number is a "combined" version number of all individual macro source files: it is the maximum version number of any individual source file's version number.

   iii. A short history of the changes made to any of the macro source files.

   iv. A complete list of *all macro source files* and their version numbers listed in *alphabetical order.*

6. Every macro source file starts out with the same standardized text, which reads as follows (the last four lines are, of course, different from file to file, also note that the file name such as `reg2.TEX` as well as the line numbers refer to my own source code files and are therefore of secondary interest for the user of the macros in this series):

```
1  % This macro source file is from the four volume series
2  % "TeX in Practice" by Stephan von Bechtolsheim, published
3  % 1993 by Springer-Verlag, New York.
4  % Copyright 1993 Stephan von Bechtolsheim.
5  % No warranty or liability is assumed.
6  % This macro may be copied freely if no fees other than
7  % media cost or shipping charges are charged and as long
8  % as this copyright and the following source code itself
9  % is not changed. Please see the series for further information.
10 %
11 % Version 1.0
12 % Date: May 1, 1993
13 %
14 %
15 % This source code is documented in 4.1.11, p. I-91.
16 % Original source in file "reg2.TEX", starting line 587.
17 \wlog{L: "absdimen.tip" ["reg2.TEX," l. 587, p. I-91]}%
18 % This file DOES belong to format "texip."
```

The previous text is 18 lines long. The text is *not* reprinted in the series itself anywhere else, in particular not with every source code listing. Therefore, to synchronize the line numbers of the source code as listed in this series and the source code of the `.tip` files, all *listings* of published source code files start with line 19, rather than line 1.

7. To *use* any of these macros, *always* use the following approach:

   (a) First load file `inputd.tip` using `\input` (only only):

```
\input inputd.tip
```

(b) Next load all macro files you want to load by calling the macro `\InputD` (do *not* use `\input` to load any `.tip` macro source files with the exception of `inputd.tip`). The `\InputD` macro has one parameter, `#1`, the name of a source code file to load.

For instance, to load file `box-mac.tip`, enter `\InputD{box-mac.tip}`. Do *not* omit the file extension `tip`. The beginning of your TeX source file would now look as follows:

```
\input inputd.tip
\InputD{box-mac.tex}
```

More `\InputD` calls could follow at this point.

8. Note that this series defines a format which has most of the relevant macros defined in this series pre-loaded. See 31.3, p. III-612, for details.
9. The series contains the reprint of numerous log files. The version of the TeX program I was running for the processing of this series was changed to print shortened log file lines to accommodate the width of the pages in this series.
10. In case you use LaTeX with any of my macros, you should not have any problems. Enter the instruction to load `inputd.tip` and the subsequent calls of the input macro `\InputD` *after* the `\documentstyle` command and *before* `\begin{document}`.

    Here is a brief example of what your LaTeX source code file might look like:

```
\documentstyle{article}
\input inputd.tip
\InputD{box-mac.tip}
\InputD{...}
...                 % Your macros and initializations go here.
\begin{document}
    ...
\end{document}
```

Two more remarks about using these macros with LaTeX:

(a) Be aware that LaTeX uses `\everypar`. Therefore, if you use any of the macros from this series which change `\everypar`, you must be aware of potential conflicts.

(b) The plain format and LaTeX both have a `\line` macro with two totally different and unrelated meanings.

11. Remember, this series teaches you how to use TeX. The macros do *not* form a complete format including style files. In a typical application you will load macros and then write yourself additional macros. This series is like a cookbook: you find lots of recipes, but you still need to get out the utensils yourself, decide on the menu and clean up later. If you need something ready to use I suggest using LaTeX.
12. I cannot assume any *liability* for the macros. But I did my best to provide error free code. Please contact me in case you find any errors (in the source

code of the presented macros or otherwise in this series). The next Section contains my address.

13. If loading individual macros, etc., seems to be a little cumbersome to you, we provide to you (as part of the macros) a special file called `texip-ex.tip` (the file name stands for `texip.tip`, expanded). Here the word expanded means that this is *one* macro source file, which (with the exception of `plain.tex`) contains *all* macro source files marked with $\mathcal{P}'$.

    Whether you run `initex` on `texip.tip` (which loads another 200 or so files) or run `initex` directly on `texip-ex.tip` does not make any difference as far as the end result is concerned. It's just easier in that if you just pick up `texip-ex.tip` from somewhere then you don't need to pick up other files, at least initially.

    I suggest that if you use `texip-ex.tip` that you rename the resulting `.fmt` file from `texip-ex.fmt` to `texip.fmt`.

6 Contacting the Author

If you wish to get in touch with me, please write to the following address. I am interested in your feedback, suggestions, clarifications, corrections and so forth. After all, one of *your* suggestions may make it into the second edition (if there is such)! Please, *write* or *send email.* Do *not* call, and please *do not* use of Springer's FAX numbers. Please do not contact me at my current employer.

Here is the address at which I can be contacted:

Stephan von Bechtolsheim
Springer-Verlag
175 Fifth Avenue
New York, NY 10010
Email: `texip@cs.purdue.edu`

The above email address will either forward to me or to someone at Springer-Verlag who will subsequently get in touch with me.

7 TeX Users Group

TeX is a great product and it's free! I do encourage you to show your support by joining the TeX Users Group, which can be contacted at the following address:

TeX Users Group
P.O. Box 869
Santa Barbara, CA 93102
(805) 899 4673
Internet: `tug@math.ams.com`

Corrections to this series will be distributed by the TeX Users Group. This is yet another reason to join this organization.

8 Rewriting Code for Improved Readability

Let me point out that I took the liberty of reformatting plain format macro code for improved readability. For instance, to set a register (counter or dimension register) to zero, the plain format declares a dimension register `\@z` which is initialized to zero:

```
\newdimen\z@
\z@ = 0pt
```

This register can be used to set another register, let's say `\dimen0`, to zero, as in `\dimen0 = \z@`. This, in turn, can be abbreviated to `\dimen0 \z@`. The *dimension* register `\z@` can also be used to set a *counter* registers to zero, as in `\count0 = \z@`. Finally, `\z@` can be used in place of a number 0, that is you can write `\count3 = \z@` or `\count3 \z@`, for short. This method of using `\z@` has also the advantage that no space needs to be written after the constant.

Now back to the changes to the plain format macros I applied in this series, when I reprint any plain format macro or macros. For instance, `\z@` is used in the definition of `\allowbreak` as follows:

```
\def\allowbreak{\penalty\z@}
```

In this series though, I state that this macro is defined as follows:

```
\def\allowbreak{\penalty 0 }
```

I think the second form of presenting this macro is more *readable*, and this is really all that this is about. I prefer readability and clarity in computer code over efficiency.

9 Summary

I hope you have a good time reading this series.

1
Before We Get Started

Let me begin with some initial remarks about TEX. TEX is such an exciting (but also sometimes tricky) program that one needs to discuss briefly what's ahead.

1.1 What Is TEX?

TEX is a computerized programmable formatting system. It facilitates the typesetting of text, mathematical formulas and tables. It is a *programmable* system, which means that the user enters the text together with instructions on how this text should be typeset. TEX then reads the input and does the typesetting.

TEX is a very powerful and general system. You will be amazed at what you can do with it, after you have learned how to use it. On the other hand, because of its power, it is a little more difficult to master than other formatting systems. But be patient, it's worth all the effort. The power and flexibility of TEX is awesome, and I hope that this series will help you to conquer it.

TEX's has many reasons, of which the most important are:

- TEX is very powerful, flexible and general.
- TEX is in the public domain. It has been ported to many different machines, from main frames over workstations to PCs. These implementations (and any of the additional software needed) are, for the most part, available for free or a nominal fee only.
- TEX's output is not restricted to one particular unit. It can be printed on laser printers and film (using phototypesetters), and it can be displayed on high-resolution bit-mapped displays connected to computers.
- TEX's typesetting quality is superb. Its typesetting of mathematical equations is, in particular, appealing.
- TEX has a powerful macro mechanism that allows the user to extend TEX's functionality in many different ways.

1.2 Complexity and Power of Systems

TEX is a little more complex (and a lot more powerful) than many other typesetting systems.

The issue of complexity versus power reveals an underlying law in nature that shows up here and cannot be defeated, and that is, *in order to solve problems of a certain complexity you need tools with a certain minimum functionality, which results in a certain minimum complexity of those tools themselves.*

For instance, you cannot use your bicycle to fly to the moon, and even your car or an airplane wouldn't do it. Those machines are simply not powerful enough. If you look at the Apollo system, a system to fly to the moon, then you have a sufficiently powerful system. You also have a fairly complex system. You may argue that certain components of the Apollo system could have been implemented more simply, but you would not be able to reduce the overall complexity of this system by an order of magnitude without affecting its functionality.

This principle also applies to a typesetting system: if you require such a system to do a lot, it will be more complicated than if you require it to do less. For instance, TEX would be simpler without its mathematical formula typesetting commands, but then you couldn't typeset mathematical formulas as conveniently as you can with TEX's math typesetting features. The list of examples go on and on, but to make a long story short:

> With TEX you have a very powerful system, which is a little more complex than other typesetting systems! **You just can't have it both ways, that is, a very simple system doing a lot of things!**

While you are learning TEX, there may be some rough days ahead of you. Remember to have fun, it's all worth the effort.

1.3 Summary

In this Chapter we learned:

- TEX is a complex computerized typesetting system which is very powerful and fully programmable producing beautiful output.
- TEX is available on a large variety of machines.
- To learn TEX is not easy, but it's worth the effort.

2
Processing with TEX

The purpose of this chapter is to familiarize the reader with the basics of TEX. I discuss how a document is processed through TEX and how it is printed afterwards. I explain TEX in a natural top-down approach. I also discuss the handling of characters that are special to TEX and give an overview of those characters and their meaning in the context of TEX.

2.1 Properties and Capabilities of TEX

Let us first discuss the basic properties and capabilities of TEX:

1. Since TEX is a *programmable* typesetting system, the text to be typeset is mixed with instructions controlling the typesetting process. TEX is *not* a WYSIWYG (What-You-See-Is-What-You-Get) system. You therefore do *not* see the typeset form of your input immediately on your screen.

   Because TEX is not a WYSIWYG system, the text and the typesetting instructions in the text must be processed by the TEX program, before the result can be printed or viewed on a screen.
2. The capabilities of TEX include the typesetting of
   (a) *Text*,
   (b) *Mathematical formulas* and
   (c) *Tables*.
3. TEX has no built-in capabilities for the generation of *diagrams* and *graphs*, but simple diagrams and graphs can generated. The best examples for this is the picture environment of LATEX in Lamport (1985). All the diagrams contained in this series were generated using the picture environment of LATEX.
4. Seen from a computer scientist's point of view, TEX is a *special purpose programming language* that is based on *macro expansion* with *instructions for the typesetting of documents*.

2.1.1 A Convention About Input and Output of TEX

In this chapter as well as everywhere else in this series, the following convention is followed: *input* (entered by the user into a file for typesetting) is reprinted using TEX's typewriter font, as, for instance, in `sample input`. The *output* is show exactly the way it comes out when processed by TEX and, if the text is rather short, it is enclosed in quotes.

2.1.2 The Structure of TEX's Input

TEX requires the user to enter two different types of information into a text file:

1. *The text.* If you want to print "the weather is nice" then enter `the weather is nice` into a text file.
2. *Formatting instructions* or *TEX instructions.* These instructions tell TEX how the text should be typeset. They come in various flavors as the following examples illustrate.

   (a) *Most* of TEX's instructions start with a backslash (\), which in TEX is also called the *escape character.*

      i. `\bf` prints the following text in **boldface**,
      ii. `\it` prints the following text in *italic*,
      iii. `\tt` prints the following text in `typewriter font`,
      iv. `\bye` is an instruction at the end of a document to tell TEX that the end of a document is reached,
      v. `\TeX` prints the TEX logo.

   (b) *Other* typesetting instructions do *not* start with a backslash. Here are some examples:

      i. Inline mathematical formulas, that is, mathematical formulas that appear inside the text of a paragraph, are enclosed by `$`'s. To print the formula $a = b - c$ input `$a=b-c$`.
      ii. The "^" is the symbol for superscripts in mathematical formulas and the underscore "_" is the symbol for subscripts. Enclose the superscript or subscript value in curly braces. Here are three examples:

Input	Output
`$a^{2}$`	a^2
`$a_{2i-1}$`	a_{2i-1}
`$x^{t}_{i-1}$`	x^{t}_{i-1}

      iii. Curly braces "{" and "}" are not only used to enclose superscripts and subscripts in mathematical formulas (see example above), but are also used in the definition of macros (see the next Subsection) and in grouping. When used for grouping, curly braces enclose a change (for instance, a font change) and they limit the change to the text within curly braces.

2.1.3 The Extensibility of TEX

There is a basic set of instructions provided to you by TEX, called *primitives*. You are allowed to *add instructions* through the definition of macros. For example, `\def\name{X. Y. Miller}` defines the control sequence `\name`. After this definition is entered each `\name` in the input will be replaced by `X. Y. Miller`, that is if you input `my name is \name`, TEX will print "my name is X. Y. Miller."

2.1.4 Processing a Document with TEX

Here is a step-by-step explanation of how the text is entered into a file, processed by TEX, and then printed. For a graphical representation of this process see Fig. 2.1 on the next page.

1. *Edit TEX source file.* The text to be typeset, together with its TEX instructions, is entered into a file with the help of a program called an *editor*. An *editor* is a program that allows you to enter and change text stored in a file.
   The file being edited is called the *TEX source file* or *source file* for short. Normally it has the *file extension* "`.tex`." If you stored your text in the file `paper.tex` then `paper` is called the *base name* of this file name.
2. *Run TEX.* The text is now processed by TEX. This is normally done by a command like `tex` ⟨file name⟩. In our case the command would be `tex paper.tex`, or simply `tex paper` (TEX appends the file extension `.tex` automatically in the second case). This step results in the generation of two files:
   - A log file, which is a record of TEX's processing containing warning messages.
   - A `dvi` file (device independent), that contains the typeset document in an (output) device independent way.
3. *Analyze log file.* You now analyze the log file generated by TEX. This file contains important information, especially error messages. If an error occurred one goes back to steps 1 and 2 to correct and run the source file again.
   The file extension of log files is normally "`.log`" (sometimes also "`.lis`"). In this case the log file's file name is `paper.log` (`paper.lis`).

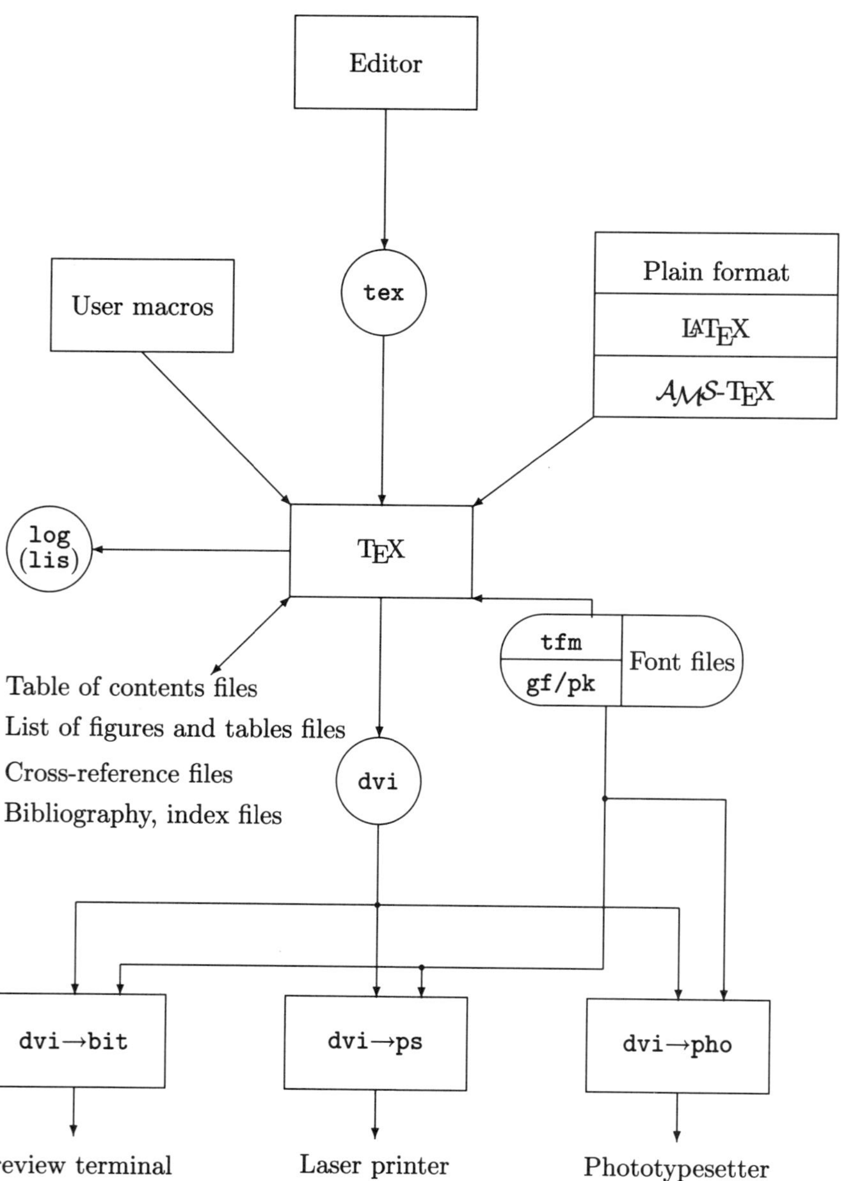

Figure 2.1. Processing documents using TEX.

4. *Preview or print the* `dvi` *file.* TEX also generates a `dvi` file. The abbreviation "`dvi`" stands for deviceindependent. A typical command to print a document might be `dvipr file.dvi` where `dvipr` stands for dvi print. In our case you would issue the command `dvipr paper.dvi`. This can be usually abbreviated to `dvipr paper` in which case `dvipr` supplies the file extension `.dvi`. Some users also have the capability to preview their output on the screen using a command such as `preview paper.dvi`. Again writing `preview paper` (without file extension) is usually sufficient.

Fig. 2.1 on the previous page shows the way a document is entered into a TEX source file with the help of an editor and processed by TEX. The resulting `dvi` file can be printed using different types of *drivers* leading to output on different devices. TEX furthermore reads in user macros and format macros (such as macros of the plain format). TEX takes its font information from `tfm` files. Drivers (which sometime also access `tfm` files) usually require access to the pixel patterns of characters which can be found in `gf` or `pk` files. All of this will be explained in detail later.

2.2 Macros, Macro Packages and Formats

2.2.1 Some Basic Terminology

Let me start with some important basic definitions in the context of TEX. The meaning of the terms presented now will become much more clear as you continue to read.

What I call the *pure* version of TEX is a version of TEX where no macro definitions are loaded. Under those circumstances TEX's instructions are limited to primitives. *Primitives* are roughly 300 instructions that are directly built into the TEX program. They are always available, regardless of any loaded macro definitions.

Typesetting with TEX would be very awkward and cumbersome if one had only primitives available (something you will be able to confirm after you have learned more about primitives and macros). Therefore TEX allows you to *define macros*. Each macro is identified by a *name* that is used to invoke the macro. When you define a macro you must also give the *replacement text*: it contains those instructions that replace any later following macro call(s). The instructions in a replacement text can contain text, primitives, or other macros that are defined somewhere else.

Here is a macro example. The standard macro package of TEX, called the *plain format*, contains a definition of a macro called `\centerline` to center a single line. To center some text `TEXT` one enters the instruction `\centerline{TEXT}`, resulting in the following output:

TEXT

If there were no `\centerline` macro and you were restricted to using primitives only, you would have to enter `\hbox to \hsize{\hfil TEXT\hfil}` to center `TEXT`. This is not only longer to write, but also more error prone, and even without a detailed knowledge of TEX, `\centerline{TEXT}` is easily understood. Macros in TEX are similar to procedures or functions in conventional programming languages.

A set of macros is called a *format.* This term normally implies that the macros are complete enough to typeset at least one type of document; see 2.2.3 on this page for a list of formats of TEX.

Macros are *loaded* before the processing of some text is initiated. Loading is a computer science term that describes the attachment of the functions contained in a program library to another program. This series introduces its own format which is discussed in 31.3, p. III-612.

2.2.2 The Different Meanings of the Word TEX

Throughout this series the expression TEX is used in a variety of related, but different meanings. Let me clarify this now (note that the context normally reveals the proper interpretation of the expression TEX).

The first important distinction we have to make is the following: when in this series it is stated that "TEX has this and that capability" then you should look at the instruction being discussed. If this instruction is a *primitive* then this statement applies to *every* format of TEX (there are some rare cases where primitives are redefined by formats, but those cases are more of an exception; if primitives are redefined anywhere in this series of four volumes, then these instances are clearly identified). If, on the other hand, the instruction being discussed is a *macro* then there are two possibilities of where this macro could have come from. If this macro is defined in this series, then its definition is actually reprinted here. Otherwise you can assume that a macro is defined as part of the simplest macro package or plain format (and our discussions of TEX in this series are based on the plain format). If in doubt, consult the index. A version of TEX with *no* format loaded is also identified as *pure TEX.*

Finally note that the term TEX also refers to the TEX program as it is stored on your machine.

2.2.3 Standard Macro Packages (Formats) of TEX

There are three standard macro packages (or formats) available with TEX. They have been included in Fig. 2.1, p. 6.

1. The *plain format.* This is the most basic macro package. Usually when you enter the command `tex` on any computer a version of the TEX program is started which has the plain format already loaded.

The plain format is usually a starting point for the design of other macro packages. Most of the macro definitions of the plain format are directly included in other formats.

The source code of the plain format can be found in Appendix B of the TEXbook (Knuth (1986a)). As already mentioned the discussion in this series centers around the plain format.

2. The LATEX *macro package.* This format offers many extensions over the plain format and is a viable alternative for producing documents with TEX over the plain format of TEX. LATEX, for instance, numbers chapters and sections of a document automatically. LATEX also generates a table of contents, a list of figures and tables on request. Furthermore, symbolic cross-references are maintained to generate text like "see Fig. 3.5 on page 34" automatically.

   Another important feature of LATEX is that the layout of the document is stored in *style files* separately from the document itself. Therefore, the layout of a document can be modified easily and independently of the text. A description of LATEX can be found in *the* LATEX *Manual*, Lamport (1985).
3. The *AMS-TEX macro package.* This is a macro package tailored towards typesetting papers for mathematical journals; see *The Joy of TEX*, Spivak (1986) for details. AMS-TEX also uses style files.

2.3 Files Accessed by TEX

The files accessed or written by TEX in the process of computing a document are of interest because they show you how TEX communicates with the outside world. TEX will read in (and in some cases also write out) the following files:

1. *Document source files.* These files contain the text of documents together with instructions to TEX how to typeset the text.
2. *(User) macro (definition) files.* These files contain the definitions of macros used in a document. (These may be your own macro definitions or somebody else's).
3. *Format files.* These files contain the macro definitions belonging to the format used for a document. The main difference between format files and files containing *user* macro definitions is that format macros are expected to be, in a certain sense, complete and cover a wider variety of different documents.
4. *Style files.* Some formats use style files to determine the layout of a document. This allows one to change the style of a document independently of the text of a document. LATEX and AMS-TEX use style files, whereas the plain format does not.
5. *Font files.* TEX has to load information about the fonts it will use. This font metric information can be found in `tfm` files (`tfm` stands for TEX font metric); see 15.2.7, p. II-238, for details. Other font files necessary for the printing of documents will be discussed later.

6. *Administrative files.* These are files generated during a TEX run to be read-in during a later TEX run of the same document. They are for TEX macros' internal bookkeeping purposes. Examples are files maintaining cross-reference information or table of contents information. Since a macro package writes and reads administrative files, you can ignore these files, unless are are interested in the internal workings of a macro package.

2.4 Preparations for Using TEX Efficiently

2.4.1 Maintaining Your Own TEX Notebook and File

I suggest getting yourself a notebook, file or folder to collect important TEX examples and other related materials. There are a couple of items you might want to put in this folder:

1. *Manual pages.* Make a copy of all TEX-related manual pages. This allows you to study those commands easily.
2. *Font catalogue.* You should have access to a font catalogue or at least a listing of the fonts contained in the TEX font directory of your machine. Chapter 15, p. II-227, discusses fonts in detail.
3. *Local macros.* You should have the *documentation* and the *source code listing* of all local macros used such as those specific to your company or university.
4. *Collection of samples of tricky TEX problems.* Whenever you have solved a complicated TEX problem such as a tricky table it is important to save a copy for future reference. Here is what you should do *now* immediately after having successfully printed the tricky table:
   (a) You should make a copy of the original source file and remove all the other text except for that tricky table.
   (b) This file should now be processed by TEX and the resulting `dvi` file should be printed.
   (c) A *verbatim listing* of the same file should also be printed so you have a copy of the source code.
   (d) The output from the two previous steps should be stapled together and saved in your folder. Later when a similar problem occurs you can access the example conveniently.

2.4.2 Choosing a Good Text Editor Is Important

While a subsection titled "Choosing a Good Editor" may at first seem inappropriate in a book on TEX, I believe that the subject of selecting a good editor is a very important and frequently overlooked issue. I continue to come across people who still use line editors. (A *line editor* is an editor where the editing commands are based on line numbers.) In a line editor, unlike in a *screen editor* where the text is constantly displayed, you can *not* use the cursor and move to the position where you want to change, add, or delete some text.

The biggest problem with a line editor is that after every change you have to issue a command to display the new text on your screen. Observe that with a screen editor the screen *always* reflects the current state of your text. You don't have to issue a command telling the editor to show the text you have entered.

Line editors are like an old pair of shoes with big holes everywhere—you throw them away, don't you!? So get rid of your line editors.

The Mercedes[1] of all screen editors is the GNU Emacs editor, provided by the Free Software Foundation. This is an editor that can be specifically programmed to help you to enter TeX sources. See Stallmann (1986) and Bechtolsheim (1988) for more details.

2.5 Utilities

A *utility* in computer programming is a program that supports a particular task. A utility for TeX is therefore a program that helps process documents with TeX. The following utilities are partially in the public domain while others can be acquired from various TeX vendors.

1. `dviselect`. This program allows you to extract a particular page or a particular set of pages from a `dvi` file. This utility is very useful for printing only the pages that were modified in a document.

   Running `dviselect` produces another `dvi` file containing only the selected pages. This reduced `dvi` file is then printed as any `dvi` file generated by TeX. A device driver will not notice the difference.

   For instance, `dviselect 3-5 report.dvi xx.dvi` copies pages 3–5 of the "old" `dvi` file `report.dvi` into a new `dvi` file `xx.dvi`. Afterwards you simply print `xx.dvi`. Pages 3–5 from `report.dvi` are then printed. Here is another example:

   ```
   dviselect 3,11,23 report.dvi xx.dvi
   ```

   extracts pages 3, 11 and 23 from `report.dvi` and writes them to `xx.dvi`.

   Most versions of `dvipr`, the program used to print a `dvi` file, provide an option to print only part of a document—in other words `dviselect` is integrated into `dvipr`.
2. `dvipr`. This program prints a `dvi` file on the printer selected by the user. Printing a `dvi` file is subdivided into two steps:

---

[1] This shows my German heritage.

(a) A *driver* converts the `dvi` file into the output device's own language. From this follows that for each different printer language, a different driver is needed (observe though that no changes to the TeX program are necessary!).
(b) The resulting file is passed to the *spooler* of the selected printer. A spooler *serializes* requests from different users to print output on the same printer. On PCs, or when previewing, you normally do not have a spooler.

Here are some desirable properties of `dvipr`.

(a) `dvipr` should have an option allowing to print *multiple copies*. Although laser printers, by far the most frequently used units for output, are no substitutes for copy machines, it is frequently convenient to be able to print multiple copies for short documents, like letters and memos.
(b) `dvipr` should *remove any intermediate files after printing*. Having temporary files in your directory after printing is very annoying. You may also want to consider letting `dvipr` remove the `dvi` file after printing.
(c) `dvipr` should allow printing a document in *landscape mode* in addition to *portrait mode*. Landscape mode is particularly useful for wide tables. See 33.4.5, p. IV-48, for more details.
(d) `dvipr` should have an option that allows you to *shift the page horizontally and vertically at printing time*. You can also shift pages by assigning the proper dimensions to `\hoffset` and `\voffset` in your TeX document, but then the entire document must be processed again if you need to adjust these dimensions. See 33.6.4, p. IV-53.
(e) `dvipr` should allow for the printing of selected pages in case there is no `dviselect` program on your computer. See the discussion about `dviselect` (item 1 on the previous page, of this list).

3. `texclean`. This program removes all intermediate TeX files, including all `dvi` and log files, so that only the source files remain. This allows you to leave a directory in a clean state after you have finished a document. Of course after you have executed `texclean`, you have to run TeX again to print the document.

   Why do I make such a fuss about it? Why should one use a separate program `texclean` and not simply remove all intermediate files "by hand" giving the commands directly? Assume the command on your computer to remove files is called `rm` (frequently also called `del` for delete). Certainly you could enter the command `rm *.dvi *.log` (or `del *.dvi *.log`) to remove all `dvi` and `log` files. But one of these days you will *accidentally* type `rm *.tex *.dvi` and *remove all your source files*. And that is going to hurt! By using `texclean` consistently you can avoid this mistake.
4. `detex`. This program makes a copy of a TeX source file and then removes all TeX constructs and macro calls from this copy. In most cases this is done to check the spelling of a source file. The next item of this list deals with spelling checkers.
5. `spell`. A spelling checker program is a must in a decent TeX environment. Of

course, the spelling checker will not discover grammatical errors nor correct homonyms.

Any good spelling checker should have two dictionaries:

(a) A *standard dictionary* containing all commonly used words.
(b) A *user dictionary* of user-specified correct words, acronyms and abbreviations. For instance, assume you write a document with a specialized vocabulary referring to acronyms which are not in the standard dictionary. If there is no user dictionary, the acronyms will *always* be listed as misspelled. This is very annoying! If there is a user dictionary, you can add these acronyms to it and they will no longer be reported as misspelled words.

To prepare for spell checking, the spell checker usually invokes `detex` automatically. Thus the application of `detex` is usually unnoticed by the user.

2.6 Information about TEX

Following are some ways you can acquire more information about TEX and TEX-related products.

2.6.1 The Original Books Describing TEX and METAFONT

The TEX and METAFONT systems are described in a five-volume set called *Computers and Typesetting.* The author of all five volumes is Donald E. Knuth, professor at Stanford University and creator of TEX and METAFONT (METAFONT is a companion program of TEX for the creation of fonts; see 17.2, p. II-315).

Volume A (Knuth (1986a)), the TEXbook, contains the description of TEX. This book is the ultimate reference manual for TEX, and whenever you are in doubt, you should check this book for the nitty gritty details. Volume C of his series (Knuth (1986c)) is the manual describing METAFONT.

The two companion volumes Knuth (1986b) and Knuth (1986d) contain the listing of the TEX-program and the METAFONT-program. Both programs have been implemented with the help of the "`WEB`-system," and these two volumes show you that computer program listings can actually look beautiful. See 17.3, p. II-317, for a brief discussion of the `WEB`-system.

METAFONT was used to generate the *Computer Modern fonts* for TEX, which are described in Volume E of *Computers and Typesetting* (Knuth (1986e)). This volume, in my opinion the most exciting volume of this series, contains a detailed description of every character of the Computer Modern fonts. Each character is presented on two facing pages of this book. On the left-hand side is a blown up reproduction of the character with all METAFONT-related reference points clearly indicated. On the right-hand side is the METAFONT program to generate the character. Check it out!!!

2.6.2 TUG, the TEX Users Group

Many TEX users are members of TUG, the TEX Users Group. TUG was originally a subgroup within the AMS, the American Mathematical Society, which has been supporting TEX from its beginning, but now TUG is independent.

TUG publishes TUGBOAT a journal which appears three times a year. Here is a brief overview of the subjects discussed in this journal:

1. General announcements, conferences, meetings, etc.
2. TEX and METAFONT courses at various locations in the U.S. and Canada, and more recently in Europe.
3. TEX macros.
4. Implementation of TEX on various computer systems, and reports by site coordinators.
5. METAFONT.
6. TEX utilities and support programs.
7. Device drivers.
8. Advertisements.

Two different memberships (individual memberships and institutional memberships) are available. At least one person in the group you are working with should be a member of TUG, because TUGBOAT provides a lot of useful information. The address of TUG can be found in the front matter of this series (Notes on "TEX in Practice") on p. xxxix.

2.6.3 TEX is a Public Domain Software Product

You should realize that the TEX and METAFONT software are *in the public domain.* In other words you can use it, modify it, sell it, or do with it whatever you want to. The software is essentially free. Let me make two important remarks though:

1. People have ported TEX to a variety of different machines and operating systems, and people can and do charge for that service (normally in the neighborhood of $250).
2. Device drivers in particular are frequently *not* in the public domain (quite a number are in the public domain). They may cost some money, but normally not very much.

In other words, TeX is essentially free.

Because there are no royalties to be paid for using TeX, you should become a member of TUG and help support TeX this way!

An inherent problem of public domain software is that because you didn't pay for it, you also don't have the right to yell at someone (or not pay someone's bill) if something doesn't work. But in the case of TeX you are in a much better situation than you typically are with public domain software. First of all, TeX is an exceptionally reliable and well-designed piece of software. Secondly, there are a number of consultants and companies that can help you out. See the advertisement in TUGBOAT for more details.

2.6.4 Electronic Mailing Lists

There are a number of electronic mailing lists you may be able to access, if you are connected to one of the large computer networks. Let me just mention **`TeXHax`** here. Talk to your local email guru or send email to **`TeXhax-request@cs.washington.edu`** for subscription information. There is also a newsgroup `comp.text.tex` you might consider reading. And finally there are other national and international mailing lists. Just ask around!

The main depository for all the TeX software is the following machine on the Internet: `labrea.stanford.edu` (please note that the date of this information is May 1992 and is subject to change).

2.7 Entering Text

You already saw that certain characters like \ or $ have a special meaning in TeX. Still, as this series shows you, the same characters can also be printed (and not interpreted by TeX). All of this needs to be discussed in detail now.

In this Section I also compare TeX typesetting with printing text on a typewriter. Certain characters are available in proportionally spaced fonts (the text in front of you is set in a proportionally spaced font), but they are usually not available in typewriter fonts (a fixed-spaced font).

Proportionally spaced fonts are fonts where different characters can and usually do have different widths, whereas in a fixed-spaced font all characters have the same width.

A character in any type of computer program is nothing more than a number, the *character code* of this character. In Figs. 16.4–16.7, pp. II-304–II-307, you find font tables from which you can determine character codes of characters. Once the character code is known, you always can use `\char` to print the character; see 16.6.1, p. II-296.

In order to print those characters that have a special meaning in TEX as they appear on your terminal screen, use a *verbatim mode*. In verbatim mode all characters are simply printed the way they are entered. So if I enter `$\?\tt{` in verbatim mode then the output will read exactly that: `$\?\tt{`. All special TEX characters, including $ and the curly braces, lose their special function and are simply printed. 18.3, p. III-26, deals with verbatim mode in more detail.

2.7.1 Letters and Digits

Let us look at the most frequently used characters first.

1. **Letters:** `A...Z, a...z`
   A letter is typeset by simply entering it.
   TEX is *case sensitive*, in other words, lowercase and uppercase characters are different. This not only applies to regular text, but also to control sequences. For instance, `\xy`, `\Xy`, `\xY` and `\XY` are four different control sequences in TEX.
2. **At sign:** `@`
   The `@` simply prints as `@`. Nevertheless this character requires special attention. It is frequently used inside macro packages as a letter, whereas in outside macro packages it is used differently. This will be discussed in 18.1.12, p. III-13.
3. **Arabic numerals:** `0...9`
   To print Arabic numerals (digits), simply input the desired numeral and it is printed.

Next is the discussion of some of the more special characters in TEX. The following list may be confusing at first. But as you get more and more familiar with TEX, you will probably appreciate this list of characters.

2.7.2 Special Characters in TEX

Some characters in TEX require special attention because they invoke a certain typesetting function instead of printing directly. Let's get started.

1. **Backslash:** \
   TEX uses the "\" character to begin *control sequences*, which are *instructions* to TEX. Control sequences are not printed in the output but interpreted by TEX to trigger some typesetting or other function. Within the context of TEX, the "\" is called the *escape character* because it allows "escaping" from the input of regular text.
   To print the backslash in some text, you can choose one of the following methods:

(a) Use a verbatim mode. In verbatim mode the interpretation of special characters is in general suspended and "`\abc`" will print "`\abc`." See 18.3, p. III-26, for details.

(b) Use `\string` in case you have to print the backslash as part of a control sequence. For instance, to print `\bye`, type `{\tt\string\bye}` or to print `\$`, write `{\tt\string\$}`. Note that the curly braces in the two examples delimit the font change to the typewriter font (`\tt`).

`\string` can only be used to print the *immediately* following control sequence. If you have two control sequences `\a\b` to print, you need to enter `\string` twice and write `{\tt\string\a \string\b}`. See 19.1.1, p. III-65, for more details.

(c) In mathmode \ can be printed by writing `\backslash`. Thus a single \ can be printed by writing `$\backslash$`.

2. **Dollar sign: `$`**
The "`$`" is used to begin and end mathematical equations: `$a=b+c$` prints $a = b + c$. See Chapter 13, p. II-155, for details. This math mode is called *inline math mode* because the mathematical equation is part of the paragraph's text.

In *display math mode* an equation appears centered on a line by itself. Display math mode is initiated and terminated by double dollar signs. The input

```
This is some text and a formula like
$$
    a = b+c^{2}
$$
shows display math mode.
```

generates the following output:
This is some text and a formula like

$$a = b + c^2$$

shows display math mode.

To print a "`$`" in regular text enter the dollar sign symbol after a backslash. For example, `the change is \$12.37` prints "the change is $12.37."

The "`$`" in the italic font, `\it`, generates the British Currency Pound Sign *£* (`{\it \$}`) and *not* an italicized "`$`."

3. **Ampersand: `&`**
The "`&`" is used as the tab character in tables built with `\halign`. See 38.2.2, p. IV-200, for details.

In case you want to print the ampersand enter "`\&`": to print Smith & Co enter `Smith \& Co`.

4. **Percent Sign: `%`**
The percent sign is used to start *comments* in a TeX source file. The comment runs to the end-of-line character. More precisely, all characters from and including the `%` to the end-of-line character are ignored by TeX. Remember: TeX will ignore everything from the `%` on the current line up to and

including the end-of-line character. The fact that the end-of-line character is also ignored is very important; see item 9, p. 27.

Here is a short example: assume you want to add information to your text that identifies the person who entered the text and when the text was modified last, but you do not want to have this information appear when the document is printed. A comment will do exactly that:

```
% This paper was coded into TeX by Alfred Miller.
% Date June 10, 1688
% Revision 500.23
% The following tables still need work:
%          2.3, 2.4, 2.9, 3.7
     And here we have the regular text of the
documentation.
% And here is another comment.
     And here is some more text. % A comment.
```

Observe that the `%` has to be repeated for each line of comment. None of the first five lines will appear in the final document.

To type `%` in regular text, as in 20%, enter `20\%`.

5. **Pound sign: `#`**
The pound sign is used in TeX in the following two instances:

   (a) To indicate a parameter in a macro definition; `#1` is the first parameter, `#2` the second, and so forth. See 21.7, p. III-180, for details.
   (b) To indicate the place of substitution in templates of tables. See 38.2.1, p. IV-200.

   If you want to print the # character, enter `\#`. For instance, to print "Apartment #3-11" enter `Apartment \#3-11`.

6. **Caret: `^`**
The caret "^" is used to indicate a superscript in mathematical formulas. For example, `$a^{2+i}$` prints a^{2+i}. See 13.1.5, p. II-160, for details.

   To print a caret in regular text write `$\hat{}$` or `\^{}`.

   Observe that "\^" prints the *accent circumflex*. For instance, in abcêde would be entered as as `abc\^ede`. See 16.5, p. II-293, for more details on accents.

   Finally, the caret is used to enter characters with character codes that are not directly represented by one of the standard characters on the keyboard. For instance, `^^I`, can be used to input the tab character. See 16.6.1, p. II-296, for details.

7. **Underscore: `_`**
The underscore "_" denotes subscripts in mathematical formulas. It is applied the same way superscripts are specified using the caret: the subscript is enclosed in curly braces. For instance, to print x_2 input `$x_{2}$`.

   To print this character in regular text, enter `\_`. For example, to print a_b, enter `a\_b`.

8. **Curly braces: `{}`**
In 2.1.2, item 2.b.iii, p. 4, it was already explained that curly braces have multiple functions. For example, they serve as grouping symbols to delimit

font changes (`This is a {\bf lot} of fun`), which prints only the word *lot* in boldface. They are also used to delimit the argument of a macro: for instance, in the case of `\centerline` the line of text to be centered is enclosed inside curly braces as in `\centerline{TEXT}`.

All the various meanings of curly braces are discussed in detail in 19.4, p. III-99.

To print curly braces, enter mathmode and use `\lbrace` or `\rbrace`. For example: the input `$\lbrace a, b, c\rbrace$` prints $\{a, b, c\}$. See 14.6.1, p. II-207, for details on curly braces.

Instead of using `\lbrace` and `\rbrace`, you can also use "`\{`" and "`\}`." The preceding example, therefore, could also have been entered as `$\{ a, b, c\}$`. I *strongly* recommend that *you do not* use `\{` and `\}`, because these two control sequences can be too easily mixed up with `{` and `}`. Use `\lbrace` and `\rbrace` only.

9. **Brackets:** `[]`
   There is nothing special about brackets: if you need to print them, just enter them: `[abc]` prints [abc].
10. **Parentheses:** `()`
   There is also nothing special about parentheses: need them, write them, print them: `(abc)` prints (abc).
11. **Plus sign:** `+`
   The plus sign is usually used inside mathematical equations. For instance, `$a+b$` prints $a+b$. The plus sign printed in math mode is the same character which is printed when a plus sign is printed in some text. However math mode should be always used for mathematical equations because among other things the spacing around a plus sign is automatically computed properly. Also, in math mode the plus sign is automatically printed in a smaller size if this is appropriate as in e^{x+y}.

   The `\+` control sequence is used in `\settabs` based tables; see 6.9, p. 198, for details.
12. **Minus sign:** –
   The minus sign is a different story than the plus sign. You *only* get the minus sign if you use math mode. For instance, `$a-b$` prints $a - b$. If you enter this same symbol not in math mode, a hyphen will be printed (discussed further below). See also 2.7.3, p. 23.
13. **Question mark:** `?`
   To print a question mark in TEX, enter "`?`."
14. **Open question:** `<`
   The *open question mark* in TEX exists *only* in proportionally spaced fonts such as the font which is currently being used. You need to enter `>` to get "¿."
15. **Exclamation point:** `!`
   There is nothing special about the exclamation point. Simply type it when you need it.
16. **Open exclamation:** ¿
   There is a counter part to the open question mark, which is the open exclamation point. You need to enter `<` to get "¡." Note that like the open

question mark there is no such symbol for fixed spaced fonts.

17. **Less than, greater than:** $<$ $>$
Let me discuss those symbols briefly.

    (a) When `<` and `>` are used in math mode they print as expected, as less than and greater than signs: the input `$a<b$` prints as $a < b$.
    (b) If you use a *fixed-space font* like `\tt` in which all characters have the same width, then the input {\tt <ABC>} prints, as expected, <ABC>.
    (c) If you use the same input with a *proportionally spaced font*, then you get the open question mark (see item 14 on the previous page of this list) and the open exclamation point (see item 16 on the previous page of this list).

    Sometimes the less than and greater than symbols are used in text, for instance, to indicate syntactic variables in programming language theory. In this case you need to go back and forth between math mode and "regular text mode": to print <expr>, enter `$<$expr$>$`. See 13.2.8, p. II-168, for a macro `\angt` to simplify things in those cases.

18. **Apostrophe or right-quote:** '
To get an apostrophe, enter an apostrophe. That applies to proportionally and fixed-spaced fonts. Two adjacent apostrophes using a proportionally spaced font are a different story; see item 21 on this page of this list.

    To get the *acute accent* enter `\'`. For instance, `abc\'ef` prints "abcéf."

    Entering an apostrophe by itself makes TeX print exactly that character as in "that's just fine." When the apostrophe is used in a case where TeX expects a numerical constant (for instance, in an assignment to a counter register), this character instructs TeX to provide the character code of the following character; see 3.3.1, p. 39, for details.

    By the way, macro `\rq` expands to a right quote.

19. **Reverse apostrophe or left quote:** ‘
To get a reverse apostrophe, enter one. That applies to proportionally and fixed-spaced fonts. Two adjacent reverse apostrophes using a proportionally spaced font are a different story; see item 20 on this page of this list.

    To get the *grave accent* enter ``\` ``. For instance, ``abc\`ef`` prints "abcèf."

    This character also has a special meaning when TeX expects a numerical constant, because then this character instructs TeX to parse the following digits as an octal number; see 3.3.1, p. 39, for details.

    By the way, macro `\lq` expands to a left quote.

20. **Left double-quotation mark:** ‘‘
Left double quotation marks in TeX are entered using two adjacent apostrophes. This applies only to proportionally spaced fonts. To quote using a proportional font such as in "quote" enter ``` ``quote.'' ```

21. **Right double-quotation mark:** ''
Right double quotation marks in TeX are entered using two adjacent right apostrophes. See the preceding explanation for an example.

22. **Double-quotation mark:** "
Since neither a left nor a right double quotation mark exists in the fixed-spaced fonts, you get a "neutral" quote when you enter `{\tt "}`. Entering "

in a proportionally spaced font generates a left double quote, but that's not the way you are supposed to generate one. See item 20 on the previous page.

`\"` generates the dieresis accent; the input `M\"unchen` prints München, a city of great beer and pretzels.

23. **En-dash:** –

Proportionally spaced fonts have en-dashes that are used to indicate a range. In TeX you need to enter `--` to get an en-dash. For instance, to print "pages 23–34" enter `pages 23--34`.

A fixed-spaced font usually only has a hyphen, so to print "`pages 23-34`" you would enter `pages 23-34`.

The usual length of an en-dash is 0.5 em. See also 2.7.3, p. 23.

24. **Em-dash:** —

Proportionally spaced fonts have an em-dash for punctuation and in TeX you need to enter `---` to get an em-dash. For instance, to print "I still like it—even now" enter `I still like it---even now`.

A monospaced font usually only has a hyphen so to print the preceding text using a monospaced font, one usually uses a hyphen surrounded by a space on both sides.

The usual length of an em-dash is 1 em. See also 2.7.3, p. 23.

25. **Hyphen:** `-`

A hyphen is used in *compound words* like daughter-in-law, A-rated, two-sided and p-y-o (which according to one of my students means "pick your own"...). The above text was input as `daughter-in-law`, `A-rated`, `two-sided` and `p-y-o`.

Of course, as the name of this character suggests, the hyphen is also used for hyphenation. For details on hyphenation see 12.7.4, p. II-139.

See also 2.7.3, p. 23.

26. **Period:** `.`

To understand the various applications of periods you must distinguish between a *regular space* as it appears between the words of a sentence, and an *extended space* as it appears after a period ending a sentence.

The way the Computer Modern fonts of TeX are set up, the difference between the two spaces is rather small. The usual interword space, when not adjusted for left and right justified text margins, is 3.33 pt for a 10 pt base font. The extended space is 4.44 pt, only 30% larger than the regular space and far less than the old typewriter rule of leaving twice the regular space after a period ending a sentence.

(a) The most frequent application of a period is to *indicate the end of a sentence.* This normally makes TeX insert some additional horizontal space (called *glue*) to increase the distance between the period and the word following the period. See 16.2.5, p. II-278, for details.

As you will see below (item 2, p. 24) multiple consecutive spaces in the input are treated as a single space. So entering two spaces after a period does *not* tell TeX that the period is to be interpreted as a period ending a sentence. However, it is still advisable to do so because it does make your input easier to read on the terminal screen.

(b) A period can *terminate an abbreviation.* Spacing after a period that ends an abbreviation should be regular and not extended (as in the case of a period ending a sentence).

Instead of discussing in detail here when TEX handles the period after an abbreviation correctly and when not, let us consider how you can tell TEX to generate a space after a period of "regular" size.

There are two ways to generate a regular space in TEX (not only after a period but also otherwise):

i. `\␣`: this simply gives you a regular space (the `\␣` construct is called a *control space*)

ii. `~`: this gives you a regular space with the additional property that this space cannot be broken across lines. In other words, there will be no line-break between the word preceding the tilde and the word following the tilde. In the case of abbreviations, this is something you typically want.

(c) Three periods together form an *ellipsis* as in "Hmmm ... why?". *Do not* enter an ellipsis as you would do on a typewriter; writing "`Hmmm ... why?`," because the output prints as follows "Hmmm ... why?" and the three periods are much too close together.

There are three different ellipses in TEX.

i. `\dots` is an ellipsis in regular text as in "Hmmm ... why?" which was entered as `Hmmm \dots{} why?`. The function of the `{}` is to force a space between the end of the ellipsis and `why` because spaces after control words like `\dots` are ignored.

ii. `\cdots` (centered dots) as in $x_1+x_2+\cdots+x_n$. To print this text enter the following: `$x_{1}+x_{2}+\cdots+x_{n}$`. `\cdots` can be used only in math mode.

iii. `\ldots` (line dots) as in $(x_1, x_2, \ldots, x_n)$ which was entered as `$(x_{1}+x_{2}+\ldots+x_{n})$`. `\ldots` can be used only in math mode.

(d) And one more remark: this series is printed with French spacing in effect, that is, spaces after periods and regular spaces are *not* different. See 16.2.5, p. II-278, for details.

27. **Tilde:** ~

As mentioned earlier the tilde is special in that it represents a non-breakable space; see 2.8.2, item 27 on this page for details.

If preceded with a backslash the tilde is one of the accents of TEX: `\~o` prints õ.

28. **French ligature œ, OE:**

The French ligature œ and Œ are generated by `\oe` and `\OE` respectively.

29. **Scandinavian A-with-circle:**

The symbols å and Å are generated by `\aa` and `\AA`.

30. **Scandinavian O-with-slash:**

The symbols ø and Ø are generated by `\o` and `\O`.

31. **Polish suppressed L:**
    The Polish suppressed L is generated by `\l` and `\L`, which print "ł" and "Ł" respectively.
32. **German "es-zet" or sharp S:**
    You get ß if you enter `\ss`.
33. **Dagger or obelisk:**
    You get † when you enter `\dag`.
34. **Double dagger or diesis:**
    You get ‡ when you enter `\ddag`.
35. **Section number sign:**
    You get the section number sign "§" when you enter `\S`.
36. **Paragraph sign or pilcrow:**
    Enter `\P` to print "¶."

2.7.3 Minus Sign, Hyphen, En-Dash and Em-Dash

The preceding list contains four types of "horizontal line characters": the hyphen, minus sign, en-dash, and em-dash. Sometimes the question arises as to which of the characters you should use. This question is very simple to answer. The applications for the hyphen (item 25, p. 21), minus sign (item 12, p. 19) and the em-dash (item 24, p. 21) can be easily determined. If none of these rules apply, use the en-dash.

2.8 The Space, Tab and End-of-Line Characters

Spaces, tabs and end-of-line characters have much in common and therefore are dealt with together. We will start out with some some basic definitions.

2.8.1 Related Definitions

1. *Space* or *space character*. The character with character code 20_{16} (in TEX one writes `"20` for hexadecimal 20). The `"` in `"20` indicated to TEX a hexadecimal constant.
2. *Visible space*. The symbol ␣ used in the TEX literature and also in this series to explicitly indicate a space.
3. *Control space*. The `\␣` primitive of TEX to force a space to be printed.

4. *Space token.* What TEX (or TEX's mouth, to be more precise) converts a space or multiple and adjacent spaces into. (The *mouth* of TEX is that part of the TEX program which is directly concerned with reading the TEX source code to convert it into tokens.)
5. *Tie.* An indication not to break a line in a paragraph between two words. In TEX the tilde is used for that. Note that the tie replaces the usual space (or end-of-line character) which is inserted between two words of some text.
6. *Return* or *end-of-line character.* The character with character code 17_{16} (`"17` in TEX notation) ends lines.
7. *Tab character* or *tab* for short. The character with character code 9, used to represent usually from 1–8 spaces.
8. *Ampersand* (`&`). This is a different tab character (which has nothing to do with the `^^I` tab character). `&` is used to separate columns of a table when this table is built with `\halign`. Usually which tab character is being referred to is clear from the context.
9. *Active* character. A character which has a macro-like function. The character does *not* print directly. Instead a macro is invoked and the effect of the character therefore depends on the macro definition for the active character.
10. *Interword glue.* The glue (a distance with the capability to stretch and shrink) inserted between the words of a paragraph in TEX.

2.8.2 Rules Governing Spaces, Tabs and End-of-Line Characters

Things are becoming a little more complicated now, but later you will perceive the following rules which explain the interpretation of spaces, tabs and the end-of-line characters as quite natural.

1. The *visible space* ␣ is used to indicate spaces in this series. This character is at position 20_{16} (hexadecimal) in the typewriter font of TEX (20_{16} is also the ASCII character code of the space character). This symbol can be generated in either of the following ways:

   (a) `{\tt\char‘\ }`.
   (b) `{\tt\char"20}`.
   (c) `\verb*+ +`. This uses an inline verbatim mode which is presented in 18.3, p. III-26.
   (d) `\VisibleSpaceTt`. This macro is defined in 18.3.1, p. III-26.

2. *Adjacent consecutive spaces in the input are reduced to simple spaces.* This is a *very* important rule. Therefore the input `This␣␣␣is␣␣␣some␣␣␣text` and the input `This␣is␣some␣text` generate the identical output of "This is some text."

   This reduction of multiple spaces to one space (it is more accurate to say to one space token) happens when the *text is read in.* Only *adjacent* multiple spaces are reduced to simple spaces. For example, `This { } is fun` prints *three* spaces between `This` and `is` because there are three spaces between these two words in the input and none of them are adjacent to each other.

If one were to type `This␣␣␣{␣␣␣}␣␣␣is␣fun`, note that there are also three spaces printed between the two words `This` and `is` because adjacent multiple spaces were reduced to simple spaces. Therefore, this is identical to the previous example `This␣{␣}␣is␣fun`.

See 10.1.1, p. II-1, for another example with spaces.

3. *The space, tab and end-of-line characters can be made* **active**. If they are made active, none of the rules given so far will apply but the following rules apply.

   (a) An active space character (see 18.2.2, p. III-16, for an explanation of the `\obeyspaces` macro, which makes the space active) can make TEX print multiple adjacent spaces as separate spaces in the output.

   (b) An active end-of-line character (see 18.2.4, p. III-18, for an explanation of the `\obeylines` macro which makes the end-of-line character active) can cause TEX's output to follow the line breaks of TEX's input.

   As a matter of accuracy one should know that, like macros, active space and end-of-line could be defined to do almost anything. The definitions just given are the definitions of the plain format.

4. *The tab character is equivalent to the space character.* When a tab character is displayed on a terminal screen then it usually represents between 1 and 8 spaces, advancing to the next horizontal character position 0 mod 8. This model of a tab character does not apply in TEX. On the other hand the display verbatim mode of this series, presented in detail in 18.3.12, p. III-43, does interpret the tab character as the "appropriate" number of spaces.

5. *The end-of-line character and the space character are normally identical in TEX.* A consequence of this is that it does not matter where you enter spaces and where you break lines (that is enter end-of-line characters) when you type a paragraph. But observe the next rule.

6. *Two consecutive end-of-line characters in the input* are converted into `\par`; `\par` terminates a paragraph in TEX. To put it into more practical terms: TEX converts an empty line (that is the way two consecutive end-of-line characters appear on the terminal screen) into a `\par` ending the previous paragraph.

   If you have multiple consecutive empty lines then only the first empty line has the effect of ending the previous paragraph. The following empty lines have no effect. See 10.5.1, p. II-13, for details.

7. *Spaces, tabs and end-of-line characters may "disappear" in a line break.* Observe that after you entered your text, TEX will take your text and make all line break decisions regardless of whether your source code contained line breaks or spaces or tabs (or a mixture of those) between the words of your paragraph.

8. *Use a* tie *(~) instead of a space to specify a space that* **cannot** *disappear in a line break.* If in your input you replace the space between two words by a tilde, then TEX will *not* generate a line break between the two words. One of the two words might be hyphenated, of course.

Here is an example. The input

```
$$
    \vbox{
        \hsize = 4.50in
        We now show how to prevent a line break in \TeX{} forcing
        \TeX{} to keep two words on the same line. This text is
        enough for the example.
    }
$$
```

generates the following output:

> We now show how to prevent a line break in TeX forcing TeX to keep two words on the same line. This text is enough for the example.

Now I will show how to instruct TeX to keep the two words `to` (currently printed at the end of the first line of the output) and `keep` (currently printed at the beginning of the second line of output) on one line. This is done by inserting a "~" between these two words in the input. Here is the new input:

```
$$
    \vbox{
        \hsize = 4.50in
        We now show how to prevent a line break in \TeX{} forcing
        \TeX{} to~keep two words on the same line. This text is
        enough for the example.
    }
$$
```

This generates the following output:

> We now show how to prevent a line break in TeX forcing TeX to keep two words on the same line. This text is enough for the example.

Here are two typical applications of `~`:

(a) Keep *initials* and last name together as in "A. Smith" (`A.~Smith`).
(b) Keep abbreviations and following text together, as in "Fig. 3.7" which was entered as `Fig.~3.7`.

9. *Spaces and tabs at the beginning of a line are ignored.* In that case they are *not* reduced to simple spaces. This is an exception to the rule of item 2, p. 24.

   A consequence of this rule is that the indentation of the first line of a paragraph cannot be generated by indenting the first line of a paragraph in the input. Nevertheless, for improved readability of the input the source code of the first line of paragraphs should be indented. See 10.7, p. II-18, for details on paragraph indentation.

It is important to look at this rule and the next rule together. Remember that the percent sign % (item 4, p. 17) introduces a comment removing all characters on the current line starting with the percent sign and ending with the end-of-line character. Observe that the end-of-line character is *also removed.* In other words, the space, which is normally introduced by the end-of-line character of regular lines, is lost too.

Let's analyze the following example where the current and previous rule are taken into account simultaneously:

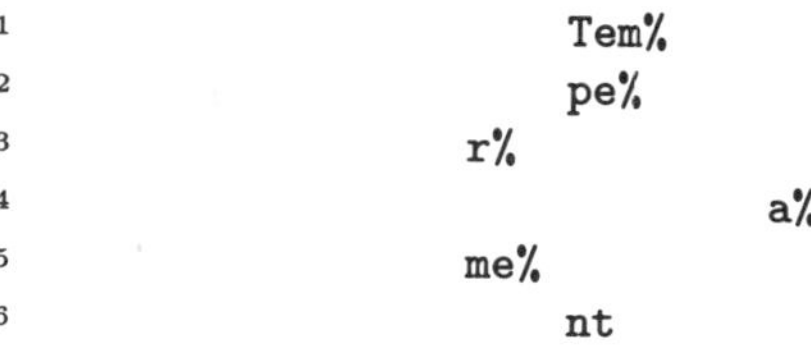

```
          Tem%
          pe%
     r%
                    a%
     me%
          nt
```

The above input will print "Temperament" as one word, without any intervening spaces in it. The spaces normally generated by the end-of-line characters are ignored due to the "%" adjacent to the last character on every line, and the spaces in the beginning of the lines are ignored because of the rule preceding this one.

10. *Spaces inside mathematical formulas are ignored.* Therefore, in math mode, many spaces are as good as no space at all. The input `$a-b=c$` and the input `$␣␣a␣-␣␣b␣␣=␣␣␣c$` result in the identical output of $a - b = c$.
11. *Spaces in vertical modes* are ignored; see 27.7, p. III-437, for details.
12. *Spaces after control words are ignored.* (However, spaces are *not ignored* after *control symbols*). A *control word* is an instruction in TeX which consists of a backslash and any number of letters (observe that I said *letters* and not *characters*) like `\TeX`. On the other hand,`\$` is a *control symbol,* because it starts with a backslash followed by exactly one non-letter character.

    For example, to write "TeX is fantastic," the input must be `\TeX{} is fantastic` rather than `\TeX is fantastic` which prints as "TeXis fantastic". On the other hand, `\$ 5` prints $ 5, not $5.

    This issue of spaces and control sequences is discussed in more detail in 18.1.3, p. III-3. The `{}` which was used to prevent TeX from further ignoring spaces is called an *empty group*; see 19.4.5, p. III-102. In the above example, `\TeX{} is ...`, these curly braces have no other effect than to make the space following `\TeX` not immediately adjacent to `\TeX`. Therefore the space is not ignored and will be printed in the output.
13. *Spaces in text are converted into interword glue.* Glue is TeX's way to describe space that can be adjusted in length (observe that the space between words is typically not fixed but varies slightly to allow for left justified and right justified text). A more accurate discussion of interword glue can be found in 16.2, p. II-275.
14. A *hard space* is a space that is explicitly programmed by the user. A hard space in TeX is generated by `\␣` (a control space).
15. When you write a space after a number, as in "23 is a nice number," then this space will not be ignored. By contrast a space after a numerical constant

which is assigned to some register is absorbed as part of the assignment and therefore in effect ignored.

For instance, in order to assign a numerical value to a register, enter

```
\count0 = 15 text...
```

rather than `\count0 = 15text...`, which is less readable. You should always leave spaces after numerical constants. See 3.3.3, p. 44, for details.

The same applies to dimensions. You can enter `\hskip 10pt More text` instead of `\hskip 10ptMore text`, which is much less readable.

16. Spaces after the following keywords in TEX are ignored:
    (a) `plus` and `minus`; see 5.1, item 5, p. 122.
    (b) `height`, `depth` and `width`; see 5.7.2, p. 156.
17. Spaces after the tab character "`&`" in tables are ignored. Spaces are also ignored after the opening curly brace of `\halign`. See 38.3.17, p. IV-229, for details.

2.9 Organizing Your TEX Sources

Let me next discuss how those files in which you enter a document to be processed by TEX, should be properly organized. We will focus upon what should be entered in the beginning of a document and how it should be arranged.

1. Start with a comment, that contains information about which document it is, what major revisions the document went through, the author, who entered the document, etc.
2. Define the values for
    (a) `\magnification`
    (b) `\hsize` and `\vsize`, `\hoffset` and `\voffset`.
    (c) `\baselineskip`, `\parindent`, `\parskip`, etc.

    If this is one document out of a series (like a departmental report), you may read in all those values from a separate file, similar to the way you read in macros from a separate file. This ensures consistency among all documents of the same class.
3. Read in all your macros. Unless you use only a very few macros, or some macros that are particular to one single document, all macro definitions should be stored in a separate file. If you use macros from this series read the instructions in "General Notes on 'TEX in Practice'" carefully.
4. Define all fonts (`\font...`) that are particular to your document.
5. Define all macros particular to the current document. As mentioned before, any macros that are also used in other documents should be stored in a separate file.
6. Then start with your text.

Here is a sample of the beginning part of a document designed according to the rules given above:

```
% Department Report 86-34, Prof. Groucho
% Marx Brothers Institute for Research on Advanced Laughter
% Author: Prof. Funny Fun
% Typist: Ms. Typee Type
% Date: February 31, 1986
% Revision -100

% Magnification and \hsize are changed. All other values
% remain unchanged compared with the settings of the plain
% format.
\mag = \magstep 1
\hsize = 6.0truein

% Read in report macros.
\input macros-report.tex

% A larger boldface font for section titles is needed.
\font\bigbf = amb10 scaled \magstep 2

% Some special macros to print some formulas in math mode.

% \fraca{x}{y} prints the fraction
%        x+y
%      -------
%        x-y
\def\fraca #1#2{%
    {#1+#2 \over #1-#2}%
}

% \fracb{x}{y} prints the fraction
%          x+y
%      ------------
%        exp(x-y)
\def\fracb #1#2{%
    {#1+#2 \over \exp{#1-#2}}%
}

% Split line macro: \splitline{Left}{Right} prints the
% first argument left justified and the second right
% justified on a line by itself.
\def\splitline #1#2{\line{#1\hfil#2}}


% Here it is where the text starts.
\centerline{How To Laugh While Taking a Bath}

This document deals with the question....
...
\bye
```

2.10 How to Experiment with TEX

I have seen it happen over and over again: someone struggles with a 50-page document and only has two more equations and one table to go (the rest of the document prints correctly). And each time a small change is made all 50 pages are processed and printed again—a huge waste of time and paper.

Let me make some suggestions on how to experiment with TEX properly. The first thing to do when you run into a problem, for example with a particular table, is to copy the table into a separate file. From now on work only with this separate file. After you succeed reinsert the corrected table back into the original file. It is much quicker to run TEX and to print just this one page.

Let me offer another suggestion: when you start to explore a new area of TEX, for instance, the typesetting of mathematical equations, do *not* start by typesetting some manuscript given to you: there will simply be too many new things at the same time. Instead start with some small examples on your own. Play around designing your own small equations, one equation at a time. This way you gradually build your confidence.

Whatever you do, collect all your examples in a binder, as I discussed earlier. This is useful for yourself and will also be useful for your colleagues when they ask you some questions.

Many people have complained about how time consuming it is to learn TEX. Yes, it *is* time consuming, but it is also a matter of *making time*! For instance, one thing you can do is to come to your office 15 minutes early every day and play with TEX, before a lot of work is dumped on your table.

A *very* good thing to do in the beginning is to use TEX to write letters. You can design your own letterhead. Since there is a lot of liberty on how to do that it gives you lots of opportunities to play around with various aspects of TEX. Also because most letters are short, if something goes wrong, it does not cost much to correct your error and to print another copy.

2.11 Summary

In this chapter you learned:

- TEX is a computer program for the typesetting of documents, including mathematical formulas, but excluding graphs and diagrams.
- TEX is also a computer programming language based on macro expansion.
- TEX has a variety of special characters with specific meanings such as `\`, `$`, `&`, `%`, `#`, `^`, `_`, `{`, `}`, `~` (and its "derivatives"), the period, spaces, tabs and end-of-line character.
- TEX source code consists of text and typesetting instructions; most typesetting instructions start with a backslash, TEX's escape character.

- Processing a TeX document involves first executing the TeX program which generates a `dvi` file. This `dvi` file is then converted into a printer-specific output file by a driver and then this printer-specific file can be printed.
- There are three standard macro packages: the plain format, LaTeX and AMS-TeX.
- Various utilities make life with TeX easier.
- A good screen editor is essential for efficiently working with TeX.
- It is worthwhile to be a member of TUG, the TeX Users Group.
- To learn TeX requires patience and endurance. It is important to start with small projects, such as using TeX to write letters.

3
Registers, Numbers, and Counter Registers In Particular

Registers are a sort of memory in TEX. There are different register types. For instance, counter registers allow the user to store numbers (such as the current section number) and to retrieve this number from a register, for instance, to print the register. This chapter discusses registers in general, counter registers in particular. It also discusses numbers and arithmetic in TEX.

3.1 Registers in General

The following rules apply to all register types:

1. There are *six types of registers* in TEX. The registers differ in what type of information they can hold. The registers of TEX are the following (in parenthesis the instruction to access a register of the specified type is listed).
   (a) *Counter* registers (`\count`); see 3.3.6, p. 49.
   (b) *Dimension* registers (`\dimen`); see 4.1.7, p. 87.
   (c) *Glue* registers (`\skip`); see 4.2, p. 91.
   (d) *Math glue* registers (`\mskip`); see 4.3, p. 93.
   (e) *Token* registers (`\toks`); see 20.1, p. III-117.
   (f) *Box* registers (`\box`, `\copy` and other instructions); see 4.5, p. 95.

   The types of the registers identify *what* can be stored in a particular register. Counter registers, for example, are used to store numerical values. A counter register can, for instance, be used to number the chapters or sections of a document automatically.

   Note that each of the above instructions such as `\count`, `\dimen` and so forth must be followed by a register index (discussed next).
2. There are 256 registers of each type available in TEX and each register is identified by a *register index*, a number in the range $0 \ldots 255$.
3. `\new...` *instructions.* Normally you do *not* refer to registers by their index, but by *names* (it would be too cumbersome to remember register indices). To

assign names automatically to register index `\new...` macros were defined in the plain format. The type of the register being reserved depends on which `\new...` instruction is called. The name of the register to be allocated is specified by the user through a control sequence that is given immediately following the `\new...` instruction.

For instance, to allocate a counter register for keeping track of chapter numbers you might write `\newcount\ChapterNo`. For a register to keep track of equation numbers you might say `\newcount\EquationNo` (`\newcount`, as the name of this macro suggests, allocates the next free *count*er register).

Let me now discuss *which register indices* are allocated by these `\new...` instructions. In TeX's plain format (and all other standard TeX formats) the allocation starts for each register type with register index 10 (the reason for this is discussed shortly). The allocated register index increases by one after each `\new...` instruction. The allocations of register indices for the various register types are completely independent of each other.

Which register index was actually allocated by a `\new...` call can be found out easily by looking in the log file. Here is a small example; the following TeX source code is used:

• `ex-regn-log.tip` •

```
\newcount\ChapterNo
\newcount\EquationNo

\bye
```

• End of `ex-regn-log.tip` •

The resulting log file reads as follows:

• `ex-regn-log.log` •

```
This is TeX, C Version 3.14 (...)
**&/usr/local/tex/lib/fmt/plain ex-regn-log.tip
(ex-regn-log.tip
\ChapterNo=\count26
\EquationNo=\count27
)
No pages of output.
```

The log file shows that TeX allocated counter register 26 for the storing the current chapter number (`\ChapterNo`), and counter register 27 (`\EquationNo`) for the storing of the current equation number. The allocation did not start with register 10 (as you might have expected) but with register 26, because other counter registers were already previously allocated by the plain format, the format that is used in the example.

4. Register numbered 0...9 have a special interpretation in TeX (this is why the allocation of registers using any `\new...` type of instruction starts with register index 10 and not with register index 0).

   (a) All registers with register indices in the range 0...9 are reserved for *temporary* use. For instance, to store a value for a very short time, one of those registers can be used. In this case one refers to these registers by their register index, rather than by a name allocated by a `\new...` type of call. The user is responsible for administering temporary registers and must make sure that a register with an index in the 0...9 range is not simultaneously used somewhere else. Grouping can be used frequently to avoid conflicts; for a detailed discussion of grouping see 19.4.2, p. III-100.

(b) Counter registers 0...9 can also be used as temporary registers, but usually contain the current page number or page numbers. These registers are written to the `dvi` file each time a page is written to the `dvi` file using `\shipout`; `\shipout` is described in 29.8, p. III-531. See 3.3.6, p. 49, for details on counter registers.

5. *Parameters.* There are a number of parameters like the various register types which were just introduced. For instance, the three counter parameters that indicated the current date, `\day`, `\month` and `\year` are initialized by TeX to the current day (in the month), the current month and the current year when the program is started. These parameters can be used in a macro which prints the current date (see 21.4.5, p. III-163). They can also be used like ordinary counter registers in that they can participate in arithmetic, can be printed and so forth.

   Parameters are maintained by TeX. They do *not* belong to the pool of 256 registers of each register type. Specifically, there is *no register index* by which parameters can be addressed; they can be addressed by their names only.

   Parameters will be discussed in more detail as the various register types are discussed. They are fairly important, because they allow the parameterization of the layout of a document in TeX. When we discuss dimensions and glue parameters this process becomes more clear. These "register like entities" are referred to as *parameters* in TeX.

   Note that the word *parameter* is used in TeX in two quite different instances:

   (a) Parameters are register-like constructs to hold values to customize TeX's processing, as was explained above.
   (b) Parameters occur in macro definitions: `#1`, `#2`, and so forth. They are called formal arguments in many programming languages.

6. The value of a register can be printed in the text. For example, if we assume counter register `\ChapterNo` contains the current chapter number, then we will want to print the current chapter number in the title of a chapter, as in "Chapter 3."

   For the purpose of printing register contents we have to distinguish between two different types of registers in TeX:

   (a) *Non-box registers.* These are all the register types with the exception of the box registers. They can be written into the text using `\the` (see 24.3, p. III-313, for complete details of applying `\the`).

      i. *Counter registers.* The current value stored in a counter register is printed as an Arabic numeral, as in `\the\ChapterNo`. For alternatives in the printing of counter registers like roman numerals, see 3.3.4, p. 47.

ii. *Dimension registers.* The value, a dimension in the case of a dimension register, is written into the text using the unit points. The user cannot specify a different unit for the output of dimensions.

The dimension value is printed in full precision. For instance, the user cannot specify to print only two digits after the decimal point.

Here is a brief example. The following input is used:

```
\newdimen\xdimen      % Allocate a dimension register.
\xdimen = 6.5in       % Assign value.
{\tt \string\xdimen} contains the following value: \the\xdimen.
```

This input generates the following output: `\xdimen` contains the following value: 469.75499pt.

iii. *Glue registers* and *math glue registers.* The value stored in such a register is obviously a glue value. A glue value can be interpreted as a triple of dimension values, and therefore, there is not much difference between printing dimension and glue values stored in registers (use `\the` followed by the specification of the glue register.)

Stretchability and shrinkability are identified by the appropriate keywords `plus` and `minus`, each followed by the stretchability or shrinkability dimension. If either of these two dimensions are zero, they are not printed (including the respective keywords). All dimensions in glue value printing are given using the unit points. For stretchability and shrinkability values the additional units, `fil`, `fill` and `filll` may occur. These units are discussed in 5.4.1, p. 135.

iv. *Token registers.* Token registers are not discussed in this chapter, because they are quite different from all the other register types; see 20.1, p. III-117, for their discussion.

(b) *Box registers.* There are a variety of different ways to extract information from a box register. However, `\the` cannot be used to print the contents of a box register. See 4.5.3, p. 96, for details.

7. Let me now discuss how you can *write* the value of a register into the *log file*, rather than the text. This is useful for a variety of purposes. Again we have to distinguish among the two different register type groups.

   (a) *Non-box registers.* `\showthe` writes the value of the following register to the log file. For instance, `\showthe\ChapterNo` writes the current chapter number on the screen, as well as into the log file. `\showthe\count0` writes the current content of counter register 0 to the log file (which is usually the current page number).

   Instead of `\showthe`, you can use `\the` (followed by a register specification) inside `\message` (see 29.5.2, p. III-521) or `\wlog` (see 29.5.5, p. III-523). The advantage of `\the` inside `\message` (instead of using `\showthe`) is that you can include additional information that is written to the log file, when using one of these instructions. See the mentioned references for further details.

(b) *Box register.* The `\showbox` primitive has a function that is very similar to `\showthe` but applies to box registers; see 4.5.14, p. 105, for details.

8. *Box register 255.* This box register is reserved for a special purpose. When a page break occurs, the current page is stored in this box register and removed by the output routine to be written to the `dvi` file; see 32.1.1, item 4, p. IV-2, for details. In general you should *not* use this box register unless you know precisely what you are doing. TeX does *not* have a "parameter box register" for storing the "current page," nor does it have any other box parameters.
9. Section 4.6, p. 112, contains an overview of all `\new...` type of instructions. Most of them are used to allocate registers, but some have nothing to do with registers.

3.2 Register Arithmetic

This Section deals with *register arithmetic.* The fact that you can do arithmetic in TeX allows you to actually compute dimensions and other values on the fly which is very useful in many applications in TeX. It also shows the power of TeX.

3.2.1 Assignments of Values to Registers

A value is assigned to a register in a way that is typical for most programming languages. First the register name is given, then an equal sign, and then the value. Here are examples of some register declarations and assignments of values to registers.

```
\newcount\acount
\acount = 12

\count0 = 20

\newdimen\xdim
\xdim = 12.4pt

\dimen0 = 3in

\newskip\xskip
\xskip = 12pt plus 2pt minus 4pt
```

```
\skip0 = 21pt plus 4pt minus 2pt

\newmskip\xmskip
\xmskip = 12pt plus 2pt minus 4pt

\mskip0 = 21pt plus 4pt minus 2pt
```

The equal sign in an assignment to a register is optional in TeX, that is, it can be omitted. The following assignments are therefore equivalent to the previously given assignments:

```
\acount 12
\count0 20
\count0 = 20
\xdim = 12.4pt
\dimen0 = 3in
\xskip = 12pt plus 2pt minus 4pt
\skip0 = 21pt plus 4pt minus 2pt
```

I recommend that you *always* enter the equal sign because it makes these assignments easier to read and makes them look similar to assignments in other programming languages. For instance, it is totally acceptable to think of `\acount` in the above example as the name of an integer variable to which the value 12 is assigned.

Note for the instructions like `\hskip` (horizontal skip, see 5.1, p. 121) or `\vskip` (vertical skip, see 5.1, p. 121) no equal sign is written between the instruction and the following glue specification. Actually writing an equal sign is illegal. This makes perfect sense because in an instruction like `\hskip 12pt` no value is assigned. Instead the value 12 pt defines the amount of horizontal skipping to be executed at this point in time.

Here a note to a reader familiar with a programming language other than TeX: TeX has *no* data type *real*, that is TeX does *not* allow for any floating point type of arithmetic. There is one exception: dimension values can be *entered* using decimal point notation. This is not really an exception though, because all computations are done using integer arithmetic (unit scaled points).

3.2.2 Arithmetic in TeX

TeX's arithmetic capabilities are restricted to the type of operations of two operands, where the first operand is replaced by the result of the operation. In TeX you *cannot* write an arithmetic expression like `\a` = (`\b` + `\c`) * `\d` where `\a`, `\b`, `\c` and `\d` are counter registers.

The following table gives you an overview of TeX's arithmetic operations. The mathematical interpretation is followed by two ways to input such instructions in TeX, a long and a short form. I recommend that you use the long form because your TeX code will be easier to read. The short form saves a couple of tokens. Assume for now that `\a` and `\b` are counter registers (that is assume you have entered `\newcount\a`, `\newcount\b` previously):

Math	Long form	Short form
$a := b$	`\a = \b`	`\a \b`
$a := a + b$	`\advance \a by \b`	`\advance \a \b`
$a := a - b$	`\advance \a by -\b`	`\advance \a -\b`
$a := a * b$	`\multiply \a by \b`	`\multiply \a \b`
$a := a/b$	`\divide \a by \b`	`\divide \a \b`

Note that in all of the preceding examples, a numerical constant could be used instead of the second operand `\b`. For instance, `\advance \a by 10` adds 10 to `\a`. But the first operand `\a` cannot be replaced by a numerical constant because `\a` will need to hold the result of the numerical operation, and therefore the first operand must be a register.

There is *no* `\subtract`.

You also *cannot* use arithmetic in a case such as the following:

```
\hskip \advance\xskip by 10pt
```

That is you cannot use the result of an `\advance` in a `\hskip` or something similar. You can only use these instructions in assignments as they are shown above.

3.3 Numbers and Counter Registers in TEX

Next is the discussion of numbers and number registers. Before we discuss number registers, though, we need to discuss the various ways you can enter numerical constants in TEX.

3.3.1 Numerical Constants

Numerical constants in TEX can be generated in four ways, three of which we will discuss now (the fourth way allows one to specify a *character*; TEX computes, and uses as a numerical constant, the character code of the given character).

1. *Decimal* constants. To specify a number in base 10, no special precautions are necessary in TEX because that is TEX's default. So to specify the numerical constant 13, simply write `13`.
2. *Octal* constants. To enter an octal constant write the number preceded by a right quote. Therefore octal 15 (which is the same as decimal 13) is written as `'15` in TEX.

Table 3.1. 7-bit ASCII code table.

<table>
<tr><td>00 nul</td><td>01 soh</td><td>02 stx</td><td>03 etx</td><td>04 eot</td><td>05 enq</td><td>06 ack</td><td>07 bel</td></tr>
<tr><td>08 bs</td><td>09 ht</td><td>0A nl</td><td>0B vt</td><td>0C np</td><td>0D cr</td><td>0E so</td><td>0F si</td></tr>
<tr><td>10 dle</td><td>11 dc1</td><td>12 dc2</td><td>13 dc3</td><td>14 dc4</td><td>15 nak</td><td>16 syn</td><td>17 etb</td></tr>
<tr><td>18 can</td><td>19 em</td><td>1A sub</td><td>1B esc</td><td>1C fs</td><td>1D gs</td><td>1E rs</td><td>1F us</td></tr>
<tr><td>20 sp</td><td>21 !</td><td>22 "</td><td>23 #</td><td>24 $</td><td>25 %</td><td>26 &</td><td>27 ’</td></tr>
<tr><td>28 (</td><td>29)</td><td>2A *</td><td>2B +</td><td>2C ,</td><td>2D -</td><td>2E .</td><td>2F /</td></tr>
<tr><td>30 0</td><td>31 1</td><td>32 2</td><td>33 3</td><td>34 4</td><td>35 5</td><td>36 6</td><td>37 7</td></tr>
<tr><td>38 8</td><td>39 9</td><td>3A :</td><td>3B ;</td><td>3C <</td><td>3D =</td><td>3E ></td><td>3F ?</td></tr>
<tr><td>40 @</td><td>41 A</td><td>42 B</td><td>43 C</td><td>44 D</td><td>45 E</td><td>46 F</td><td>47 G</td></tr>
<tr><td>48 H</td><td>49 I</td><td>4A J</td><td>4B K</td><td>4C L</td><td>4D M</td><td>4E N</td><td>4F O</td></tr>
<tr><td>50 P</td><td>51 Q</td><td>52 R</td><td>53 S</td><td>54 T</td><td>55 U</td><td>56 V</td><td>57 W</td></tr>
<tr><td>58 X</td><td>59 Y</td><td>5A Z</td><td>5B [</td><td>5C</td><td>5D]</td><td>5E ^</td><td>5F _</td></tr>
<tr><td>60 ‘</td><td>61 a</td><td>62 b</td><td>63 c</td><td>64 d</td><td>65 e</td><td>66 f</td><td>67 g</td></tr>
<tr><td>68 h</td><td>69 i</td><td>6A j</td><td>6B k</td><td>6C l</td><td>6D m</td><td>6E n</td><td>6F o</td></tr>
<tr><td>70 p</td><td>71 q</td><td>72 r</td><td>73 s</td><td>74 t</td><td>75 u</td><td>76 v</td><td>77 w</td></tr>
<tr><td>78 x</td><td>79 y</td><td>7A z</td><td>7B {</td><td>7C |</td><td>7D }</td><td>7E ~</td><td>7F del</td></tr>
</table>

Note that for TeX to interpret the right quote as a symbol beginning an octal constant, TeX has to "expect" a numerical constant in the first place, as in `\count0 = '15`. The term *expect* means here, that TeX's syntax requires an integer to follow as it is in the case of an assignment where so far only the left hand side of the assignment was parsed. If, on the other hand, you simply write "`It's fun to write '15`," TeX will print exactly that: "It's fun to write '15."

3. *Hexadecimal* constants. To enter a hexadecimal constant, precede the constant with a double quote. For instance, to enter the hexadecimal number DA3, write `"DA3`. Lowercase and uppercase letters can be used and actually mixed in hexadecimal constants.

   TeX interprets a leading double-quotation mark as an indicator to interpret a number as a hexadecimal number, only if TeX "expects" a numerical constant in the first place.

3.3.2 Characters, Character-Based Constants, etc.

TeX uses the ASCII code for its character encodings. A *code* defines which number is used to represent which character. The 7 bit ASCII code can be found in Table 3.1 on this page.

If you look at Figure 16.4, p. II-304, then the next question arises is the following: how do you *print* a character where the character is not represented directly on the keyboard? For instance, the character with character code 9 (you can read the 9 as a decimal or hexadecimal number, though not as an octal one, obviously) is the tab character, and tabs are treated as spaces in TeX. On the other hand according to this font table there is a character (the greek Ψ) at that position, and this character has nothing to do with the tab character.

3.3.2.1 Using `\char` To Print Characters

One way to print such a character is to use `\char`. This control sequence must be followed by the character code of the character to be printed. Therefore ȷcan be generated by `\char17`, `\char"11` or `\char'21`.

The main problem with this approach is that characters generated with `\char` are regarded as single entities and do not, for instance, participate in hyphenation. For more information on `\char` see 16.6.1, p. II-296.

3.3.2.2 A Short Form of Character Definition `\chardef`

Instead of defining a macro to declare a special character the `\chardef` primitive can be used as follows:

```
\def\X{\char9 }
```

can be abbreviated to

```
\chardef\X = 9
```

A `\chardef` based macro definition can be also used where TeX expects a numerical value. Using the preceding example `\count0 = \X` would assign the value of 9 to `\count0`.

This form of defining numerical constants is common in the plain format. Here is a list of cases in the plain format, where `\chardef` is used to define numerical constants. For instance, `\@ne` stands for 1, and so forth.

```
\chardef\active=13 \catcode`\~=\active % tilde is active
\chardef\@ne=1
\chardef\tw@=2
\chardef\thr@@=3
\chardef\sixt@@n=16
\chardef\@cclv=255
```

3.3.2.3 Escape Sequences To Print Characters in TeX 2.9

Since `\char`-generated characters do not participate in hyphenation, and because `\char` cannot be used to define characters in hyphenation patterns, TeX defines escape sequences. These escape sequences differ in different versions of TeX (the distinctions made below are related to the issue of escape sequences to print characters only).

- First we will discuss TEX 2.9 as a representative of all versions before TEX 3.0.
- Then we will discuss TEX 3.0 as a representative of all versions of TEX including and after TEX 3.0.

Preceding TEX 3.0 (TEX 2.9 is used as a generic version number for that purpose below) and version TEX 3.0.

TEX 2.9 is based on a 7-bit ASCII code. Therefore, characters with codes in the range of `0`..."`7F` must be accommodated. This range is subdivided into three subranges:

- For characters with a character code in the range of `20`...`5f` use the corresponding printable ASCII character. See Figure 16.4, p. II-304, and Figure 16.5, p. II-305.
- For characters with a character code in the range of `0`...`1f` write `^^X` where character `X` is defined as follows: *add* `40"` to the character code of the character that you want to print (this new number is now in the range `40`...`5f`). This new number determines the character code of the character to be used for `X` according to the first rule.
- For characters with a character code in the range of `60`...`7f` write `^^X` where character `X` is defined as follows: *subtract* `40"` from the character code of the character that you want to print (this new number is now in the range `20`...`3f`). This new number determines the character code of the character to be used for `X` according to the first rule.

Note that the second and third of the preceding rules are quite similar. However, the codes of the characters `X` being generated according to these two rules fall into two disjoint intervals, these two rules do not conflict with each other.

3.3.2.4 Escape Sequences To Print Characters in TEX 3.0

The rules in TEX 3.0 are much simpler: you can generate *any* character by writing `^^xy`, where `x` and `y` are the two hexadecimal digits of the character code of the character you want to generate. There are two important details: if `x` is zero, it must not be omitted, and `x` and `y` must be written as lower case hexadecimal digits.

Furthermore TEX 3.0 still allows the input format of TEX 2.9, which under some rather bizarre circumstances leads to incompatibilities: for instance, the input `^^01` would cause TEX 2.9 to print *two* characters: the first is character `^^0` (the character code of `0` is `"30`, therefore `^^0`, according to rule 3 of the preceding rules on TEX 2.9, generates the character with character code `"70`). This character would be followed by a `1`. In contrast TEX 3.0, `^^01` prints *one* single character, the character with character code `"01`. We will follow the TEX 3.0 conventions for most of this series.

3.3.2.5 Character Code Based Constants

Recall that TeX's characters are based on the ASCII code, with character codes in the range of 0...255. For instance, in the ASCII code the character "A" is assigned character code 65.

Given a *character* you have two choices to determine the *character code* of this character:

1. As mentioned in 3.3.2, p. 40, you could use an ASCII code table and *look up* the character code. The ASCII code information is contained in font tables of this series (see Figs. 16.4–16.7, pp. II-304–II-307).
2. Let TeX *compute* the character code. This method is in general preferable, because it makes the TeX source more readable and avoids potential errors in a table lookup. Let me discuss this approach in more detail now.

To implement the *second* approach you have two different (very closely related) choices. Both approaches *only* work, if TeX *expects* a numerical value in the first place. Here are the two approaches:

1. Enter a left quotation mark in front of the character for which you would like to generate the character code. In the following example grouping is used to preserve the current value of counter register 0. The example also shows two different ways of getting the character codes, one by assignment to a counter register and the other using `\number`.

```
{%
    \count0 = `A%
    the character code of {\tt A} is~\the\count0, and the~{\tt B}
    has character code~\number`B.
}%
```

   The preceding source prints the following text: the character code of `A` is 65, and the `B` has character code 66.
2. Instead of a left quotation mark followed by a character you can use a left quotation mark followed by a *one character long control sequence.* For instance, in the preceding example you could have written ``\count0 = `\A`` instead of ``\count0 = `A``.

   For the preceding example this is really irrelevant. It is important though if you need to "disable" the special meaning of a character in TeX, in which case you need to escape the character by using the backslash. Here is an example to print the character codes of the curly braces:

```
{%
    the character code of opening curly and closing curly
    brace is \number`\{ \space and \number`\} \space respectively%
}%
```

   The output generated by this source code reads as follows: "the character code of opening curly and closing curly brace is 123 and 125 respectively."

The inverse operation to computing the character code of a character is, of course, to print a character of which the character code (rather than the character itself) is given. In TeX this can be done using \char followed by the character code of the character to be printed. For instance, \char`\A prints A: first the character code of "A" is computed (`\A does that), and then this character code is passed to \char to print the character with this character code, which is, of course, the "A."

There are more things to be discussed as far as characters and character codes are concerned. For instance, with an 8-bit character code as TeX uses it (since TeX 3.0 was introduced all characters can be accessed directly), there must be the possibility of entering 256 different characters, far more characters than you find keys on your keyboard (even if you take the shift key into account, you are still quite a bit away from being able to generate 256 characters). A discussion of these matters can be found in 16.6, p. II-295.

3.3.3 The Different Notations of Numerical Constants

For TeX to read a numerical constant, the constant must be "intentionally terminated." This can be accomplished by a space, by \relax, or by an empty group (there are other possibilities, but I limit the discussion to the preceding choices). Therefore, when TeX reads in a numerical constant it must read something terminating the constant; since the user's notion of what terminates a number may be different from TeX's, we need to discuss the applicable rules. We will begin with a sample problem that demonstrates the potential confusion of register values.

3.3.3.1 An Example Explaining the Pitfalls

The preceding explanation may have sounded very theoretical, so consider this an example. Look at the following TeX source code:

```
\def\ANumber{14}%
\def\Text{15 is a nice number}%
\count0 = \ANumber
\Text.
The value of counter register~0 is~\the\count0
```

The text generated by the preceding example reads as follows (note that a value of 1415 and not 14 is printed): "is a nice number. The value of counter register 0 is 1415." Here is what happened:

1. TeX reads-in and saves the two macro definitions of \ANumber and \Text.
2. TeX then begins the assignment to counter register 0 (\count0 =).
3. TeX expands \ANumber. It expands to 14.

4. The space character (actually it is an end-of-line character but spaces and returns are equivalent in this context) after `\ANumber` in `\count0 = \ANumber` is a space after a control word. Therefore, the space is *ignored* (see 18.1.3, p. III-3). So far nothing was found to tell TeX to terminate reading-in a number.
5. TeX *continues* to expand. `\Text` is expanded next generating the number `15` followed by some additional text. This `15` is tagged on to the `14`, so far collected, resulting in the number 1415. This number 1415 is now assigned to the counter register.

   A space follows the `15` in the TeX source code. This space is significant, because

   (a) The space terminated TeX's process of building a number.
   (b) The space, because it *terminated a numerical constant*, is *removed* by TeX.

6. The end result is that counter register 0 is assigned the value of 1415, and not the value of 14 which you might have expected from an initial reading of the preceding TeX source code.
7. The preceding analysis is also consistent with the fact that the text printed reads "`is a nice number`," rather than "`15 is a nice number`."

3.3.3.2 Using Delimiters for Numerical Constants

The question that arises now is how such problems can be avoided by the proper use of delimiters for numerical constants.

1. Note first that a space is a desirable terminator of a constant, and because it is removed after the assignment is completed, such a constant terminating space does not appear in the output.
2. If you cannot add a space (for instance, because spaces after a control word are ignored), you have three alternatives:

   (a) Use `\space`. This macro expands to a space, which will cause the constant to be terminated. The space subsequently is removed according to the previous rules.
   (b) Use `\relax`. This control sequence causes TeX to terminate the numerical constant; see 27.4, p. III-431, for other applications of `\relax`.
   (c) Use an empty group by inserting a pair of curly braces.

3. As noted before, the space terminating a numerical constant is removed by TeX. This can lead to problems; for example, assume the following TeX source code:

```
\count0 = 12
\count1 = 24
The current values of counter registers~0 and~1 are
\the\count0 and \the\count1
```

The TeX code generated by this example reads as follows: "The current values of counter registers 0 and 1 are 12and 24" (note that there is no space between "12" and "and").

What happened? The space after `\count0` in `\the\count0` was ignored by TeX because it acted as a delimiter of the counter register index 0 in `\the\count0`.

Therefore a second space must be introduced in the preceding example, and because two adjacent spaces are reduced to one by TeX, such space must be actually "programmed in." This can be done using `\space`. Here is the corrected example:

```
The current values of counter registers~0 and~1 are
\the\count0 \space and \the\count1
```

Note that `\space` expands to a space token, and a space token will delimit numerical constants. Therefore, the original problem would occur, if the following input were used (note that there should have been a space between `\count0` and `\space`):

```
The current values of counter registers~0 and~1 are
\the\count0\space and \the\count1.
```

On the other hand, the following works (not that I would recommend it...):

```
The current values of counter registers~0 and~1 are
\the\count0\space\space and \the\count1.
```

3.3.3.3 Taking up the Preceding Example

Let us take up the example of 3.3.3.1, p. 44, here. According to what we just said there are a variety of ways how this example can be fixed:

1. Redefine `\ANumber` to `\def\ANumber{14␣}`.
2. Redefine `\ANumber` to `\def\ANumber{14\relax}`.
3. Change the assignment to `\count0` from `\count0 = \ANumber` to `\count0 = \ANumber\relax`.

3.3.3.4 Some More Tricky Examples

Here is another, and even more tricky, example illustrating the same problem. The following TeX source code is used:

```
\newcount\c
\c = 10
\advance\c by 1\the\c   \the\c
The value of {\tt \string\c} is \the\c
```

The output generated by this source code reads as follows: "The value of `\c` is 11020."

TEX does *not* advance `\c` by 1 and then print the new value (`\the\c`) of `\c`. Instead, it advances `\c` by 11010 because `\the\c` expands to 10 and `\the\c` occurs twice. The problem can be corrected by leaving a space after the `1` of `\advance\c by 1`.

Here is an even more subtle example. The following input was used:

```
\newcount\cco
\def\xx{\ifnum\cco=1 2\else 3\fi}%
\cco = 1
\cco = 3\xx
The value of {\tt\string\cco} is \the\cco
```

The output generated by the preceding source reads as follows: "The value of `\cco` is 32." `\cco` contains a value of 32 after the above code was executed because the conditional of `\xx` was evaluated and produced the number 2, which was tagged on to the 3 of `\cco = 3`. At the time `\xx` is expanded, `\cco` still has a value of 1.

Enough confusion? Let's do something else!

3.3.4 Printing Numerical Values, `\number`, `\romannumeral`

I will now discuss the *printing* of numerical values in TEX. For instance, you might want to use Roman numbers instead of Arabic numbers, or you might want to label a list (a), (b), (c), ... rather than 1, 2, 3, ...

Here is an overview of TEX's capabilities of printing numerical values:

1. *Arabic numerals.* `\number` ⟨number⟩ prints ⟨number⟩ as an Arabic numeral. ⟨number⟩ can be a counter register (`\number\counta`) or a numerical constant (`\number 12`) in which case you could simply have written `12`).

   Instead of `\number\counta` you can write `\the\counta`. But `\the` *cannot* be used with a numerical constant, like `\the 12`. However, `\number` can be used with a numerical constant as in `\number 12`.

   Here are some examples, all of which print the number 10.

```
\newcount\counta
\counta = 10
\number\counta
\the\counta
\number 10
\number 0010
```

   Note that `\number` can be also used with *dimension* registers. In this case, the dimension stored in the dimension register is printed using the unit scaled points. The abbreviation for the unit itself though (that is the string `sp`) is not printed. See 4.1.7, item 9.b, p. 88, for details.

2. *Roman numerals.* Uppercase and lowercase roman numerals can be generated in TEX.

(a) *Lowercase roman numerals* are printed with `\romannumeral`. For instance, `\romannumeral 23` prints xxiii. `\romannumeral` can be also used to print the contents of a counter register. To print the contents of `\counta` as a roman numeral, for example, enter `\romannumeral\counta`.

(b) The printing of *uppercase roman numerals* is discussed in 3.4.1, p. 68.

3. *Hexadecimal numbers.* The macro `\Hex` of 27.1.4, p. III-404, can be used to print hexadecimal numbers.
4. *Octal numbers.* The macro `\Oct` discussed in 27.1.4.3, p. III-405, can be used to print octal numbers.
5. *Characters derived from numbers.* To convert a number into a character with that number as character code use `\char`. See 16.6.1, p. II-296, and the next Subsection.

3.3.5 Printing a Character Based on Its Character Code, `\char`, `\PrintAlph`

Given a *character code*, you can print the corresponding character using `\char` as previously mentioned. `\char"45` prints E because the hexadecimal number `"45` is the character code of E. For a table of characters and character codes see Figs. 16.4–16.7, pp. II-304–II-307.

`\char` is used in the font tables just mentioned. It also can be used to label a list (a), (b), (c), ... rather than (1), (2), (3), ... In this case one has to convert the number of a counter register (let's use `\counta`) into a character. If `\counta`'s value is 1 "(a)" should be printed, if the value of this counter register is 2, "(b)" should be printed, and so forth.

The macro `\PrintAlph` takes a numerical value (typically stored in a counter register) and prints the "corresponding" lowercase letter. This macro has one parameter, `#1`, a number. When this parameter is 1, the macro prints an "a," if this parameter is 2 it prints a "b," and so forth.

$\mathcal{P}'$ • `pralph.tip` •

```
\def\PrintAlph #1{%
```

The following curly brace starts a group. Because counter register 0 is used in this macro, its change must be kept limited to the execution of this macro.

```
    {%
        \count0 = #1%
```

The character code of the character which should be printed is computed as follows: #1 + '\a − 1 (remember `'\a` produces the character code of the "a.") The macro does *not* contain an "overflow" test; thus, if a number exceeding 26 is used as the argument ("z" is the 26th character), no error message is printed, but some seemingly unrelated character is printed instead.

```
        \advance\count0 by -1
```

```
            \advance\count0 by `\a
```

Now print the character, terminate the group and the macro is done.

```
            \char\count0
        }%
}
```

• End of `pralph.tip` •

Here is a brief example application of this macro. The following input is used:

```
(\PrintAlph{1}), (\PrintAlph{2}), (\PrintAlph{3}) and so forth
```

This input generates the following output:

"(a), (b), (c) and so forth."

There are certain problems with the preceding macro in some specific applications; see 3.4, p. 68, for another way to define a macro like the one given above.

3.3.6 Counter Registers, `\newcount`

TEX provides a set of 256 *counter registers.* Such registers are identified by `\count` followed by a register index. The macro `\newcount` followed by the name of a counter register allocates a private counter register. For instance, `\newcount\acount` reserves a private counter register naming it `\acount`.

Registers 0...9 are reserved for *temporary use* as is the case with all other registers. In the case of counter registers however recall that the first ten registers have another special meaning: their values are written to the `dvi` file each time a `\shipout` instruction is performed (the `\shipout` instruction is used by the output routine to write a page to the `dvi` file). It is a commonly used convention that counter register 0 contains the page number, and in the case of double page numbers like "3–45" (page 45 of the third chapter), counter register 0 might be used to store the chapter number, and counter register 1 might be used to store the page number with each chapter. See 29.8, p. III-531, for important additional details on these counter registers.

3.3.7 Assign a Name to a Counter Register, `\countdef`

`\countdef` allows you to define a name for a particular counter register. For instance, `\countdef\xx = 23` would make `\xx` an abbreviation for counter register 23. This instruction is rarely used directly by the user. Instead, it is used by the `\newcount` macro to assign the next free counter register index to the user specified name.

There is an example in the plain format where this instruction is used directly. Remember that counter register 0 contains the page number (a TEX convention). The plain format contains the instruction `\countdef\pageno = 0`. This tells TEX that counter register 0 is also to be known under the name `\pageno`. This allows one to refer to the "page number counter register" by `\pageno` instead of `\count0`.

3.3.8 Arithmetic with Counter Registers

TEX only knows about integers (whole numbers without a decimal point); there are *no* floating point numbers (numbers with a decimal point) in TEX. *Dimensions* can be *entered* using decimal points, but are internally treated as integers; see later for details. This implies that the result of a division in TEX is also always an integer. Therefore, the result of dividing 3 by 2 in TEX is 1, and *not* 1.5.

More examples of arithmetic with counter registers follow, also using numerical conditionals discussed in 25.1.4, item 1, p. III-320.

3.3.8.1 The Definition of Macro `\LeadingZ`

Let us first consider macro `\LeadingZ`. This macro has one parameter, `#1`, which must be a number in the range 0...99. `\LeadingZ` will always print this number with *two* digits. In other words, a leading zero is added if the number is in the range 0...9.

Here is the definition of macro `\LeadingZ`:

$\mathcal{P}'$ • `leadingz.tip` •

```
\catcode`\@ = 11
\newcount\@LeadingZCount
\def\LeadingZ #1{%
```

If the number is less than 10, print a leading zero now. The `\fi` terminates the conditional. The print the number.

```
     \@LeadingZCount = #1\relax
     \ifnum \@LeadingZCount < 10
         0%
     \fi
     \the\@LeadingZCount
}
\catcode`\@ = 12
```

• End of `leadingz.tip` •

3.3.8.2 The Definition of Macro `\PrintMilTime`

The macro `\PrintMilTime` (no parameters) prints the current time in military format, that is, as a 24-hour clock. TEX's parameter `\time` is used. This parameter is loaded at the beginning of each TEX job with the number of *minutes* after midnight (see 3.3.10, p. 53, for a brief discussion of `\time`). TEX has *no* parameters `\hour` or `\minute`. In other words, you have to do the arithmetic yourself. See Chapter 26, p. III-357, for a whole set of date and time related macros.

$\mathcal{P}'$ • `pmtime.tip` •

```
\InputD{leadingz.tip}                      % 3.3.8.1, p. 50.
```

Allocate two counter registers to save the hour and minutes of the current time.

```
\newcount\Hour
\newcount\Minute
```

Now define macro `\PrintMilTime`:

```
\def\PrintMilTime{%
```

Compute the current hour by dividing `\time` by 60.

```
    \Hour = \time
    \divide\Hour by 60
```

Compute the number of minutes left in the current hour (`\time` mod 60). Then print the time.

```
    \Minute = \Hour
    \multiply\Minute by 60
    \advance\Minute by -\time
    \Minute = -\Minute
    \LeadingZ{\the\Hour}:\LeadingZ{\the\Minute}%
}
```

• End of `pmtime.tip` •

This macro is used in the following example. The input

```
\input inputd.tip
\InputD{pmtime.tip}                        % 3.3.8.2, p. 51.
\medskip
\centerline{The current time is \PrintMilTime.}
```

generates the text:

The current time is 01:06.

3.3.9 Modulo Arithmetic, the Definition of Macro `\ModuloOneAdvanceNumCond`

Arithmetic modulo some number n is occasionally needed in TEX ($n > 0$ is an integer). In modulo n arithmetic, only numbers in the range $0 \dots n-1$ are used.

I will discuss a macro to *increment a counter* mod n, where the counter *wraps around* that is after $0, 1, \ldots, n-1$, the counter loops back to 0. That is the counter cycles through numbers $0, 1, \ldots, n-1$.

Here is a macro which advances a register by 1 mod n. In most practical applications when the counter "wraps around" some special action has to take place. To be able to distinguish between an ordinary increment and a wrap around this macro is defined as a *conforming conditional.* It must be used with `\ifnum` (see 25.2.2, p. III-351, for details on conforming conditionals). To be precise: first the counter is advanced (mod n), and then its value is returned so it can be used in an `\ifnum` comparison.

The macro `\ModuloOneAdvanceNumCond` has the following two parameters:

- `#1`. The counter register that should be incremented by one modulo n. This increment (and the wrap around if it occurs) is done on a *global basis* that is it does *not* following grouping, if a group is currently established.
- `#2`. The modulo basis, that is, n.

The macro returns the value after the increment to be used in an `\ifnum` comparison.

The macro source file begins here.

$\mathcal{P}'$ • `modonead.tip` •

```
\def\ModuloOneAdvanceNumCond #1#2{%
```

A "closing formula" like for conforming conditional macros presented in this series (see 25.2.2, p. III-351) is used. The macro presented here must be called with `\ifnum` and therefore the closing formula is `0=0\fi`.

```
        0=0\fi
```

Increment the counter on a global basis.

```
        \global\advance #1 by 1
```

If incrementing the counter by 1 caused it to overflow, that is to become n, then the counter is reset to zero. Also the conditional evaluates to true. Otherwise (no wrap around) the conditional generates the result false.

```
        \ifnum #1 = #2\relax
            \global #1 = 0
        \fi
        \ifnum #1%
}
```

• End of `modonead.tip` •

Here is an application of this macro. The following input was used (the macro `\XCountFun` has one parameter, `#1`, which identifies the call to this macro).

```
\input inputd.tip
\InputD{modonead.tip}                   % 3.3.9, p. 52.
\newcount\XCount
\XCount = 0

```

```
\def\XCountFun #1{%
    #1.~%
    \ifnum\ModuloOneAdvanceNumCond{\XCount}{3} = 0
        Counter wrapped around (zero now).
    \else
        Current value of counter {\tt \string\XCount}
        is~\the\XCount.
    \fi
}

\XCountFun{A}%
\XCountFun{B}%
\XCountFun{C}%
\XCountFun{D}%
\XCountFun{E}%
\XCountFun{F}%
\XCountFun{G}%
\bye
```

This input generates the following output:

A. Current value of counter `\XCount` is 1. B. Current value of counter `\XCount` is 2. C. Counter wrapped around (zero now). D. Current value of counter `\XCount` is 1. E. Current value of counter `\XCount` is 2. F. Counter wrapped around (zero now). G. Current value of counter `\XCount` is 1.

3.3.10 Counter Parameters

I now present a list of all the counter parameters of TEX. This list mainly consists of cross-references that you should follow to find out more about the various registers. You may skim through the list simply to get an impression of which counter parameters are available in TEX.

1. Time-related counter parameters.
   - (a) `\time`. The *Minutes* after midnight when the current job was started. There are no counter parameters `\hour` and `\minute` in TEX.
   - (b) `\day`. The current day in the month. There is *no* access to the day of the week (Monday, Tuesday, ...); see 26.16, p. III-381, for how to do this.
   - (c) `\month`. The current month.
   - (d) `\year`. The current year.
2. Line breaking counter parameters (see also item 3):
   - (a) `\pretolerance`. The maximum allowable tolerance in pass 1 of the line breaking algorithm; see 12.7.2, p. II-137.
   - (b) `\tolerance`. The maximum allowable tolerance in pass 2 of the line breaking algorithm; see 12.7.2, p. II-137.

(c) `\doublehyphendemerits`. Demerits added if two consecutive hyphenated lines occur; see 12.7.15, item 4.b, p. II-143.
(d) `\finalhyphendemerits`. Demerits added if the second to the last line of a paragraph is hyphenated; see 12.7.15, item 4.c, p. II-144.
(e) `\adjdemerits`. Demerits added for two adjacent and visually incompatible lines; see 12.7.15, item 4.a, p. II-143.
(f) `\linepenalty`. Penalty added to the demerit formula of each line; see 12.7.15, item 4.d, p. II-144.
(g) `\looseness`. TeX will try to make the paragraph `\looseness` lines longer than it would ordinarily (`\looseness = 0`) without exceeding any of the given tolerances; see 12.8.1, p. II-149.

3. Implicit horizontal penalties stored in counter parameters (the term "implicit horizontal penalties" is defined in 5.8, p. 157).

(a) `\linepenalty`. Amount added to the *badness* of every line in a paragraph; see 12.7.10, item 4.d, p. II-144. The term badness is defined in 5.3, p. 127.
(b) `\hyphenpenalty`. Penalty of a line break after a discretionary hyphen; see 12.7.10, item 1, p. II-144.
(c) `\exhyphenpenalty`. Penalty of a line break after an explicit hyphen; see 12.7.10, item 2, p. II-144.
(d) `\binoppenalty`. Penalty for a line break at a binary operator in a mathematical equation; see 12.7.10, item 3, p. II-144.
(e) `\relpenalty`. Penalty for a line break at a math relation in a mathematical equation; see 12.7.10, item 4, p. II-144.

4. Implicit vertical penalties (this term is defined in 5.8, p. 157).

(a) `\clubpenalty`. Penalty for creating a club line at the bottom of a page; see 32.5.4.2, item 1.b, p. IV-20.
(b) `\widowpenalty`. Penalty for creating a widow line at the top of the page; see 32.5.4.2, item 1.c, p. IV-20.
(c) `\displaywidowpenalty`. Penalty for creating a widow line before a displayed equation; see 32.5.4.2, item 2.a, p. IV-21.
(d) `\brokenpenalty`. Penalty inserted between a hyphenated line and the following line; see 32.5.4.2, item 1.a, p. IV-20.
(e) `\predisplaypenalty`. Penalty inserted before a displayed equation; see 32.5.4.2, item 2.b, p. IV-21.
(f) `\postdisplaypenalty`. Penalty inserted after a displayed equation; see 32.5.4.2, item 2.c, p. IV-21.
(g) `\interlinepenalty`. Penalty inserted between every pair of two lines of a paragraph; see 32.5.4.2, item 1.d, p. IV-21.
(h) `\floatingpenalty`. Penalty split insertions; see 32.7.7, p. IV-35.
(i) `\outputpenalty`. The penalty associated with the current page breakpoint as reported to the output routine; see 33.6.1, p. IV-52.

5. Debugging and tracing related counter parameters:

(a) `\pausing`. If positive, TeX pauses after each line read-in from the file;

see 27.12, p. III-443.

(b) `\tracingonline`. This counter register is usually zero. If positive, the output of `\showbox` and the output generated by setting `\tracingcommands`, and so forth which *usually* only appears in log files, is *also* written to the terminal screen; see 22.2.4, p. III-217, for details.

(c) `\tracinglostchars`. If positive, characters that are not in a font are shown; see 16.6.4, p. II-297, for details.

(d) `\tracingmacros`. If positive, the showing of the expansion of macros is enabled; see 22.2.1, p. III-216, for details.

(e) `\tracingstats`. If positive, the statistics about memory use is shown.

(f) `\tracingparagraphs`. If positive, it shows line-break calculations.

(g) `\tracingpages`. If positive, it shows page break computations.

(h) `\tracingoutput`. If positive, it shows all boxes that are shipped out (using `\shipout`).

(i) `\tracingcommands`. If positive, it shows commands before they are executed.

(j) `\tracingrestores`. If positive, it shows de-assignments if groups end.

(k) Finally, there is `\tracingall` which is *not* a counter parameter but a plain format macro which sets all the preceding counter parameter to a positive value; see 27.11, p. III-441, for details.

6. Counter parameters relating to characters and fonts:

   (a) `\mag`. The global magnification factor of a document; see 15.1.2, p. II-228.

   (b) `\uchyph`. If positive, then the second part of a hyphenated word will be printed beginning with a capital letter; see 12.7.8, p. II-143.

   (c) `\defaulthyphenchar`. The default character code of the hyphenation character. It is obviously initialized to the character code of the hyphen ("-"); see 12.7.7, p. II-142.

   (d) `\lefthyphenmin` and `\righthyphenmin`: the minimum number of characters before and after the hyphen of a hyphenated word; see 12.7.4, item 8, p. II-141, for details.

   (e) `\defaultskewchar`: the default skew character code; see 14.5.9, p. II-207.

   (f) `\escapechar`. Character code of the character used by `\string` to print the escape character; see 19.1.2, p. III-66. This has nothing to do with what the current escape character is (usually the backslash, of course).

   (g) `\endlinechar`. Character code of the character placed at the end of every line; see 18.1.13, p. III-14.

   (h) `\newlinechar`. Character code of a character that generates a new line in the output of a `\write`; see 29.5.3, p. III-522.

   (i) `\fam`. The current family number when typesetting mathematical equations; see 14.5.5, p. II-204.

7. Box related counter parameters:

   (a) `\hbadness`, `\vbadness`. These registers contain a threshold value for the badness of hboxes and vboxes. If the badness of an hbox or vbox when built exceeds the corresponding value, then the box involved is reported as overfull, or whatever is appropriate. See 5.3.5, p. 131, for details.

(b) `\badness`. The badness of the most recently constructed box; see 5.3.3, p. 129, for details.

(c) There are two registers relating to the writing of box information to the log file:

   i. `\showboxdepth` (maximum number of items per level shown).
   ii. `\showboxbreadth` (maximum level when boxes are shown).

   See 4.5.14, p. 105, for details on both.

8. Other counter parameters:

   (a) `\deadcycles`. Counter register that is incremented each time the output routine is called *without* output to the `dvi` file, and reset to zero, each time the output writes a page to the `dvi` file; see 29.8, p. III-531.
   (b) `\maxdeadcycles`. Upper bound on `\deadcycles`, before an error is reported by TeX; see 29.8, p. III-531.
   (c) `\holdinginserts`. If this register is set to a positive value (and is not zero), insertion material is *not* passed on to the output routine (in the related insertion box registers). See 32.7.8, p. IV-35, for details.
   (d) `\hangafter`. Parameter determining the number of lines to which hanging indentation applies; see 11.4, p. II-80.
   (e) `\globaldefs`. Determines whether any type of definitions and assignments are handled globally or not; see 19.4.12, p. III-108.
   (f) `\delimiterfactor`. Ratio for variable delimiters, times 1000; for details see 13.6.5, p. II-184.
   (g) `\inputlineno`. Line number (of the source code file) which would be reported if TeX generated an error message. See 28.3.5, p. III-460.
   (h) `\language`. Register to be set to the current language to control the hyphenation patterns to be applied; see 12.7.4, p. II-139.

3.3.11 Numerical Conditionals, `\ifnum`, `\ifcase`

We will now discuss numerical conditionals. Conditionals are an important part of TeX's macro mechanism and are discussed in further detail in Chapter 25, p. III-317.

TeX has three numerical conditionals:

1. TeX's conditional `\ifnum` allows the comparison of numbers. This conditional can be used to test whether one number is less than, equal to, or greater than another number. The macro `\LeadingZ` presented a simple application of `\ifnum`. See 25.1.8, p. III-327, for another example.

2. TEX's conditional `\ifodd` allows you to test whether a number is odd. See 25.1.1, p. III-318, for an application of this macro.
3. There is also `\ifcase`, a construct similar to case statements in other programming languages. This construct has strong similarities to conditionals and, therefore, is listed here. For a general description of this instruction, see item 2, 25.1.4, p. III-321.

For all of the above references, see 25.1.4, p. III-320, for details on conditionals in general.

3.3.12 Computing the Absolute Value

The following macro `\AbsoluteValue` computes the absolute value of a number. It has two parameters:

- `#1`. A number.
- `#2`. A counter register which is loaded with the absolute value of `#1`. Note: `#1` and `#2` may be identical.

A macro to compute the absolute value of a dimension can be found in 4.1.11, p. 91.

Here is the source code of this macro:

$\mathcal{P}'$ • `absval.tip` •

```
\def\AbsoluteValue #1#2{%
    \ifnum #1<0
        #2 = -#1\relax
    \else
        #2 = #1\relax
    \fi
}
```

• End of `absval.tip` •

The following example shows an application of this macro:

• `ex-absval.tip` •

```
\InputD{absval.tip}                         % 3.3.12, p. 57.
\newcount\exabs
\AbsoluteValue{12}{\exabs}%
    The absolute value of 12 is \the\exabs.
\AbsoluteValue{-13}{\exabs}%
    The absolute value of $-13$ is \the\exabs.
```

• End of `ex-absval.tip` •

This source code generates the following output: The absolute value of 12 is 12. The absolute value of -13 is 13.

3.3.13 Modulo Computation, \IModN

The macro \IModN computes #1 mod #2 and stores the result in counter register #3. Here is a more precise description of its parameters:

- #1. A number $i \geq 0$. If this number is stored in a counter register, then this register can be the same as the register specified for #3.
- #2. A number $n > 0$. If this number is stored in a counter register, this register can be the same as the register specified for #3.
- #3. A counter register, which after the preceding macro was called, contains the value of i mod n.

Here is the source code for macro \IModN:

$\mathcal{P}'$ • imodn.tip •

```
\catcode`\@ = 11
```

In the following two counter registers initially the value of #1 is saved.

```
\newcount\@IModNCount
\newcount\@IModNCountCopy
```

The macro definition itself starts here.

```
\def\IModN #1#2#3{%
    \@IModNCount = #1\relax
    \@IModNCountCopy = #1\relax
```

Check whether the arguments make sense. #1 must be ≥ 0 and #2 must be > 0.

```
    \ifnum \@IModNCount < 0
        \errmessage{\string\IModN: \string#1
            (value \the\@IModNCount) is negative.}%
    \fi
    \ifnum #2< 1
        \errmessage{\string\IModN: \string#2
            (value #2) is negative or zero.}%
    \fi
```

Here is where the modulo computation really takes place.

```
    \divide\@IModNCount by #2\relax
    \multiply\@IModNCount by #2\relax
    #3 = \@IModNCountCopy
    \advance #3by -\@IModNCount
}
\catcode`\@ = 12
```

• End of imodn.tip •

The following test program shows examples applications of \IModN.

• ex-imodn.tip •

```
\InputD{imodn.tip}                          % 3.3.13, p. 58.
\newcount\IModNTestCount
```

Macro `\IModNTest` takes two arguments `#1` and `#2`. It computes `#1` mod `#2` and prints out the result of this computation together with the values of `#1` and `#2`.

```
\def\IModNTest #1#2{%
    \IModN{#1}{#2}{\IModNTestCount}%
    {\tt \string\IModNTest}:
    #1 mod #2 = \the\IModNTestCount.\par
}
```

And here are a number of calls to macro `\INumNTest`.

```
\IModNTest{0}{10}%
\IModNTest{3}{10}%
\IModNTest{9}{10}%
\IModNTest{10}{10}%
\IModNTest{100}{10}%
\IModNTest{107}{10}%
```

• End of `ex-imodn.tip` •

The preceding source code generates the following output:

`\IModNTest`: 0 mod 10 = 0.
`\IModNTest`: 3 mod 10 = 3.
`\IModNTest`: 9 mod 10 = 9.
`\IModNTest`: 10 mod 10 = 0.
`\IModNTest`: 100 mod 10 = 0.
`\IModNTest`: 107 mod 10 = 7.

3.3.14 Compute the Value in a Certain Position, `\ValueOfDecimalPosition`

In this and the following Subsection we discuss macros relating to the decimal representation of integers. Let w be a positive decimal number with a decimal representation written as $w = \sum_{i=0}^{k} d_i 10^i$. We call d_i the *digit at position i*. We call i the *digit position*. Furthermore we assume that (with the exception of number 0, which is a special case, of course), d_k, the digit at the highest position, is non-zero. The preceding discussion can be extended to negative numbers using their absolute value instead. d_i can be easily computed as $(w/10^i)$ mod 10, where "/" stands for *integer* division.

The macro `\ValueOfDecimalPosition` which we will define now has three arguments:

- `#1`. Some number, positive or negative.
- `#2`. A digit position.
- `#3`. A counter register. This counter register, after the completion, contains the value of d_i where i is the same as `#2`.

The source code of this macro begins here.

$\mathcal{P}'$ • valdecpo.tip •

```
\InputD{imodn.tip}                      % 3.3.13, p. 58.
\InputD{absval.tip}                     % 3.3.12, p. 57.
\InputD{rangetst.tip}                   % 25.1.9, p. III-328.
\InputD{doloop.tip}                     % 27.1.8, p. III-412.
\catcode`\@ = 11
```

A counter register private to this macro is needed.

```
\newcount\@ValueOfDecimalPosition
```

The following counter register is used for a loop counter.

```
\newcount\@ValueOfDecimalPositionLoopCount
```

The macro definition starts here.

```
\def\ValueOfDecimalPosition #1#2#3{%
```

`#2` must be a positive number, and not greater or equal 10 (the largest positive number one can represent in TeX is $2^{31}-1$). Generate an error message if that is not true.

```
    \CheckRange{#2}{0}{9}{\string\ValueOfDecimalPosition:
        \#2 must be in the range 0 .. 9}%
```

Put the absolute value of the provided number into `\@ValueOfDecimalPosition`.

```
    \AbsoluteValue{#1}{\@ValueOfDecimalPosition}%
```

Now divide the number by 10 as often as determined by `#2`. Use a loop to do so (`\DoLoop` macro).

```
    \DoLoop{\@ValueOfDecimalPositionLoopCount}{1}{1}{#2}%
        {\global\divide\@ValueOfDecimalPosition by 10}%
```

Now take this value mod 10 and return it. We are done.

```
    \IModN{\@ValueOfDecimalPosition}{10}{#3}%
}
\catcode`\@ = 12
```

• End of valdecpo.tip •

Here is an example application of macro `\ValueOfDecimalPosition`:

• ex-valdecpo.tip •

```
\InputD{valdecpo.tip}                   % 3.3.14, p. 60.
\InputD{doloop.tip}                     % 27.1.8, p. III-412.
```

The following macro takes as argument an integer value and computes the numbers of weights $0\ldots3$ for these numbers.

```
\def\TestValueOfDecimalPosition #1{%
    The number is {\it #1}.
    \DoLoop{\count0}{0}{1}{6}{%
        \ValueOfDecimalPosition{#1}{\count0}{\count1}%
        (P:~\the\count0, V:~\the\count1)
    }%
}
```

And here are a few calls of `\TestValueOfDecimalPosition`.

```
\BeginItemize
    \Item\TestValueOfDecimalPosition{17}
    \Item\TestValueOfDecimalPosition{243}
    \Item\TestValueOfDecimalPosition{-243}
    \Item\TestValueOfDecimalPosition{4122}
\EndItemize
```

• End of `ex-valdecpo.tip` •

The preceding source code generates the following output:

- The number is *17.* (P: 0, V: 7) (P: 1, V: 1) (P: 2, V: 0) (P: 3, V: 0) (P: 4, V: 0) (P: 5, V: 0) (P: 6, V: 0)
- The number is *243.* (P: 0, V: 3) (P: 1, V: 4) (P: 2, V: 2) (P: 3, V: 0) (P: 4, V: 0) (P: 5, V: 0) (P: 6, V: 0)
- The number is *-243.* (P: 0, V: 3) (P: 1, V: 4) (P: 2, V: 2) (P: 3, V: 0) (P: 4, V: 0) (P: 5, V: 0) (P: 6, V: 0)
- The number is *4122.* (P: 0, V: 2) (P: 1, V: 2) (P: 2, V: 1) (P: 3, V: 4) (P: 4, V: 0) (P: 5, V: 0) (P: 6, V: 0)

3.3.15 The Definition of Macro `\LargestDecimalPlace` and Its Use

The following macro `\LargestDecimalPlace` determines the largest non-zero digit position of an integer. It has two parameters.

- `#1`. A number (positive or negative). If negative, the absolute value of `#1` is used.
- `#2`. A counter register to hold the result from the evaluation of this macro. The macro's result is the highest decimal position of the decimal representation of this number. For instance, for number 9 the result would be zero, whereas for numbers 10 through 99 the result would be 1.

The source code of this macro begins here.

$\mathcal{P}'$ • `largdp.tip` •

```
\InputD{valdecpo.tip}                         % 3.3.14, p. 60.
\InputD{absval.tip}                           % 3.3.12, p. 57.
\catcode`\@ = 11
```

We need one private counter register.

```
\newcount\@LargestDecimalPlaceCount
```

The macro definition itself starts here.

```
\def\LargestDecimalPlace #1#2{%
```

Convert number into a positive number by taking the absolute value.

```
        \AbsoluteValue{#1}{\@LargestDecimalPlaceCount}%
```

The initial value for the result is zero, then we start a recursive macro.

```
        \wlog{We make progress}%
        #2 = 0
        \@LargestDecimalPlaceMore{#2}%
}
```

The following macro `\@LargestDecimalPlaceMore` has one argument which is identical to `#2` of the preceding macro. The following macro generates recursive calls and divides `\@LargestDecimalPlaceMore` by 10 until this register is less than 10.

```
\def\@LargestDecimalPlaceMore #1{%
        \wlog{One round: \the#1}%
        \ifnum\@LargestDecimalPlaceCount < 10
```

We are done and `#1` contains the result.

```
                \def\@LargestDecimalPlaceMoreNext{}%
        \else
```

One (or more) recursion necessary.

```
                \advance #1 by 1
                \divide\@LargestDecimalPlaceCount by 10
                \def\@LargestDecimalPlaceMoreNext{%
                        \@LargestDecimalPlaceMore{#1}%
                }%
        \fi
```

Recursion, if at all, is restarted here. Or macro terminates.

```
        \@LargestDecimalPlaceMoreNext
}
\catcode`\@ = 12
```

• End of `largdp.tip` •

Here is a short example application of this macro:

• `ex-largdp.tip` •

```
\input inputd.tip
\InputD{largdp.tip}                          % 3.3.15, p. 61.
\nonstopmode
\newcount\TestLargestDecimalPlaceCount
```

The following macro has one argument, `#1`, a number. `\LargestDecimalPlace` is invoked and the result from this macro call together with the number itself is printed.

```
\def\TestLargestDecimalPlace #1{%
        {%
                \LargestDecimalPlace{#1}
                        {\TestLargestDecimalPlaceCount}%
                Number #1: largest decimal place
                        is~\the\TestLargestDecimalPlaceCount.
```

```
    }%
}
\TestLargestDecimalPlace{9}
\TestLargestDecimalPlace{10}
\TestLargestDecimalPlace{10000}
\TestLargestDecimalPlace{99999}
\TestLargestDecimalPlace{100000}
```

• End of `ex-largdp.tip` •

The output from the preceding source code reads as follows:

> Number 9: largest decimal place is 0. Number 10: largest decimal place is 1. Number 10000: largest decimal place is 4. Number 99999: largest decimal place is 4. Number 100000: largest decimal place is 5.

3.3.16 Printing a Number in Textual Form

The following macro `\NumberToText` prints a number in its textual form. So, for instance, if called with argument 123 the macro will generate "one hundred and twenty three."

The source code for this macro starts here.

$\mathcal{P}'$ • `ntotext.tip` •

```
\InputD{imodn.tip}                        % 3.3.13, p. 58.
\catcode`\@ = 11
```

The following auxiliary macro prints a number in the range of $0 \ldots 9$ in textual form. If this number is zero, the printing of text "zero" *can* be suppressed. The macro has two parameters:

- `#1`. A control code. If this parameter is zero *and* the number to be printed (`#2`) is zero, no output is generated.

  If this parameter is non-zero then `#2` will be printed in textual form, regardless of `#2`'s value.
- `#2`. The number of which the textual representation is to be printed. Must be in the range $0 \ldots 9$.

```
\def\@OneDigitNumberText #1#2{%
    \ifcase #2\relax
        \ifnum #1=0
        \else
            zero%
        \fi
        \or
        one\or
        two\or
        three\or
```

```
        four\or
        five\or
        six\or
        seven\or
        eight\or
        nine%
    \else
        \errmessage{\string\@OneDigitNumberText: number
            \number#2 out of range.}%
    \fi
}
```

Two private counter registers are needed below.

```
\newcount\@NumberToConvert
\newcount\@NumberToConvertTwo
```

The following counter register is used as a flag. If its value is non-zero, then this means that some text has already been generated; therefore any new text to be generated must be preceded by "and."

```
\newcount\@NumberToConvertAndFlag
```

The source code for macro `\NumberToText` starts here.

```
\def\NumberToText #1{%
    \@NumberToConvert = #1\relax
```

If the number is negative, the word "minus" is printed. Then the number is made positive.

```
    \ifnum\@NumberToConvert < 0
        minus
        \@NumberToConvert = -\@NumberToConvert
    \fi
```

If the number is $\geq$ 1.000.000, then let's forget it. This macro is intended for writing the textual representation of the face value of a check: if you should ever need to use this macro to fill out checks with a face value above $1.000.000, then please hire me as consultant to extend the macro (you obviously can afford it!)[1].

```
    \CheckRange{\@NumberToConvert}{0}{999999}%
        {\string\NumberToText: numbers >= 1.000.000
            not handled.}%
```

If the number is $\geq$ 1000, then the "thousand part" of the number will be printed first.

```
    \@NumberToConvertAndFlag = 0
    \ifnum\@NumberToConvert > 999
```

Save the number, divide it by 1000, print the text of the thousand part.

```
        \@NumberToConvertTwo = \@NumberToConvert
        \divide\@NumberToConvert by 1000
```

[1] Thank you!

```
        \@NumberToText
```

Append the word "thousand and" now to the text so far generated.

```
        \space thousand and
```

Compute "number mod 1000" and then print that number.

```
        \IModN{\@NumberToConvertTwo}{1000}{\@NumberToConvert}%
    \fi
```

Now the number is < 1000.

```
    \CheckRange{\@NumberToConvert}{0}{999}%
        {\string\NumberToText: internal error 1}%
```

Print the number.

```
    \@NumberToText
}
```

A temporary register for the following macro.

```
\newcount\@NumberToTextTmp
```

The following macro `\@NumberToText` prints out numbers < 1000 in textual representation.

```
\def\@NumberToText{%
    \ifnum\@NumberToConvert > 99
```

The number is in the range $100 \ldots 999$. Print out the text relating to the hundred position of the number.

```
        \ValueOfDecimalPosition{\@NumberToConvert}{2}%
            {\@NumberToTextTmp}%
        \@OneDigitNumberText{1}{\@NumberToTextTmp}%
```

Append the word "hundred."

```
        \space hundred and
```

Take the number mod 100 and then initiate a recursive call.

```
        \IModN{\@NumberToConvert}{100}{\@NumberToConvert}%
    \fi
```

Now deal with the ten position. Load `\@NumberToTextTmp` with the value of the number at position 1 (in other words compute d_1 in $\sum_{i=0}^{n} d_i * 10^i$).

```
    \ValueOfDecimalPosition{\@NumberToConvert}{1}%
        {\@NumberToTextTmp}%
    \ifnum\@NumberToTextTmp > 1
```

The number is ≥ 20 (and < 100).

```
        \ifcase\@NumberToTextTmp
```

Internal error: number is obviously not ≥ 20.

```
                \errmessage{\string\@NumberToText:
                    internal error 1.}%
            \or
```

Still same error.

```
                \errmessage{\string\@NumberToText:
                    internal error 2.}%
            \or
            twenty\or
            thirty\or
            forty\or
            fifty\or
            sixty\or
            seventy\or
            eighty\or
            ninety%
        \else
            \errmessage{\string\@NumberToText:
                internal error 4.}%
        \fi
```

The number is ≥ 20, print the last position of it.

```
        \IModN{\@NumberToConvert}{10}{\@NumberToTextTmp}%
            \@OneDigitNumberText{0}{\@NumberToTextTmp}%
    \else
```

Now we know the number is < 20.

```
        \ifnum\@NumberToTextTmp = 1
```

The number is in the range $10 \ldots 19$. To simplify the `\ifcase` below subtract 10.

```
            \advance\@NumberToConvert by -10
            \ifcase\@NumberToConvert
                ten\or
                eleven\or
                twelve\or
                thirteen\or
                fourteen\or
                fifteen\or
                sixteen\or
                seventeen\or
                eighteen\or
                nineteen%
            \fi
        \else
```

The number is in the range $0 \ldots 9$.

```
            \@OneDigitNumberText{1}{\@NumberToConvert}%
        \fi
```

The end of `\ifnum\@NumberToTextTmp > 1`.

```
    \fi
}
\catcode`\@ = 12
```

• End of `ntotext.tip` •

Here are some examples using the preceding macro.

• `ex-ntotext.tip` •

```
\InputD{ntotext.tip}                            % 3.3.16, p. 63.
\InputD{doloop.tip}                             % 27.1.8, p. III-412.
\input doloop.tip
```

The following macro prints out its argument, `#1`, a number, and then calls `\NumberToText`.

```
\def\TestN #1{%
    \the#1: ``\NumberToText{#1}.''
}
```

Loops are used to generate a number of calls to the preceding macro.

```
{
    I.~\DoLoop{\count0}{0}{1}{32}{\TestN{\count0}}

    II.~\DoLoop{\count0}{98}{1}{104}{\TestN{\count0}}

    III.~\DoLoop{\count0}{101}{100}{1001}{\TestN{\count0}}

    IV.~\DoLoop{\count0}{1000}{849}{19000}{\TestN{\count0}}
}
```

• End of `ex-ntotext.tip` •

The preceding source code produces the following output:

I. 0: "zero." 1: "one." 2: "two." 3: "three." 4: "four." 5: "five." 6: "six." 7: "seven." 8: "eight." 9: "nine." 10: "ten." 11: "eleven." 12: "twelve." 13: "thirteen." 14: "fourteen." 15: "fifteen." 16: "sixteen." 17: "seventeen." 18: "eighteen." 19: "nineteen." 20: "twenty." 21: "twentyone." 22: "twentytwo." 23: "twentythree." 24: "twentyfour." 25: "twentyfive." 26: "twentysix." 27: "twentyseven." 28: "twentyeight." 29: "twentynine." 30: "thirty." 31: "thirtyone." 32: "thirtytwo."

II. 98: "ninetyeight." 99: "ninetynine." 100: "one hundred and zero." 101: "one hundred and one." 102: "one hundred and two." 103: "one hundred and three." 104: "one hundred and four."

III. 101: "one hundred and one." 201: "two hundred and one." 301: "three hundred and one." 401: "four hundred and one." 501: "five hundred and one." 601: "six hundred and one." 701: "seven hundred and one." 801: "eight hundred and one." 901: "nine hundred and one." 1001: "one thousand and one."

IV. 1000: "one thousand and zero." 1849: "one thousand and eight hundred and fortynine." 2698: "two thousand and six hundred and ninetyeight." 3547: "three thousand and five hundred and fortyseven." 4396: "four thousand and three hundred and ninetysix." 5245: "five thousand and two hundred and fortyfive." 6094: "six thousand and ninetyfour." 6943: "six thousand and nine hundred and fortythree." 7792: "seven thousand and seven hundred and ninetytwo." 8641: "eight thousand and six hundred and fortyone." 9490: "nine thousand and four hundred and ninety." 10339: "ten thousand and three hundred and thirtynine." 11188: "eleven thousand and one hundred and eightyeight." 12037: "twelve thousand and thirtyseven." 12886: "twelve thousand and eight hundred and eightysix." 13735: "thirteen thousand and seven hundred and thirtyfive." 14584: "fourteen thousand and five hundred and eightyfour." 15433: "fifteen thousand and four hundred and thirtythree." 16282: "sixteen thousand and two hundred and eightytwo." 17131: "seventeen thousand and one hundred and thirtyone." 17980: "seventeen thousand and nine hundred and eighty." 18829: "eighteen thousand and eight hundred and twentynine."

3.4 Generic Counter Register Macros

Generic macros to administer counters can be divided into two parts. Some macros *print counter register values* (actually these macros work for any number, but in ordinary applications it is the value of a counter register that is printed). Other powerful macros administer and manipulate counter registers in order to number a document by chapter, section, subsection, etc.

3.4.1 Printing Counter Registers, `\arabic`, `\roman`, `\Roman`, `\alph`, `\Alph`

I present the following counter value printing macros (all macros have one parameter, `#1`, a counter register or a number; the way this counter register or number is printed depends on which macro is called):

1. `\arabic`. The number stored in the counter register, or the given numerical constant, is printed as an Arabic numeral.
2. `\roman` and `\Roman`. The number is printed as lowercase or uppercase Roman numeral.
3. `\alph` and `\Alph`. The number is printed as a lowercase or uppercase letter (if the number is 0, an "a" or an "A" is printed, if the number is 1, a "b" or "B" is printed, and so forth).

Here is the definition of the macros just listed.

$\mathcal{P}'$ • `printco.tip` •

```
\catcode`\@ = 11
\def\arabic #1{\number#1}
\def\roman #1{%
    \romannumeral #1%
}
```

Next is the definition of `\Roman`.

```
\def\Roman #1{%
    \ifcase #1\or
        I\or II\or III\or IV\or V\or
        VI\or VII\or VIII\or IX\or X\or
        XI\or XII\or XIII\or XIV\or XV\or
        XVI\or XVII\or XVIII\or XIX\or XX\or
        XXI\or XXII\or XXIII\or XXIV\or XV%
    \else
        \errmessage{\string\Roman: argument \number#1 out
            of range, larger than 25.}%
    \fi
}
```

Please note that `\Roman` was *not* defined as follows:

```
\def\Roman #1{%
    \uppercase\expandafter{\romannumeral#1}%
}
```

This reason for this is that the latter definition would *not* produce a single roman numeral when expanded inside an `\edef`, but the first definition does (the first definition, of course, has a disadvantage in that it only produces a roman numeral for numbers within a certain range).

Next is the definition of `\alph`, which does *not* resort to using `\char` out of the same reasons `\Roman` did not use `\uppercase`. If you want to produce a *character token* instead of *an instruction to print a character* (`\char`), you need to use the following macro definition instead of using `\char`.

```
\def\alph #1{%
    \ifcase #1%
        \or a\or b\or c\or d\or e\or f\or g\or h\or i%
    \else
        \@Morealph{#1}%
    \fi
}
\def\@Morealph #1{%
    \ifcase #1%
        \or  \or  \or  \or  \or  \or  \or  \or  \or
        \or j\or k\or l\or m\or n\or o\or p\or q\or r%
        \or s\or t\or u\or v\or w\or x\or y\or z%
    \else
        \errmessage{\string\@Morealph: argument too large.}%
    \fi
}
```

Note that the definition of `\alph` could include "the complete `\ifcase` statement" instead of splitting the `\ifcase` statement into two separate `\ifcase` statements, one in `\alph` and the other in `\@Morealph`. The reason for this split is to keep `\alph`'s definition short: in most cases `\alph` is used with small arguments, let's say *not greater* than 7. However, if it is greater than 7, `\@Morealph` does the printing.

Here is the definition of `\Alph` along the lines of the definition of `\alph` which prints uppercase letters.

```
\def\Alph #1{%
    \ifcase #1%
    \or A\or B\or C\or D\or E\or F\or G\or H\or I%
    \else
        \@MoreAlph{#1}%
    \fi
}
\def\@MoreAlph #1{%
    \ifcase #1%
        \or  \or  \or  \or  \or  \or  \or  \or  \or
        \or J\or K\or L\or M\or N\or O\or P\or Q\or R%
        \or S\or T\or U \or V\or W\or X\or Y\or Z%
    \else
        \errmessage{\string\@MoreAlph: argument too large.}%
    \fi
}
\catcode`\@ = 12
```

• End of `printco.tip` •

3.4.2 Macros to Administer Counter Registers

The macros presented in the preceding Subsection (`\arabic`, `\roman`, `\Roman`, `\alph`, and `\Alph`) are used in the macros of this Subsection. The macros presented in this subsection are:

- `\NewCounter`. Establish a new counter.
- `\ReassignCounter`. Redefine (in particular the format in which output from this counter appears) an existing counter.
- `\TheCounter`. Basic macro to print a counter.
- `\TheArabicCounter`. Basic macro to print a counter as an arabic number.
- `\PrintCounter`. Another way to print a counter.
- `\RefCounter`. Yet another way (usually used in a reference to the counter).
- `\AddCounterToResetList`. Instruct TeX to reset the counter when another counter is incremented.
- `\StepCounter`. Increment a counter by one.
- `\SetCounter`. Set a counter to a specific value.
- `\AssignCounterToReg`. Assign the counter's value to a register.

There are significant differences in manipulating the counter registers administered by the following macros compared with using counter registers allocated by `\newcount`. Be aware of these differences.

1. The counters administered through the following macros should be manipulated using *these macros only*, not in any other way.

2. The counters are identified by *names* which can be chosen by the user. A counter's name can be almost any string as long as it does not contain spaces or curly braces. For instance, `ChapterNo` or `Chap-Num` are legal counter names.

   Counter names as used in the following macros are *not* control sequences, so they are *not* preceded by a backslash.
3. All the counter related arithmetic and assignments are done on a *global basis.* There are no provisions for disabling this (it would be no problem to add this feature).

This is the source code of these macros.

$\mathcal{P}'$ • `counters.tip` •

```
\InputD{newoutfr.tip}                     % 4.6.2, p. 113.
\InputD{printco.tip}                      % 3.4.1, p. 68.
\InputD{namedef.tip}                      % 19.1.8, p. III-73.
```

3.4.2.1 `\NewCounter`

The `\NewCounter` macro is used to allocate a new counter. Note that `\NewCounter` is used to allocate a new counter register administered by the macros presented here, whereas `\newcount` can be used to allocate one individual counter register from TEX's pool of 256 counter registers.

`\NewCounter` has the following four parameters:

- `#1`. The counter's name. A counter name is an arbitrary string without spaces and curly braces. It is *not* a control sequence. See the preceding Subsection for details.
- `#2`. This parameter must be one of `\arabic`, `\roman`, `\Roman`, `\alph` or `\Alph`. The parameter specifies the way the counter "should be looked at" when the counter is referenced later.
- `#3`. This parameter consists of the TEX instructions to print the counter's value in a document in the location of the counter's "original and central appearance." The preceding statement seems to be a little vague: later following examples will clarify this.

  The question is how this differs from the preceding second parameter. Assume you have a counter for section numbers. When the section counter value is actually printed, it should be preceded by the current chapter number, if your document is divided into chapters, which are then divided into sections.

  With this parameter, you can now specify in this example to print the chapter number followed by a period, and then the section number "itself." The "itself" refers to the format of the section counter printing as established by the second parameter (`#2`) of a call to this macro.
- `#4`. This parameter is very similar to the third parameter in that it contains the same type of instructions. However, this parameter is supposed to define

the way a counter is printed if it occurs in a *cross-reference.*

The same question as before arises: why should a different format be used for a counter when the counter occurs in a cross-reference? Assume a list in a document, where item 2 of this list has a sublist. When you print the sublist, the items of this sublist should be enumerated "(a)," "(b)," and so forth, but when you *refer* to an item, then such reference should read "see 2.a", for instance (rather than simply "a" or "(a)"). You would specify an appropriate format for this parameter so that the output would read "2.a" indeed.

For more insight into the usage of this macro and its parameters, `#3` and `#4` in particular, refer to 3.4.4, p. 77.

Note that the preceding parameters `#3` and `#4` can refer to any other counter registers administered by the following macros.

Although `\NewCounter` was introduced as having four parameters, it only has one as defined here. Note though that the remaining three parameters become the second to fourth parameter of `\ReassignCounter`. See 22.3, p. III-218, for an explanation of this technique. Here is the macro definition of `\NewCounter`.

```
\catcode`\@ = 11
\def\NewCounter #1#2#3#4{%
    \wlog{\string\NewCounter: allocating new counter "#1."}%
```

Test whether the counter was already allocated before; if so generate an error.

```
    \if\NameDefinedConditional{@C-#1}%
        \errmessage{\string\NewCounter: counter "#1" was
            allocated previously.}%
    \fi
```

Allocate a new counter register now. This is done by calling `\newcountOF` with a counter register name formed as follows: concatenate `@C-` and the name of the counter register as specified by the user (`#1`). If you assume the user's counter name is `XXX`, the counter register allocated is therefore called "`\@C-XXX`." You have to look at the counter register name as one token. See 19.1.4, p. III-69, for some additional information.

```
    \expandafter\newcountOF\csname @C-#1\endcsname
```

The counter has been declared now, so `\ReassignCounter` can be used which does all the work. Then the reset list is cleared.

```
    \ReassignCounter{#1}{#2}{#3}{#4}%
    \NameDef{@ResetC-#1}{}%
}
```

3.4.3 The Definition of Macro `\ReassignCounter`

`\ReassignCounter` is almost identical to `\NewCounter`. The only difference is that `\ReassignCounter` is used to "redefine" an existing counter. By this we mean that TeX is instructed to use an already existing counter (defined by `\NewCounter`), but to use this counter somehow differently, that is, with new settings for parameters `#2`, `#3` and `#4`. If you try to use `\NewCounter` to "redefine" an existing counter, an error message is generated by `\NewCounter`.

```
29 \def\ReassignCounter #1#2#3#4{%
30     \if\NameDefinedConditional{@C-#1}%
31     \else
32         \errmessage{\string\ReassignCounter: counter "#1"
33             not defined before.}%
34     \fi
```

If you read the explanation for source code line 21 of this macro source file and assume a counter called `XXX` is allocated, then the `\NewCounter` macro allocates a counter register called `\@C-XXX`.

The following four macros are defined with the assumption that the counter is called `XXX` and tokens formed with `\csname` are used.

1. `\@TheC-XXX`. This macro, when called, expands to the current value of the counter using the format established by parameter `#2` to `\NewCounter`.
2. `\@TheArabicC-XXX`. This macro, when called, expands to the current value of the counter printed as an arabic number.
3. `\@PriC-XXX`. This macro, when called, expands to the current value of the counter using the format established by parameter `#3` to `\NewCounter` or `\ReassignCounter`.
4. `\@RefC-XXX`. This macro, when called, expands to the current value of the counter using the format established by parameter `#4` to `\NewCounter` or `\ReassignCounter`.
5. `\@ResetC-XXX`. This macro, when expanded, will reset all the counters of counter `XXX` which belong to the reset list of that counter. Initially this reset list is empty, and therefore, the initial definition of `\@ResetC-XXX` is empty.

```
35     \NameDef{@TheC-#1}{%
36         \expandafter\expandafter\expandafter#2%
37         \expandafter{\csname @C-#1\endcsname}%
38     }%
39     \NameDef{@TheArabicC-#1}{%
40         \expandafter\the\csname @C-#1\endcsname
41     }%
42     \NameDef{@PriC-#1}{#3}%
43     \NameDef{@RefC-#1}{#4}%
44 }
```

3.4.3.1 The Definition of Macro `\TheCounter`

Macro `\TheCounter` has one parameter, `#1`, the name of a counter. It uses the *second* parameter of the most recent call to `\NewCounter` or `\ReassignCounter` of this counter to print the counter's value. The following `\NameUse` call matches the `\NameDef` call of line 23.

```
45  \def\TheCounter #1{%
46        \NameUse{@TheC-#1}%
47  }
```

3.4.3.2 The Definition of Macro `\TheCounter`

Macro `\TheArabicCounter` has one parameter, `#1`, the name of a counter. It prints this counter as an arabic numeral regardless of any format specified when the counter was defined.

```
48  \def\TheArabicCounter #1{%
49        \NameUse{@TheArabicC-#1}%
50  }
```

3.4.3.3 The Definition of Macro `\PrintCounter`

`\PrintCounter` is almost identical to `\TheCounter` (it also has one parameter, `#1`, a counter's name), except now it uses the *third* parameter of the most recent `\NewCounter` or `\ReassignCounter` call for this counter to print its value.

```
51  \def\PrintCounter #1{%
52        \NameUse{@PriC-#1}%
53  }
```

3.4.3.4 The Definitions of Macros `\RefCounter` and `\RefCounterTwo`

`\RefCounter` uses the *fourth* parameter of the most recent call to `\NewCounter` or `\ReassignCounter` for this counter to print the counter's value. Otherwise, it is identical to `\TheCounter` or `\PrintCounter`. The `\Ref` in `\RefCounter` stands for "refer" because this macro is usually used in cross-referencing applications.

```
54  \def\RefCounter #1{%
55        \NameUse{@RefC-#1}%
56  }
```

There is an instance in this series (see 30.8.7, p. III-575) where `\RefCounter` must be redefined, but its functionality must still be available. Therefore a macro `\RefCounterTwo` is defined here, which is identical to `\RefCounter` as just defined.

```
57  \let\RefCounterTwo = \RefCounter
```

3.4.3.5 Loading a Counter Value into a Counter Register, \CounterToRegister

The following macro \CounterToRegister loads the value of a counter into a counter register. This macro has two arguments:

- #1. A counter register such as \count0. Specify \global before the register if you would like to have a global assignment.
- #2. The name of a counter (as understood in this Section).

```
\def\CounterToRegister #1#2{%
    #1 = \csname @C-#2\endcsname\relax
}
```

3.4.3.6 The Definition of Macro \AddCounterToResetList

The macro \AddCounterToResetList is used to add a counter to the *reset list* of another counter. A reset list of a counter contains all the counters that need to be reset to zero, if the main counter (of that the reset list is discussed here) is incremented by one. The reset list of a counter is initially empty when the counter is either established through a \NewCounter call, or redefined through a \ReassignCounter call. This reset list contains calls to the macro \@ResetCounter for each counter there is to reset, and each call to \AddCounterToResetList adds a counter to this list.

The \AddCounterToResetList macro has the following two parameters:

- #1. This is the name of a counter A. This is the counter that will be reset to zero; for the answer to the question "when and why" see the explanation of #2.
- #2. This is the name of a second counter B. When this counter is incremented by one by calling \StepCounter, then counter A is reset to zero.

```
\def\AddCounterToResetList #1#2{%
    {%
        \def\@ResetCounter{\noexpand\@ResetCounter}%
        \expandafter\xdef\csname @ResetC-#2\endcsname{%
            \csname @ResetC-#2\endcsname\@ResetCounter{#1}%
        }%
    }%
}
```

For instance, \AddCounterToResetList{Section-No}{ChapterNo} tells TEX to reset the section number counter when the chapter number is incremented. Assuming that the *reset list* of counter ChapterNo was initially empty, the reset list of this counter now contains \@ResetCounter{SectioNo}.

Please note that if you want to add counter A to the reset list of counter B, then you must declare counter `B` before `A`, because the declaration of a counter such as `B` clears out the reset list of `A` (regardless of whether this list was empty before or not).

3.4.3.7 The Definition of Macro `\StepCounter`

The macro `\StepCounter` is a macro with one parameter, `#1`, a counter's name. This counter is incremented by one. This is as stated before done on a global basis. Any counters contained in this counter's reset list (such counters are added to this counter's reset list by calling `\AddCounterToResetList`) are reset to zero. `\expandafter` is used here to allow TEX to form the name of the counter register using `\csname` and `\endcsname` first (see 19.1.4, p. III-69).

```
\def\StepCounter #1{%
    \global\expandafter\advance\csname @C-#1\endcsname by 1
```

Evaluate the reset list of this counter now.

```
    \NameUse{@ResetC-#1}%
}
```

3.4.3.8 The Definition of Macro `\SetCounter`

The macro `\SetCounter` is used to set a counter to a particular value. The macro has two parameters:

- `#1`. The name of a counter.
- `#2`. The value to which the counter will be set (on a global basis as it is the case with all macros in the context of the macros presented here).

The reset list of `\SetCounter` is ignored for this operation:

```
\def\SetCounter #1#2{%
    \global\expandafter\csname @C-#1\endcsname = #2\relax
}
```

3.4.3.9 Macro `\AssignCounterToReg`

Macro `\AssignCounterToReg` (two arguments) assigns the value of one of the counters administered through the macros here to another counter register:

- `#1`. Counter name.
- `#2`. Counter register to which the value stored in `#1` is assigned. If you precede the counter register specification with `\global`, then a global assignment will take place.

```
\def\AssignCounterToReg #1#2{%
     #2 = \expandafter\csname @C-#1\endcsname
     \relax
}
```

3.4.3.10 Macro \@ResetCounter

The macro \@ResetCounter is the macro which is called by the reset list of one counter to reset another counter. This macro has one parameter, #1, the name of a counter, which is reset to zero on a global basis.

```
\def\@ResetCounter #1{%
     \global\csname @C-#1\endcsname = 0
}
\catcode`\@ = 12
```

• End of counters.tip •

3.4.4 Examples Using the Counter Register Macros

31.1, p. III-581, presents an extensive application of the counter register macros. Let us look at a very short example here to give you an idea of how these macros are applied.

First of all, here is the source code of the examples:

• ex-counters.tip •

```
\input inputd.tip
\InputD{counters.tip}                          % 3.4.2, p. 71.
```

Declare a *chapter counter*. All chapter numbers are printed as uppercase Roman numerals. All cross-references to chapter numbers are preceded by "C-."

```
\NewCounter{Chapter-No}%
          {\Roman}%
          {\TheCounter{Chapter-No}}%
          {C-\TheCounter{Chapter-No}}%
```

Now declare a section number counter. Sections are enumerated by *uppercase letters*. They are reset each time a new chapter is started. Section number cross-references are preceded by "S-."

```
\NewCounter{Section-No}
          {\Alph}%
          {\TheCounter{Chapter-No}.\TheCounter{Section-No}}%
          {S-\TheCounter{Section-No}}
\AddCounterToResetList{Section-No}{Chapter-No}
```

Define a macro \Chapter which prints a chapter heading. This macro has one parameter, #1, the chapter title.

```
\def\Chapter #1{%
    \bigskip
    \StepCounter{Chapter-No}%
    \leftline{\hskip 1.0in \bf Chapter \PrintCounter{Chapter-No}}
    \medskip
    \leftline{\hskip 1.0in \bf ``#1''}
    \bigskip
}
```

Define a macro `\Section` which prints a section heading. The section heading is the macro's only parameter.

```
\def\Section #1{%
    \StepCounter{Section-No}%
    \leftline{%
        \hskip 1.0in
        \bf Section \PrintCounter{Section-No}\space\space #1}
    \medskip
}
```

Here is where the example itself begins. We generate some chapter and section headings:

```
\Chapter{First Chapter Heading}
\Section{Some Heading}
\Section{Some Heading II}
\Section{Some Heading III}
\Section{Some Heading IV}

\Chapter{Second Chapter Heading}
\Section{Some Heading V}
\Section{Some Heading VI}
\Section{Some Heading VII}
\Section{Some Heading VIII}
\Section{Some Heading IX}

\newcount\testcount
\AssignCounterToReg{Chapter-No}{\testcount}
The value of {\tt \string\testcount} is \the\testcount.
\bye
```

• End of `ex-counters.tip` •

The above TeX source generates the following output:

Chapter I

“First Chapter Heading”

Section I.A Some Heading

Section I.B Some Heading II

Section I.C Some Heading III

Section I.D Some Heading IV

Chapter II

"Second Chapter Heading"

Section II.A Some Heading V

Section II.B Some Heading VI

Section II.C Some Heading VII

Section II.D Some Heading VIII

Section II.E Some Heading IX

The value of `\testcount` is 2.

3.5 Summary

In this chapter we learned:

- TEX has counter, dimension, glue, math glue, token, and box registers. For each register type there are 256 registers, where each register is identified by a register index in the range of $0 \ldots 255$.
- Register indices are normally not used directly, with the exception for addressing registers with the index in the range $0 \ldots 9$. Registers with an index in this range are for temporary usage and the user is responsible for the proper administration of values contained in those registers.

  Counter registers 0 through 9 are special in that they are written to the `dvi` file of each page. Counter register 0 typically contains the page number of a document.
- Counter registers can be addressed by the `\count` primitive.
- It is possible to reserve a counter register index and to assign a symbolic name to a counter register using `\newcount`.
- There are a variety of parameters (not only counter parameters but others too). These parameters can be accessed by the user; they are independent from the the registers provided by TEX. In particular parameters have no register index and can be addressed by name only.
- Arithmetic in TEX works with registers, parameters and constants. The result of an arithmetic operation is always stored in a register or parameter. It is possible to compute the absolute value of a number or to compute an expression like $i \bmod n$.
- TEX allows numerical constants to be written to the base of 8, 10 and 16. Furthermore, it is possible to specify a character of which TEX will provide the ASCII code as a numerical constant. `\char` allows the conversion backwards, from the character code to a character. Numerical constants in TEX must be properly terminated.
- Numerical values can be printed as Arabic and Roman numerals.

- It is possible to compare two numbers and to test whether a number is odd or even. `\ifcase` offers a multiway branch facility in TeX.
- A macro was offered which converts a number such as 100 into text ("one hundred").
- Generic counter macros allow, among other things, specifications of how a counter's value is printed, and what other counters should be reset to zero in case this counter's value is incremented by one.

4
More on Registers, Dimensions

This chapter continues the discussion of registers. We will look at dimensions, dimension units and registers, glue registers and related parameters.

4.1 Dimensions and Dimension Units

In TEX there are *three* different types of *dimension units*:

1. "Absolute" dimension units.
2. "Font relative" dimension units.
3. "Infinite" dimension units.

4.1.1 "Absolute" Dimension Units

Absolute dimension units define distances; these dimension units never change. These units are *font independent*, since they do not depend on the font currently used.

All "absolute" dimension units that TEX knows about are listed in a table below. When you look at this table you will see an extremely small unit called scaled points (abbreviated "sp"). This unit is only used in TEX, that is, it is an otherwise unknown unit. All other dimension units are commonly used units in the world of typesetting.

Internally, TEX maintains all dimensions in the unit scaled points. So if you specify a dimension in any other unit (which is what you do normally), TEX converts the dimension into scaled points when the dimension is read-in.

On the other hand, if you instruct TEX to print out an internally stored dimension, then TEX prints this value in points after it converts the dimension from scaled points back into points. Points are the most commonly used unit in typesetting which is the reason why TEX prints values in points.

Table 4.1. Dimension Conversion Table.

Unit	Explanation
`pt`	Point. This unit is most frequently used to specify font sizes. Conversion factor (to inches): 0.013837.
`in`	Inch (1 in = 72.27 pt).
`pc`	Pica (1 pc = 12 pt). A fairly common unit in typesetting; for instance, used in the specifications of linewidth or page length. Conversion factor (to inches): 0.16604.
`bp`	Big point (1 in = 72 bp). Big points are the base unit of PostScript. Conversion factor (to inches): 0.013888. The difference compared with "regular" points is minor (less than 0.5%), but still there is a difference. In PostScript this unit is called *points* and *not* big points!
`cm`	Centimeter (2.54 cm = 1 in). The easiest unit (at least for me). Conversion factor (to inches): 0.39370.
`mm`	Millimeter (10 mm = 1 cm). Also a very easy unit. Conversion factor (to inches): 0.039370.
`dd`	Didot point (1157 dd = 1238 pt). An old typesetting unit. Conversion factor (to inches): 0.0148057.
`cc`	Cicero (1 cc = 12 dd). Another old typesetting unit. Conversion factor (to inches): 0.17766.
`sp`	Scaled point (65536 sp = 1 pt). A unit specific to TeX. Conversion factor (to inches): $2.1111 * 10^{-7}$.

Note that because scaled points are such a small unit, TeX can afford to use only integer arithmetic to store and manipulate dimensions. The decision to do all arithmetic using integers (rather than using floating point arithmetic) was a conscious one and actually was the motivation behind defining the unit scaled points in the first place. Floating point arithmetic has the disadvantage that implementations of this arithmetic differ slightly from machine to machine. By using integer arithmetic the `dvi` files produced from the same TeX source code on different machines will be identical on all machines, not just "approximately identical."

Table 4.1 on this page lists the absolute dimension units of TeX. Each dimension unit contains a conversion factor to inches at the very end. If you *multiply* a dimension value given in a particular unit by the conversion factor of this unit, you will get a dimension value based on the unit inch. Therefore, if you need to convert a dimension from unit a to unit b, *multiply* the dimension value with the conversion factor of unit a and *divide* the result by the conversion factor of unit b.

4.1.2 "Font Relative" Dimension Units

The second set of dimension units depends on the current font in use. Therefore, how large one of those units "really is" is determined by the currently active font. The precise information can be found in the `.tfm` file of the current font.

TeX has three font relative units.

1. *em*. The width of a "quad" in the *current font*. Usually 1 em is the same as the font size. For a few fonts this value may vary slightly: for instance, for very broad fonts (extended bold face type of fonts), 1 em may be slightly *larger* than the font size (vice versa it may also be smaller in very narrow fonts).

   Here is a small experiment: the following macro prints the value of 1 em for a particular font. The font to be used is specified by a parameter, `#1`.

   • `ex-emunit.tip` •

```
\newdimen\WidthOfOneEm
\def\OneEmLength #1{%
    \font\testfont = #1
    {%
        \testfont
        \global\WidthOfOneEm = 1em
    }%
    The width of 1~em for {\tt #1} is~\the\WidthOfOneEm.
}
```

   Now show an example application of this macro and call it with a couple of fonts.

```
\BeginEnumerate
    \Item \OneEmLength{cmr10}
    \Item \OneEmLength{cmb10}
    \Item \OneEmLength{cmbx10}
\EndEnumerate
```

   • End of `ex-emunit.tip` •

   Executing the preceding source code generates the following text:

   (a) The width of 1 em for `cmr10` is 10.00002pt.
   (b) The width of 1 em for `cmb10` is 10.00002pt.
   (c) The width of 1 em for `cmbx10` is 11.49994pt.

   This unit is used for *font dependent horizontal measures*. This also explains the reason for the fact that 1 em is slightly larger in "broad" fonts and slightly smaller in very "narrow" fonts.

   The plain format, for instance, defines the following horizontal spacing macros with references to this unit (see 5.4.9, p. 141, for the descriptions and definitions of all of these macros).

   (a) `\thinspace`
   (b) `\negthinspace`
   (c) `\enspace`
   (d) `\enskip`
   (e) `\quad`
   (f) `\qquad`

2. *ex.* The "x-height" of the current font, in other words, the height of the lowercase "x" of the current font. This dimension unit is normally used for font dependent *vertical* movements or spacing.
3. *mu* (mathematical units spacing). This dimension unit can only be used in math modes, and then only with the `\mskip` instruction. There are 18 mu to 1 em. The unit em is defined by the font used in font family 2 (math mode). The following math glue registers are loaded using this unit in the plain format (for details see 4.3, p. 93):)

```
\thinmuskip  = 3mu
\medmuskip   = 4mu plus 2mu minus 4mu
\thickmuskip = 5mu plus 5mu
```

In whatever way you use font relative dimensions, note that the current font defines how large, for instance, 1 em is. If you load a dimension or glue register with a font relative dimension, then this assignment becomes absolute, because the font relative dimension (based on the currently active font) is translated into an absolute dimension. Afterwards, when you change fonts, this absolute dimension, stored in a dimension register, is not changed.

4.1.3 Writing Dimensions in TEX

The following rules apply for entering dimensions in TEX (for example, `+12pt`, `+ 12pt`, `+ 12 pt`, `12 pt`, and `12pt` are all legal.):

1. First list the *value* of the dimension. If the dimension is negative a minus sign precedes the number, and there may be a space between the minus sign and the number. The plus sign for positive dimensions is optional. You are allowed to specify dimension values using numbers with a decimal point (note that this applies to dimensions only and that TEX does not otherwise allow for numbers with decimal point).
2. After the dimension value is specified you may leave a space before you specify the dimension unit. You must specify a dimension unit (if not, an error will be generated by TEX); there is no default dimension unit; in case you do not provide a proper unit or none at all TEX will use unit points.
3. A space after the dimension unit of a dimension specification is ignored by TEX. This rule is very similar to the rule that a space after a numerical constant is ignored.

4.1.4 "Infinite" Dimension Units

There are some "infinite" dimension units in TEX. These units have special applications only in the specifications of stretchabilities and shrinkabilities of glue.

Glue is an item in TEX that allows a specification of a distance which can vary (shrink and stretch) within limits specified by you (these limits in the case of stretching may be exceeded, see below for details). In the case of infinite units these distances can actually vary without limit; see 5.4, p. 135, for details. There is a hierarchy within those infinite dimension units which is explained in 5.4.4, p. 137.

For the infinite units `fil`, `fill` and `filll` some special rules apply which I would like to discuss now.

1. You can use lowercase as well as uppercase letters in those units and you can mix lowercase and uppercase letters.
2. You can leave a space between the unit letters `l`, but not anywhere else.

Therefore, for instance, the following glue specification is legal, although not very readable: `\hskip 12pt plus 1FiL minus 1 FIL l L`. Usually one would write `\hskip 12pt plus 1fil minus 1filll`, of course.

I would not mention these rules if not observing them couldn't get you into trouble. Let me present an example to make the point. To understand what follows, you must understand glue and infinite units to specify the shrinkability or stretchability of glue; see 5.4, p. 135.

Here is a simple piece of TEX source code (`\HboxR` generates "visible hboxes" surrounded by rules with a marked base line and base point):

```
1  $$
2      \vbox{
3          \hsize = 4.0in
4          \HboxR to \hsize{%
5              \hskip 0pt plus 1fil
6              Like it or not (1).%
7              \hskip 0pt plus 1fil
8          }
9          \centerline{Like it or not (2).}
10         \HboxR to \hsize{%
11             \hskip 0pt plus 1fil\relax
12             Like it or not (3).%
13             \hskip 0pt plus 1fil
14         }
15     }
16 $$
```

When you print the output generated by the previous source code you will be surprised by the output:

ike it or not (1).

Like it or not (2).

Like it or not (3).

What happened in the first line of output? The `L` of `Like it or not` in line 6 of the source code was added as another "l" to the `1fil` of the previous line. This happened *despite the fact that these two characters are separated by an end-of-line character.* In other words, the `\hskip` instruction of line 5 is interpreted as `... plus 1fill` by TeX, and the text of the following line reads "`ike it or not`. See also 5.4.4, p. 137.

Inserting a `\relax` after the dimension fixes the problem: it separates the glue specification from the following text. The same problem does *not* exist when `\centerline` is used, because `\centerline` uses `\hss` and does not rely directly on units `fil` and `fill`.

4.1.5 `True` Dimensions and Global Magnification

Section 15.1, p. II-227, discusses global magnification which leads to the magnification of all dimensions. For instance, if you write `\hskip 1.0in` to skip 1 in horizontal direction, then if a magnification of 2.0 (or 2000 in TeX's notation) is in effect, TeX will actually skip 2.0 in. TeX allows the specification of "true" dimensions which are "magnification factor free." `\hskip 1.0 true in` will tell TeX to skip 1.0 in, regardless of the current global magnification. The keyword `true` can be used with any other unit.

The keyword `true` it *cannot* be used with the infinite units `fil`, `fill`, and `filll`, where the application of `true` would not make any sense anyway, if you think about it briefly.

4.1.6 Saving Tokens When Writing Dimension Values

There are two standard ways to save tokens when writing dimension related macros (see also 22.7.5, p. III-232):

1. Abbreviate the dimension unit by using by a macro. Typically the unit "pt" is abbreviated by `\@pt`, which is defined as `\def\@pt{pt}`.

   This reduces the number of tokens from two to one and you can judge yourself whether it's worth it or not. On the other hand this technique because it is used in most macro packages has to be mentioned.
2. Use a dimension register to specify a distance instead of specifying the value of a dimension explicitly. So instead of writing

```
\def\largeskip{\hskip 2.0 in}
```

   write

```
\newskip\largeskipamount
\largeskipamount = 2.0in
\def\largeskip{%
    \hskip\largeskipamount
}
```

The advantage of this approach is that the space skipped by `\largeskip` can be "redefined" easily by assigning a new dimension to the glue register `\largeskipamount` which is used by the macro.

4.1.7 Dimension Registers, `\dimen`

TEX has 256 dimension registers and also some dimension parameters. Following are some general points about dimension registers.

1. Dimension registers are specified using `\dimen` followed by the register index.
2. `\dimendef` can be used to assign a name to a dimension register. For instance, `\dimendef\adimen = 2` makes `\adimen` the name for dimension register 2. This instruction corresponds to the `\countdef` instruction used with counter registers.
3. `\newdimen` allocates a new dimension register: for instance, `\newdimen\xdim` makes `\xdim` the name of a new dimension register. The register number allocated can be found in the log file of the TEX job.
4. A value can be assigned to a dimension register in the following ways:
   (a) A dimension can be assigned directly, as in `\xdim = 12pt` or `\dimen0 = 12pt`.
   (b) A value from another dimension register, as in `\ydim = \dimen1`, can be assigned. Such an assignment might include a multiplication factor as in `\ydim = 0.45\xdim`, which assigns to dimension register `\ydim` 0.45 times the dimension contained in dimension register `\xdim`.
   (c) Such an assignment can include a (unary) minus sign. Here is an example: `\xdim = -\ydim` or `\ydim = -2.4\xdim`.
5. There is a special set of dimension registers which are "attached" to box registers. The width, height and depth of a box stored in a box register is accessible through these registers. These "box dimension registers" are totally independent of the regular dimension registers.

   To access any of those box dimension registers, use `\ht`, `\dp` and `\wd` each followed by a box register index. They access the height, depth, or width of a box stored in a box register. For example, `\xdim = \ht\abox` copies the height of the contents of box register `\abox` to dimension register `\xdim`.
6. A dimension register can be used in glue specifications to skip horizontally or vertically as in `\hskip\xdim` or `\vskip\ydim`. Naturally the stretchability and shrinkability of such glue will be zero because a dimension and not a glue value was specified.
7. There are a number of dimension parameters that will be discussed in 4.1.9 on the next page.
8. The current value of a dimension register can be printed in some text using `\the` as in `\the\xdim`. The dimension will be printed out using the unit points.

9. If you would like to print out the value of a dimension register's content as a number (in unit scaled points, although *not* printing the unit), then there are two methods:
   (a) Assign the dimension register to a counter register and print the counter register's content using `\the`; see 4.4, p. 94, for details.
   (b) Use `\number` instead of `\the`. Writing `\number\xim` after `\xdim = 1pt`, causes TeX to print 65536 because there are 65536 scaled points to 1 pt. See 3.3.4, item 1, p. 47, for the application of `\number` with counter registers and numbers.

10. The current value of a dimension register can be written to the log file using `\showthe` as in `\showthe\xdim`. The value can also be written to the log file using `\the` in `\message` or `\wlog`; see 29.5.2, p. III-521, and 29.5.5, p. III-523.

4.1.8 The Largest Legal Dimension, `\maxdimen`

The largest dimension value that can be represented inside the TeX program is 16383.99999pt. This value is assigned to a dimension register `\maxdimen` in the plain format. To this effect the plain format contains the following TeX source code:

```
\newdimen\maxdimen
\maxdimen=16383.99999pt
```

In 4.4, p. 94, it is explained that if you assign the contents of a dimension register to a counter register, the value stored in the dimension registers, interpreted as scaled points, is stored in the counter registers. In TeX, therefore, integers and dimensions stored in the unit scaled points are essentially the same. Out of this reason `\maxdimen` can be and is also used as a kind of "`\maxint`," an abbreviation for the largest possible integer in TeX. See 27.11, p. III-441, where `\maxdimen` is used in this way.

4.1.9 Dimension Parameters

TeX's dimension parameters are not part of the set of 256 "standard" dimension registers. These parameters can only be addressed by their names (no register indices exist for them)

1. Overfull and underfull box-related dimension parameters.
   (a) `\hfuzz`. A threshold dimension for the reporting of overfull hboxes; see 5.3.7, p. 132.
   (b) `\vfuzz`. A threshold dimension for the reporting of overfull vboxes; see 5.3.7, p. 132.

(c) `\overfullrule`. An overfull hbox is marked by a rule of the thickness of this dimension register; see 5.3.6, p. 132, for details.

2. Line-spacing-related dimension parameters.

   (a) `\prevdepth`. The depth of the preceding box; see 7.3.9, p. 227.
   (b) `\lineskiplimit`. Threshold value which determines in TEX whether TEX should regard two boxes as (vertically) too close or not; see 7.3.4, p. 220, for details.

3. The following parameters influence the building of boxes by TEX.

   (a) `\maxdepth`. The maximum depth of the current page. See 32.6.1, item 2, p. IV-28, for details.
   (b) `\splitmaxdepth`. The maximum depth of a box generated through an application of `\vsplit`. See 8.2.11, p. 293. This glue is also used in the case of the splitting of insertion material; see the same reference for details.
   (c) `\boxmaxdepth`. The maximum depth of a vbox being built explicitly using `\vbox`, `\vtop` or `\vcenter`; see 7.5.4, p. 246.

4. Mathmode-related dimension registers. The following dimension registers relate to the typesetting of mathematical equations.

   (a) `\delimitershortfall`. A dimension in the computation of delimiters; see 13.6.5, p. II-184.
   (b) `\nulldelimiterspace`. The width reserved by TEX in case of an omitted delimiter; see 13.6.2, p. II-182.
   (c) `\scriptspace`. The extra space after a subscript or superscript; see 13.1.5, item 17, p. II-162, for details.
   (d) `\mathsurround`. Horizontal space added to an inline math equation, before and after it; see 13.8.1, p. II-186.
   (e) `\predisplaysize`. Length of the last line preceding a displayed equation. See 14.9.4, p. II-219.
   (f) `\displaywidth`. Available line length for a displayed equation; see 14.9.4, p. II-219.
   (g) `\displayindent`; Indentation of the displayed equation; see 14.9.4, p. II-219.

5. Paragraph related dimension parameters.

   (a) `\parindent`. The current paragraph's indentation of the first line. See 10.7, p. II-18).
   (b) `\hangindent`. The amount of a paragraph's hanging indentation. See 11.4, p. II-80.

6. Offset dimension registers allow for the shifting of the page horizontally and vertically before the page is written out to the `dvi` file.

   (a) `\hoffset`. The horizontal offset by which each page is shifted (left or right) before being written to the `dvi` file; see 33.6.4, p. IV-53.
   (b) `\voffset`. A similar *vertical* offset.

4.1.10 A Rounding Error Problem

Here is a very simple example to make you aware of "problems" with dimension computations in TEX. I mentioned before that TEX converts all dimensions into scaled points (sp) and then uses integer arithmetic to do any dimension arithmetic. Here is the source code of an example that got me into trouble once. Note that **\hfuzz** (5.3.7, p. 132) is ignored in the discussion here.

• `ex-rounderr.tip` •

```
\hbox to 2in{%
    \hskip 1in
    \hskip 1in
}
\bye
```

• End of `ex-rounderr.tip` •

The log file generated by this example reads as follows:

• `ex-rounderr.log` •

```
This is TeX, C Version 3.14 (...)
**&/usr/local/tex/lib/fmt/plain ex-rounderr.tip
(ex-rounderr.tip
Underfull \hbox (badness 10000) detected at line 4

\hbox(0.0+0.0)x144.54
.\glue 72.26999
.\glue 72.26999

[1] )
Output written on ex-rounderr.dvi (1 page, 200 bytes).
```

Where does the message about an underfull hbox with badness of 10000 come from? After all $1\text{ in} + 1\text{ in} = 2\text{ in}$, or not?

Now let us look at the following example:

• `ex-rounderr-2.tip` •

```
\dimen0 = 1in
\wlog{1in is \number\dimen0 \space sp}
\dimen1 = 2in
\wlog{2in is \number\dimen1 \space sp}

\dimen2 = \dimen0
\advance\dimen2 by \dimen0
\wlog{Adding 1in to 1in is \number\dimen2 sp}
\bye
```

• End of `ex-rounderr-2.tip` •

• `ex-rounderr-2.log` •

```
This is TeX, C Version 3.14 (...)
**&/usr/local/tex/lib/fmt/plain ex-rounderr-2.tip
```

```
(ex-rounderr-2.tip
1in is 4736286 sp
2in is 9472573 sp
Adding 1in to 1in is 9472572sp
)
No pages of output.
```

This example should explain what happened in the first example. TeX converted the two relevant dimensions into scaled points. The 2 `in` of the `\hbox to 2in` are converted into 9472573 sp, and the 1 in of each of the `\hskip 1ins` is converted into 4736286 sp. Now note that $4736286 + 4736286 + 1 = 9472573$; in other words the sum of the two 1 in glues in the first example is short by 1 sp compared with the required length of 2.0 in, and no other glue to stretch is available in this box. Therefore, an underfull box is generated and also reported.

4.1.11 Computing an Absolute Dimension

The following macro `\AbsoluteDimension` has two parameters:

- `#1`. A dimension.
- `#2`. A dimension register which is loaded with the absolute value of `#1`. Note: `#1` and `#2` may be identical.

Here is the source code of this macro:

$\mathcal{P}'$ • `absdimen.tip` •

```
\def\AbsoluteDimension #1#2{%
```

Test whether the dimension is negative. If so, assign positive value.

```
     \ifdim #1 < 0pt
          #2 = -#1\relax
     \else
```

Dimension positive, simple assignment is all that is needed.

```
          #2 = #1\relax
     \fi
}
```

• End of `absdimen.tip` •

4.2 Glue Registers

TeX has a set of 256 glue registers. These registers are identified by `\skip` followed by a register index. Registers with index 0 ... 9 are intended for temporary use as is the case with all other register types. Glue registers and dimension registers are very much alike, but they are not completely interchangeable.

4.2.1 Glue Registers in General

Here are the basic rules about glue registers.

1. The `\skipdef` instruction allows the user to assign a symbolic name to a glue register. For instance, `\skipdef\skipa = 2` makes `\skipa` a name for glue register 2. This instructions corresponds to the `\countdef` instruction in counter registers.
2. The `\newskip` macro can be used to allocate a new dimension register. For example, `\newskip\xskip` allocates the next free glue register and names it `\xskip`.
3. A value can be assigned to a glue register in the following ways:
   (a) Directly, as in `\skip0 = 12pt plus 2pt minus 3pt`. If no stretchability or shrinkability values are defined they will default to zero.
   (b) From another glue register as in `\yskip = \xskip`. This might include a multiplication factor as in `\yskip = 0.45\skip0`. When a multiplication factor is used, only the natural length of the glue is multiplied and the resulting stretchability and shrinkability are set to zero.
   (c) Such an assignment can include a unary minus sign as in `\xskip = -\yskip` or `\yskip = -2.4\xdim`.
   (d) Such assignment can use a dimension register as in `\xskip = \xdim`. This will generate a glue value of zero stretchability and shrinkability, of course.
4. The value that is stored in a glue register can be used in horizontal or vertical skip instructions, as in `\hskip\xskip` or `\vskip\yskip`.
5. There is a set of glue parameters. These are discussed in the next Subsection.
6. The current value of a glue register can be written into the text using `\the`; see 24.3, p. III-313. If stretchability or shrinkability values are zero these values are *not* printed. There is no way for the user to specify "print `plus 0pt`" or "print `minus 0pt`" in this case.
7. The current value of a glue register can be written to the log file using `\showthe`, as in `\showthe\xskip`. Also `\the` can be used inside of `\message` or `\wlog`; see 29.5.2, p. III-521, and 29.5.5, p. III-523.

4.2.2 Glue Parameters

There are four general types of glue parameters in TeX. They are used in line-spacing computations, split operations, in paragraphs and in math mcode. Let me list all the glue parameters now.

1. The following glue parameters are relevant for line spacing computations:
   (a) `\baselineskip`. This glue parameter (not a dimension parameter as you might assume) determines the desired distance between consecutive boxes and in particular between lines of a paragraph; see 7.3.4, p. 220, for details.
   (b) `\lineskip`. This glue parameter register determines the interline glue if TeX regards two lines as too close together; see 7.3.4, p. 220.
2. The following glue registers have to do with split operations:
   (a) `\topskip`. Glue inserted at the top of the main vertical list, that is the top of the current page; see 32.4.2, p. IV-12.
   (b) `\splittopskip`. Glue inserted at the beginning of the source box of a `\vsplit` operation after the material to be split off was removed by the `\vsplit` operation; see 8.2.7, p. 282. This glue is also used in the case of the splitting of insertions; see the same reference for details.
3. Here is an overview of all paragraph-related glue parameters:
   (a) `\parskip`. The value in this glue register determines the amount of vertical space inserted at the beginning of each paragraph (and therefore it determines the vertical space between paragraphs). See 10.8, p. II-25, for details.
   (b) `\leftskip` and `\rightskip`. Glues inserted to the left and right of each line in a paragraph; see 10.6, p. II-14, for details.
   (c) `\emergencystretch`. Additional stretchability in especially difficult to typeset paragraphs; see 12.8.3, p. II-151, for details.
4. Here are four math mode-related glue parameters:
   (a) `\abovedisplayskip`, `\abovedisplayshortskip`. Vertical glue inserted before displayed equations. Which of the two glues is inserted depends on the length of the line preceding a displayed equation and the width of the displayed equation. See 14.9.1, p. II-216, for details.
   (b) `\belowdisplayskip`, `\belowdisplayshortskip`. Glue inserted below displayed equations. See 14.9.1, p. II-216, for details.

4.3 Math Glue Registers

Math glue registers, to a large extent, are identical to regular glue registers introduced in the previous subsection. Let me point out the important differences:

1. The instruction to name a math glue register is `\muskipdef`. For instance, `\muskipdef\ma = 2` makes `\ma` stand for math glue register 2.
2. To allocate a new math glue register use `\newmskip`. `\newmskip\am` makes `\am` stand for a math glue register.

3. Math glue registers can only be used with `\mskip` to generate glue, for example, `\mskip\am`. Using a math glue register with `\hskip` and `\vskip` is illegal. Note that `\mskip` can be used only inside mathematical equations; see 13.7.1, item 4, p. II-185, for details on `\mskip`.

4.4 Mixing Counter, Dimension and Glue Registers

It is possible in TEX to mix counter, dimension, and glue values and registers. For instance, in `\hskip\xdim` (`\xdim` is assumed to be a dimension register) TEX generates glue where the length of the glue is determined by the dimension in the dimension register. Shrinkability and stretchability of this glue are set to zero.

Let us discuss mixing the various register types in more detail. First assume the following register declarations are given:

```
\newcount\counta
\newdimen\dimena
\newskip\skipa
```

Here is a table explaining the various combinations (math glue registers are treated identically to regular glue registers and, therefore, are not included below):

- `\dimena = \counta`: This assignment is illegal. You must provide some dimension unit as, for instance, in `\dimena = \counta in`.
- `\skipa = \counta`: This assignment is illegal. Again you must provide a dimension unit.
- `\counta = \dimena`: The number of scaled points of the dimension stored in the dimension register is assigned to the counter register.
- `\skipa = \dimena`: The dimension register's dimension is used for the natural width in the glue register. Stretchability and shrinkability of the glue are set to zero.
- `\counta = \skipa`: The counter register is loaded with the number of scaled points of the natural width of the glue value of the glue register. Stretchability and shrinkability are ignored.
- `\dimena = \skipa`: The dimension register is loaded with the natural width of the glue stored in the glue register. Stretchability and shrinkability of the glue are ignored.

In this context let me explain one more item: `\ifdim` can be used to compare glue values, in which case only the natural widths of the glues are compared. For example, if you write

```
\ifdim\skip0 < \skip1 ... \fi,
```

then this is equivalent to:

```
\dimen0 = \skip0
```

```
\dimen1 = \skip1
\ifdim\dimen0 < \dimen1 ... \fi.
```

Now consider the following comparison of two glue values:

```
\ifdim 12pt plus 2pt minus 3pt < \skip1 ... \fi
```

The preceding TeX code is *illegal*, because after the `12 pt`, TeX expects one of the operators `<`, `=` or `>`. You might argue that it is not necessary to write `plus 2pt minus 3pt` in the first place, but the glue value used in such a comparison may be the argument of a macro, and the stretchability and shrinkability of this glue value may be used somewhere else. To fix this problem, assign the glue `12pt plus 2pt minus 3pt` to some glue register, and then use this glue register in the comparison instead of the glue value directly. The following code is legal and compares the natural width of the two glues involved:

```
\skip0 = 12pt plus 2pt minus 3pt    \skip1 = 24pt plus 1pt minus 1pt
\ifdim\skip0 < \skip1 ... \fi.
```

4.5 Box Registers

Box registers are an important ingredient of TeX. To fully understand the following, one needs to understand boxes in general (which is the subject of Chapters 6–8).

Many applications of box registers can be found in the Chapters on output routines (Chapters 33–37).

There are 256 box registers, as is the case with all other register types. Box register 255 is reserved for a special purpose; in it TeX stores the current page before it ships the current page out to the `dvi` file. See 32.1.1, item 4, p. IV-2, for details. This register should only be used by the output routine, but not otherwise.

Box registers 0–9 are reserved for temporary use, as is the case with registers in that register index range in general.

There are *no* box parameters.

4.5.1 Allocating a New Box Register, `\newbox`

A new box register can be allocated with `\newbox` as in `\newbox\abox`. Now `\abox` stands for the box register index allocated by `\newbox`. As usual the allocation of box registers using `\newbox` starts with register 10.

If you assume that TeX allocated box register 16, then `\the\abox` prints 16, the box register index, *not* the content of box register 16. The command `\the` cannot be used to print the content of a box register; you must use `\box` or `\copy` instead. See 4.5.3 on the next page for how this is done.

4.5.2 Box Register States

A box register is in precisely *one of the following states* at all times:

1. The box register can contain a *horizontal box*. How this horizontal box is loaded into the box register in the first place will be discussed shortly.
2. The box register can contain a *vertical box*.
3. The box register is *empty*, or *void*, as it is called in TeX. The following remarks apply to a void box register, no error messages appear.
   (a) All of the dimensions of a void box register are zero.
   (b) The opposite of (a) is not true: there are cases where the dimensions of a box stored in a box register are zero, but the box register contains a box, and therefore the box register is not empty.
   (c) It is *not* an error in TeX to print a *void* box register, in which case nothing happens and no error message is printed.

The state of a box register can be determined using the conditionals of 4.5.7, p. 99.

4.5.3 Retrieving the Content of a Box Register, `\box`, `\copy`

Let us first discuss how the content of a box register can be retrieved. How a box is loaded into a box register in the first place will be discussed shortly. For the following, assume `\abox` is a box register index (`\newbox\abox`).

1. `\box` ⟨box register index⟩. This instruction prints the content of the specified box register. Afterwards the content of the box register is destroyed. In other words, the box register is void after it is printed. Destroying the box register's content is done to free some of TeX's internal memory.

   This instruction is the most frequently used instruction to extract a box from a box register.

   Here are two examples: `\box0` prints the content of box register 0 and `\box\abox` prints the content of box register `\abox`.
2. `\copy` ⟨box register index⟩. This instruction is identical to `\box` with the exception that the content of the box register is not destroyed after it is printed.

   For instance, `\copy0` prints box register 0, and `\copy\abox` prints box register `\abox`.
3. `\unhbox` ⟨box register index⟩ and `\unvbox` ⟨box register index⟩. These instructions retrieve the content of a box register, and produce a copy of the horizontal or vertical list of that box. These instructions do not produce a copy of the box stored in the box register. The content of the box register is lost. See 8.1, p. 261, for details.

4. `\unhcopy` ⟨box register index⟩ and `\unvcopy` ⟨box register index⟩. These instructions relate to `\unhbox` and `\unvbox` the same way `\copy` relates to `\box`: they have the same functionality as `\unhbox` and `\unvbox` but do not destroy the content of the box register. See 8.1, p. 261, for details.

4.5.4 Loading Box Registers, `\setbox`

For the following assume that two box registers `\abox` and `\bbox` are declared. Box registers can be loaded in a number of ways which will be discussed now. Any previous content of a box register is lost.

The format of `\setbox` is `\setbox` ⟨box register index⟩ `=` ... where the "..." indicates an instruction that produces a box. Let us look at some alternatives now.

1. A box register can be loaded directly using `\setbox` where the box being loaded is generated directly using `\hbox`, `\vbox` or `\vtop`: `\setbox\abox = \hbox{AB}` loads the specified hbox into box register `\abox`.
2. A box register can also be loaded from another box register using `\setbox`: `\setbox\bbox = \box\abox` or `\setbox\bbox = \copy\abox`.

   Note that `\vcenter` is not a vbox in the most general sense, because `\vcenter` can only be used in math mode. Therefore, `\setbox 0 = \vcenter{...}` is illegal, even if this assignment is executed inside math mode; see 7.5.5, p. 248.

Let me now discuss in a separate list those cases where a box register is also loaded (or at least modified) but this time *not* using `\setbox`:

1. A box register can be loaded through `\vsplit`. `\vsplit` actually affects two box registers simultaneously, in many applications, when it is used together with `\setbox`; see 8.2, p. 267, for details.
2. Two special cases of loading box registers should be mentioned here:
   (a) The page breaking algorithm of TeX loads box register 255 when the current page is read-in to be written to the `dvi` file; see 32.1.1, p. IV-1.
   (b) If insertions are used, insertion related box registers are loaded with insertion material similar to box register 255 before the output routine is called. See 32.7.4, p. IV-31, for details.

4.5.5 Exchanging Two Box Registers, `\SwapBoxRegs`

An example using `\setbox` will be presented now. It shows how the contents of two box registers can be exchanged. The macro `\SwapBoxRegs` has two parameters, `#1` and `#2`. These represent the indices of two box registers which are to be exchanged. Here is the definition of this macro:

$\mathcal{P}'$ • swapbox.tip •

```
\catcode'\@ = 11
```

A temporary box register to store a copy of the content of the first box register, when \SwapBoxRegs is called, is allocated now.

```
\newbox\@SwapBox
```

The macro definition starts now.

```
\def\SwapBoxRegs #1#2{%
```

Save the first box.

```
        \setbox\@SwapBox = \box#1%
```

Replace the first box by the second box.

```
        \setbox#1 = \box#2%
```

Get the first box back and use it to replace the second box.

```
        \setbox#2 = \box\@SwapBox
}
\catcode'\@ = 12
```

• End of swapbox.tip •

4.5.6 Clearing a Box Register, \ClearBoxReg

A box register is initially void. The macro \ClearBoxReg can be used to clear (that is, make void) any box register. This macro has one parameter, #1, the index of the box register to be cleared.

Note that the plain format allocates a permanently void box register as follows (and therefore there is no need to allocate such a register for the purpose of the following macro): \newbox\voidb@x.

Here is the definition of macro \ClearBoxReg:

$\mathcal{P}'$ • clearb.tip •

```
\catcode'\@ = 11
\def\ClearBoxReg #1{%
        \setbox #1 = \box\voidb@x
}
\catcode'\@ = 12
```

• End of clearb.tip •

4.5.7 Conditionals Related to Box Registers, `\ReportBoxType`

Let us discuss conditionals relating to box registers. There are three such conditionals (for a general discussion of conditionals see 25.1.4, p. III-320). These three conditionals correspond to the three states of a box register; see 4.5.2, p. 96. Precisely one of the conditionals will always be true for any fixed box register.

1. `\ifvoid` ⟨box register index⟩. This conditional is true if the box register is void, that is contains *no box.*
2. `\ifhbox` ⟨box register index⟩. This conditional is true if the box stored in the box register is a *horizontal box.*
3. `\ifvbox` ⟨box register index⟩. This conditional is true if the box stored in the box register is a *vertical box.* Whether this vertical box was generated by `\vbox`, `\vtop` or `\vcenter` is irrelevant.

The macro `\ReportBoxType` uses all three conditionals to print the type of the box stored in a box register. This macro has one parameter, `#1`, the index of a box register.

$\mathcal{P}'$ • `rboxt.tip` •

```
\def\ReportBoxType #1{%
    \message{\string\ReportBoxType: }%
    \ifvoid #1\message{Box register #1 is void.}\fi
    \ifhbox #1\message{Box register #1 contains a horizontal box.}\fi
    \ifvbox #1\message{Box register #1 contains a vertical box.}\fi
}
```

• End of `rboxt.tip` •

Here is a brief example application of this macro. The following source code is used in this example.

• `ex-rboxt.tip` •

```
\input inputd.tip
\InputD{rboxt.tip}                      % 4.5.7, p. 99.
\setbox0 = \vbox{This is fun}
\ReportBoxType{0}
\bye
```

• End of `ex-rboxt.tip` •

The log file generated from this example reads as follows (the message at the very end about no output written to the `dvi` file is caused because no text on any page is generated).

• `ex-rboxt.log` •

```
This is TeX, C Version 3.14 (...)
**&/usr/local/tex/lib/fmt/plain ex-rboxt.tip
(ex-rboxt.tip (inputd.tip
(namedef.tip
) (inputdl.tip
```

```
\@InputDStream=\write0
))
(rboxt.tip
) \ReportBoxType:
Box register 0 contains a vertical box. )
No pages of output.
```

4.5.8 Accessing the Dimensions of a Box Register's Content, `\ht`, `\dp`, `\wd`

The height, depth and width of a box register's content can be accessed by the user. There are two purposes in doing so:

1. One might *retrieve* those dimensions.
2. One might *change* those dimensions.

These dimensions are accessed in the following way (assume that `\abox` is a box register index):

1. `\ht\abox`. The height of the box stored in box register `\abox`.
2. `\dp\abox`. The depth of the box stored in box register `\abox`.
3. `\wd\abox`. The width of the box stored in box register `\abox`.

Here is a very brief example using `\the` to print those dimensions (`\the` can be used with any other dimension register). The TeX source code of the example reads as follows:

```
\setbox 0 = \hbox{A}%
The height of~``A'' is~\the\ht0, the depth is~\the\dp0 \space
and the width is~\the\wd0
```

This input generates the following text: "The height of "A" is 6.83331pt, the depth is 0.0pt and the width is 7.50002pt."

4.5.9 Modifying the Dimensions of a Box Stored in a Box Register

The dimensions of a box register can be changed after a box register is loaded. This does *not* affect the content of the box register. For instance, if you reduce the width of a box in a box register, TeX will not clip off any material. But the change of the dimension affects TeX's "thinking"; it makes TeX "think" that the box stored in a box register actually has different dimensions.

TeX, therefore, can be tricked into "thinking" that an item has different dimensions than is actually true. For the following example you have to understand that if you pack things into an hbox (`\hbox{ABC}`), TeX will print the items of this hbox left to right, adjacent to each other. In other words, TEX will print "ABC" if you input `\hbox{ABC}`.

Now let me rewrite this example as follows:

```
\setbox 0 = \hbox{A}
\setbox 1 = \hbox{B}
\setbox 2 = \hbox{C}
\hbox{\copy0 \copy1 \copy2}
```

The output is identical, that is, "ABC," because all we did was extract the three characters from three box registers 0, 1 and 2, where these three characters are stored as individual boxes.

Now let us modify the dimensions of the three box register. In this example we will modify the width only (the height and depth are modified in later examples, but the principle stays the same). Let me set the width of box register 0 to zero and then print the contents of box register 0 and 1. Here is the source code of the example:

```
\wd0 = 0pt
\hbox{\copy0 \copy1 \copy2}
```

This time the output reads differently: "BC." Why? Because when the width of box register 0 was set to zero, it made TEX think that the "A" has width zero. Therefore, TEX did not move to the right after it printed the contents of box register 0, and therefore, it printed the "B" on top of the "A."

Note that the preceding assignment `\wd0 = 0pt` is inherently global that even if executed within a group the dimensions of the outermost box are changed.

Now let me present a different version of the preceding example. This time the widths of all three boxes are set to 25 pt (which is roughly two and a half times the width of what the box registers really contain). Therefore, the three characters appear to be completely spread-out when printed.

In addition, I use the `\HboxR` macro which draws rules around a box to indicate the dimensions of the box. You can now clearly see the increased width of the box.

Here is the source code for the next example:

```
\setbox 0 = \HboxR{A}%
\setbox 1 = \HboxR{B}%
\setbox 2 = \HboxR{C}%
\wd0 = 25pt      \wd1 = 25pt      \wd2 = 25pt
\hbox{\box0 \box1 \box2}%
```

The previous source code generated the following output: "A B C ."

4.5.10 Arithmetic with Dimensions of Box Registers, `\AdvanceBoxDimension`, `\OverallSize`

The box dimension registers are very similar to regular dimension registers. For example, their value can be printed using `\the` and so forth. One restriction is that they cannot participate in regular arithmetic instructions using `\advance`, `\multiply`, and so forth. Therefore, it is *illegal* to write `\advance\wd0 by 10pt`.

Instead, one must use a regular dimension register as intermediate storage (`\dimen0` is used below) and then use this "regular" dimension register to do the arithmetic. Here is how the width of box register 0 can be increased by 10 pt:

```
\dimen0 = \wd0
\advance\dimen0 by 10pt
\wd0 = \dimen0
```

I defined the macro `\AdvanceBoxDimension` to make changing of dimensions of box registers easy. This macro has two parameters:

- `#1`. An instruction to access the value of a box dimension register, such as `\wd0` or `\wd\abox`.
- `#2`. The amount by which this dimension should be changed.

Here is the macro definition:

$\mathcal{P}'$ • `chboxd.tip` •

```
\catcode`\@ = 11
```

Allocate a dimension register.

```
\newdimen\@AdvanceBoxD
```

Define macro `\AdvanceBoxDimension` now.

```
\def\AdvanceBoxDimension #1#2{%
    \@AdvanceBoxD = #1\relax
    \advance\@AdvanceBoxD by #2\relax
    #1 = \@AdvanceBoxD
}
\catcode`\@ = 12
```

• End of `chboxd.tip` •

The macro `\OverallSize` computes the sum of the height and depth of a box stored in a box register; it has the following two parameters:

- `#1`. A dimension register, which is assigned the result of the computations performed by this macro.
- `#2`. The number of a box register. The sum of the height and depth of the box stored in this box register will be assigned to the dimension register specified under `#1`.

$\mathcal{P}'$ • `sumhd.tip` •

```
\def\OverallSize #1#2{%
    #1 = \ht#2\relax
    \advance#1 by \dp#2\relax
}
```

• End of `sumhd.tip` •

4.5.11 Dimensions of Void Box Registers

Note that the dimensions of a void box register are zero, but the opposite is not necessarily true. A box register where all three dimensions are zero is not always empty. For instance, you can load a box register and then set all three dimensions to zero without affecting the contents of this register. See 4.5.13 on the next page for the definition of a macro which does exactly that.

4.5.12 Generating an Empty Box, `\EmptyBox`

Macro **`\EmptyBox`** generates an empty hbox. The dimensions of this box are specified by the user; they are *not* zero. This macro has the following three parameters:

- `#1`. The height of the box to be generated (the box itself is empty, as just mentioned).
- `#2`. The depth of the box to be generated.
- `#3`. The width of the box to be generated.

Here is the macro source file for this macro:

$\mathcal{P}'$ • `emptybox.tip` •

```
15 \def\EmptyBox #1#2#3{%
```

Begin to build an hbox.

```
16         \hbox{%
```

Assign an empty box to box register 0. Because the content of an hbox forms an implicit group, any other content of box register 0 will be restored after line 8 of this source code.

```
17                 \setbox 0 = \hbox{}%
```

Set the dimensions specified by the user.

```
18                 \ht0 = #1%
19                 \dp0 = #2%
20                 \wd0 = #3%
```

"Print" this empty box now.

```
21                 \box 0%
```

The hbox started in line 2 now contains an empty hbox of the dimensions as specified by the user.

```
22         }%
23 }
```

• End of `emptybox.tip` •

Let me discuss a different definition of the preceding macro. To avoid any confusion I use a different name for this macro (\EmptyBoxX).

```
\newbox\EmptyBoxRegister
\def\EmptyBoxX #1#2#3{%
     \setbox\EmptyBoxRegister = \hbox{}%
     \ht\EmptyBoxRegister = #1%
     \dp\EmptyBoxRegister = #2%
     \wd\EmptyBoxRegister = #3%
     \box\EmptyBoxRegister
}
```

This definition is *not* quite as useful as the preceding definition (although in many cases it would not matter which definition would actually be used), because it cannot be used in the following application:

```
\setbox 0 = \EmptyBoxX{3pt}{4pt}{5pt}
```

The preceding \setbox command is illegal, because when \EmptyBoxX is expanded, it does not produce a box generating command right away (ultimately it will), but TeX expects some box right after \setbox. If \EmptyBox is used, everything works because in source code line 16 of the definition of \EmptyBox, an hbox is started immediately, before any other computations are performed.

4.5.13 Setting All Dimensions of a Box Register to Zero, \ZeroBox, \ZeroBoxOut

Macros \ZeroBox and \ZeroBoxOut are used frequently in this series. Let me introduce these macros now.

1. \ZeroBox. This macro has one parameter, #1, a box register index. All dimensions of the specified box register are set to zero. The content of the box register is *not* affected.
2. \ZeroBoxOut. This macro also has one parameter, #1, which again is a box register index. This macro first calls \ZeroBox to set all its dimensions to zero. Then the content of this box register is printed, using \box. Note that, because \box is used, the content of the box register is lost after it was printed.

Here are the two macro definitions. First the definition of \ZeroBox.

$\mathcal{P}'$ • box-zero.tip •

```
\def\ZeroBox #1{%
     \wd#1 = 0pt
     \ht#1 = 0pt
     \dp#1 = 0pt
}
```

And here is the definition of \ZeroBoxOut.

```
\def\ZeroBoxOut #1{%
     \ZeroBox{#1}%
     \box#1%
}
```

• End of box-zero.tip •

4.5.14 Dumping the Contents of a Box Register into the Log File: \showbox, \showboxdepth, \showboxbreadth

The `\showbox` command dumps the contents of a box register into the log file. To understand this command, it is necessary to define the following two terms:

1. The *depth* of a box is the maximum number of nested boxes contained in a box. For instance, `\hbox{A}` is of depth 1, because it contains only one other box (take the character A as a box here).

   On the other hand, in `\hbox{A\hbox{B}}`, the outermost hbox contains another hbox of depth 1 (and no other box of any higher depth). Therefore, the outermost box is of depth 2.

   Note that `\hbox{\hbox{A}\hbox{BCD}}` is also only of depth 2, because only the *maximum depth* of any of its components matters and not how many boxes there are of a specific depth.
2. The *breadth* of a box is the number of elements on its list. For instance, `\hbox{AB\hbox{CDEFG}}` is of breadth 3 because this box contains two characters and another hbox. Note that the number of boxes in one of the sub boxes, in other words the breadth of a component box such as `\hbox{CDEFG}`, is not important.

When you want to dump the contents of an hbox into the log file, you can use the `\showbox` command. The following two parameters are relevant in this context:

1. `\showboxdepth`. Limits the depth to which components of a box are shown. If you set this parameter to 1, you will see the components of the main box which is displayed using `\shoxbox`, but you will not see any of the component boxes be printed in any further detail.

   If you set `\showboxdepth` to 2, any subboxes of the main box are dumped into the log file showing their internal list, but the contents of those boxes would not be displayed in any further detail, and so forth.
2. `\showboxbreadth`. This parameter defines how many of the elements of a list of each box are shown. If you set this parameter to a rather large value, all elements of the list of a box are shown.

Let me make some additional remarks:

1. The `\showbox` command is the command that allows you to write the necessary box dimensions into the log file. The `\showbox` command is followed by the index of a box register and the contents of the index are written to a log file. You cannot write the contents of a box directly to a log file. You must assign it to a box register first.
2. TeX will normally stop and ask you for further input after it has processed `\showbox` the same way it does when you use `\showthe`. This can be avoided using `\nonstopmode` or `\batchmode`; see 27.12, p. III-442.
3. By default the output of `\showbox` appears *only* in the log file. If you set `\tracingonline` to a positive value, the output will also occur on the terminal screen. See 22.2.4, p. III-217, for details.
4. `\showboxdepth` and `\showboxbreadth` also determine the level of detail displayed when a math list is written to the log file using `\showlists`. For an example see 14.1.1, p. II-189.

Here is the source code of an example:

• ex-showbox.tip •

```
\nonstopmode
```

First load box register 0 with a sample box. This sample box will be used throughout the whole example.

```
\setbox 0 = \hbox{%
     A%
     B%
     \hbox{ABCD}%
     \hbox{%
          X%
          \hbox{ABCDEFGHIJKLM}%
     }%
}
```

Now use `\showbox` and various values of the registers related to `\showbox`. The following macro `\ShowMeTheBox` has two parameters:

- #1. The value `\showboxdepth` will be set to.
- #2. The value `\showboxbreadth` will be set to.

```
\def\ShowMeTheBox #1#2{%
     \showboxdepth = #1
     \showboxbreadth = #2
     \wlog{\string\ShowMeTheBox: \noexpand\showboxdepth is #1,
                                  \noexpand\showboxbreadth is #2.}
     \showbox 0
}
\wlog{** Depth 1 Log File Output **}
\ShowMeTheBox{1}{1}
\ShowMeTheBox{1}{2}
\ShowMeTheBox{1}{3}
```

```
\ShowMeTheBox{1}{4}
\ShowMeTheBox{1}{5}
```

Any value larger than 4 (as shown above using the value 5) would generate the same output.

Now switch to depth 2.

```
\wlog{** Depth 2 Log File Output **}
\ShowMeTheBox{2}{1}
\ShowMeTheBox{2}{4}
```

If we had a call `\ShowMeTheBox{2}{5}` or with any larger breadth, the output (sticking to depth 2) would be the same, of course.

Depth 3 is next.

```
\wlog{** Depth 3 Log File Output **}
\ShowMeTheBox{3}{1}
\ShowMeTheBox{3}{4}
```

The following example shows that for the box given breadth 5 is not enough, because the `\hbox{ABCDEFGHIJKLM}` box has breadth 13.

```
\ShowMeTheBox{3}{5}
```

Lucky number 13 is next!

```
\ShowMeTheBox{3}{13}
\bye
```

• End of `ex-showbox.tip` •

The log file generated by the preceding example is reprinted next. You have to study this log file carefully to see the effect of different settings of `\showboxdepth` and `\showboxbreadth`. In the first group of examples, `\showboxdepth` remains 1, and `\showboxbreadth` is increased by 1 after each example. Note that TeX will print "`.etc.`" if a box cannot be displayed in full detail because `\showboxbreadth` is too small.

• `ex-showbox.log` •

```
This is TeX, C Version 3.14 (...)
**&/usr/local/tex/lib/fmt/plain ex-showbox.tip
(ex-showbox.tip
** Depth 1 Log File Output **
\ShowMeTheBox: \showboxdepth is 1, \showboxbreadth is 1.
> \box0=
\hbox(6.83331+0.0)x141.31975
.\tenrm A
.etc.

\ShowMeTheBox ...} \showbox 0

l.19 \ShowMeTheBox{1}{1}

\ShowMeTheBox: \showboxdepth is 1, \showboxbreadth is 2.
> \box0=
\hbox(6.83331+0.0)x141.31975
```

```
.\tenrm A
.\tenrm B
.etc.

\ShowMeTheBox ...} \showbox 0

l.20 \ShowMeTheBox{1}{2}

\ShowMeTheBox: \showboxdepth is 1, \showboxbreadth is 3.
> \box0=
\hbox(6.83331+0.0)x141.31975
.\tenrm A
.\tenrm B
.\hbox(6.83331+0.0)x29.4445 []
.etc.

\ShowMeTheBox ...} \showbox 0

l.21 \ShowMeTheBox{1}{3}

\ShowMeTheBox: \showboxdepth is 1, \showboxbreadth is 4.
> \box0=
\hbox(6.83331+0.0)x141.31975
.\tenrm A
.\tenrm B
.\hbox(6.83331+0.0)x29.4445 []
.\hbox(6.83331+0.0)x97.29187 []

\ShowMeTheBox ...} \showbox 0

l.22 \ShowMeTheBox{1}{4}

\ShowMeTheBox: \showboxdepth is 1, \showboxbreadth is 5.
> \box0=
\hbox(6.83331+0.0)x141.31975
.\tenrm A
.\tenrm B
.\hbox(6.83331+0.0)x29.4445 []
.\hbox(6.83331+0.0)x97.29187 []

\ShowMeTheBox ...} \showbox 0

l.23 \ShowMeTheBox{1}{5}

** Depth 2 Log File Output **
\ShowMeTheBox: \showboxdepth is 2, \showboxbreadth is 1.
> \box0=
\hbox(6.83331+0.0)x141.31975
.\tenrm A
.etc.

\ShowMeTheBox ...} \showbox 0
```

```

l.25 \ShowMeTheBox{2}{1}

\ShowMeTheBox: \showboxdepth is 2, \showboxbreadth is 4.
> \box0=
\hbox(6.83331+0.0)x141.31975
.\tenrm A
.\tenrm B
.\hbox(6.83331+0.0)x29.4445
..\tenrm A
..\tenrm B
..\tenrm C
..\tenrm D
.\hbox(6.83331+0.0)x97.29187
..\tenrm X
..\hbox(6.83331+0.0)x89.79185 []

\ShowMeTheBox ...} \showbox 0

l.26 \ShowMeTheBox{2}{4}

** Depth 3 Log File Output **
\ShowMeTheBox: \showboxdepth is 3, \showboxbreadth is 1.
> \box0=
\hbox(6.83331+0.0)x141.31975
.\tenrm A
.etc.

\ShowMeTheBox ...} \showbox 0

l.28 \ShowMeTheBox{3}{1}

\ShowMeTheBox: \showboxdepth is 3, \showboxbreadth is 4.
> \box0=
\hbox(6.83331+0.0)x141.31975
.\tenrm A
.\tenrm B
.\hbox(6.83331+0.0)x29.4445
..\tenrm A
..\tenrm B
..\tenrm C
..\tenrm D
.\hbox(6.83331+0.0)x97.29187
..\tenrm X
..\hbox(6.83331+0.0)x89.79185
...\tenrm A
...\tenrm B
...\tenrm C
...\tenrm D
...etc.

\ShowMeTheBox ...} \showbox 0
```

```

1.29 \ShowMeTheBox{3}{4}

\ShowMeTheBox: \showboxdepth is 3, \showboxbreadth is 5.
> \box0=
\hbox(6.83331+0.0)x141.31975
.\tenrm A
.\tenrm B
.\hbox(6.83331+0.0)x29.4445
..\tenrm A
..\tenrm B
..\tenrm C
..\tenrm D
.\hbox(6.83331+0.0)x97.29187
..\tenrm X
..\hbox(6.83331+0.0)x89.79185
...\tenrm A
...\tenrm B
...\tenrm C
...\tenrm D
...\tenrm E
...etc.

\ShowMeTheBox ...} \showbox 0

1.30 \ShowMeTheBox{3}{5}

\ShowMeTheBox: \showboxdepth is 3, \showboxbreadth is 13.
> \box0=
\hbox(6.83331+0.0)x141.31975
.\tenrm A
.\tenrm B
.\hbox(6.83331+0.0)x29.4445
..\tenrm A
..\tenrm B
..\tenrm C
..\tenrm D
.\hbox(6.83331+0.0)x97.29187
..\tenrm X
..\hbox(6.83331+0.0)x89.79185
...\tenrm A
...\tenrm B
...\tenrm C
...\tenrm D
...\tenrm E
...\tenrm F
...\kern-0.27779
...\tenrm G
...\tenrm H
...\tenrm I
...\tenrm J
...\tenrm K
```

```
...\tenrm L
...etc.

\ShowMeTheBox ...} \showbox 0

l.31 \ShowMeTheBox{3}{13}

)
No pages of output.
```

4.5.15 The Definitions of Macros \ShowBoxAll, \ShowBoxDepthOne and \ShowBoxDepthTwo

Macro \ShowBoxAll has one parameter, #1, a box register index. The box stored in this register will be dumped into the log file "in all detail," that is, this macro sets \showboxdepth and \showboxbreadth to very large values and then applies \showbox.

$\mathcal{P}'$ • shboxes.tip •

```
\def\ShowBoxAll #1{%
    {%
        \nonstopmode
        \showboxdepth = 10000
        \showboxbreadth = 10000
        \showbox #1%
    }%
}
```

Macro \ShowBoxDepthOne also has one parameter, #1, the register index of a box register. The box is "shown" with depth 1 but at a very large breadth. This means that the sizes of all the components of the main box are shown, but these components boxes in turn are not listed in more detail (that is the boxes, glue or characters contained in them are not listed).

```
\def\ShowBoxDepthOne #1{%
    {%
        \nonstopmode
        \showboxdepth = 1
        \showboxbreadth = 10000
        \showbox #1%
    }%
}
```

Macro \ShowBoxDepthTwo is modeled after \ShowBoxDepthOne, but this time the depth is set to 2. The breadth is again set to a very large value.

```
\def\ShowBoxDepthTwo #1{%
    {%
        \nonstopmode
```

```
            \showboxdepth = 2
            \showboxbreadth = 10000
            \showbox #1%
        }%
}
```

• End of shboxes.tip •

The preceding macros contain calls to \nonstopmode to prevent TeX from stopping after the \showbox call contained in these macros.

4.5.16 Grouping and Box Register Dimensions

The details of grouping and box register dimensions are rather peculiar; see 19.4.14, p. III-110, for details.

4.6 Summary of the \new... Macros

A summary of all \new... type of macros is presented now. Most of these but not all are for the allocation of new registers.

4.6.1 A List of All \new... Macros

Here is a list of *all* \new... macros, not only those that have to do with registers. All these macros are defined using \outer; see 21.6, p. III-179.

1. **\newbox** is used to allocate a new *box register*; see 4.5, p. 95.
2. **\newcount** is used to allocate a new *counter register*; see 3.3.6, p. 49.
3. **\newdimen** allocates a new *dimension register*; see 4.1.7, p. 87.
4. **\newfam** allocates a *new family* in mathmode; see 14.5.4, p. II-203.
5. **\newif** defines a new \if like construct; see 25.1.7, p. III-324.
6. **\newinsert** allocates registers for a new *insertion class*; see 32.7.2, p. IV-29.
7. **\newmskip** allocates a new \mskip register; see 4.3, p. 93.
8. **\newread** allocates a new *input stream*; see 28.2, p. III-448.
9. **\newskip** is used to define a new *glue register*; see 4.2, p. 91.
10. **\newtoks** allocates a new *token register*; see 20.1.1, p. III-117.
11. **\newwrite** allocates a new *output stream*; see 28.5.2, p. III-473.
12. **\newlanguage** allocated a new *language* (this is important as far as hyphenation patterns are concerned); see 12.7.4, p. II-139.

4.6.2 \outer-free Definitions of the \new... Macros

The following source code when loaded defines macros `\newcountOF`, `\newdimenOF`, and so forth, where `OF` stands for `\outer`-free. That is, the macro source code below does *not* replace `\newcount`, and so forth, but provides functionally equivalent macros.

$\mathcal{P}'$ • newoutfr.tip •

```
\catcode`\@ = 11
\def\newcountOF{\alloc@0\count\countdef\insc@unt}
\def\newdimenOF{\alloc@1\dimen\dimendef\insc@unt}
\def\newskipOF{\alloc@2\skip\skipdef\insc@unt}
\def\newmuskipOF{\alloc@3\muskip\muskipdef\@cclvi}
\def\newboxOF{\alloc@4\box\chardef\insc@unt}
\def\newhelpOF#1#2{\newtoksOF#1#1\expandafter{\csname#2\endcsname}}
\def\newtoksOF{\alloc@5\toks\toksdef\@cclvi}
\def\newreadOF{\alloc@6\read\chardef\sixt@@n}
\def\newwriteOF{\alloc@7\write\chardef\sixt@@n}
\def\newfamOF{\alloc@8\fam\chardef\sixt@@n}
\def\newifOF#1{\count@\escapechar \escapechar\m@ne
  \expandafter\expandafter\expandafter
   \edef\@if#1{true}{\let\noexpand#1=\noexpand\iftrue}%
  \expandafter\expandafter\expandafter
   \edef\@if#1{false}{\let\noexpand#1=\noexpand\iffalse}%
  \@if#1{false}\escapechar\count@} % the condition starts out false
\def\newlanguageOF{\alloc@9\language\chardef\@cclvi}
\catcode`\@ = 12
```

• End of newoutfr.tip •

For the more *radically* inclined people (like me), I suggest loading the following macro source code file. This redefines *all* macros of the plain format that use `\outer` to macros which *no more* use `\outer`. Here is the source code of the file `outf-rad.tip` which does that. `\outer` is not only used for the macros but also used for two other macros (which are also made "-free" below).

$\mathcal{P}$ • outf-rad.tip •

```
\catcode`\@ = 11
\def\newcount{\alloc@0\count\countdef\insc@unt}
\def\newdimen{\alloc@1\dimen\dimendef\insc@unt}
\def\newskip{\alloc@2\skip\skipdef\insc@unt}
\def\newmuskip{\alloc@3\muskip\muskipdef\@cclvi}
\def\newbox{\alloc@4\box\chardef\insc@unt}
\def\newtoks{\alloc@5\toks\toksdef\@cclvi}
\def\newhelp#1#2{\newtoks#1#1\expandafter{\csname#2\endcsname}}
\def\newread{\alloc@6\read\chardef\sixt@@n}
\def\newwrite{\alloc@7\write\chardef\sixt@@n}
\def\newfam{\alloc@8\fam\chardef\sixt@@n}
\def\newif#1{\count@\escapechar \escapechar\m@ne
  \expandafter\expandafter\expandafter
   \edef\@if#1{true}{\let\noexpand#1=\noexpand\iftrue}%
```

```
  \expandafter\expandafter\expandafter
   \edef\@if#1{false}{\let\noexpand#1=\noexpand\iffalse}%
  \@if#1{false}\escapechar\count@} % the condition starts out false
\def\newlanguage{\alloc@9\language\chardef\@cclvi}
\def^^L{\par}
\def\newinsert#1{\global\advance\insc@unt by\m@ne
  \ch@ck0\insc@unt\count
  \ch@ck1\insc@unt\dimen
  \ch@ck2\insc@unt\skip
  \ch@ck4\insc@unt\box
  \allocationnumber=\insc@unt
  \global\chardef#1=\allocationnumber
  \wlog{\string#1=\string\insert\the\allocationnumber}}
\def\+{\tabalign}
\def\beginsection#1\par{\vskip\z@ plus.3\vsize\penalty-250
  \vskip\z@ plus-.3\vsize\bigskip\vskip\parskip
  \message{#1}\leftline{\bf#1}\nobreak\smallskip\noindent}
\def\proclaim #1. #2\par{\medbreak
  \noindent{\bf#1.\enspace}{\sl#2\par}%
  \ifdim\lastskip<\medskipamount \removelastskip\penalty55
        \medskip\fi}
\def\bye{\par\vfill\supereject\end}
\catcode`\@ = 12
```

• End of `outf-rad.tip` •

4.6.3 Name Conflicts in `\new...` Macros

Let me point out that none of the `\new...` macros test whether a particular name requested for a register is already in use. For instance, the input

```
\newbox\abox
\newbox\abox
\newcount\xx
\newdimen\xx
```

does not generate any warnings or error messages.

This can lead to obvious problems. The `\new...` macros can be easily extended to include a test of whether the proposed name of a register or other entity has already been used. See 21.5.7, p. III-174, for details.

If you read in the following TeX source code then your plain format will be patched in such a way that the accidental allocation of registers with names previously used will cause TeX to report an error. The code offered below is identical to the plain format definition of `\alloc@` with the exception of lines 19-22 which were added.

Macro `\alloc@`, by the way, has the following parameters:

- `#1`. Each register group for which new registers are assigned is allocated one counter register. This counter register's index is in the range 10...19. `#1` is the last digit of this counter register index, that is it is "mod 10" of the register index.

- #2. \count if a counter register is allocated, \dimen if a dimension register is allocated and so forth.
- #3. \countdef if a counter register is allocated, \dimendef if a dimension register is allocated and so forth.
- #4. The insertion index counter. This facilitates to ensure than when a new register is allocated it does not conflict with an existing insertion index. See 32.7.2, p. IV-29, for details.
- #5. The name of the new register which is being allocated.

$\mathcal{P}$ • allocat.tip •

```
\catcode`\@ = 11
\def\alloc@#1#2#3#4#5{%
```

Increment the register which holds the index of the next register to be allocated by 1.

```
        \global\advance\count1#1by\@ne
```

Check whether there is still room. \ch@ck is defined as part of the plain format.

```
        \ch@ck#1#4#2%
```

Get the allocation number.

```
        \allocationnumber=\count1#1%
```

Check whether already a register of that name is allocated.

```
        \ifx #5\@allocUndef
        \else
            \errmessage{\string\alloc@: \string#5 already defined}%
        \fi
```

Do the allocation.

```
        \global#3#5=\allocationnumber
```

Report the allocation

```
    \wlog{\string#5=\string#2\the\allocationnumber}%
}
\catcode`\@ = 12
```

• End of allocat.tip •

Here is an example application of the preceding macro. The following source code is used.

• ex-allocat.tip •

```
\nonstopmode
\input inputd.tip
\InputD{allocat.tip}                          % 4.6.3, p. 115.
\newbox\abox
\newbox\bbox
```

```
\newbox\cbox
\newbox\abox
\bye
```

• End of `ex-allocat.tip` •

The preceding source code generates the following output.

• `ex-allocat.log` •

```
This is TeX, C Version 3.14 (...)
**&/usr/local/tex/lib/fmt/plain ex-allocat.tip
(ex-allocat.tip
(inputd.tip
(namedef.tip
) (inputdl.tip
\@InputDStream=\write0
)) (allocat.tip
)
\abox=\box16
\bbox=\box17
\cbox=\box18

! \alloc@: \abox already defined.
\alloc@ ...#5 already defined}
\fi \global #3#5=\allocatio...
l.7 \newbox\abox

This error message was generated by an \errmessage
command, so I can't give any explicit help.
Pretend that you're Hercule Poirot: Examine all clues,
and deduce the truth by order and method.

\abox=\box19
)
No pages of output.
```

4.7 Dumping All Parameters into the Logfile

Sometimes in life (although rarely) a brute force approach works best. Here is a "brute force macro." The macro `\DumpAllPars` (no argument) writes all parameters to the log file.

$\mathcal{P}'$ • `dumppars.tip` •

Macro `\DumpOneReg` has one argument, `#1`, a parameter. It writes the names of the parameter to the log file.

```
\def\DumpOneReg #1{%
    \wlog{Parameter "\string#1", value = \the#1}%
```

```
}
```

The following list of counter parameters is taken from 3.3.10, p. 53.

```
\def\DumpAllRegs{%
    \wlog{\string\DumpAllRegs: Counter parameters first.}%
    \DumpOneReg{\time}%
    \DumpOneReg{\day}%
    \DumpOneReg{\month}%
    \DumpOneReg{\year}%
    \DumpOneReg{\pretolerance}%
    \DumpOneReg{\tolerance}%
    \DumpOneReg{\doublehyphendemerits}%
    \DumpOneReg{\finalhyphendemerits}%
    \DumpOneReg{\adjdemerits}%
    \DumpOneReg{\linepenalty}%
    \DumpOneReg{\looseness}%
    \DumpOneReg{\linepenalty}%
    \DumpOneReg{\hyphenpenalty}%
    \DumpOneReg{\exhyphenpenalty}%
    \DumpOneReg{\binoppenalty}%
    \DumpOneReg{\relpenalty}%
    \DumpOneReg{\clubpenalty}%
    \DumpOneReg{\widowpenalty}%
    \DumpOneReg{\displaywidowpenalty}%
    \DumpOneReg{\brokenpenalty}%
    \DumpOneReg{\predisplaypenalty}%
    \DumpOneReg{\postdisplaypenalty}%
    \DumpOneReg{\interlinepenalty}%
    \DumpOneReg{\floatingpenalty}%
    \DumpOneReg{\outputpenalty}%
    \DumpOneReg{\pausing}%
    \DumpOneReg{\tracingonline}%
    \DumpOneReg{\tracinglostchars}%
    \DumpOneReg{\tracingmacros}%
    \DumpOneReg{\tracingstats}%
    \DumpOneReg{\tracingparagraphs}%
    \DumpOneReg{\tracingpages}%
    \DumpOneReg{\tracingoutput}%
    \DumpOneReg{\tracingcommands}%
    \DumpOneReg{\tracingrestores}%
    \DumpOneReg{\mag}%
    \DumpOneReg{\uchyph}%
    \DumpOneReg{\lefthyphenmin}%
    \DumpOneReg{\righthyphenmin}%
    \DumpOneReg{\defaultskewchar}%
    \DumpOneReg{\escapechar}%
    \DumpOneReg{\endlinechar}%
    \DumpOneReg{\newlinechar}%
    \DumpOneReg{\fam}%
    \DumpOneReg{\hbadness}%
    \DumpOneReg{\vbadness}%
    \DumpOneReg{\badness}%
```

```
        \DumpOneReg{\showboxdepth}%
        \DumpOneReg{\showboxbreadth}%
        \DumpOneReg{\deadcycles}%
        \DumpOneReg{\maxdeadcycles}%
        \DumpOneReg{\holdinginserts}%
        \DumpOneReg{\hangafter}%
        \DumpOneReg{\globaldefs}%
        \DumpOneReg{\delimiterfactor}%
        \DumpOneReg{\inputlineno}%
        \DumpOneReg{\language}%
```

Next are dimension parameters from 4.1.9, p. 88.

```
        \wlog{\string\DumpAllRegs: Dimension parameters next.}%
        \DumpOneReg{\hfuzz}%
        \DumpOneReg{\vfuzz}%
        \DumpOneReg{\overfullrule}%
```

Note that `\prevdepth` inside a `\write` is illegal in TeX. Therefore `\prevdepth` is not written to the log file and commented out.

```
%       \DumpOneReg{\prevdepth}%
        \DumpOneReg{\lineskiplimit}%
        \DumpOneReg{\maxdepth}%
        \DumpOneReg{\splitmaxdepth}%
        \DumpOneReg{\boxmaxdepth}%
        \DumpOneReg{\delimitershortfall}%
        \DumpOneReg{\nulldelimiterspace}%
        \DumpOneReg{\scriptspace}%
        \DumpOneReg{\mathsurround}%
        \DumpOneReg{\predisplaysize}%
        \DumpOneReg{\displaywidth}%
        \DumpOneReg{\displayindent}%
        \DumpOneReg{\parindent}%
        \DumpOneReg{\hangindent}%
        \DumpOneReg{\hoffset}%
        \DumpOneReg{\voffset}%
```

Last are all the glue parameters from 4.2.2, p. 92.

```
        \wlog{\string\DumpAllRegs: Glue parameters last.}%
        \DumpOneReg{\baselineskip}%
        \DumpOneReg{\lineskip}%
        \DumpOneReg{\topskip}%
        \DumpOneReg{\splittopskip}%
        \DumpOneReg{\parskip}%
        \DumpOneReg{\leftskip}%
        \DumpOneReg{\rightskip}%
        \DumpOneReg{\emergencystretch}%
        \DumpOneReg{\abovedisplayskip}%
        \DumpOneReg{\abovedisplayshortskip}%
        \DumpOneReg{\belowdisplayskip}%
        \DumpOneReg{\belowdisplayshortskip}%
```

And we are done.

```
        \wlog{\string\DumpAllRegs: done.}%
    }%
```

• End of **dumppars.tip** •

No sample call of this macro is offered: just try it out yourself. Let's cut down a little bit at least on the length of this series ....

4.8 Summary

In this chapter we learned:

- Arithmetic in TEX allows the use of counter, dimension and glue registers in addition to numerical constants and dimension and glue constant values.
- It is possible to compare dimensions and glue values in TEX.
- TEX has dimension units, which are absolute, font relative, or infinite. Infinite dimension units are only for the specifications of stretchabilities and shrinkabilities of glue. Note that dimensions are usually magnified by the current magnification and can be suppressed using the keyword `true` with any dimension specification. The unit scaled point (sp) was introduced by TEX. It is a very small unit, and all dimensions internally in TEX are represented using this unit and integers only.
- Box registers allow the user to store boxes in registers. A box register is loaded using `\setbox`. The commands `\box` and `\copy` duplicate the content of a box register. The content of the original box is lost in the case of `\box`, but not in the case of `\copy`.
- It is possible to inquire about the state of a box register. It is also possible to inquire about, and change the dimensions of a box stored in a box register. By setting the dimensions of a box register to zero, TEX can be tricked into printing material without moving its reference point.
- `\showbox` can be used to dump the content of a box register into the log file. `\showboxdepth` and `\showboxbreadth` can be used to control what information is dumped into a file and what not.

5
Glue, Leaders and Rules

As mentioned in Chapter 4, *glue* is an entity in TEX that is used to describe *spacing*. For instance, the horizontal space between words is taken up by *horizontal glue*, and the vertical space between lines is occupied by *vertical glue*. An example of *leaders* are the dots in a table of contents, which "lead the eye" from the table of contents entry to the page number on the right-hand side. The term *rules* in typesetting means vertical or horizontal lines as they are used, for instance, in tables.

5.1 Basic Properties of Glue

Since among other things, glue controls the spacing between words in paragraphs, it is a very important concept in TEX. Among other things, it controls the spacing between words in paragraphs. The concept of glue can be explained more clearly once we look at glue and boxes together.

The basic goal of the concept of glue is to be able to describe in mathematical terms either a vertical or horizontal distance that contrary to a usual definition of a distance, is *not rigid* but can *shrink* and *stretch*, if that should be necessary.

Here are some basic properties of glue (kern is not included in the discussion below; see 5.4.8, p. 140, for details):

1. Glue can extend in either of *two directions*:
   (a) *Horizontal glue.* Horizontal glue fills up white space horizontally.
   (b) *Vertical glue.* Vertical glue fills up white space vertically.
2. Glue can be generated in two different ways.
   (a) *Explicit glue* is explicitly specified by the user. *Explicit horizontal glue* is specified with `\hskip` followed by a glue value specification. *Explicit vertical glue* is specified with `\vskip` followed by a glue value specification.

The term *skip* means that TeX will move the current reference point horizontally or vertically by the specified distance.

(b) *Implicit glue* is glue that is inserted by TeX under precisely defined circumstances. The user has control over the amount of glue being inserted, but the insertion itself is handled automatically by TeX.

The most prominent example for *implicit horizontal glue* is the glue between words or the *interword glue*, the *interword space* for short. TeX converts space characters in the input to horizontal glue. The user does *not* use the `\hskip` command to instruct TeX to insert glue between each pair of words in a paragraph.

Interline glue, on the other hand, is *implicit vertical glue*. TeX will insert this glue between the lines of a paragraph to insure constant line spacing of the text in a paragraph.

The amount of implicit glue is determined by a value assigned to a *glue parameter*. For instance, `\baselineskip` specifies the amount of interline glue. `\baselineskip = 12pt` gives a 12 pt line spacing size. The line spacing distance is measured as the distance between two consecutive lines. See 7.3, p. 217, for a detailed discussion of TeX's line spacing.

3. A *glue value* consists of *three dimensions* (the notation used to write down a glue value is discussed under item 5 of this list).

   (a) The *natural length* or *space*. This is the ideal amount of white space to be inserted at the current location.
   (b) The *stretchability* is the amount by which the glue can be stretched. This value specifies how much the glue can stretch relative to the natural length of the glue.
   (c) The *shrinkability* is the amount by which the glue can be pushed together. This value specifies how much the glue can shrink relative to the natural length of the glue.

4. The *natural length* of a glue is *usually positive*:

   (a) Positive *horizontal* glue tells TeX to skip to the *right*.
   (b) Positive *vertical* glue tells TeX to skip *downwards*.

   The natural length can be *negative*:

   (a) Negative *horizontal* glue tells TeX to skip to the *left*.
   (b) Negative *vertical* glue tells TeX to skip *upwards*.

5. The notation of *glue values* is as follows. First the natural length, a dimension, is given. This is followed by the keyword `plus` and the stretchability of the glue, a dimension. This in turn is followed by the keyword `minus` and the shrinkability of the glue, again a dimension. For instance, a glue with a natural length of 12 pt, a stretchability of 10 pt and a shrinkability of 4 pt is written as follows:

```
12pt plus 10pt minus 4pt
```

   Observe that `plus` and `minus` are keywords of TeX after which spaces are ignored. It does not make any difference whether you write `plus␣10pt` or `plus10pt`.

Four potential applications of this particular glue value follow:

(a) *Explicit horizontal* glue (`\hskip 12pt plus 10pt minus 4pt`). TEX will skip horizontally by 12 pt, and if stretched out, it will skip up to an additional 10 pt (resulting in a skip of 22 pt), or it will skip by up to 4 pt less than 12 pt, that is, down to 8 pt if pushed together. The circumstances under which the glue will be stretched or pushed together are discussed in 5.2.2, p. 125.

5.2.3, p. 126, discusses potential overstretching of glue. For instance, the maximum of 12 pt as specified with `plus 12pt` is not a strict maximum; see 5.2.3, p. 126, for details.

(b) *Implicit horizontal* glue (`\tabskip = 12pt plus 10pt minus 4pt`). The `\tabskip` glue specifies the distance between the columns of a table built with `\halign`. The distance between the columns of a table can be adjusted by TEX according to the established limits.

(c) *Explicit vertical* glue (`\vskip 12pt plus 10pt minus 4pt`). A vertical skip will be performed within the given limits.

(d) *Implicit vertical* glue (`\parskip = 12pt plus 10pt minus 4pt`). This implicit vertical glue is inserted at the beginning of each paragraph. It is responsible for the white space between paragraphs. The above specification tells TEX to leave one empty line between paragraphs, which can be extended to become almost two empty lines, but which also can be pushed down to become about 2/3rds of a line.

Observe that when a glue value is assigned to a glue parameter, an equal sign, as in `\parskip =` , is written. This is consistent with the issue of assigning values to registers (see 3.2.1, p. 37). On the other hand, no equal sign is used with explicit glues, that is, with `\hskip` or `\vskip`.

6. The specifications of natural length, stretchability, and shrinkability must be done in this order. If stretchability and/or the shrinkability are not specified, they *default to zero.* There is no default for the natural length of a glue. Here is another set of examples:

(a) `\hskip 12pt plus 10pt minus 4pt` is a legal glue specification.

(b) `\hskip 12pt` is equivalent to `\hskip 12pt plus 0pt minus 0pt`.

(c) `\hskip 12pt plus 3pt` is equivalent to `\hskip 12pt plus 3pt minus 0pt`.

(d) `\hskip 12pt minus 3pt` is equivalent to `\hskip 12pt plus 0pt minus 3pt`.

(e) `\hskip 2pt minus 4pt plus 10pt` is *not* a legal glue specification. It is interpreted as `\hskip 12pt plus 0pt minus 4pt`, followed by the text "`plus 10pt`."

(f) `\hskip 12pt \relax minus ....` Here the control word `\relax` separates the glue specification `\hskip 12pt` from subsequent text that starts with the word "minus."

(g) `\hskip 12pt {}minus more`. Here an empty group separates the glue specification `\hskip 12pt` from the following text that starts with the word "minus."

The last two examples show how a glue specification can be separated from the following text which might start with one of the two keywords `plus` or `minus`: either use `\relax` (see 27.4, p. III-431) or insert an empty group (see 19.4.5, p. III-102).

7. The stretchability and shrinkability of glue specifications can make use of the "infinite units" `fil`, `fill`, and `filll`, which are discussed in 5.4, p. 135. These infinite units cannot be used to specify the natural length of a glue (see preceding reference for details).
8. There is a very important difference between the stretchability and shrinkability of glue, when it comes to *exceeding* the specified values:
   (a) Glue can *shrink only as far as specified.* It will not shrink at all if the shrinkability is zero.
   (b) Glue can *stretch beyond the specified value.* The value for the stretchability of a glue is the *desired* but *not the absolute* maximum of stretching. If the stretchability is zero it will not stretch at all. The benefit of specifying maximum stretchability even though TeX will stretch beyond this value if necessary, is discussed
9. *Glue is a special case of leaders.* While glue fills up some space with "white space," leaders fill up space with either a rule or repeated copies of some user-specified box. See 5.6, p. 145, for details.

5.2 Horizontal Glue

Since horizontal glue is a little easier to work with than vertical glue the following examples use horizontal glue exclusively. All of the examples below could be modified to using vertical glue. For examples using vertical glue see 5.5, p. 142.

To understand the examples you will need some knowledge of boxes (explained in Chapter Chapter 6). For the purposes of discussion here, know that the instruction `\hbox` generates a horizontal box. This box is a ... and can be .... The contents of an hbox is enclosed inside curly braces following `\hbox`, so `\hbox{ABC}` forms a horizontal box containing the three characters `ABC`. The width of this box is the sum of the widths of the three characters `A`, `B`, and `C`.

6.2, p. 162, gives a brief introduction into hboxes (see also Fig. 6.1, p. 162).

5.2.1 Glue Without Stretch- and Shrinkability, Negative Glue

In this Subsection, examples using glue *without* stretchability and shrinkability are given. In these examples we enclose three items inside a horizontal box or hbox: the character "A," varying amounts of explicit horizontal glue (`\hskip`), and the character "B." Observe that positive horizontal glue skips to the right and negative horizontal glue skips to the left.

Also note that spaces after dimensions in general (therefore also after dimensions that are part of glue specifications) are ignored. This allows us to write `\hskip 25pt B` instead of `\hskip 25ptB`, which is less readable.

The examples use glue without stretchability and shrinkability. Therefore `\hskip 10pt plus 0pt minus 0pt` can be abbreviated to `\hskip 10pt` (see item 6, p. 123).

Finally here are the examples:

	Input	Output
1:	`\hbox{A\hskip -25pt B}`	B A
2:	`\hbox{A\hskip -15pt B}`	BA
3:	`\hbox{A\hskip -10pt B}`	BA
4:	`\hbox{A\hskip - 5pt B}`	AB
5:	`\hbox{A\hskip 0pt B}`	AB
6:	`\hbox{A\hskip 5pt B}`	A B
7:	`\hbox{A\hskip 10pt B}`	A B
8:	`\hbox{A\hskip 15pt B}`	A B
9:	`\hbox{A\hskip 25pt B}`	A B

5.2.2 Getting Glue to Stretch and Shrink

Note that glue will not stretch or shrink unless it is forced to do so. Specifying stretchability or shrinkability values is not enough to make TeX stretch or shrink glue. Consequently, in any of the above examples we could have specified any stretchability or shrinkability value, and the results would have been as if we had not specified such values. For instance, if we had modified the last example and written

```
\hbox{A\hskip 25pt plus 20pt minus 10pt B}
```

"A" and "B" would still be printed 25 pt apart.

The *natural width* of a box is defined in TeX as the sum of the widths of all components in this box. Stretchabilities and shrinkabilities of glues are ignored when it comes to computing the natural width of a horizontal box. The natural width, if you use the `\hbox` command as in `\hbox{ABC}`, is the width of this box. That is width and natural width are the same, which in turn is the sum of the widths of the three characters `A`, `B`, and `C`.

Using hboxes there are two ways to instruct TeX to *stretch or shrink it* (assume for now that sufficient glue to stretch or shrink is available in an hbox):

1. `\hbox spread` ⟨dimen⟩ `{...}` instructs TeX to build an hbox which is wider by ⟨dimen⟩ than an hbox constructed by `\hbox{...}`. Thus the width of this hbox is ⟨dimen⟩ larger than the natural width of this box.

⟨dimen⟩ can be negative in which case any glue in the box is pushed together and the box is made less wide than its natural width.

As mentioned before you can use any of TEX's units to specify such dimensions (units point and inches are the most commonly used units in this book).

2. `\hbox to` ⟨dimen⟩ `{...}` tells TEX to make the hbox as wide as it is specified by ⟨dimen⟩. `\hbox to` and `\hbox spread` relate to each other as follows. Assume, for instance, that the natural width of an hbox is 1.5 in and that the following instruction is given: `\hbox to 2.0in{...}`. This makes this hbox 0.5 in wider than its natural width and therefore one could also have written `\hbox spread 0.5in{...}` instead.

In both cases, `spread` and `to`, the adjustment of the width will be made with any glue inside the box; it is not possible to adjust the width of a character. The next Subsection presents some `\hbox spread` examples.

5.2.3 Stretching, Overstretching, Shrinking and Overshrinking of Glue

Glue can be stretched and pushed together in basically four different ways. Fig. 5.1 on the next page gives examples of the following four categories: stretching, overstretching, shrinking and overshrinking. Each example contains exactly one glue, which is the only item of the box of which the length can be adjusted. Later examples with more than one glue will be discussed.

1. Examples 1–3. The glue in these examples has zero stretchability and shrinkability. Examples 2 and 3 show that the glue will neither stretch nor shrink (although the width of the hbox is being modified).
2. Examples 4–9. The glue in these examples can stretch, but cannot shrink. Therefore in Example 4, the distance between the two characters remains unchanged. Examples 8 and 9 show that the glue can be overstretched. This is consistent with rule 8.a, p. 124.
3. Examples 10–14. The glue in these examples can shrink, but not stretch. Here we see that contrary to overstretching, a glue cannot overshrink (example 10). This is consistent with rule 8.b, p. 124.
4. Examples 15–23. The glue in those examples can stretch and shrink. It therefore will not overshrink (example 15), but it will overstretch (examples 22 and 23). See the same rule mentioned previously.

All preceding examples are consistent with rules 8.a and 8.b, p. 124. If you were to actually run the example itself you would realize that a number of warnings of overfull and underfull boxes are generated by TEX (simply enter the following examples, run TEX, and see yourself). We ignore those in the discussion here. Some of the hboxes of the examples are marked with a black rule. This will

In this figure `\hs` is used as an abbreviation for `\hbox spread`. If this abbreviation had not been used, some of the example lines would have been too wide for this text page.

```
\def\hs{\hbox spread}
```

	Source code	Output
1:	`\hs 0pt {A\hskip 20pt plus 0pt minus 0pt B}`	A B
2:	`\hs 5pt {...}`	A B
3:	`\hs -5pt {...}`	A B■
4:	`\hs -5pt {A\hskip 20pt plus 20pt minus 0pt B}`	A B■
5:	`\hs 0pt {...}`	A B
6:	`\hs 10pt {...}`	A B
7:	`\hs 20pt {...}`	A B
8:	`\hs 30pt {...}`	A B
9:	`\hs 40pt {...}`	A B
10:	`\hs -15pt {A\hskip 20pt plus 0pt minus 10pt B}`	A B■
11:	`\hs -10pt {...}`	A B
12:	`\hs -5pt {...}`	A B
13:	`\hs 0pt {...}`	A B
14:	`\hs 5pt {...}`	A B
15:	`\hs -15pt {A\hskip 20pt plus 20pt minus 10pt B}`	A B■
16:	`\hs -10pt {...}`	A B
17:	`\hs -5pt {...}`	A B
18:	`\hs 0pt {...}`	A B
19:	`\hs 5pt {...}`	A B
20:	`\hs 10pt {...}`	A B
21:	`\hs 20pt {...}`	A B
22:	`\hs 30pt {...}`	A B
23:	`\hs 40pt {...}`	A B

Figure 5.1. Glue examples.

be discussed shortly. The issue we are focusing upon now is simply what TEX does with glue under extreme circumstances of stretching and shrinking.

5.3 Badness of Boxes

To be able to compute the best line breaks, TEX has to assign a quality grade to each line based on how much that line has to be stretched out or pushed together to achieve left and right justified text. This grade is called *badness*. This grade is a "reverse grade," as the name already suggests: the *higher* the grade (which is a number) the *worse* the line is.

When TEX typesets a paragraph with left and right justified lines, it uses the glue between words (called the interword glue) to adjust the line length. A line that comes out too long is pushed together, and a line that comes out too short is spread out. TeX tries to *minimize* this stretching and shrinking—the less stretching and shrinking happens, the more uniform the text appears and therefore, the better it looks.[1] The concept of glue was developed among other purposes for the precise description of stretchable and shrinkable dimensions.

What good does it do to specify the maximum stretchability of glue if TeX will stretch the glue as far as needed anyway? Also, what do the messages in the log file tell us about underfull and overfull boxes?

Note that in paragraphs the badness of a line and the badness of an hbox are identical because lines (after the computation of line breaks) are treated as hboxes in TeX.

One final remark: the badness computations of horizontal and vertical boxes are identical, and because horizontal boxes are easier to grasp, the badness discussion is limited to horizontal boxes in this chapter.

5.3.1 Computing the Badness

Let us look now at the computation of the badness of a box. The *badness* is an integer value in the range of 0...10000, where badness 0 stands for a "perfect" box and 10,000 for a "terrible" box. The special penalty value of 1,000,000 was introduced in TeX 3.0 and is discussed in 5.3.3 on the next page.

For instance, the hboxes of examples 2, 3, 4 and 15 of Fig. 5.1 on the previous page have badness 10,000: in those cases we tried to make a box wider and narrower, but none of those boxes contained glue that could stretch or shrink. Therefore those boxes "deserve" the highest badness of 10,000.

Now let us assume an hbox with one glue in it which can stretch. Assume that the box is to be spread out by x pt, and that the glue in it has a stretchability of y pt. If $x = 0$ (no stretching) then obviously we have a perfect box with a badness of zero.

Now assume $x \neq 0$ and $y \neq 0$. Then x/y defines what we call the *stretch ratio*. For instance, in Example 8 of Fig. 5.1 on the previous page (`\hbox spread 30pt{A\hskip 10pt plus 20pt B}`) the stretch ratio is 30 pt/20 pt = 1.5.

The badness of a box is computed from the stretch ratio of the box by taking the cube of the stretch ratio (1.5^3 in our example) and multiplying it by 100 (leading to a badness of $1.5^3 * 100 \approx 367$). If the so-far computed value exceeds 10,000 then it is reduced to 10,000. For another example, if the same box were spread out 300 pt, the badness of the box would be computed as follows: the stretch ratio is 300 pt/20 pt = 15. Therefore the badness is at first computed as $15^3 * 100 = 367500$. This value is subsequently reduced to 10,000 because it exceeds the maximum value of 10,000.

---

[1] Actually TeX takes one more factor into account, and that is the sequence of lines—TeX tries to avoid a very tight (pushed together) line followed by a very loose (pulled out) line. But this is irrelevant for the discussion here.

Here is the complete formula for computing the badness *bad* of a box. The variable x is the amount by which the box is spread out, y is the amount of *stretchability* of the glue in this box, "min" computes the minimum of two numbers, and "round" rounds a real number to the nearest integer.

$$bad = \begin{cases} 0 & \text{if } x = 0 \\ 10{,}000 & \text{if } y = 0 \text{ and } x \neq 0 \\ \min\left(10000, \text{round}\left((x/y)^3 * 100\right)\right) & \text{otherwise} \end{cases}$$

Observe that a stretch ratio of 1 corresponds to a badness of 100. A stretch ratio > 1 (equivalent to $bad > 100$) means that glue in this box is overstretched. Therefore if the badness of a box exceeds 100, glue in it is being overstretched.

5.3.2 Computing the Badness When Shrinking Occurs

The formula of the previous Subsection assumes that glue is being stretched. Let us now discuss the badness computation of a box where the box is *pushed together* (`\hbox spread` $x$pt, $x < 0$) and where the available *shrinkability* of the glue is z with $z \geq 0$ (note that the shrinkability of some glue is specified by giving a positive (non-zero) value z). The actual amount of shrinking, z, is a negative value. Note that according to item 8, p. 124, glue cannot be overpushed and therefore when the stretch ratio exceeds 1, the badness immediately jumps to its maximum value of 10,000.

The badness computation is therefore done according to the following formula:

$$bad = \begin{cases} 0 & \text{if } x = 0 \\ 10000 & \text{if } x \neq 0 \text{ and } -x > z \\ \text{round}\left((x/z)^3 * 100\right) \end{cases}$$

See 5.3.3 on this page for a small modification of this formula in TeX 3.0.

5.3.3 The Counter Parameter `\badness`

One of the extensions of TeX 3.0 is to provide a counter parameter `\badness`. This counter register is read-only so it cannot be modified by a user (such modification would not make any sense anyway). This counter register contains the badness of the most recently built box. If the most recent box was overfull, the `\badness` register is loaded with the value of 1,000,000 (which according to the preceding rules is not a badness value TeX would assign) rather than 10,000, if the most recent box was *overfull*.

The next Subsection contains an example where this register is actually used.

5.3.4 Examples of TeX's Badness Computations

The following series of examples will demonstrate TeX's computation of badness. TeX only reports the badness of an hbox, if this badness exceeds the threshold value stored in the `\hbadness` register.

• **badness.tip** •

By setting `\hbadness` to zero, the badness of *all* hboxes, except those with a badness of zero, is written to the log file.

```
\hbadness = 0
```

Define a macro `\PrintBadness` which prints the badness of the most recently built box.

```
\def\PrintBadness{%
    {%
        \nobreak
        \count0 = \badness
        \leftline{%
            \hskip 20pt
            (Badness of preceding box: \the\count0)%
        }%
        \smallskip
    }%
}
```

Create some loose and underfull boxes first. Terms *loose* and *underfull* are discussed in 5.3.5 on the next page.

```
\hbox spread 100pt {A\hskip 10pt plus 10pt B}\PrintBadness
\hbox spread 50pt  {A\hskip 10pt plus 10pt B}\PrintBadness
\hbox spread 20pt  {A\hskip 10pt plus 10pt B}\PrintBadness
\hbox spread 10pt  {A\hskip 10pt plus 10pt B}\PrintBadness
\hbox spread 5pt   {A\hskip 10pt plus 10pt B}\PrintBadness
\hbox spread 1pt   {A\hskip 10pt plus 10pt B}\PrintBadness
```

Now create some tight and overfull boxes. Terms *tight* and *overfull* are discussed in 5.3.5 on the next page.

```
\hbox spread -10pt {A\hskip 10pt minus 5pt B}\PrintBadness
\hbox spread -5pt  {A\hskip 10pt minus 5pt B}\PrintBadness
\hbox spread -2pt  {A\hskip 10pt minus 5pt B}\PrintBadness
\hbox spread -1pt  {A\hskip 10pt minus 5pt B}\PrintBadness
\bye
```

• End of **badness.tip** •

The output generated by the execution of the preceding source code is reprinted in Figure 5.2 on the next page.

The log file generated by the execution of the preceding source code is not reprinted here. It contains messages about the badness of the various boxes.

A B
(Badness of preceding box: 10000)
A B
(Badness of preceding box: 10000)
A B
(Badness of preceding box: 800)
A B
(Badness of preceding box: 100)
A B
(Badness of preceding box: 12)
A B
(Badness of preceding box: 0)
A B■
(Badness of preceding box: 1000000)
A B
(Badness of preceding box: 100)
A B
(Badness of preceding box: 6)
A B
(Badness of preceding box: 1)

Figure 5.2. Output of box badness example source code.

5.3.5 Overfull and Underfull Boxes, `\hbadness`, `\vbadness`

For the following definitions remember that a badness of exactly 100 implies that the glue inside a box has been stretched out or pushed together exactly to the specified values, because a badness of 100 corresponds to a stretch ratio of 1. Therefore, the cutoff point in the following definitions, between underfull and loose boxes (or overfull and tight boxes), is a badness of 100.

A box is called

1. *Underfull*, if the box is spread out and the badness of the box exceeds 100.
2. *Loose*, if the box is spread out and the badness of the box is below or equal to 100, but not 0.
3. *Overfull*, if the box is pushed together and the badness of the box exceeds 100.
4. *Tight*, if the box is pushed together and the badness is below or equal to 100, but not 0.

TeX will only report, to the log file, those hboxes (vboxes) in which the badness exceeds the value of `\hbadness` (`\vbadness`). The default for both values is 1000. Overfull boxes of badness 10,000 are always reported, even if `\hbadness` or `\vbadness` are set to values above 10,000.

There are two cases where overfull boxes occur *frequently.* I point out those two cases now because they deserve special attention.

1. Inside a paragraph, when TEX cannot find a suitable line break, it will report an overfull line. See 12.8.2, p. II-150, for details.
2. Inside the output routine, overfull `\vbox`es occur and the relating error message in the log file reads: `Overfull \vbox (...) occurred while \output active`). See 33.7, p. IV-54, for details.

5.3.6 The Marking of Overfull Horizontal Boxes, `\overfullrule`

Overfull horizontal boxes are marked with a vertical rule of thickness, `\overfullrule`. The default for this parameter in the plain format is 5 pt. Examples for boxes marked this way can be found in Fig. 5.1, p. 127; see, for instance, Example 3. Here is another example: `\hbox spread -1pt {A\hskip 10pt B}` will print A B■ . By the way, the period ending the last sentence had to be moved to the right, because otherwise it would have disappeared in the overfull rule.

In case you don't like to have your overfull hboxes marked with a rule (the black box printed in the preceding example), set the thickness of the overfull rule to zero: `\overfullrule = 0pt`.

Overfull vertical boxes and any underfull boxes are not marked by TEX.

5.3.7 Dimension Parameters `\hfuzz`, `\vfuzz`

There is one additional factor which needs to be taken into account when *reporting overfull* boxes (the following remarks do *not* apply to underfull boxes): a box is only reported as overfull if the excess width, after shrinking by the maximum available shrinkability, is greater than `\hfuzz` (for horizontal boxes) or `\vfuzz` (for vertical boxes). The plain format's default for both parameters is 0.1 pt. Here is a short example involving `\hfuzz`.

• `ex-hfuzz.tip` •

```
\nonstopmode
```

Print the default values.

```
The default value for {\tt\string\hfuzz} is~\the\hfuzz\space
and the default for {\tt\string\vfuzz} is~\the\vfuzz.\par
```

Now print the same box twice, each time with different `\hfuzz` values. The box we will use contains no glue. By trying to push together its content, we generate an overfull box.

```
\hfuzz = 0.0pt
```

```
5 \centerline{\hbox spread -1.0pt{XXX}}
6 \hfuzz = 2.0pt
7 \centerline{\hbox spread -1.0pt{XXX}}
8 \bye
```

• End of **ex-hfuzz.tip** •

The output generated by the preceding source code reads as follows:

> The default value for `\hfuzz` is 0.1pt and the default for `\vfuzz` is 0.1pt.
>
> XXX█
>
> XXX

The log file generated by the preceding example reads as follows. Note that only *one* overfull box is reported, the one caused by the execution of line 5. The same box in line 7 does not generate a message because the threshold value of 2 pt (`\hfuzz`) is *above* the required (and unavailable) amount of shrinkage of 1 pt.

• **ex-hfuzz.log** •

```
This is TeX, C Version 3.14 (...)
**&/usr/local/tex/lib/fmt/plain ex-hfuzz.tip
(ex-hfuzz.tip

Overfull \hbox (1.0pt too wide) detected at line 5
\tenrm XXX|

\hbox(6.83331+0.0)x21.50005
.\tenrm X
.\tenrm X
.\tenrm X
.\rule(*+*)x5.0

[1] )
Output written on ex-hfuzz.dvi (1 page, 376 bytes).
```

5.3.8 Stretching of Multiple Glues

What happens if there is more than one glue inside a box which is stretched or shrunk? The amount of spreading or shrinking is *proportionally* divided among the stretchabilities or shrinkabilities of the glues. Here is a series of short examples. The examples begin with the definition of a macro `\hskipa` which generates a specific glue. This macro was defined as a matter of convenience.

```
    \def\hskipa{\hskip 0pt plus 20pt}
1:  \hbox spread 0pt {A\hskipa B\hskipa C}    ABC
2:  \hbox spread 15pt{A\hskipa B\hskipa C}    A  B  C
3:  \hbox spread 40pt{A\hskipa B\hskipa C}    A     B     C
4:  \hbox spread 60pt{A\hskipa B\hskipa C}    A       B       C
```

In Example 3, the desired amount of spreading is 40 pt. Because the two glues inside the box have the same stretchability, both will stretch by the same amount, 20 pt, adding up to the requested 40 pt.

Now let us repeat the above examples with a different second glue which has twice the stretchability of the first one. The second glue, therefore, will be stretched by twice the amount of the first glue. In other words, the distance between A and B is half the distance between B and C.

```
    \def\hskipa{\hskip 0pt plus 20pt}
    \def\hskipb{\hskip 0pt plus 40pt}
1:  \hbox spread  0pt{A\hskipa B\hskipb C}  ABC
2:  \hbox spread 15pt{A\hskipa B\hskipb C}  A B  C
3:  \hbox spread 40pt{A\hskipa B\hskipb C}  A   B     C
4:  \hbox spread 60pt{A\hskipa B\hskipb C}  A    B         C
```

The sum of the available stretchability from glues generated by `\hskipa` and `\hskipb` is 20 pt + 40 pt = 60 pt (this statement applies to both glues). In Example 2 we need to stretch the box by a fourth of this value (15 pt/60 pt). Therefore `\hskipa` will stretch by 20 pt/4 = 5 pt, and `\hskipb` by 40 pt/4 = 10 pt. Both values add up to 15 pt, the desired amount.

The following example is a little more complicated.

```
\hbox spread 30pt{%
      A%
      \hskip 20pt plus 20pt
      B%
      \hskip 30pt plus 40pt
      C%
}
```

The overall available stretchability is 60 pt (20 pt + 40 pt). The desired amount of stretching is 30 pt (`\hbox spread 30pt`). Both glues will therefore stretch by 1/2 of their stretchability: the first glue will stretch by 10 pt, the second one by 20 pt. One has to add the natural length of each of the glues to the amount by which they stretch to get the final distance the two glues stretch. The first glue's length will ultimately be 30 pt (20 pt + 10 pt) and the second glue's length will be 50 pt (30 pt + 20 pt).

The above box therefore generates the same printed result as the following box. The boxes are not equivalent, however. The badness of the preceding box is non-zero (because its glue is stretched), but zero for the following box:

```
\hbox{%
      A%
      \hskip 30pt
      B%
      \hskip 50pt
      C%
}
```

5.4 Glue with Infinite Stretchability and Shrinkability

So far, we have always associated the stretching and shrinking of glue with the badness of a box. There are some cases however, where one would like to call a box "perfect" (and give it badness of zero) despite the fact that there is glue being stretched or shrunk.

Glue of this type is needed to center text, for example. One constructs an hbox, which is as wide as the current line. In order to center some text, glue is added to this text on the left and right side. Both glues have equal stretchability and therefore they will stretch by the same amount when centering the text.

Here is an example where glue of "regular" stretchability is used.

```
\hbox to \hsize{\hskip 0pt plus 4in XXX\hskip 0pt plus 4in}
```

This input generates the following output:

XXX

Why use a stretchability of 4 in? Why not more, or less? While a stretchability of 4 in would be sufficient for the usual value of `\hsize` of 6.5 in, it would be insufficient for the case where `\hsize` is set to a much larger value. While the glue would still stretch as far as needed and the desired printed result would be generated, the resulting error message in the log file reporting an underfull hbox would be misleading. Therefore we will introduce glue of infinite stretchability and shrinkability in TEX where the badness of a box stays zero regardless of the amount of stretching and shrinking.

5.4.1 "Infinite" Units of Dimension

To define glues with infinite stretchabilities and shrinkabilities, new units `fil`, `fill` and `filll` are defined. Let us limit the discussion to the unit `fil` for now. Here is an example leading to some text being centered:

```
\hbox to \hsize{\hskip 0pt plus 1fil XXX\hskip 0pt plus 1fil}
```

The stretchability of the glue on the left side and on the right side are equal and therefore the amount of required stretching is subdivided equally among both glues, as was discussed in 5.3.8, p. 133. The text will be centered as requested.

As long as we do not change the ratio of the stretchabilities of the glue on the left and on the right side the output will not change. Therefore the following two examples will print the same centered text.

```
\hbox to \hsize{\hskip 0pt plus 0.1fil XXX\hskip 0pt plus 0.1fil}
\hbox to \hsize{\hskip 0pt plus 5fil   XXX\hskip 0pt plus 5fil}
```

The main difference between the boxes presented previously using a glue with a stretchability of 4 in and the boxes presented in this Subsection using infinite stretchability is that the *badness* of the boxes in this Subsection is *zero* in all cases. In particular the badness is zero regardless of how much the glue is finally stretched. Note that to achieve a badness of zero was one of our original motivations for the introduction of infinite stretchabilities for glues!

Let us now repeat the above examples using the other two infinite dimension units `fill` and `filll`. As long as we do not mix infinite stretchabilities referring to different units, there will be no difference. In other words, the following three examples will produce exactly the same output, the centering of "XXX."

```
\hbox to \hsize{\hskip 0pt plus 1fil XXX\hskip 0pt plus 1fil}

\hbox to \hsize{\hskip 0pt plus 1fill XXX\hskip 0pt plus 1fill}

\hbox to \hsize{\hskip 0pt plus 1filll XXX\hskip 0pt plus 1filll}
```

If you mix different units, then the result will be quite different; see 5.4.4 on the next page for details.

Here are show examples, where non-centered text results: in each case, the space on the left side of the text "XXX" is twice the space on the right side of the text "XXX."

```
\hbox to \hsize{\hskip 0pt plus 2fil XXX\hskip 0pt plus 1fil}

\hbox to \hsize{\hskip 0pt plus 4fil XXX\hskip 0pt plus 2fil}

\hbox to \hsize{\hskip 0pt plus 0.6fil XXX\hskip 0pt plus 0.3fil}
```

The preceding source code generates the following output:

XXX
XXX
XXX

5.4.2 More on the Use of Infinite Units

Infinite glues are used in macros like `\centerline`, `\leftline` and `\rightline`. The discussion of those macros is delayed until we discuss infinite glues `\hfil`, `\hss`, and others.

Note that the "infinite units" `fil`, `fill` and `filll` can only be used in the connection of specifying the stretchability or shrinkability of some glue. They cannot be used to define the natural length of some glue or to specify an "ordinary" dimension somewhere else.

5.4.3 `\hfil`, `\hfill`, `\hss`, `\hfilneg`

There are a number of horizontal glues that are used very frequently in TeX. Therefore, as a matter of convenience, the following four *primitives* are defined in TeX (if these primitives did not exist, the plain format would have probably defined macros `\hfil`, and so forth).

```
\hfil      \hskip 0pt plus 1fil
\hfill     \hskip 0pt plus 1fill
\hss       \hskip 0pt plus 1fil minus 1fil
\hfilneg   \hskip 0pt plus -1fil
```

Similar primitives for vertical glues (`\vfil`, `\vfill`, `\vss` and `\vfilneg`) also exist; see 5.5.3, p. 143, for details.

5.4.4 The Hierarchy in the Dimensions Units of the Stretchability and Shrinkability of Glues

We already went through examples with more than one glue inside a box. Then the required amount of stretchability or shrinkability was divided proportionally among the different stretchabilities or shrinkabilities. As we have seen, when glues are involved, things get a little more complicated.

As we already know, the specification of the stretchability or shrinkability of a glue can make use of the following four units:

1. Some specific dimension using `pt`, `in` or some other "finite" dimension unit. A complete overview of the available units can be found in 4.1, p. 81 (hierarchy value 1);
2. `fil` (hierarchy value 2);
3. `fill` (hierarchy value 3);
4. `filll` (hierarchy value 4).

The preceding list forms a *hierarchy*. The *hierarchy value* defines the position within this hierarchy.

The following two rules clarify the difference between the various units:

1. First the *glue reduction rule* of TeX is applied:

   - Look at all available stretchabilities and determine the largest hierarchy value *hmax* (if there is no glue with stretchability, go to step item 1).
   - Eliminate (ignore) the stretchabilities of all glues where the stretchability hierarchy value is smaller than the maximum determined in the first step.
   - Do the same for all the shrinkabilities.

   After this reduction rule has been applied the stretchabilities and shrinkabilities of all remaining glues (or the only remaining glue) are (is) now at level *hmax*.
2. The next step is to apply the *glue simplification rule*. This rule basically states that all units are treated in an identical manner. Glues with finite dimension units in their stretchabilities or shrinkabilities are dealt with as discussed before in 5.3.8, p. 133.

If, on the other hand, glues with infinite stretchabilities or shrinkabilities remain, then these glues are treated as if their stretchabilities or shrinkabilities were specified with some finite unit (choose any unit you like).

We now discuss the difference between infinite and finite stretchabilities (the following discussion also applies to the shrinking of glue): when the badness of a box is computed, then the formulas presented before are used for finite units ($hmax = 1$) only. For *infinite* units ($hmax > 1$), the badness of a box is always set to zero.

5.4.5 Examples Involving Glue with Infinite Stretchabilities

Let us study some examples to illustrate the rules of the previous Subsection. Assume that ⟨glue_1⟩ and ⟨glue_2⟩ are two glues enclosed inside the same hbox. When reading the following examples be careful to distinguish among the three units `fil`, `fill` and `filll`. Also assume for all examples below that the glues are being stretched and not pushed together (as indicated before there is no real difference between stretching and shrinking of glue except when it comes to exceeding the specified stretchabilities or shrinkabilities) and that both glues are the only glues enclosed in an hbox:

1. ⟨glue_1⟩: `\hskip 10pt plus 20pt`, ⟨glue_2⟩: `\hskip 10pt plus 20pt`.
   Both glues stretch by the same amount (their stretchabilities are on the same level in the hierarchy). The badness of the resulting box will not be zero, because glues with finite dimension units in the specifications of their stretchabilities are involved.
2. ⟨glue_1⟩: `\hskip 10pt plus 20pt`, ⟨glue_2⟩: `\hskip 10pt plus 1fil`.
   ⟨glue_1⟩'s stretchability is ignored due to the glue reduction rule. ⟨glue_1⟩ in this example therefore could be replaced by `\hskip 10pt`. ⟨glue_2⟩ will stretch as far as necessary. The resulting box will have badness zero.
3. ⟨glue_1⟩: `\hskip 10pt plus 20pt`, ⟨glue_2⟩: `\hskip 10pt plus 1fill`.
   The first glue's stretchability is ignored (glue reduction rule), so ⟨glue_1⟩ can be replaced by `\hskip 10pt`. Now apply the glue simplification rule. ⟨glue_2⟩ is the only glue which will stretch (as far as necessary). The badness of the resulting box will again be zero.
4. ⟨glue_1⟩: `\hskip 20pt plus 1fil`, ⟨glue_2⟩: `\hskip 20pt plus 1fil`.
   Both glues are of the same level in the hierarchy, so applying the glue reduction rule does not change anything. Both glues will stretch by the same amount; the badness of the resulting box will be zero because the stretchability of both glues is specified using an infinite unit.
5. ⟨glue_1⟩: `\hskip 20pt plus 1fill`, ⟨glue_2⟩: `\hskip 20pt plus 1fill`.
   Both glues are of the same hierarchy, so no glue reduction is possible. The result is the same as in the previous example, because the glue simplification rule states that there is no real difference between the infinite units `fil`, `fill` or `filll`.

6. $\langle\mathrm{glue}_1\rangle$: `\hskip 20pt plus 1filll`, $\langle\mathrm{glue}_2\rangle$: `\hskip 20pt plus 1filll`.
   This example is very similar to the previous example with the same result.
7. $\langle\mathrm{glue}_1\rangle$: `\hskip 20pt plus 1fil`, $\langle\mathrm{glue}_2\rangle$: `\hskip 20pt plus 1fill`.
   Because of the glue reduction rule $\langle\mathrm{glue}_1\rangle$'s stretchability is eliminated. Therefore $\langle\mathrm{glue}_2\rangle$ which will stretch as far as necessary. The badness of the resulting box is zero.
8. $\langle\mathrm{glue}_1\rangle$: `\hskip 0pt plus 1fil`, $\langle\mathrm{glue}_2\rangle$: `\hskip 0pt plus 1fill`.
   This example is almost identical to the previous one except that the first glue can be in effect eliminated completely because its stretchability is ignored and its natural length is zero.
9. $\langle\mathrm{glue}_1\rangle$: `\hfil`, $\langle\mathrm{glue}_2\rangle$: `\hfill`.
   Because `\hfil` and `\hfill` are abbreviations for `\hskip 0pt plus 1fil` and `\hskip 0pt plus 1fill` this example is identical to the previous one.

You may also want to read 6.12, p. 205, for a more mathematical way of looking at glues of infinite stretchabilities or shrinkabilities.

5.4.6 Glue Is a Discardable Item

It is important to realize that glue is a *discardable item*. The term *discardable* means that it could in certain cases eventually discarded by TEX. See, for instance, 16.2, p. II-275, on interword glue: if a line break occurs between two words, then the interword glue originally inserted between these two words disappears.

Similarly, the vertical "interline" glue between the last line of a page and the first line on top of the next page disappears in the page break. Also in case a paragraph happens to start on top of a page, the `\parskip` glue (which is responsible for any additional vertical space between paragraphs) of this paragraph is not inserted into the page.

5.4.7 Zero Glue Versus No Glue

There is an important difference in TEX between the following two situations:

1. When there is *no* glue between two items.
2. When there is glue of *zero amount* between two items.

For that purpose we will present the following example:

• `ex-nz-glue.tip` •

```
\InputD{box-mac.tip}                      % 9.3.14, p. 343.
    \VboxR{%
```

For this experiment to work we need to instruct TEX *not* to hyphen the "word" ABCDEFGHIJKLM. This can be done with the `\hyphenation` primitive as follows: `\hyphenation{ABCDEFGHIJKLM}`.

```
        \hyphenation{ABCDEFGHIJKLM}
```

`\hsize` is set to a small value.

```
        \hsize = 0.5in
        \parindent = 0pt
```

Print the "word" ABCDEFGHIJKLM, hyphenation disabled. The word is *not* enclosed in an hbox; in addition because no glue is inserted between two consecutive characters of any word, the word *cannot* be broken across lines.

```
        1:~ABCDEFGHIJKLM

```

Repeat the experiment: instead of no glue between each pair of characters, zero glue is inserted. Now TEX can break the "word" ABCDEFGHIJKLM up.

```
        2:~A\hskip 0pt
        B\hskip 0pt
        C\hskip 0pt
        D\hskip 0pt
        E\hskip 0pt
        F\hskip 0pt
        G\hskip 0pt
        H\hskip 0pt
        I\hskip 0pt
        J\hskip 0pt
        K\hskip 0pt
        L\hskip 0pt
        M
    }
```

• End of `ex-nz-glue.tip` •

This source code generates the following output:

1: ABCDEFGHIJKLM
2: ABCD
EFGHIJ
KLM

5.4.8 Kern, `\kern`

TEX knows an item, which is very similar to glue, which is called "kern." As in the case of glue there are two different ways such kerning is inserted by TEX:

1. There is *explicit* kerning inserted by using the `\kern` primitive. `\kern` must be followed by a dimension.

2. There is *implicit* kerning inserted by TeX. This is the case when kerning is used to change the space between characters selectively. See 16.4.2, p. II-291.

Let us describe the properties of `\kern` and compare it with glue:

1. There is no distinction between "horizontal kern" and "vertical kern" when the kerning is generated. `\kern` will generate vertical kerning if TeX is in one of the vertical modes, otherwise it will generate horizontal kerning.
2. Kern cannot stretch and shrink. The syntax of the `\kern` command is `\kern` ⟨dimension⟩ and *not* `\kern` ⟨glue⟩.
3. Contrary to glue kern is *not* a discardable item, unless it is immediately followed by glue.

The following is an application where `\kern` is used instead of `\hskip`, so TeX will not generate a line break later. The macro `\TeX` which generates the TeX logo is defined as follows:

```
\def\TeX{T\kern-.1667em\lower.5ex\hbox{E}\kern-.125emX}
```

If `\hskip` instead of `\kern` had been used, then if the TeX logo ended up at the end of a line TeX might insert a line break between the "T" and the lowered "E," or between the lowered "E" and the "X." This is avoided by using `\kern`.

Another way to define the TeX logo using `\hskip` would be to enclose the whole logo inside an hbox because TeX will not break an hbox across lines. Let me define macro `\TeXX` therefore as follows:

```
\def\TeXX{%
     \leavevmode
     \hbox{T\hskip-.1667em\lower.5ex\hbox{E}\hskip-.125emX}%
}
```

See 7.2.3, p. 214, for an explanation of `\leavevmode` and an explanation of the necessity of including it into this macro definition if a call to macro `\TeXX` occurs at the beginning of a paragraph.

Note that there is also a "math kern" instruction `\mkern`. See 13.7.1, item 5, p. II-185, for details.

5.4.9 Macros of the Plain Format Relating to Horizontal Glue and Kern

Here are some horizontal glue and kern macros defined by the plain format:

```
\def\thinspace{\kern .16667em }
\def\negthinspace{\kern -.16667em }
\def\enspace{\kern .5em }

\def\enskip{\hskip .5em\relax}
\def\quad{\hskip 1em\relax}
```

```
\def\qquad{\hskip 2em\relax}
```

The macros **\thinspace**, **\negthinspace** and **\enspace** insert kern of $\frac{1}{6}$ em, $-\frac{1}{6}$ em and $\frac{1}{2}$ em. The macros **\enskip**, **\quad** and **\qquad** insert horizontal glue (which cannot stretch) in the amount of $\frac{1}{2}$ em, 1 em and 2 em respectively. All these dimensions are font relative (for details on "em," see 4.1.2, p. 82), and therefore the preceding spacing instructions scale properly, if the current font size is changed.

5.5 Vertical Glue, \vskip

Vertical glue is specified the same way horizontal glue is except that **\vskip** is used instead of **\hskip**. Therefore `\vskip 10pt plus 2pt minus 2pt` instructs TeX to skip 10 pt down, with 2 pt less or 2 pt more if needed. The same remarks about overstretching or overshrinking, etc., as made in the context of horizontal glues apply. Note that *positive* vertical glue skips *downwards* (this is the direction text is accumulated on a page) and not upwards (coordinate systems in mathematics normally have their y-axis pointing *upwards*).

5.5.1 Implicit Vertical Glues, Glue Parameters

Following is a list of important *implicit vertical glues.* I will not explain those glues in all detail at this point in time.

1. **\baselineskip** (sometimes also **\lineskip**) is the glue inserted between the lines of some text. See 7.3.4, p. 220, for details.
2. **\parskip** glue is inserted at the beginning of every paragraph; see 10.8, p. II-25.
3. **\abovedisplayskip** and related glues are inserted before and after displayed equations; see 14.9.1, p. II-216.

5.5.2 Macros of the Plain Format Generating Vertical Glue, \smallskip, \medskip, \bigskip

There are three important macros defined in the plain format that generate vertical glue. These macros are **\smallskip**, **\medskip** and **\bigskip**. The relevant code of the plain format dealing with the definitions of those macros reads as follows:

```
\newskip\smallskipamount \smallskipamount = 3pt plus 1pt minus 1pt
```

```
\newskip\medskipamount   \medskipamount   = 6pt plus 2pt minus 2pt
\newskip\bigskipamount   \bigskipamount   =12pt plus 4pt minus 4pt
\def\smallskip{\vskip\smallskipamount}
\def\medskip{\vskip\medskipamount}
\def\bigskip{\vskip\bigskipamount}
```

Here is an example using the preceding macros. The following input was used:

```
$$
    \vbox{
        \hbox{1: This is a box.}
        \hbox{2: This is another one.}
        \hbox{3: This box is followed by a {\tt\string\smallskip}.}
        \smallskip
        \hbox{4: This is a box.}
        \hbox{5: This is another one.}
        \hbox{6: This box is followed by a {\tt\string\medskip}.}
        \medskip
        \hbox{7: This is a box.}
        \hbox{8: This is another one.}
        \hbox{9: This box is followed by a {\tt\string\bigskip}.}
        \bigskip
        \hbox{10: This is the last box.}
    }
$$
```

The following output results from this example:

1: This is a box.
2: This is another one.
3: This box is followed by a `\smallskip`.

4: This is a box.
5: This is another one.
6: This box is followed by a `\medskip`.

7: This is a box.
8: This is another one.
9: This box is followed by a `\bigskip`.

10: This is the last box.

5.5.3 \vfil, \vfill, \vss, \vfilneg

Similar to the special horizontal glue instructions `\hfil`, `\hfill`, `\hss` and `\hfilneg` (5.4.3, p. 136) primitives `\vfil`, `\vfill`, `\vss` and `\vfilneg` are defined in TEX. They do not add any real new functionality, because macros along the same lines could have been defined.

```
\vfil       \vskip 0pt plus 1fil
\vfill      \vskip 0pt plus 1fill
\vss        \vskip 0pt plus 1fil minus 1fil
\vfilneg    \vskip 0pt plus -1fil
```

Examples of the application of those primitives follow in Chapter 7. For an application of `\vfilneg` in particular see 32.5.2, item 1, p. IV-18.

5.5.4 Examples of Explicit Vertical Glue

The same way we had explicit horizontal glue there is explicit vertical glue in TeX for which examples are presented next. As mentioned before, the same rules apply to vertical glue as they do to horizontal glue. For example, while you can overstretch a vertical glue you cannot overpush it.

For the examples a new box type needs to be introduced, called vbox (vertical box). The height of vertical boxes can be modified using the `\vbox spread` or `\vbox to` construct. Again examples frequently refer to "visible vboxes" using macro `\VboxR`, the same way `\HboxR` was used before to produce "visible hboxes."

The source code of the first example reads as follows:

```
\InputD{box-mac.tip}                    % 9.3.14, p. 343.
$$
    \def\VboxExample #1{%
        \VboxR spread #1{
            \hbox{Line 1}
            \vskip 10pt plus 10pt minus 40pt
            \hbox{Line 2}
        }%
    }
    \hbox{%
        \VboxExample{10pt}%
        \hskip 18pt
        \VboxExample{0pt}%
        \hskip 18pt
        \VboxExample{-5pt}%
        \hskip 18pt
        \VboxExample{-10pt}%
        \hskip 18pt
        \VboxExample{-18pt}%
        \hskip 18pt
        \VboxExample{-35pt}%
    }%
$$
```

This source code generated the following output:

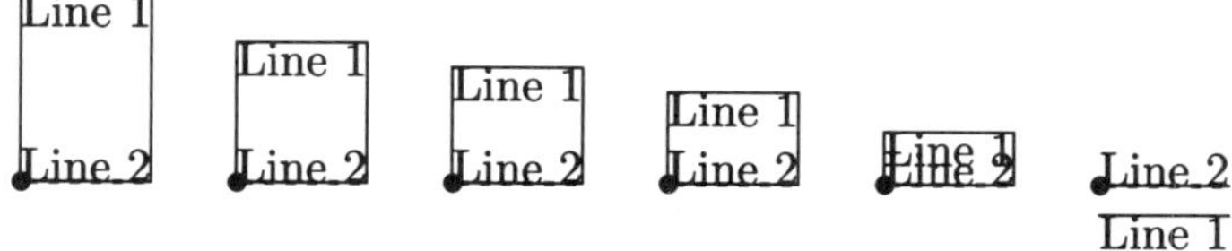

5.6 Leaders

Leaders in printing are dots, dashes, etc., in a line used to direct the eye across the page, such as in a table of contents. TeX's definition of leaders is more mathematical (although the goal is, of course, to allow the printing of leaders). Here is a brief description of TeX's leader's concept:

1. Leaders are a *generalization of glue*: instead of filling up some space with "nothing," leaders fill up this space with "something."
2. This "something" that fills white space can be either a rule or the repeat copy of a box. Because a TeX box can contain almost anything TeX's leader construct is very general. The number of copies of the replicated box as it is inserted by TeX naturally depends on the size of the box and the amount of space to be filled up.

   This replicated replicated, is called a *leader replication box* in this series.
3. The space being filled up by a leader has to be of positive length. In the case the length is negative, nothing is inserted. Leaders in this case behave like the equivalent amount of glue.
4. Similar to horizontal and vertical glue there are *horizontal* and *vertical leaders.* We will deal with horizontal leaders only. Vertical leaders would use `\vskip` instead of `\hskip` in the examples below. Vertical leaders are much less important than horizontal leaders and therefore vertical leaders are not discussed further.
5. Unlike *implicit glue* there are no "implicit leaders." All leaders are "explicit leaders."
6. The three leader generating primitives in TeX which are `\leaders`, `\cleaders` and `\xleaders`. Each instruction is followed by a rule or box specification (used for filling up the white space), followed in turn by a glue specification.

   The format for horizontal or vertical leaders is therefore as follows:

   `\leaders` ⟨box or rule⟩ ⟨glue specification⟩
   `\cleaders` ...
   `\xleaders` ...

   If we restrict ourselves to horizontal leaders, then ⟨glue specification⟩ can be either `\hskip` followed by the amount of glue of this `\hskip`, or one of `\hfil`, `\hfill`, `\hss` or `\hfilneg`.

In case of a rule-based horizontal leader the rule must be specified using `\hrule` (`\vrule` would be used with vertical leaders). If a box is specified for ⟨box or rule⟩, you can do so either using a command like `\hbox` or you can retrieve such a box from a box register, for instance, using `\box`.

7. Similar to the preceding definitions vertical leaders can be defined (in this case vertical glue must be specified instead of horizontal glue and `\hrule` must be used for the specification of a leader rule; otherwise there are no other changes).

Let us examine leaders based on rules in more detail. This will be followed by a discussion of leaders based on the replication of boxes.

5.6.1 Leader Definitions Based on Rules, "Visible Glue"

Leaders based on rules are rather easy to understand. There is no difference between leaders built with `\leaders`, `\cleaders` and `\xleaders` in this case. I will use `\leaders` in the examples below. What happens is straightforward: the space normally filled up by some glue is now replaced by a horizontal rule.

Here is the source code of Figure 5.3 on the next page.

• `ex-f-rule-leaders.tip` •

```
\vbox{
    \hsize = 3.0in
    \hbox to \hsize{\hfil                XXX}
    \hbox to \hsize{\leaders\hrule\hfil XXX}
    \smallskip
    \hbox to \hsize{\hfil                XXX\hfil}
    \hbox to \hsize{\leaders\hrule\hfil XXX\leaders\hrule\hfil}
    \smallskip
    \hbox to \hsize{XXX\hfil}
    \hbox to \hsize{XXX\leaders\hrule\hfil}
    \smallskip
    \hbox          {A\hskip 10pt B}
    \hbox          {A\leaders\hrule\hskip 10pt B}
    \bigskip
    \hbox spread 10pt {A\hskip 10pt plus 10pt B}
    \hbox spread 10pt {A\leaders\hrule
                        \hskip 10pt plus 10pt B}
    \hbox spread 10pt {A\leaders\hrule height 2pt depth 2pt
                        \hskip 10pt plus 10pt B}
    \hbox spread 10pt {A\leaders\hrule height 6pt depth 3pt
                        \hskip 10pt plus 10pt B}
    \hbox spread 10pt {A\leaders\hrule height 6pt depth -4pt
                        \hskip 10pt plus 10pt B}
    \hbox spread 10pt {A\leaders\hrule height 6pt depth -2pt
                        \hskip 10pt plus 10pt B}
}
```

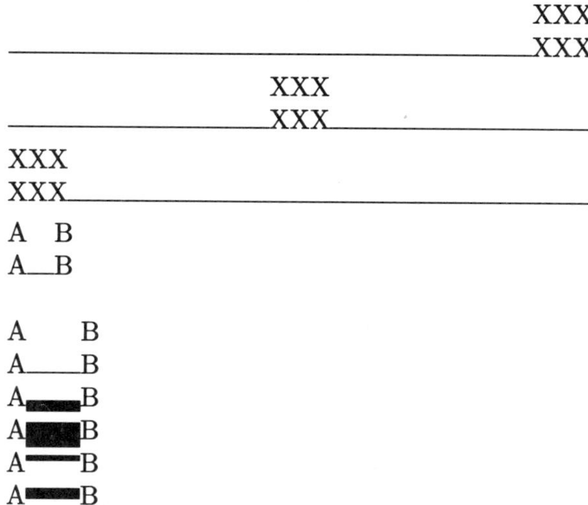

Figure 5.3. Rule-based leader examples.

• End of `ex-f-rule-leaders.tip` •

Leaders based on rules are *very* useful for making glue visible. For instance, to see the effect of an `\hfil` glue, simply replace `\hfil` by `\leaders\hrule\hfil`. The amount of space filled up by the `\hfil` glue is now marked by a horizontal line! This idea of using leaders to make glue visible is useful when you are developing complicated boxes and you would like to "see" the glue in these boxes.

5.6.2 Leaders Based on Boxes

Leaders can also be constructed from replication of boxes. This method will also demonstrate the necessity of having three different leader types `\leaders`, `\cleaders` and `\xleaders` (as previously stated, there is no difference among these leader types when rule-based leaders are involved).

Using replicated boxes to fill up white space we face the following dilemma: the distance to fill up with replications of the "leader box" should be an integral multiple of the width of the leader box, but for all practical purposes will be not.

Assume, for instance, that the amount of space to be filled up is 87 pt and that the leader box is 10 pt wide. We have room for 8 boxes, but now the question is what happens to the remaining 7 pt ($= 87\text{ pt} - 8 * 10\text{ pt}$). There are three possibilities in TEX which correspond to the three leader primitives `\leaders`, `\xleaders` and `\cleaders`. In the following we refer to these 7 pt as the "remaining space."

1. `\leaders`. TEX applies an imaginary window, and only those leader boxes are printed which fully fit into the window. For an example see Fig. 5.4, p. 151. This way of generating leaders is used to generate the dots in a table of contents where you want to ensure that the leader dots of different lines line up vertically.
2. `\cleaders`. The remaining space is divided equally as white space before the first and as white space after the last leader box. Therefore, the space between the leader boxes is zero. For an example see Fig. 5.5, p. 151.
3. `\xleaders`. The remaining space is divided equally between

   (a) White space inserted before the first leader box.
   (b) White space inserted between the leader boxes.
   (c) White space added after the last leader box.

   For an example see Fig. 5.6, p. 152.

After having discussed leaders we now show some example. These examples show how the preceding commands are applied. You may also want to look at 12.4, p. II-118, for a "real application" of leaders in a table of contents.

5.6.3 Leader Example Macros

Next we will discuss the macros used for generating Figs. 5.4–5.6. These macros show some simple and straightforward applications of leaders.

• `ex-leadermac.tip` •

1. Macro `\MyLBox` defines the leader box used in the examples. `\MyLBox` prints .

```
\def\MyLBox{%
    \hbox{%
        \vrule height 3pt depth 0pt width 15pt
        \vrule height 6pt depth 1pt width 15pt
    }%
}
```

2. Macro `\cl` generates an hbox. This macro has the following three parameters:

   - `#1`. The amount by which the hbox generated by this macro will be spread (unit points).
   - `#2`. The text printed before the leader itself.
   - `#3`. The leader primitive to be used: one of `\leader`, `\cleader` and `\xleader`.

```
\def\cl #1#2#3{%
    \hbox spread #1pt{%
```

```
        \hskip 60pt
        #2%                        % Text before the leader.
        #3\MyLBox\hfil             % The leader
        BBB%                       % Text after the leader
    }%
}
```

3. Define macro `\BunchOfLeaders` to generate a bunch of leader examples. This macro has the following two parameters:

   - `#1`. The text inserted into the line before the leader is printed.
   - `#2`. The leader type to be used.

```
\def\BunchOfLeaders #1#2{%
    \cl{100}{#1}{#2}
    \cl{103}{#1}{#2}
    \cl{106}{#1}{#2}
    \cl{109}{#1}{#2}
    \cl{112}{#1}{#2}
    \cl{115}{#1}{#2}
    \cl{118}{#1}{#2}
    \cl{121}{#1}{#2}
    \cl{124}{#1}{#2}
    \cl{127}{#1}{#2}
    \cl{130}{#1}{#2}
    \cl{133}{#1}{#2}
    \cl{136}{#1}{#2}
    \cl{139}{#1}{#2}
}
```

• End of `ex-leadermac.tip` •

5.6.4 Sample Figure Source Codes

This Subsection lists the source code of all sample figures. The following source code generates Figure 5.4, p. 151.

• `ex-f-leaders.tip` •

```
\InputD{ex-leadermac.tip}                 % 5.6.3, p. 148.
\vbox to 37pt{}
\BunchOfLeaders{AAA}{\leaders}

\cl{100}{}{\leaders}
\cl{100}{A}{\leaders}
\cl{100}{AA}{\leaders}
\cl{100}{AAAAAA}{\leaders}
\vbox to 12pt{}
```

• End of `ex-f-leaders.tip` •

The following source code generates the output of Figure 5.5 on the next page.

• `ex-f-cleaders.tip` •

```
\InputD{ex-leadermac.tip}                    % 5.6.3, p. 148.
\vbox to 37pt{}
\BunchOfLeaders{AAA}{\cleaders}
\vbox to 12pt{}
```

• End of `ex-f-cleaders.tip` •

The following source code generates the output of Figure 5.6, p. 152.

• `ex-f-xleaders.tip` •

```
\InputD{ex-leadermac.tip}                    % 5.6.3, p. 148.
\BunchOfLeaders{AAA}{\xleaders}
```

• End of `ex-f-xleaders.tip` •

5.6.5 Leader Related Macro Definitions in the Plain Format

Following are six standard leader definitions of the plain format. Note that all these leader definitions are equivalent to an `\hfill` (note two "`l`"s and not one) type of horizontal glue.

The following leaders are defined by the plain format and they generate the following output:

Name	Sample
`\hrulefill`	
`\dotfill`	....
`\leftarrowfill`	
`\rightarrowfill`	
`\upbracefill`	
`\downbracefill`	

Here are the macro definitions of these leaders. The instructions were reformatted to improve their readability. Macro **`\m@th`** is called below. This macro sets **`\mathsurround`** to zero, thus instructing TeX *not* to insert any additional horizontal space before and after "mathematical equations." Because **`\@math`** is invoked inside the following mathematical equations themselves and because mathematical equations form implicit groups, the effect of **`\m@th`** is limited to the leaders below; see 13.8.1, p. II-186.

Also note that the following macro definitions are in some cases not pure leader generating macros: other material is also generated.

1. The definition of `\hrulefill` is as follows:

```
\def\hrulefill{\leaders\hrule\hfill}
```

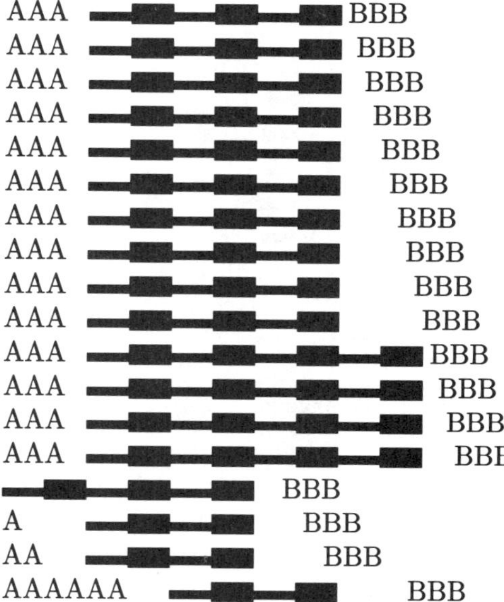

Figure 5.4. `\leaders` examples.

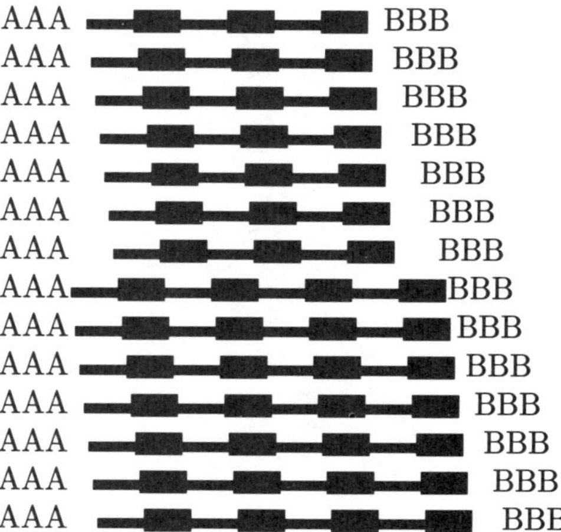

Figure 5.5. `\cleaders` examples.

Figure 5.6. `\xleaders` examples.

2. The definition of `\dotfill` is as follows:

```
\def\dotfill{%
    \cleaders\hbox{%
        $%
        \m@th
        \mkern 1.5mu
        .%
        \mkern 1.5mu
        $%
    }%
    \hfill
}
```

3. The definition of `\rightarrowfill` is next (note that the horizontal line of this symbol is composed of minus signs and that before `\cleaders` is invoked, a single minus sign is printed to guarantee a minimum length arrow; also note that a right hand arrow is appended after `\cleaders`):

```
\def\rightarrowfill{%
    $%
    \m@th
    \mathord-%
    \mkern -6mu
    \cleaders\hbox{%
        $%
        \mkern -2mu
        \mathord-%
        \mkern -2mu
        $%
    }%
    \hfill
    \mkern -6muf
    \mathord\rightarrow
```

```
        $%
}
```

4. The definition of `\leftarrowfill` is quite similar to the preceding definition of `\rightarrowfill`. Here it is:

```
\def\leftarrowfill{%
        $%
        \m@th
        \mathord\leftarrow
        \mkern -6mu
        \cleaders\hbox{%
            $%
            \mkern -2mu
            \mathord-%
            \mkern -2mu
            $%
        }%
        \hfill
        \mkern -6mu
        \mathord-%
        $%
}
```

5. The definition of `\downbracefill` is (all together there are six separate steps executed: four pieces of braces and two invocations of `\leaders` to generate a connecting horizontal line):

```
\mathchardef\braceld="37A
\mathchardef\bracerd="37B
\mathchardef\bracelu="37C
\mathchardef\braceru="37D
\def\downbracefill{%
        $%
        \m@th
        \braceld
        \leaders\vrule\hfill
        \braceru
        \bracelu
        \leaders\vrule\hfill
        \bracerd
        $%
}
```

6. The definition of `\upbracefill` is very similar to the definition of the preceding macro:

```
\def\upbracefill{%
        $%
        \m@th
        \bracelu
        \leaders\vrule\hfill
        \bracerd
        \braceld
```

```
        \leaders\vrule\hfill
        \braceru
        $%
    }
```

5.7 Rules

A rule in printing terminology is a vertical or horizontal line as it used, for instance, in tables. TEX obviously must allow for the printing of rules which is the subject of this Section.

Note that TEX has two different rule generating commands and despite the fact that `\hrule` (for horizontal rule) seems to suggest that it can be only used to print horizontal rules, that is *not* true. This command can be (and is) used quite frequently to print vertical rules. A similar remark applies to the `\vrule` (vertical rule) command.

There are two types of rules in TEX.

1. `\vrule` (vertical rule). This type of a rule is used in either of the horizontal modes (in other word, inside a paragraph or inside an `\hbox`).

   As you will see shortly the dimensions of a `\vrule` can be set in any possible way. For example, the dimensions can be set so that the rule looks like a horizontal rule, despite the fact that it is still called a `\vrule`. Note that when TEX is in horizontal mode (inside an hbox or inside a paragraph) TEX *requires* the use of the `\vrule` primitive, regardless of whether the rule *looks like* a horizontal or a vertical rule.

   Note that an `\hrule` will begin a paragraph if applied in vertical mode; see 10.4, p. II-11.
2. `\hrule` (horizontal rule). This type of rule is used in any of the vertical modes, therefore in particular between paragraphs or inside vboxes.

   The opposite remark compared to `\vrule`s applies now: an `\hrule` with properly set dimensions may actually look like a vertical rule.

5.7.1 Rule Dimensions

A rule has a height, depth and width, very similar to the dimensions of a box (which has a height, depth and a width, see Fig. 6.1, p. 162).

1. The three dimensions height, depth and width of a rule can be specified explicitly as follows:

   (a) `\vrule width 10pt` generates a `\vrule`, which is 10 pt wide.
   (b) `\vrule height 10pt` generates a `\vrule` rule, which is 10 pt high.

   (c) `\vrule depth 10pt` generates a `\vrule`, which is 10 pt deep.

   The same specifications can be used with `\hrule`s. Note also that any of those dimensions can be negative, although this is the exception rather than the rule. For details see 5.7.3 on the next page.

2. The dimension specifications of a rule (its height, depth and width) can be given *in any order*. Therefore the following six specifications of a `\vrule` are all identical:

```
\vrule height 10pt  depth 4pt   width 6pt
\vrule height 10pt  width 6pt   depth 4pt
\vrule depth 4pt    height 10pt width 6pt
\vrule depth 4pt    width 6pt   height 10pt
\vrule width 6pt    height 10pt depth 4pt
\vrule width 6pt    depth 4pt   height 10pt
```

3. It is possible to have more than one width, height or depth specification. In this case the *last* specification prevails (all previous specifications are simply ignored). The following two rule specifications are therefore identical:

```
\vrule width 10pt height 2pt width 14pt height 6pt depth 3pt
    depth 4pt width 11pt
\vrule width 11pt height 6pt depth 4pt
```

   Later we will see that this handling of multiple dimension specifications of rules is a useful feature of TEX. See 39.5.1, p. IV-275, for an example.

4. If any of the three dimension specifications of a rule are missing, TEX uses default values. Here are the rules for our rules[2]. These defaults depend on the type or rules:

   (a) The default dimensions for `\vrule`s are determined as follows.

   - The default *width* of a `\vrule` is 0.4 pt. This value cannot be changed, that is it is hard-wired (computer jargon for *built into*) into the TEX program.
   - The default *height* of a `\vrule` is the height of the hbox or line of the paragraph, that this rule belongs to.
   - The default *depth* of a rule is determined the same way the default height of a rule is determined. The depth of the hbox or the depth of the line of the paragraph, the rule belongs to, is also applied to the rule.

   (b) The default dimensions for `\hrule`s are determined as follows:

   - The default *width* of a `vrule` is the width of the enclosing vbox (it is `\hsize`, if the `vrule` command occurs in vertical mode, between two paragraphs, for instance).
   - The default *height* of a `\vrule` is 0.4 pt. This value is hard-wired

---

[2] You know, Germans like rules...

into the TeX program and cannot be changed.

- The default *depth* of a **\vrule** is 0.0 pt.

5. Usually the values for height, depth and width of a rule are positive. There are cases though where they can be negative. For instance, assume the following specification of an **\hrule**:

```
\hrule height 10pt depth -4pt width 12pt
```

This horizontal rule will be 12 pt wide. It will appear as being 12 pt + (−4 pt) = 8 pt thick, positioned 4 pt *above* the baseline (the depth specification "−4 pt below the baseline" means "4 pt above the baseline").

6. In macro packages sometimes a more compact writing of glue specifications is used; see 22.7.5, p. III-232, for details.

5.7.2 Keywords **height**, **depth** and **width**

The term *keyword* in programming means a word with a special meaning. Most items with a special meaning in TeX start with the backslash, but there are exceptions and such are the keywords **height**, **depth** and **width** in rule specifications.

Spaces after keywords are ignored in TeX, so whether you write **height 2pt** or **height2pt** (less readable and therefore not advisable) is irrelevant. Spaces after the keywords **plus** and **minus** in glue specifications are also ignored; see 5.1, item 5, p. 122.

5.7.3 Examples of Rules

I will now present some examples using rules. For that purpose remember that the height and depth of an hbox is the height and depth of the highest and deepest item in the box in which this rule is enclosed.

1. **\hbox{\vrule A\vrule}** prints |A|.
   Because the height and depth of the rules are not explicitly specified, they are determined by the size of the "A."
2. **\hbox{\vrule e\vrule}** prints |e|.
   The height and depth of the rules are determined by the size of the "e."
3. **\hbox{\vrule g\vrule}** prints |g|.
   The height and depth of the rules are determined by the size of the "g."
4. **\hbox{\vrule Age\vrule}** prints |Age|.
   The height of the **\hbox** is now determined by the height of the "A," and the depth of the **\hbox** by the depth of the "g." The rules inherit this height and depth.

5. `\hbox{\vrule width 2pt Age\vrule width 1pt}` prints |Age|.
   This example is identical to the previous example with the exception that the widths of the rules are now 2 pt and 1 pt respectively. Note that the space after the "2pt" is ignored by TeX.
6. `\hbox{\vrule width 6pt height 3pt depth 3pt A}` prints ■A.
   The rule is as a little square, half of it below and half above the baseline.
7. `\hbox{\vrule width 10pt height 10pt depth 0pt A}` prints ■A.
   Now the rule appears as a little square sitting on the baseline.
8. `\hbox{\vrule width 10pt height  0pt depth 10pt A}` prints ■A.
   Now the rule appears as a little square hanging off the baseline.
9. `\hbox{\vrule width 18pt height 1pt depth 0pt A}` prints ——A.
   By defining the dimensions properly it is obviously possible to print horizontal rules despite the fact that the specification says `\vrule`.
10. `\hbox{\vrule width 18pt height 0pt depth 1pt A}` prints ——A.
    The above rule has a thickness of 1 pt, hanging off the baseline.
11. `\hbox{\vrule width 18pt height 2pt depth 2pt A}` prints ▬A.
    The above rule has a thickness of 4 pt with 2 pt above and 2 pt below the baseline.
12. `\hbox{\vrule width 18pt height 7pt depth -4pt A}` prints ▬A.
    The above rule has a thickness of 4 pt with the bottom edge of the rule 3 pt above the baseline.
13. `\hbox{\vrule width 18pt height -2pt depth 4pt A}` prints ▬A.
    The above rule has a thickness of 2 pt with the top edge of the rule 2 pt below the baseline.
14. `\hbox{\vrule width 1pt\relax height 3pt}` prints |height 3pt. A glue specification can be separated from any subsequent text using `\relax`, which prevents TeX from further interpreting the words `width`, `height` and `depth` as keywords of rule specifications. See 27.4, p. III-431, for details on `\relax`.

5.8 Penalties

Penalties are indicators to TeX that tell it about the desirability or undesirability of a break point. The discussion of penalties at this point will be very brief, because penalties can be really only understood in the context of line breaks and page breaks which are subjects of later chapters.

There are, similar to glue, two different penalties: *horizontal* penalties to influence line breaks and *vertical* penalties controlling page breaks.

Also very similar to glue there are *two* different ways such penalties are generated:

1. An *explicit* penalty. An explicit penalty is inserted by the user with the `\penalty` control sequence.

There is only one control sequence generating both horizontal and vertical penalties. If TEX is in vertical mode, a `\penalty` is interpreted as a vertical penalty. Otherwise it is interpreted as a horizontal penalty.

2. An *implicit* penalty. An implicit penalty is inserted by TEX automatically. For instance, there is an implicit vertical penalty called `\widowpenalty` which is inserted between the two last lines of a paragraph. This penalty is used to prevent the generation of widow lines in a document.

The terms *horizontal* and *vertical penalty*, as well as the terms *implicit* and *explicit* penalty are not used in the TEXbook, but I found these terms useful for the explanation of the penalty idea in this series. See item 3 (item 4) in 5.8, p. 54, for a list of all implicit horizontal (vertical) penalties.

5.8.1 Penalty Values

Penalties are integer values in the range $-10,000\ldots+10,000$. Values greater than $+10,000$ are allowed, but a value greater than 10,000 is interpreted as a value of 10,000, when a break point is computed by TEX. Similarly values less than $-10,000$ are legal and equivalent to a value of $-10,000$.

There are three different ranges of values of penalty p:

1. $p < 0$: a negative penalty means that *a break at this point is encouraged.* The smaller the value the more desirable is a break. The value of $-10,000$ *forces* a break. The `\break` macro, which is used to force break points, is therefore an abbreviation of `\penalty-10000`.
2. $p = 0$: a value of zero determines a neutral break point. There are a few cases where having no penalty and having a penalty of zero makes a difference (frequently a zero penalty can be discarded); see 8.2.10, p. 290, for an example.
3. $p > 0$: a positive penalty *discourages breaking at the current point.* The higher the value the less desirable is a break point with $p = 10000$ preventing a break completely. The `\nobreak` macro therefore is an abbreviation of `\penalty 10000`.

5.8.2 Macros Involving Penalties

A brief overview of the plain format macro definitions involving penalties is next. Note that some of those macros do *more* than just defining a penalty. The following discussion presents plain format macros which involve horizontal and vertical glue together with penalties.

5.8.2.1 `\break`, `\nobreak`, `\allowbreak`

The three macros mentioned in this Subsection's title line define three basic penalties:

1. `\def\break{\penalty -10000 }`. Forces a *line break* when in *horizontal mode* or a *page break* when in *vertical mode.*
2. `\def\allowbreak{\penalty 0 }`. Inserts a "neutral penalty."
3. `\def\nobreak{\penalty 10000 }`. Forbid a *line break* at the current point (if in *horizontal mode*) or a *page break* (if in *vertical mode*).

All three penalties can be applied to horizontal and vertical mode.

5.8.2.2 `\slash` and Tilde

The following two macros involve a horizontal penalty.

1. `~`. The "~" in TEX prints as a space where the space cannot be broken across lines. Therefore, "~" is an abbreviation for `\nobreak \space`, since a space preceded by a "do not break here" instruction is generated. For details of how a character such as "~" can be made to print as an actual character; see 18.2.1, p. III-15.
2. `\def\slash{/\penalty\exhyphenpenalty}`. This macro prints a slash after which a break can occur as is the case after a hyphen.

5.8.2.3 `\filbreak`, `\goodbreak`, `\eject`, `\supereject`

The four macros `\filbreak`, `\goodbreak`, `\eject` and `\supereject` are plain format macros controlling page breaks. Their definitions always start with a `\par` to force TEX into vertical mode, if it should not already be in vertical mode (`\par` has no effect if TEX is already in vertical mode). For the definitions of these macros plus additional details see 32.5.2, p. IV-17.

5.9 Summary

In this chapter we learned:

- Glue is a central ingredient in TEX to allow the specification of horizontal and vertical white space which can stretch and shrink.
- TEX has horizontal and vertical glue.

- Each of these two types of glue can be either generated explicitly by the user (using `\hskip` or `\vskip`), or inserted by TEX under precisely defined circumstances thus being called implicit glue.
- A glue value specification requires the specification of three dimensions: the desired distance, the maximum stretchability and the minimum shrinkability. The stretchability and shrinkability are defined using the keywords `plus` and `minus`. They default to zero if not specified.
- Glue will only stretch and shrink if there is an incentive to stretch and shrink. Glue can be "enticed" to stretch and shrink using the `\hbox to` and `\hbox spread` type of constructs.
- The badness of boxes is computed from the amount of stretching or shrinking of any glues in it. Multiple glues stretch proportionally to their specified stretchabilities or shrinkabilities.
- Infinite units `fil`, `fill` and `filll` can be used to allow glue to stretch and shrink by infinite amounts. The badness of boxes which contain glue of infinite stretchabilities and shrinkabilities is always zero.
- `\hfil`, `\hfill`, `\hss` and `\hfilneg` are abbreviations of `\hskip` type of glues with infinite stretchability and shrinkability.
- Vertical glue is defined using `\vskip`; there are `vfil`, `\vfill`, `\vss` and `\vfilneg` instructions which are the vertical equivalents of `\hfil`, `\hfill`, etc.
- TEX provides leaders, a generalization of the glue concept. These leaders can be used conveniently to generate "visible glue," a sometimes useful item in the development of macros.
- Two different types of rules are provided in TEX: `\vrules` and `\hrules`. The dimensions of those rules are determined by defaults, but explicit specifications by the user using the keywords `height`, `depth` and `width` are also possible.

6
Boxes

Boxes are a very basic component of TEX. We will discuss boxes in quite some detail in this Chapter, because boxes allow the user of TEX to construct and position text in almost any possible way. While boxes are a rather low level entity of TEX, a thorough understanding of boxes is very important for a variety of reasons.

6.1 Basics About Boxes, Box Types

There are two different types of boxes in TEX:

1. *Horizontal boxes* (or *hboxes*) are generated with the help of the `\hbox` instruction.
2. *Vertical boxes* (or *vboxes*) are generated by one of the following three instructions: `\vbox`, `\vtop` and `\vcenter`.

Distinguishing between the two box types is only important *while* the box is being built, because in a horizontal box the material of this box is collected left to right (in what is called the *restricted horizontal mode*), while in vertical boxes the material is collected top to bottom (the *inner vertical mode*). Once a particular box has been built TEX will treat both box types in an identical fashion.

The discussion in this Chapter focuses on horizontal boxes, because they are a little easier to understand than vboxes.

6.1.1 Coding a Box

Recall that a box is generated in TEX by giving the corresponding box instruction followed by the content of the box enclosed inside curly braces. Here is the

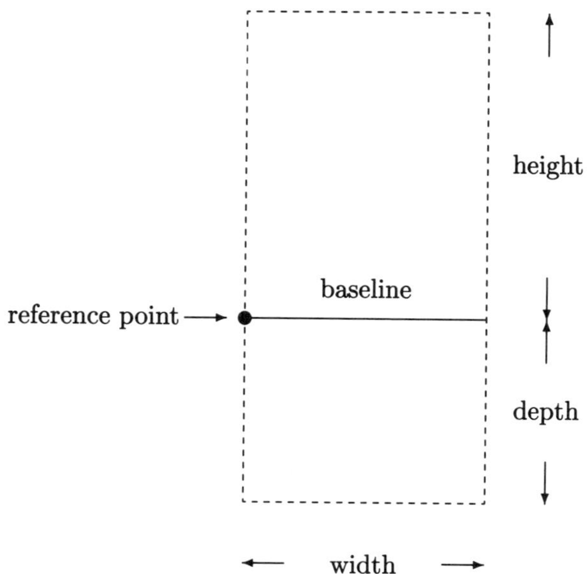

Figure 6.1. A TEX box.

example of a horizontal box containing the three characters "ABC": `\hbox{ABC}`.

6.2.8, p. 167, discusses the fact that the curly braces used to delimit the contents of `\hbox` can be replaced by `\bgroup` and `\egroup`, so the preceding hbox could also have been generated by entering `\hbox\bgroup ABC\egroup`.

6.1.2 Reference Point and Dimensions of Boxes

Fig. 6.1 on this page presents TEX's model of a box. Whether it is a horizontal or a vertical box is irrelevant in this context.

Each box has a *reference point* and a *baseline*. The *three dimensions* which are measured with respect to the reference point are *height*, *depth* and *width*.

Note that a box does *not* have a "left width" and "right width" that is the reference point of the box is located on the left vertical boundary of the box.

6.2 Horizontal Boxes (Hboxes)

We will now analyze horizontal boxes in detail. The next two chapter discuss vertical boxes.

6.2.1 Making Boxes Visible

For the discussion of hboxes (and later also for the discussion of vboxes) it is very useful to make boxes "visible." By that we mean the following.

1. Rules are drawn around the box indicating the size of the box.
2. The baseline is indicated by a dashed line.
3. The reference point is marked with a "•."

We do this with a set of macros which will be presented later; see 9.3, p. 318, for details.

The application of the above mentioned macros is straightforward. You are *strongly* encouraged to use these macros yourself in your own experiments. After you have loaded these macros simply write `\HboxR` (`\hbox` with rules) instead of `\hbox` and a horizontal box identical to the one using `\hbox` will be generated. The main difference is that rules around the box are drawn, a "•" marks the reference point and the baseline is indicated using a dashed line, as mentioned before.

There are similar instructions `\VboxR`, `\VtopR` and `\VcenterXR` that print the three different types of "visible vboxes."

In this chapter in particular (but also others) I will take the liberty to interchange `\hbox` and `\HboxR` freely. So a sentence may read "the input `\hbox{ABC}` prints ABC," but also "the input `\hbox{ABC}` prints ABC," without an explicit recognition of the fact that `\HboxR` was used for the output of this box instead of `\hbox`.

6.2.2 The Contents of an Hbox

The content of an hbox follows the `\hbox` command and is enclosed in curly braces (or a pair of `\bgroup` and `\egroup`).

An hbox can contain the following items:

1. *Characters.* To store a character inside an hbox simply list the character. Naturally you are allowed to change fonts inside an hbox. As we will see shortly hboxes (actually also vboxes) form implicit groups. Therefore such font changes are always limited to the content of one box.
2. *Horizontal glue and leaders.*
   (a) *Horizontal glue.* `\hskip` ⟨glue⟩ inserts the specified amount of glue inside the hbox.
   (b) *Horizontal leaders.* 5.6, p. 145, discusses leaders. For instance, `\leaders\hrule\hskip` ⟨glue⟩ inserts a *horizontal rule*, which is a leader as far as TeX is concerned, at the specified place inside an hbox. Remember that leaders are a form of visible glue, and when we explore hboxes in this chapter leaders are frequently used as a form of visible glue.

3. *Other boxes.* Other boxes can be stored inside an hbox which leads to *nested boxes* (boxes inside boxes).
   (a) While in many cases these other boxes will also be horizontal boxes, this is *not* necessarily the case. They can be vertical boxes too.
   (b) Such a box can be retrieved from a box register using `\box`, `\copy`, `\unhbox` or `\unhcopy` (`\unvbox` and `\unvcopy` can only be used in a vertical box).
   (c) Boxes can be moved up and down with `\raise` or `\lower`. Each of these specifications is followed by a dimension indicating the distance by which the boxes are moved up and down.
4. *Vertical rules (`\vrule`).* In order to specify a rule inside an hbox, `\vrule` must be used. See 5.7, p. 154, for an explanation of how the dimensions of such a rule are determined.
5. *Math mode material.* Mathematical formulas can be inserted into an hbox using inline math mode only (see 6.3.9, p. 175). Display math mode *cannot* be used, but it can be simulated using inline math mode and the `\displaystyle` command; see 14.4.1, p. II-195.

6.2.3 The Building of an Hbox

TEX builds an hbox as follows. First the reference point for the box being built is established. Then the material of this box is collected *left to right.* After an item is added to the box (more precisely to the horizontal list of the box) TEX moves to the right by the width of the last item just added and inserts the following material at that point.

6.2.4 Implicit Grouping and Hboxes

When an hbox is specified by `\hbox`, then processing the contents of the hbox occurs inside a group as already briefly indicated (that is called *implicit grouping*). In other words, changes inside the argument of an `\hbox` command are local unless explicitly declared as being global using `\global` (see 19.4.11, p. III-107). If you, for instance, generate an hbox in which you change to an italics font then writing `\hbox{\it ABC}` is sufficient. The text following the `\hbox{...}` will *not* be printed in italics, but in the font which was previously in effect.

6.2.5 Characters Are Almost Hboxes

Characters are treated by TEX as a special kind of horizontal box (see 15.2.3, p. II-231).

The dimensions of a "character horizontal box" are normally those of a minimum bounding box (the box is rarely *precisely* that, the box is usually a little larger than a strictly defined minimum bounding box). Obviously the baseline of the character and the baseline of its character box coincide. The width of the character box is the width of the character. The dimensions of the character boxes of a font are stored in the font's `TFM` file; see 15.2.7, p. II-238.

This discussion leads to a very simple example. To build an hbox of the three characters "ABC," simply write `\hbox{ABC}`, building a horizontal box with the three characters (character boxes) "ABC" in it. To build a box "*ABC*" write `\hbox{\it ABC}`, and to build a box containing the three characters `ABC` write `\hbox{\tt ABC}`.

A macro to print the size of characters is presented in 15.2.4, p. II-232. You might want to look into this macro definition. The character is stored inside an hbox which is assigned to a box register, and then the dimensions of the hbox can be determined by reading the dimension registers of the box register.

6.2.6 The `\null` Macro

`\null` is a macro of the plain format which generates an empty hbox. Here is the definition of `\null`, simple and easy.

```
\def\null{\hbox{}}
```

6.2.7 How to Structure the Source Code of an `\hbox` Command

Properly formatting the input to an `\hbox` command is important, so that the TeX source code of an `\hbox` specification is clearly readable. What follows is necessary for generating readable TeX code. It is also important out of another reason: my own experience tells me that once you have understood how to input hboxes properly (according to the rules listed below), you understand hboxes also conceptually, and vice versa.

We need to recall some of the rules about spaces (see 2.8, p. 23, for complete details):

1. Spaces at the beginning of a line are ignored; see item 9 of the list on p. 26.
2. The end-of-line character is equivalent to the space character; see item 5, p. 25.
3. The space introduced by the end-of-line character can be eliminated by a percent sign (`%`) at the end of the line; see item 9, p. 27.
4. Spaces after dimensions are ignored; see item 15, p. 27.
5. Spaces at the beginning of a line are ignored.

Here is a properly indented hbox. Observe the indentation of the input and the placement of the curly braces. The general rules of inputing hboxes properly follow the example.

```
\hbox to \hsize{%
    \hskip 10pt
    $a+b = c$
    Here we even have some text.
    \raise 4pt \hbox{%
        ABC%
        \hskip 23pt
        \raise 5pt \hbox{x?1}%
    }%
    \hfil
}
```

Here are the rules for entering an hbox.

1. The input should give only one "major item" per line such as one **\hbox**, **\hskip** or **\raise** and **\lower** per line. An exception to this rule would be some text stored inside an **\hbox**. This text would normally be entered on one line and one would not write each character on a separate line.
2. A closing curly brace terminating a box-generating command like **\hbox** should line up vertically with the backslash of "its" **\hbox** command (the same statement applies to curly braces of other box types also, of course). This rule allows the reader of your TeX source to locate immediately the beginning and end of the content of a box.

   This rule should be applied "within reason." For a "miniature hbox" like **\hbox{A}** it would be inappropriate to waste three lines and to write

```
\hbox{%
    A%
}
```

3. The content of any type of box, if this content is entered according to the previous rule (not on one line) should be indented with respect to the original box-generating command. For instance, the proper input is

```
\hbox{%
    ABC
    \hskip 10pt
}
```

   and not

```
\hbox{%
ABC
\hskip 10pt
}
```

4. Don't forget %s at the end of lines, especially after opening and closing curly braces or other text. Otherwise the end-of-line character will result in a horizontal space being added to the box.

   Let me focus now on this rule briefly comparing four examples:

```
% Example 1a.
\hbox{%
    A%
    \raise 5pt \hbox{B}%
    \raise 10pt\hbox{C}%
}

% Example 1b.
\hbox{A\raise 5pt \hbox{B}\raise 10pt\hbox{C}}

% Example 2a.
\hbox{
    A
    \raise 5pt \hbox{B}
    \raise 10pt\hbox{C}
}

% Example 2b.
\hbox{ A \raise 5pt \hbox{B} \raise 10pt\hbox{C} }
```

Note that examples 1a and 1b produce the same output, which is "A$^{\mathrm{B}^{\mathrm{C}}}$." On the other hand examples 2a and 2b produce a different output that reads " A ^{B} ^{C} ." This time there is a space after every character and before the first one (spaces after dimensions don't matter; see 2.8.2, item 15, p. 27).

6.2.8 `\hbox\bgroup` ... `\egroup`

It is possible to replace the curly braces of an `\hbox` with `\bgroup` and `\egroup`. Therefore the following two boxes are equivalent:

```
\hbox{ABC}
\hbox\broup ABC\egroup
```

The same `\bgroup` and `\egroup` ideas can be applied to vertical boxes, of course, as, for instance, in

```
\vbox\bgroup
    ...
\egroup
```

What we gain from using `\bgroup` and `\egroup` instead of curly braces is discussed in 19.4.7, p. III-103, in detail. The `\bgroup` and `\egroup` control sequences allow you to define macros that begin but do not end a box, and macros that end an box that was not started by the same macro but another macro.

Here is a brief example for some macros which can be defined to generate some boxes.

```
\def\Abox{\hbox\bgroup A\More}%
```

```
\def\More{B\EvenMore}%
\def\EvenMore{C\egroup}%
```

After the preceding definitions were entered, `\Abox` will print the following output: "ABC."

6.3 Examples of Building Horizontal Boxes

In 6.2.2, p. 163, we discussed what can be stored inside an hbox. Now we will look at some examples for the various items.

6.3.1 Characters in Hboxes

To store characters inside an hbox, simply list the characters of the hbox enclosed in curly braces. Thus `\hbox{ABC}` generates `\HboxR{ABC}`. Font changes may be included. For instance, `\hbox{A\it B\bf C}` prints A*B***C**.

Because the curly braces that delimit the content of an hbox also have a grouping function (implicit grouping, see 6.2.4, p. 164), no additional curly braces are needed to delimit the effect of font changes inside hboxes.

6.3.2 Other Boxes Inside an Hbox

Other boxes can be printed inside an hbox. For instance, `\hbox{A\hbox{BC}D}` prints "ABCD." The outermost hbox contains three entities; the second one is another hbox containing "BC."

More complicated (and also more interesting) examples follow shortly.

6.3.3 Using Boxes Stored in Box Registers

Box registers can be used inside hboxes. First a horizontal box containing the two characters "AB" is assigned to box register 0. Then three copies of this box register are printed.

```
\setbox 0 = \hbox{AB}
\hbox{%
    \copy0
    \copy0
    \copy0
}
```

The above input generates the following text: ABABAB.

Observe that there are no spaces between the "AB"s despite the fact that there are spaces between the `\copy0`s. The reason for this is that TeX ignores spaces after numerical constants. In the above case the space after the numerical constant `0` of `\copy0` is ignored. Having spaces in the input improves the readability over the equivalent input `\hbox{\copy0\copy0\copy0}`.

Let us discuss the following ways of printing spaces between the above boxes:

1. Use `\␣`. The input `\hbox{\copy0\␣\copy0\␣\copy0}` prints AB AB AB.
2. Use `\space`. Let me explain this in some additional detail:
   (a) `\hbox{\copy0␣\space\copy0␣\space\copy0}` prints AB AB AB.
   (b) `\hbox{\copy0\space\copy0\space\copy0}` prints ABABAB *without* any spaces between the "AB"s. In this case the `\space` is absorbed because of the space skipping behavior of TeX after numerical constants.
   In example 2.a, writing `\copy0␣\space` causes TeX to actually insert *two* space tokens into the input. The first one is ignored because it occurs after a numerical constant. The second space token is *not* ignored and prints as a space in the output.
   (c) Note that `\hbox{\copy0\space\space\copy0\space\space\copy0}` prints AB AB AB, because this example is identical to 2.(a).
3. Use an *empty group* `{}` to stop TeX from skipping spaces after numerical constants: `\hbox{\copy0{} \copy0{} \copy0}` prints AB AB AB.

6.3.4 Raising and Lowering Boxes, `\raise`, `\lower`

Boxes can be raised and lowered by `\raise` or `\lower`. Each of these instructions must be followed by a *dimension*, which specifies the amount of raising or lowering. This dimension in turn must be followed by a box, which is raised or lowered. For instance, `\hbox{A\raise 4pt\hbox{C}}` prints A^{C}.

One *cannot* raise or lower a single character or a rule, in other words the preceding example could *not* have been abbreviated to `\hbox{A\raise 4pt C}`. Also to raise a rule ▬(`\vrule width 10pt height 3pt depth 0pt`) by 5 pt one *cannot* write `\raise 5pt \vrule ...`, but one must write `\raise 5pt \hbox{\vrule ...}` instead and include the rule inside a box.

Following is a list of examples of the use of `\raise` and `\lower`.

	Input	Output

1	`\hbox{%`
	`    A%`
	`    \raise 0pt\hbox{BC}%`
	`    D%`
	`}`
		ABCD

2

```
\hbox{%
    A%
    \raise 5pt\hbox{BC}%
    D%
}
```

$\mathrm{A^{BC}D}$

3

```
\hbox{%
    A%
    \raise 10pt\hbox{BC}%
    D%
}
```

$\mathrm{A^{BC}D}$

4

```
\hbox{%
    A%
    \raise 15pt\hbox{BC}%
    D%
}
```

$\mathrm{A^{BC}D}$

5

```
\hbox{%
    A%
    \raise -7pt\hbox{BC}%
    D%
}
```

$\mathrm{A_{BC}D}$

6

```
\hbox{%
    A%
    \lower 7pt\hbox{BC}%
    D%
}
```

$\mathrm{A_{BC}D}$

7

```
\hbox{%
    A%
    \raise 5pt\hbox{BC}%
    D%
    \raise 10pt\hbox{XX}%
    Y%
    \lower 5pt\hbox{123}%
    T%
}
```

$\mathrm{A^{BC}D^{XX}Y_{123}T}$

8

```
\hbox{%
    A%
    \raise 5pt\hbox{A}%
    \raise 2pt\hbox{B}%
    \raise 7pt\hbox{C}%
    \raise 2pt\hbox{D}%
    \raise 9pt\hbox{E}%
    \raise 2pt\hbox{F}%
    \raise 11pt\hbox{G}%
    \raise 2pt\hbox{H}%
    X%
}
```

$\mathrm{A^{A}B^{C}D^{E}F^{G}HX}$

9

```
\hbox{%
    A
    \raise 5pt\hbox{BC}
    \raise 7pt\hbox{DE}
    \raise 5pt\hbox{XX}
    X
}
```

A BC DE XX X

10

```
\hbox{%
    A
    \raise 5pt\hbox{%
        \vrule height 2pt width 20pt
    }%
    \raise 7pt\hbox{%
        \vrule height 3pt width 10pt
    }%
    \raise 5pt\hbox{%
        \vrule height 4pt width 5pt
    }%
    X
}
```

A X

Observe that after a box has been raised TEX will return to the original baseline; see example 9. The "BC" in this example is raised by 5 pt, and "DE" is *not* raised by an *additional* 7 pt but by 7 pt with respect to the baseline.

Furthermore, note that the output of examples 5 and 6 are identical: raising by a negative amount is obviously identical to lowering by the same positive amount.

6.3.5 More `\raise` and `\lower` Examples

Let us discuss how to generate $\mathrm{A}^{\mathrm{B}^{\mathrm{C}}}$. The "A" is printed on the baseline, the "B" is raised by 5 pt, and the "C" is raised by another 5 pt with respect to the "B." There are *two different ways* to look at this: one is to raise the "B" by 5 pt, and then to raise the "C" by twice this amount, similar to what was done in example 9 on the preceding page. The other possibility is to construct an hbox, which contains a "B" with a raised "C," and then to raise this box with respect to the "A."

Here are both solutions:

- Solution 1 with a "raised B" and a "double-raised C."

```
\hbox{%
    A%
    \raise 5pt \hbox{B}%
    \raise 10pt\hbox{C}%
}
```

- Solution 2 with the "A" followed by a raised box containing a "B" and a raised "C."

```
\hbox{%
    A%
    \raise 5pt \hbox{%
        B%
        \raise 5pt\hbox{C}%
    }%
}
```

The second solution could be written differently using a box register:

```
\setbox 0 = \hbox{%
    B%
    \raise 5pt\hbox{C}%
}
\hbox{%
    A%
    \raise 5pt \box0
}
```

6.3.6 Vertical Boxes Inside Horizontal Boxes

Vertical boxes can be contained in horizontal boxes. A detailed discussion of vboxes will follow later. In this subsection we show two such examples. Note here that boxes can be nested in arbitrary ways: an hbox can contain other hboxes *or* vboxes, and in turn a vbox can contain other hboxes and vboxes.

For the first example the following input is used (the emphasis is not on the contents of the vertical boxes):

```
\hbox {%
    ABC:%
    \hskip 10pt
    \VtopR{%
        \hsize = 1.5in
        \raggedright
        This is a little paragraph inside a {\tt\string\vtop}.
    }%
    \hskip 10pt
    More text.
}
```

This input generates the following output:

ABC: This is a little para-graph inside a \vtop. More text.

Replacing \vtop with \vbox prints the following text:

ABC: This is a little para-graph inside a \vbox. More text.

6.3.7 Horizontal Glue Inside Hboxes

Now I will present some examples where the main emphasis is upon horizontal glue inside hboxes. I already gave some examples before when we discussed horizontal glue (5.2.1, p. 124). Remember that negative horizontal glue skips to the left (allowing the overprinting of previously printed text), and positive horizontal glue skips to the right.

Also remember that any glue's stretchability or shrinkability is ignored, unless the box is told to stretch and shrink (by `\hbox to / spread`.

The examples below show that by using horizontal glue in conjunction with `\raise` and `\lower` items can be positioned at any arbitrary location on the paper: the horizontal glue is used to shift the item to the left or right to whatever horizontal position is desired, and `\raise` and `\lower` is used to shift the item up and down to whatever vertical position is desired.

Input / Output

1

```
\hbox{%
    AB%
    \hskip 5pt
    \raise 5pt\hbox{CD}%
    E%
}
```

Output: AB CD E

2

```
\hbox{%
    AB%
    \hskip -5pt
    \raise 5pt\hbox{CD}%
    E%
}
```

Output: ABCDE

3

```
\hbox{%
    AB%
    \hskip 5pt
    \raise -5pt\hbox{CD}%
    E%
}
```

Output: AB CDE

4

```
\hbox{%
    AB%
    \hskip -5pt
    \raise -5pt\hbox{CD}%
    E%
}
```

Output: ABCDE

5

```
\hbox{%
    AB%
    \hskip -10pt
    \raise 5pt\hbox{CD}%
    E%
}
```

Output: ABCDE

6

```
\hbox{%
    AB%
    \hskip -20pt
    \raise 5pt\hbox{CD}%
    E%
}
```

Output: CDABE

7

```
\hbox{%
    AB%
    \hskip -15pt
    \raise -7pt\hbox{CD}%
    \hskip -30pt
    E%
}
```

Output: E AB CD

It is illegal to use vertical glue to shift an item up and down inside an hbox. For instance, you *cannot* print A^B by entering `\hbox{A\vskip -3pt B}`.

6.3.8 Vertical Rules Inside Hboxes

The discussion of vertical rules in hboxes will be a little complicated because the height and depth of such rules (if not specified explicitly) default to the height and depth of the box these rules are contained in. See 5.7, p. 154, for a detailed discussion.

6.3.8.1 Rules with Default Dimensions

The first set of examples illustrates that the height and depth of an hbox determines the height and depth of rules contained in this hbox if those dimensions are not specified.

Input Output

1

```
\hbox{%
    \vrule
    AB%
    \raise 2pt \hbox{BC}%
    \vrule
}
```

Output: |ABBC|

2

```
\hbox{%
    \vrule
    AB%
    \raise 8pt \hbox{BC}%
    \vrule
}
```

Output: |AB BC|

3

```
\hbox{%
    \vrule
    AB%
    \raise 12pt\hbox{BC}%
    \vrule
}
```

BC
AB

4

```
\hbox{%
    \vrule
    AB%
    \raise -2pt \hbox{BC}%
    \vrule
}
```

ABBC

5

```
\hbox{%
    \vrule
    AB%
    \raise -5pt \hbox{BC}%
    \vrule
}
```

ABBC

6

```
\hbox{%
    \vrule
    AB%
    \raise -8pt \hbox{BC}%
    \vrule
}
```

AB
BC

7

```
\hbox{%
    \vrule width 3pt
    AB%
    \raise -5pt \hbox{BC}%
    \vrule width 5pt
}
```

ABBC

6.3.8.2 Rules with Explicit Dimension Specifications

For examples involving rules with explicit dimension specifications see 5.7.3, p. 156. If the height and/or depth of a rule is specified, then TEX will print a rule with such a dimension. TEX will also take these dimensions into account when determining the overall height and depth of the box in which the rule is contained.

6.3.9 Mathematical Formulas Inside Hboxes

Mathematical formulas, in inline math mode only, can appear in hboxes. Display mathmode can be "simulated" using `\displaystyle`. Here is an example:

	Input	Output

1	`\hbox{%`
	`    Text`
	`    $a^{2} + b^{2} = c^{2}$`
	`    text.`
	`}`
		Text $a^2 + b^2 = c^2$ text.

2	`\hbox{%`
	`    Text`
	`    ${a+b\over c} + d$,`
	`    text.`
	`}`
		Text ${a+b\over c} + d$, text.

3	`\hbox{%`
	`    Text`
	`    $\displaystyle {a+b\over c}`
	`            + d$,`
	`    text.`
	`}`
		Text $\displaystyle \frac{a+b}{c} + d$, text.

Incidentally, a mathematical formula can contain an hbox, and this hbox can contain a mathematical formula, and so forth.

6.4 Determining the Dimensions of Hboxes

The purpose of this Section is to explain the computation of dimensions of hboxes in detail after the informal discussion offered so far.

6.4.1 A Little Bit of Theory

When computing the dimensions of hboxes, one may assume that the components of a box are all built before the box itself is built. Thus, the dimensions of all components of a box are known when the box's dimensions itself are computed (an exception to this occurs under some circumstances with rules; see below for details). When a component box is built according to the rules below before the real box, is assembled and its dimensions are determined, a recursive situation occurs. Here is a concise description of this computation:

1. The *width* computation proceeds in two steps.

   First the so-called *natural width* w_n is computed: the widths of all components of the box are simply added up. At this point stretchabilities and shrinkabilities of glues are simply disregarded. Note that the width of a

`\vrule` is always known, either because it is specified explicitly (e.g., `\vrule width 2pt`), or because TEX uses the default value of 0.4 pt.

Now note that there are three different ways for the user to actually *specify* what the width of an hbox should be.

(a) One could not specify the width at all by using the "simple form" of the `\hbox {...}` construct (no `to` or `spread` after `\hbox`). In this case the box's width will be the natural width (of which the computation was just explained).

Observe that in this case the stretchabilities and shrinkabilities of any glues contained in the hbox are irrelevant.

(b) The user could explicitly instruct TEX to assign a specific width ⟨dimen⟩ to the box by using the `\hbox to` ⟨dimen⟩ `{...}` construct.

This results in an hbox of width ⟨dimen⟩ being constructed. TEX will now adjust the width of the box built so far as follows (assume the dimension ⟨dimen⟩ is w_u):

i. If $w_n < w_u$ (meaning that the box constructed so far must be *stretched out* because the natural width is too small) then TEX will stretch out the total of any glue or leaders in the box by $w_u - w_n$. 5.2.3, p. 126, discusses what happens if there is an insufficient amount of stretchability in the box (actually there may be no stretchability available at all).

An important point however is that *regardless* of whether there is sufficient glue to stretch or not TEX will assign w_u as the final width to the box.

ii. If $w_n = w_u$, then obviously no changes are necessary. But, of course, this will happen only in one out of a million cases.

iii. If $w_n > w_u$ (meaning the box must be *pushed together*) then TEX will push together any glue or leaders in the box by $w_n - w_u$. Subsection 5.2.3, p. 126, discusses what happens if there is an insufficient amount of shrinkability in the box (actually there may be none at all).

Similar to the case $w_n < w_u$ whether there is sufficient glue to shrink or not TEX will assign w_u as the final width to this box.

(c) The specification `\hbox spread` ⟨dimen⟩ `{...}` tells TEX to build an hbox, which is ⟨dimen⟩ wider than the natural width w_n. Assume this ⟨dimen⟩ by which the box is spread out is w_s. Then this construct is equivalent to `\hbox to` w_u where $w_u = w_n + w_s$.

Here is an easy example: assume the natural width w_n of a box is 1.5 in, and that this box is to be spread out by 0.5 in. This specification is obviously equivalent to instructing TEX to build a box which is 2.0 in wide (`\hbox to 2.0in{...}`).

2. The *height* of an hbox is the *maximum* height of any component in the box. If this box contains a *raised box* as a component, this component's height is the height of the raised box plus the amount by which the component box was raised.

The *height of a rule* is a factor in computing the height of the box only if the height is explicitly specified (`\vrule height ...`). Therefore, a rule can only influence the height of a box if the rule carries an explicit height specification.

3. The *depth* of an hbox is determined similar to the way the height is determined. The depth of the box is therefore the maximum depth of any component of the box. If this box contains a box that is lowered, the depth of the lowered box plus the amount by which the box is lowered must be added together.

   Rules (`\vrules`) are again only taken into account if their depth is specified.

6.4.2 Examples of Width Computations of Hboxes

Let us study width computation examples now. Writing `\hbox{A}` will build an hbox which is 7.5 pt wide, because this is the width of the "A." The hbox built by `\hbox{AA}` is therefore 15 pt wide, `\hbox{AAA}` will generate an hbox which is 22.5 pt wide, and so forth.

The letter "Q" has a width of 7.77 pt, the letter "A" has a width of 7.5 pt, but the width of `\hbox{AQ}` is *not* 15.27 pt as expected but only 15 pt. What happened? The answer is simple: *kerning* (a character pair and font specific correction of the space between two characters) reduced the distance between these two characters resulting in an hbox which is slightly smaller; see 16.4.2, p. II-291, for details.

If, on the other hand, you write `\hbox{A{}Q}`, then kerning is prevented, and the width of this hbox is 15.27 pt as expected.

The degree a box is raised or lowered has no influence on the width computations. In the following example (using Computer Modern Fonts), TEX also does not insert any kerning between characters A and B, or B and C:

1:	`\hbox{ABC}`	ABC
2:	`\hbox{A\raise 4pt\hbox{B}C}`	A^{B}C
3:	`\hbox{AB\raise -3pt\hbox{C}}`	AB$_{\mathrm{C}}$

If `\hskips` are included in an hbox their width is added to the width of the box. Observe that when the natural width of a box is computed, any of the shrinkabilities or stretchabilities of those glues are disregarded. In the following examples therefore *all boxes have the same width*, which is the sum of the width of the two characters "A" and "B" plus an additional 20 pt from the natural width of the horizontal glue contained in each of the following boxes.

```
1: \hbox{A\hskip 20pt B}
2: \hbox{A\hskip 20pt plus 20pt B}
3: \hbox{A\hskip 20pt plus 1fil B}
4: \hbox{A\hskip 20pt plus 1fill minus 1fil B}
```

5: `\hbox{A\hskip 20pt minus 30pt B}`

Note that the width of a vertical rule inside an hbox is always known: it is either specified or defaults to 0.4 pt.

6.4.3 Computing Height and Depth of an Hbox

Note that height and depth dimensions are computed along the same lines: the height of an hbox is determined by the highest component of the box, and the depth is determined by its deepest component. The only slight complication comes from rules that are treated differently depending on whether or not their height or depth is specified or not.

There are two different ways the height or depth of a rule is determined, if a rule is contained in an hbox (note that the word "depth" could be substituted for "height" and both methods would still be valid):

1. If the height of a rule is *not specified* then the height of the *box* is computed *disregarding* the height of that rule. The height of the rule is then set to the height of the box, *after* the height of the box was computed.
2. If the height of a box is *specified* then the height (depth) of the rule will be as specified. When TeX determines the height of the hbox by computing the maximum height of the box that rule's height will be also taken into account!

Note how in the first three examples below the height and depth of the rule changes as the height and depth of the box is changed by raising and lowering "XXX." The fourth through sixth examples include a second rule with height set to 10 pt. The depth of that rule is not specified. In the fourth example this height determines the height of the whole box. In the fifth example the raised "XXX" controls the height of the whole box but causes only the first rule to stretch to this height, not the second rule. Note that in the sixth example the depth of both rules is determined by the depth of the lowered "XXX."

Input — Output

1

```
\hbox{%
    \vrule width 1pt
    AAA%
    \raise 0pt\hbox{XXX}%
}
```

Output: |AAAXXX

2

```
\hbox{%
    \vrule width 1pt
    AAA%
    \raise 10pt\hbox{XXX}%
}
```

Output: |AAA XXX (XXX raised)

3

```
\hbox{%
    \vrule width 1pt
    AAA%
    \raise -7pt\hbox{XXX}%
}
```

AAA XXX

4

```
\hbox{%
    \vrule width 1pt
    AAA%
    \raise 0pt\hbox{XXX}%
    \vrule width 1pt height 10pt
}
```

AAAXXX

5

```
\hbox{%
    \vrule width 1pt
    AAA%
    \raise 12pt\hbox{XXX}%
    \vrule width 1pt height 10pt
}
```

XXX
AAA

6

```
\hbox{%
    \vrule width 1pt
    AAA%
    \raise -8pt\hbox{XXX}%
    \vrule width 1pt height 10pt
}
```

AAA XXX

6.4.4 Empty Hboxes Built with `\hbox to` ⟨dimen⟩

Note that it is possible to generate an empty hbox of a specified width. For instance, `\hbox to 1.0in{}` generates an empty box which is 1 in wide, with zero height and depth. The main difference between this and 1 in long glue (`\hskip 1.0in`) is that the hbox is *not* a discardable item. See 5.4.6, p. 139.

6.5 Hboxes of Zero or Nearly Zero Width, `\hbox to 0pt {...}`

Hboxes of zero width can be, for instance, used to print two characters on top of each other. The following examples also demonstrate that dimensions of a box can be different from what the contents of the box suggests it should be.

6.5.1 The Problem of Overprinting Two Characters

We will try to solve the following problem: print an "A" and a "V" on top of each other as in "X." These two characters were chosen because they have the identical width of 7.5 pt. For this problem three different solutions will be presented, each one an improvement over the preceding one.

1. *The two characters are printed with a negative* `\hskip` *between them.* First the "A" is printed, then a horizontal skip to the left by the width of the "A" occurs. This positions TEX back to where the printing of the "A" originally occurred. Then the "V" is printed, this time on top of the "A" of course. To print "A" and "V" on top of each other we therefore would have to write `\hbox{A\hskip -7.5pt V}`.

   See 15.2.4, p. II-232, for how the width of a character can be determined.
2. *Now let me rewrite the previous solution* as follows. The first two items of the previous hbox are packed into a separate hbox as follows:

```
1 \hbox{%
2     \hbox{A\hskip -7.5pt}%
3     V%
4 }
```

   The output will obviously be identical.

   Let us look now at the inner hbox (line 3) built by `\hbox{A\hskip -7.5pt}`. This box has a natural width of zero, because the width of an hbox is the sum of the widths of its components. The components are the character "A" (width 7.5 pt) and `\hskip -7.5pt` (width -7.5 pt).

   If you think about this for a moment, you will realize that this is what you wanted to do in the first place. The character "A" should be printed with an *effective width of zero* which means that the current reference point will not move. Afterwards the "V" should be printed now of course moving the current reference point to the right by the width of the "V."
3. *Now rewrite the previous solution once more.* The inner hbox will be built using an hbox with the following two properties:

   (a) The hbox contains the character "A."
   (b) The width of the hbox will be set to zero.

   There are two ways to construct a zero width hbox:

   (a) Use the "`\hbox to`" type of construct, in which case the instruction would obviously be `\hbox to 0pt{...}`. TEX must be provided with some glue, which can shrink backwards after the character "A" has been printed. By using glue which can shrink backwards as far as necessary, we will allow TEX to insert the right amount of backspacing. The following command is therefore used to build an hbox of zero width: `\hbox to 0pt{A\hskip 0pt minus 1fil}` or simply `\hbox to 0pt{A\hss}`.

   To print the two characters "A" and "V" on top of each other we therefore would enter the following instructions:

```
\hbox{%
    \hbox to 0pt{A\hss}%
    V%
}
```

Note the main advantage of this approach compared to the previous two approaches: it is *not* necessary to determine the width of the "A."

(b) Assign the box to a *box register* and then set the width of this box register to zero; see 4.5.4, p. 97, for details.

6.5.2 Macros `\rlap` and `\llap`

The `\rlap` and `\llap` macros of the plain format are based on the ideas discussed in the previous Subsection. Both macros build horizontal boxes of zero width. For simplicity the `\hss` glue instead of a `\hskip 0pt minus 1fil` glue is used. Note that the fact that the `\hss` glue can also stretch is irrelevant as far as ordinary applications of these macros are concerned.

Both macros have one parameter (`#1`), some text that that will be inserted into an hbox of zero width, with infinite glue to the right in the case of the `\rlap` macro and infinite glue to the left in the case of the `\llap` macro.

Here are the definitions of the macros `\rlap` and `\llap`.

```
\def\rlap #1{\hbox to 0pt{#1\hss}}
\def\llap #1{\hbox to 0pt{\hss#1}}
```

Using the `\rlap` macro the two characters "A" and "V" can be printed on top of each other as follows: `\hbox{\rlap{A}V}` prints AV (overprinted).

In the case of `\llap` note that the glue is inserted *before* the text and not after the text (as it is with `\rlap`). In `\llap` the glue will first stretch to the left by the width of the text which will be printed and then the text will be printed. Therefore using `\llap` the text is printed with the text's right end ending at the current point, whereas using `\rlap` the text is printed to the right of the current point with the left end of the text printed at the current point.

Using `\llap` the preceding AV-example could have been written as follows. This time first the "A" is printed followed by the "V" which is printed to the *left* of where the "A" ends: `\hbox{A\llap{V}}`. It is important that you understand the difference between the `\rlap` and `\llap` approach of solving this problem.

Here are some additional examples using `\rlap` and `\llap`. Note in particular where the "***" are printed in the case of `\rlap` versus `\llap`.

	Input	Output
1:	`\hbox{222 333\rlap{***} 444 555}`	222 333***444 555 (*** over 444)
2:	`\hbox{222 333\llap{***} 444 555}`	222 333 444 555 (*** over 333)
3:	`\hbox{222 333\raise 5pt\rlap{***} 444 555}`	222 333 444 555 (*** raised above 444)
4:	`\hbox{222 333\lower 5pt\llap{***} 444 555}`	222 333 444 555 (*** lowered below 333)

6.5.3 Poor Man's Boldface, Macro \BoldfaceFake

Now we will discuss a little trick to generate boldface-like characters of some font, for which no boldface version is available. As the title of this Subsection suggests, the resulting characters don't look great, and you should not use the approach below if a boldface version of your font is available.

The idea of simulating boldface characters is to print each character three times, each time shifted by some small amount to the right. The amount of shifting of course determines the appearance of the text.

Here is the source code of an example:

```
    \hbox{%
        \hbox to 0.3pt{This is poor man's boldface\hss}%
        \hbox to 0.3pt{This is poor man's boldface\hss}%
        \hbox          {This is poor man's boldface}%
    }
```

This generates the following text: **This is poor man's boldface**.

Let me now define a macro which also allows us to experiment with different shift amounts. Here is the definition of macro \BoldFaceFake. This macro has two parameters:

- #1. The text to be printed three times.
- #2. The amount of shifting done after each printing of the text (#1).

$\mathcal{P}'$ • poorbold.tip •

```
\def\BoldfaceFake #1#2{%
    \hbox{%
        \hbox to #2{#1\hss}%
        \hbox to #2{#1\hss}%
        \hbox {#1}%     % Last time print text with reg. width.
    }%
}
```

• End of poorbold.tip •

Here is an example using this macro. The following input was used:

```
\InputD{poorbold.tip}                        % 6.5.3, p. 183.
$$
    \vbox{                                          \tabskip = 5pt
        \halign{
            \hfil #pt&
            \BoldfaceFake{test text}{#pt}\relax \tabskip = 10pt&
            \hfil #pt\relax                     \tabskip = 5pt&
            \BoldfaceFake{test text}{#pt}%
        \cr
            \omit\hfil({\tt \#2})\hfil&\omit&
            \omit\hfil({\tt \#2})\hfil\cr
            0.0& 0.0&               0.1& 0.1\cr
            0.2& 0.2&               0.3& 0.3\cr
```

```
                0.4& 0.4&                      0.5& 0.5\cr
                0.6& 0.6&                      0.7& 0.7\cr
                1.0& 1.0&                      2.0& 2.0\cr
          }
     }
$$
\bye
```

This generates the following text:

(#2)		(#2)	
0.0pt	test text	0.1pt	test text
0.2pt	**test text**	0.3pt	**test text**
0.4pt	**test text**	0.5pt	**test text**
0.6pt	**test text**	0.7pt	**test text**
1.0pt	**test text**	2.0pt	test text

6.5.4 Constructing a Special Symbol

The following example shows an application where we construct a special summation sign with an asterisk printed in the top line of the summation sign. To print $\sum_{i=1}^{*n} x_i$, define macro `\xsum` as follows (the dimensions for the `\hskip` and the `\raise` instructions were found by trial and error):

```
\def\xsum{%
    \hbox to 0pt{%
        \hskip 6pt
        \raise 2pt\hbox{*}%
        \hss
    }%
    \sum
}
```

Now `$\xsum_{i=1} x_{i}$` generates $\sum_{i=1}^{*} x_i$.

There is one problem not solved by this macro: when the size of the summation sign changes (for instance, it does so in display math mode), then the dimensions to place the asterisk would have to change too. This issue is addressed in 14.4.5, p. II-198.

Note that the macro uses a zero width hbox to "pretend" that no movement has taken place although some text was indeed printed.

6.5.5 Solving the Same Problem Using Box Registers

Using box registers we can *rewrite* the `\rlap` macro. The simplest way to achieve the same effect is simply to force the width of the box to be zero. Here is the definition of macro \Rlap, identical in its function to \rlap, just implemented differently.

```
\def\Rlap #1{%
     \setbox 0 = \hbox{#1}%
     \wd0 = 0pt
     \box0
}
```

There is yet another approach of defining an \rlap like macro. This method uses a negative \hskip to compensate for the width of the text, thus generating a zero width hbox. The width of the text is available because the text is stored inside box register 0. Note that to extract the text from box register 0 \copy0 is used rather than \box0 because \box0 would destroy the content of box register 0 and the width of the text which is accessed through \wd0 would be lost (after \box0 the width of box register 0, \wd0, is zero). Here is macro \RlapX to implement our ideas.

```
\def\RlapX #1{%
     \setbox 0 = \hbox{#1}%
     \hbox{%
          \copy0
          \hskip -\wd0
     }%
}
```

A rewriting of \llap is also possible along the lines of \RlapX. This defines a new macro \LlapX. Now \box0 instead of \copy0 can be written, because \wd0 is used before the contents of box 0 is extracted.

```
\def\LlapX #1{%
     \setbox 0 = \hbox{#1}%
     \hbox{%
          \hskip -\wd0
          \box0
     }%
}
```

The idea of setting the width of a box to zero can be generalized to setting the height and depth of a box to zero; see 34.6, p. IV-80.

6.6 \...line Macros \line, \leftline, \rightline and \centerline

6.6.1 The Definitions of the \...line Macros

There are four macros defined in the plain format of TeX that typeset a single line of text. Following are the descriptions of all four macros.

Three of these macros have one parameter, **#1**, the text of the line to be printed (what appears to be a parameter for **\line** is really not a parameter of this macro but forms the direct specification of the input of the hbox built by **\line**. See 22.3, p. III-218, for a detailed explanation).

1. **\line**. Generate an hbox which is **\hsize** wide. This macro is simply an abbreviation for **\hbox to \hsize**.
2. **\leftline**. Generate a left justified line, that is an hbox which is **\hsize** wide with the content of this hbox shifted all the way to the left. This macro has one parameter, **#1**, the material to be shifted to the left.
3. **\rightline**. This macro is identical to **\leftline**, and it also has one parameter, **#1**, the contents of an hbox which is being built, but this time the content is shifted all the way to the right.
4. **\centerline**. This macro is identical to **\leftline** and **\rightline** with the exception that the content of the hbox being generated is centered inside this hbox.

Here are the definitions of these four macros:

```
\def\line{\hbox to \hsize}
\def\leftline   #1{\line{#1\hss}}
\def\rightline  #1{\line{\hss#1}}
\def\centerline #1{\line{\hss#1\hss}}
```

6.6.2 The Definitions of Macros \LeftLeaderLine, \RightLeaderLine, and \CenterLeaderLine

Following are examples using the above macros with slightly modified definitions, using leaders as visible glues. Consequently we will define macros **\LeftLeaderLine**, **\RightLeaderLine** and **\CenterLeaderLine** which are identical to **\leftline**, **\rightline** and **\centerline** except that they use leaders instead of ordinary glues. All three macros have one parameter, **#1**, the text to be printed on one line. The text will be shifted all the way to the right or to the left or it will be printed centered on the current line.

$\mathcal{P}'$ • leadline.tip •

Here are the definitions of the macros **\LeftLeaderLine** and so forth.

```
\def\RightLeaderLine #1{%
    \line{\leaders\hrule\hss #1}%
}

\def\LeftLeaderLine #1{%
    \line{#1\leaders\hrule\hss}%
}
```

```
\def\CenterLeaderLine #1{%
    \line{\leaders\hrule\hss #1\leaders\hrule\hss}%
}
```

• End of leadline.tip •

6.6.3 Examples

Now we present some applications of the macros of the preceding SubSection. If we had, for instance, used macro `\leftline` instead of `\LeftLeaderLine`, the output would have been identical except for the leaders which are printed when macro `\LeftLeaderLine` is used. Printing leaders makes the workings of `\leftline` easier to understand.

The following sample source code reduces the `\hsize` to 26 pc and centers the output horizontally on the page using display math mode:

```
\input inputd.tip
\InputD{leadline.tip}                    % 6.6.2, p. 186.
$$
    \vbox{
        \hsize = 26pc
        \line{Left flush and right flush%
            \leaders\hrule\hfil on the same line.}
        \line{This is left%
            \leaders\hrule\hfil oh well\leaders\hrule\hfil
            and this is right.}
        \RightLeaderLine{A sample of calling
            {\tt \string\RightLeaderLine}.}
        \LeftLeaderLine{A sample of calling
            {\tt \string\LeftLeaderLine}.}
        \CenterLeaderLine{A sample of calling
            {\tt \string\CenterLeaderLine}.}
    }
$$
```

The preceding input generates the following output:

Left flush and right flush on the same line.
This is left oh well and this is right.
A sample of calling `\RightLeaderLine`.
A sample of calling `\LeftLeaderLine`.
A sample of calling `\CenterLeaderLine`.

6.6.4 Paragraphs Preceding `\...line` Calls

There is an important point about the definition of the `\centerline` macro in the previous example (note that the same comment also applies to the other three macros). Assume you would like to center a line following a paragraph. The following input is *illegal* because the \hbox to \hsize (which is generated by the expansion of \centerline) will be interpreted as *part of the paragraph.*

```
A paragraph...
      ... the last line.
\centerline{***}
```

The problem is corrected by first finishing the paragraph (insert an empty line between the end of the paragraph and \centerline). The following input generates the desired result:

```
A paragraph...
      ... the last line.

\centerline{***}
```

6.6.5 \line... Macros and Glue Used

The second comment refers to the fact that all three macros \centerline, \leftline and \rightline use \hss glue instead of \hfil glue. A consequence is that if, for instance, \centerline is used with text as an argument of which the width exceeds \hsize the text will be centered, the text will obviously stick out on the left and right side and *no warning* (in form of a message about an overfull hbox) will be generated by TEX. This overwide text is actually a legal argument for the \centerline macro. The same remark applies to \leftline and \rightline.

6.6.6 Using the \line... Macros Inside a Vbox

You also can use the \line... macros inside a vbox. Here is the source code of such an example (note that the change to \hsize is limited to inside the vbox being built below because of the implicit grouping of box contents).

```
\InputD{leadline.tip}                              % 6.6.2, p. 186.
$$
      \vbox{
            \hsize = 3.0in
            \LeftLeaderLine{This is left flush}
            \leftline       {This is left flush}
            \RightLeaderLine{This is right flush}
            \rightline      {This is right flush}
            \CenterLeaderLine{This is centered}
            \centerline      {This is centered}
      }
$$
```

This generated the following output:

```
This is left flush______________________________
This is left flush
______________________________This is right flush
                              This is right flush
_______________This is centered_______________
               This is centered
```

6.7 Generating More Hboxes

More examples of the use of the `\hbox` command are presented here.

6.7.1 Hboxes Prevent Hyphenation

One application of hbox is the prevention of hyphenation, if a word is enclosed inside an hbox in a paragraph, that word will not be hyphenated. If you enclose more than one word inside an hbox then none of the words will be hyphened; also TeX will not generate a line break between any of these words. Also note that if you use left and right flush text, the interword spaces between the words enclosed in that hbox will not be adjusted.

6.7.2 Generating the TeX Logo

Here is the definition of the TeX logo:

```
\def\TeX{T\kern-.1667em\lower.5ex\hbox{E}\kern-.125emX}
```

The TeX logo does not use negative horizontal glue (`\hskip`), but kern to move the two characters "T" and "E" and the two characters "E" and "X" closer to each other. The reason is that kern, at least by itself, does not form a legal break point for a line break, when the TeX logo is printed inside a paragraph (by contrast negative horizontal glue could form a legal break point). See 5.4.8, p. 140, for details on kern.

An alternative would have been to enclose the whole logo inside an hbox. Here is the definition of `\TeXX`:

```
\def\TeXX{\hbox{T\hskip-.1667em\lower.5ex\hbox{E}\hskip-.125emX}}
```

6.7.3 Building Letterheads

I will now present a series of letterhead examples. These examples may be of interest to you when you start playing around with TEX, since designing letterheads is a good way to begin learning TEX.

For the first example the following input is used (it's a rich university, listing an 800 number as its regular phone number).

```
\vbox{
    \font\bigbf = cmbx12
    \medskip
    \centerline{\bigbf Ecila Bluewald}
    \medskip
    \centerline{\it Department of Goofistics}
    \centerline{\it Lost University}
    \centerline{\it Moth Ball Bldg}
    \smallskip
    \centerline{\bf West Northcity, XX 00000-4790}
    \smallskip
    \centerline{\tt (800) 123-4567}
}
```

The preceding input generated the following letterhead:

Ecila Bluewald

Department of Goofistics
Lost University
Moth Ball Bldg

West Northcity, XX 00000-4790

(800) 123-4567

Observe the `\smallskip` and `\medskip` instructions, which improve the vertical spacing in this letterhead.

Here is another example. The following input was used (note the advanced approach of the following university by the use of a 900 number).

```
\vbox{
    \line{{\bf Ecila Bluewald}\hfil Department of Goofistics}
    \rightline{No University}
    \rightline{Moth Ball Bldg}
    \line{{\bf West Northcity, XX 00000-9999}\hfil
        \tt (900) 123 4567}
}
```

This generates the following letterhead:

Ecila Bluewald Department of Goofistics
No University
Moth Ball Bldg
West Northcity, XX 00000-9999 (900) 123 4567

6.7.4 Removing Glue from a Horizontal List, `\unskip`

The primitive **`\unskip`** will be explained in detail later (see 8.5.3, p. 308), but here is a brief discussion. Assume you are currently building a horizontal list. Then if the most recent item on this list is horizontal glue (or a horizontal leader), TeX will remove it upon an **`\unskip`**. Otherwise **`\unskip`** has no effect.

Assume, for instance, that you would like to write a macro **`CenterlineP`** (the `P` stands for period), which centers some text *and* terminates this text with a period. Furthermore assume that the text you center *may* end with some trailing horizontal space (that you would like to remove). Nothing could be easier than that.

First here is the source code of **`\CenterlineP`**:

$\mathcal{P}'$ • **`centerlp.tip`** •

```
\def\CenterlineP #1{%
    \centerline{#1\unskip .}
}
```

• End of **`centerlp.tip`** •

And here is a short example application of this macro. The following source code is used.

```
\input inputd.tip
\InputD{centerlp.tip}                          % 6.7.4, p. 191.
\CenterlineP{Text A}
\CenterlineP{Text B }
```

This source code generates the following output:

Text A.
Text B.

6.8 A Table Generated with Hboxes

I will now discuss building a table using hboxes. The table we will typeset is fairly simple and the use of hboxes is more or less straightforward. Later we will show typesetting tables using **`\halign`** which offers significant advantages over using hboxes directly. But to typeset a table using hboxes is very educational and of tremendous help when trying to understand **`\halign`** later.

Here is the table we will try to typeset:

XXXXXX	YYY	Z	TTT
XXXXX	YY	ZZ	TTTT
XXXX	Y	ZZZZZ	TTTTTT
X	YYYYYY	ZZ	TTT

6.8.1 An Outline of Printing a Table Using Hboxes

The approach to typesetting the above table can be described as follows (later you will see that `\halign`'s computations proceed along the same lines):

1. Normally a table to be typeset with TeX is not given as "neatly" (i.e., typeset) as it is here. Therefore you should go through the following steps before you actually try to typeset the table using TeX:
   (a) Sketch the layout of the table.
   (b) Decide on the alignment of each column. Right now let us restrict ourselves to left aligned, right aligned and centered entries; we will also use only one type of alignment within each column.
   (c) Decide on the distance between the columns. Let d_i be the distance between columns i and $i + 1$.
2. *Find the widest entry within each column*, because the widest entry determines the width of each column. We use "eyeballing". Of course, you could let TeX *measure the width of each entry* and determine the widest entry.
3. *Find the width of each widest entry.* Let us call w_i the width of the widest entry of column i. Whatever method you used in the previous step, now you have to actually find the width of these widest entries (it is insufficient to just know which entry in each column is the widest).
4. *Typeset the table.* Each row becomes one individual hbox. Inside each such "row hbox" you find the following components:
   (a) `\hbox to` w_1 `{...}` for the entry of the first column in the current row. Horizontal glue must be added to this box to achieve the desired justification of the table entries in this column.
   (b) `\hskip` d_1. This is the glue which determines the distance d_1 between the first and second column.
   (c) `\hbox to` w_2 `{...}` for the entry of the second column. Horizontal glue must be added to achieve the desired justification for entries in that column.
   (d) `\hskip` d_2. This glue obviously determines the distance d_2 between the second and the third column.
   (e) The above steps must be repeated for all the remaining columns.
5. *Center the whole table* by enclosing it into a vbox which is subsequently centered using display math mode.

6.8.2 An Example Table Built Using Hboxes

Let me go through an example step by step.

1. *Sketch layout.* It is important that you have a clear idea of what your table

should look like. For the example table in particular the following decisions were made:

(a) It is a four column table.
(b) The four columns are left justified, right justified, centered and left justified.
(c) The distances between the columns are 45 pt, 15 pt and 30 pt.

2. The *widest entries* within each column are easily identified

   - First column: **XXXXXX**.
   - Second column: YYYYYY.
   - Third column: ZZZZZ.
   - Fourth column: `TTTTTT`.

3. Now *find the width of each of the widest entries.* Each entry will be stored inside an hbox, which is assigned to a box register. Then the width of the box can be printed. The following TeX source code was used.

• `boxes-tw.tip` •

```
\nonstopmode
\setbox 0 = \hbox{\bf XXXXXX}   \showthe\wd0
\setbox 0 = \hbox{YYYYYY}       \showthe\wd0
\setbox 0 = \hbox{ZZZZZ}        \showthe\wd0
\setbox 0 = \hbox{\tt TTTTTT}   \showthe\wd0
\bye
```

• End of `boxes-tw.tip` •

This generated the following log file:

• `boxes-tw.log` •

```
This is TeX, C Version 3.14 (...)
**&/usr/local/tex/lib/fmt/plain boxes-tw.tip
(boxes-tw.tip
> 52.16638pt.
l.2 ... XXXXXX}^^I\showthe\wd0

> 45.00009pt.
l.3 ...YYYY}^^I^^I\showthe\wd0

> 30.55557pt.
l.4 ...ZZZZ}^^I^^I\showthe\wd0

> 31.49973pt.
l.5 ... TTTTTT}^^I\showthe\wd0

)
No pages of output.
```

In other words (we will round those values up to the next full point), the widths of the columns are 53 pt, 46 pt, 31 pt and 32 pt respectively.

4. Here is the source code for the table:

```
$$\vbox{
    \hbox{%     Row 1
        \hbox to 53pt {\bf XXXXXX\hfil}%
        \hskip 45pt
        \hbox to 46pt {\hfil YYY}%
        \hskip 15pt
        \hbox to 31pt {\hfil Z\hfil}%
        \hskip 30pt
        \hbox to 32pt {\tt TTT\hfil}%
    }
    \hbox{%     Row 2
        \hbox to 53pt {\bf XXXXX\hfil}%
        \hskip 45pt
        \hbox to 46pt {\hfil YY}%
        \hskip 15pt
        \hbox to 31pt {\hfil ZZ\hfil}%
        \hskip 30pt
        \hbox to 32pt {\tt TTTT\hfil}%
    }
    \hbox{%     Row 3
        \hbox to 53pt {\bf XXXX\hfil}%
        \hskip 45pt
        \hbox to 46pt {\hfil Y}%
        \hskip 15pt
        \hbox to 31pt {\hfil ZZZZZ\hfil}%
        \hskip 30pt
        \hbox to 32pt {\tt TTTTTT\hfil}%
    }
    \hbox{%     Row 4
        \hbox to 53pt {\bf X\hfil}%
        \hskip 45pt
        \hbox to 46pt {\hfil YYYYY}%
        \hskip 15pt
        \hbox to 31pt {\hfil ZZ\hfil}%
        \hskip 30pt
        \hbox to 32pt {\tt TTT\hfil}%
    }
}$$
```

6.8.3 Adding Headers to an Hbox-Based Table

Now it is time to add some headers to the previous tables. The widths of columns 1 and 2 together with the glue in between the two columns is 53 pt + 45 pt + 46 pt = 144 pt. The width of columns 2 and 3 together with their intermediate glue is 31 pt + 30 pt + 32 pt = 93 pt.

Here are the TEX instructions to add a header over columns 1 and 2, and a header over columns 3 and 4. Both headers are centered.

```
\hbox{%
    \hbox to 144pt{\hfil\bf Header 1\hfil}%
    \hskip 15pt                          % Between col. 2 and 3.
    \hbox to 93pt{\hfil\bf Header 2\hfil}%
}
```

Similarly we could add a header over all four columns (the width of the whole table is 53 pt + 45 pt + 46 pt + 15 pt + 31 pt + 30 pt + 32 pt = 252 pt).

```
\hbox to 252pt{\hfil \bf Header for the Whole Table\hfil}
```

The table including the headers will be printed shortly, after we add some additional vertical glue to improve the vertical spacing.

6.8.4 Adding Vertical Glue to an Hbox-Built Table

The vertical spacing of the above table is currently unsatisfactory. More space between the first and the second header row as well as between the second header row and the first table body row is desirable. This leads to the following new table. First the source code:

```
$$
\vbox{
    \hbox to 252.8pt{\hfil \bf Header for the Whole Table\hfil}
    \medskip
    \hbox{%
        \hbox to 144pt{\hfil\bf Header 1\hfil}%
        \hskip 15pt                          % Between col. 2 and 3.
        \hbox to 93pt{\hfil\bf Header 2\hfil}%
    }
    \bigskip
    \hbox{%                                  hbox of row 1
        \hbox to 53pt {\bf XXXXXX\hfil}%
        \hskip 45pt
        \hbox to 46pt {\hfil YYY}%
        \hskip 15pt
        \hbox to 31pt {\hfil Z\hfil}%
        \hskip 30pt
        \hbox to 32pt {\tt TTT\hfil}%
    }
    \hbox{%                                  hbox of row 2
        \hbox to 53pt {\bf XXXXX\hfil}%
        \hskip 45pt
        \hbox to 46pt {\hfil YY}%
        \hskip 15pt
        \hbox to 31pt {\hfil ZZ\hfil}%
        \hskip 30pt
        \hbox to 32pt {\tt TTTT\hfil}%
```

```
    }
    \hbox{%                                    hbox of row 3
        \hbox to 53pt {\bf XXXX\hfil}%
        \hskip 45pt
        \hbox to 46pt {\hfil Y}%
        \hskip 15pt
        \hbox to 31pt {\hfil ZZZZZ\hfil}%
        \hskip 30pt
        \hbox to 32pt {\tt TTTTTT\hfil}%
    }
    \hbox{%                                    hbox of row 4
        \hbox to 53pt {\bf X\hfil}%
        \hskip 45pt
        \hbox to 46pt {\hfil YYYYY}%
        \hskip 15pt
        \hbox to 31pt {\hfil ZZ\hfil}%
        \hskip 30pt
        \hbox to 32pt {\tt TTT\hfil}%
    }
}
$$
```

The new table looks as follows:

Header for the Whole Table

Header 1		**Header 2**	
XXXXXX	YYY	Z	TTT
XXXXX	YY	ZZ	TTTT
XXXX	Y	ZZZZZ	TTTTTT
X	YYYYY	ZZ	TTT

6.8.5 Using a Macro Building Table Rows

In the previous examples you have seen that a lot of repeated TEX code had to be entered to generate the table rows. Let me define a macro `\TableLine`, where the four parameters `#1` through `#4` determine the entries of the four columns:

```
\def\TableLine #1#2#3#4{%
    \hbox{%
        \hbox to 53pt {\bf #1\hfil}%
        \hskip 45pt
        \hbox to 46pt {\hfil #2}%
        \hskip 15pt
        \hbox to 31pt {\hfil #3\hfil}%
        \hskip 30pt
        \hbox to 32pt {\tt #4\hfil}%
    }
}
```

The table (excluding the headers just discussed) now can be generated as follows:

```
$$
    \vbox{
        \TableLine{XXXXXX}{YYY}{Z}{TTT}
        \TableLine{XXXXX}{YY}{ZZ}{TTTT}
        \TableLine{XXXX}{Y}{ZZZZZ}{TTTTTT}
        \TableLine{X}{YYYYY}{ZZ}{TTT}
    }
$$
```

6.8.6 Adding Horizontal Rules

Adding horizontal rules is rather straightforward. We simply use `\hrule` in the vbox which encloses the whole table. The width of the vbox is as wide as any table row (all table rows are of the same width the way the table is built). Therefore the length of the horizontal rule comes out correctly.

6.8.7 Modifications to the Discussed Table

Two additional modifications of our table should be noted:

1. In selective places `\HboxR` will be used instead of `\hbox`, printing visible hboxes. This should give you a better idea of how this table is put together.
2. Selective glues are replaced by leaders to make these glues visible.

The following source code was used in the example:

```
$$
\vbox{
    \HboxR{%                                  Row 1
        \hbox to 53pt {\bf XXXXXX\hfil}%
        \hskip 45pt
        \hbox to 46pt {\hfil YYY}%
        \hskip 15pt
        \hbox to 31pt {\hfil Z\hfil}%
        \hskip 30pt
        \hbox to 32pt {\tt TTT\hfil}%
    }
    \hbox{%                                   Row 2
        \HboxR to 53pt {\bf XXXXX\hfil}%
        \hskip 45pt
        \HboxR to 46pt {\hfil YY}%
        \hskip 15pt
        \HboxR to 31pt {\hfil ZZ\hfil}%
```

```
        \hskip 30pt
        \HboxR to 32pt {\tt TTTT\hfil}%
    }
    \hbox{%                                    Row 3
        \hbox to 53pt {\bf XXXX\hfil}%
        \leaders\hrule\hskip 45pt
        \hbox to 46pt {\hfil Y}%
        \leaders\hrule\hskip 15pt
        \hbox to 31pt {\hfil ZZZZZ\hfil}%
        \leaders\hrule\hskip 30pt
        \hbox to 32pt {\tt TTTTTT\hfil}%
    }
    \hbox{%                                    Row 4
        \hbox to 53pt {\bf X\leaders\hrule\hfil}%
        \hskip 45pt
        \hbox to 46pt {\leaders\hrule\hfil YYYYY}%
        \hskip 15pt
        \hbox to 31pt {\leaders\hrule\hfil ZZ\leaders\hrule\hfil}%
        \hskip 30pt
        \hbox to 32pt {\tt TTT\leaders\hrule\hfil}%
    }
}
$$
```

This source code generates the following table:

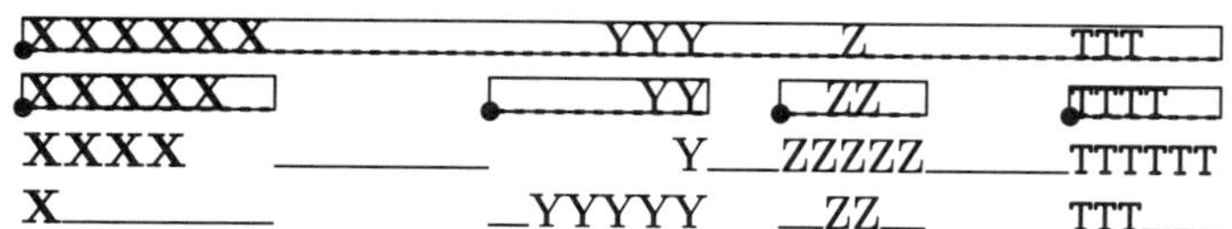

6.9 Building Tables Using `\settabs`

The `\settabs` macro of the plain format allows one to build tables using hboxes. The main difference compared to the approach for building tables shown in the previous Section is that the input is slightly simplified. The main disadvantage of the approach using `\settabs` *and* using hboxes remains the same, that you need to specify the width of columns ahead of time (this is overcome when building tables using `\halign`; see Chapters 38–41 for details).

I will only give a very brief overview of the use of `\settabs` here; for details see the TEXbook (pages 231–234). Here are the rules of building a table using `\settabs`:

1. Each line of the table, when entered, is structured as follows:

   `\+` ⟨text$_1$⟩ `&` ⟨text$_2$⟩ `&` ... `\cr`

   This should be interpreted as follows:

   (a) `\+` begins a table line. Spaces after `\+` are ignored.

(b) **&** (ampersand) advances to the next tab stop.

There is a very important difference compared with the tab key on a typewriter: assume you are currently in column i. After you have entered an ampersand, the following text will be typeset in column $i+1$, *even if* the length of the text you just entered (that is the text for column i) is *wider* than the width of column i. If that is true *overprinting* will happen (see below for an example).

Note that spaces after the ampersand are ignored.

(c) **\cr** ends a table line.

(d) You don't need to specify entries for all columns; you can enter **\cr** before you have reached the last column.

2. The *width* of all columns must be specified ahead of time. There are two possibilities of how this can be done.

   (a) After **\settabs** enter k **\columns**, where k stands for the number of columns your table is supposed to have. All columns have the same width.

   (b) Right after **\settabs** enter a *sample line* (starting with **\+** and ending with **\cr**). This line does *not* appear in the output. Instead the entries of this sample line determine the width of each column.

3. Note that **\settabs** does *not* allocate any space between columns. In particular, if you use the approach just described, where you specify the width of each column by specifying a sample line, the entries of the sample line should be the widest entries of each column "plus a little extra space."
4. The alignment of column entries are determined as follows:

   (a) Columns by default are *left justified.*

   (b) For any other type of justification use **\hfill** type of glue. For instance, **\hfill XX\hfill** will generate a centered entry **XX**. Note that **\hfil** glue will not work because it is not able to "overpower" **\hfil** glue; see 5.4.4, p. 137, for a discussion of this issue.

Here is a very short **\settabs** example which illustrates the most important features of **\settabs** (see the TEXbook for additional details). Tables generated by **\settabs** can be easily centered using display math mode.

• **ex-settabs.tip** •

```
$$
    \vbox{
```

A sample line is specified first. The table has three columns.

```
        \settabs
            \+ XXXXXXXXXX& YYY YYY YYY YYY& ZZZZZ\cr
```

Two rows, all entries are left flush. The third row has right flush entries.

```
            \+ XXX& YYY& ZZZ\cr
            \+ XXXXXX& YY& ZZZZ\cr
```

```
              \+ \hfill ABCD& \hfill EF& \hfill GHIJ\cr
```

Show that if an entry is too wide, it will extend into the next column.

```
              \+ --- --- --- --- --- --- --- --- --- --- --- ---&
                  SOMETHING& K\cr
```

You don't need an entry for all columns.

```
              \+ ABC\cr
```

That's it.

```
      }
  $$
```

• End of `ex-settabs.tip` •

The preceding source code generates the following output:

```
XXX            YYY                 ZZZ
XXXXXX         YY                  ZZZZ
          ABCD                    EFGHIJ
— — — — — — SOMETHING —            K
ABC
```

6.10 More Hbox Examples

6.10.1 Underlining, \underbar

The `\underline` primitive of TEX allows the underlining of mathematical formulas. By enclosing text in an hbox, it can be underlined as if it were a mathematical formula. For that purpose the macro `\underbar` was defined. This macro has one parameter, the text to underline. After the text was stored in box register 0, the depth of this register is set to zero, so that the underlining line is independent of any descenders in the text.

```
\def\underbar #1{%
    $
        \setbox0 = \hbox{#1}
        \dp0 = 0pt
        \m@th
        \underline{\box0}
    $%
}
```

Here is an example using this macro: `\underbar{ABC ggg}` generates ABC ggg. See 16.7, p. II-297, for more details on underlining.

6.10.2 A Macro for Signature Lines, `\SignatureLine`

Here is an example of generating signature lines: a name in parentheses is printed with a centered line above this name. The dimension in this macro by which the name is lowered below the signature line (`\lower 10pt`) was found by trial and error.

The macro `\SignatureLine` has two parameters:

- `#1`. The overall width of the line.
- `#2`. The text which is printed centered below the line.

Note that instead of the `\hbox to 0pt` construct below `\rlap` could have been used.

$\mathcal{P}'$ • `sigline.tip` •

```
\def\SignatureLine #1#2{%
    \hbox{%
        \hbox to 0pt{%
            \vrule width #1 height 0.6pt depth 0pt
            \hss        % Equivalent to \hskip -#1.
        }%
        \lower 10pt \hbox to #1{\hfil #2\hfil}%
    }%
}
```

• End of `sigline.tip` •

Here is an example using this macro. The following input was used

```
\input inputd.tip
\InputD{sigline.tip}                    % 6.10.2, p. 201.

\line{%
    \hskip 0.5in
    \SignatureLine{1.5in}{X.\ Y.\ Goofball}%
    \hfil
    \SignatureLine{1.5in}{A.\ B.\ Smith}%
    \hskip 0.5in
}
```

prints the following text:

X. Y. Goofball A. B. Smith

6.10.3 A Form Line Macro, `\FormLine`

In the next example we present a macro to print a line as it is typically used in forms: some text followed by a rule, and above this rule some entry (centered with respect to the rule). The macro \FormLine which we will define now, has the following three parameters:

- #1. The width of the whole box which will be generated by the macro (the text preceding the rule and the rule itself).
- #2. The text preceding the rule.
- #3. The text to be centered above the rule.

Note that this macro generates an hbox of width #1. Here is the definition of this macro.

$\mathcal{P}'$ • formline.tip •

```
\def\FormLine #1#2#3{%
```

Start a group to keep all changes local.

```
    {%
```

First compute in \dimen0 the length of the rule by subtracting the width of the text preceding the rule from the width of the whole text. The length of the text is determined by storing the text inside an hbox which is assigned to box register 0. Therefore, \wd0 can be used to retrieve the width of the text.

```
        \setbox0 = \hbox{#2}%
        \dimen0 = #1%
        \advance\dimen0 by -\wd0
```

Now construct the desired hbox.

```
        \hbox{%
```

Print the text preceding the rule.

```
            \box0
```

Print the rule with an effective width of zero. Macro \rlap could have been used.

```
            \hbox to 0pt{%
                \vrule width \dimen0 height 0.4pt depth 0pt
                \hss
            }%
```

Now print the text #3 centered above the rule.

```
            \raise 3pt \hbox to \dimen0 {\hfil #3\hfil}%
```

End the hbox.

```
        }%
```

End the group.

```
    }%
```

End the macro definition.

```
}
```

• End of formline.tip •

Now here is a sample application of this macro. The input

```
\InputD{formline.tip}                        % 6.10.3, p. 202.
\centerline{\FormLine{3in}{Amount: }{\tt\$23,000}}
```

generated the following output:

Amount: $23,000

Here is another example. The following input

```
    \line{%
        \hskip 20pt
        \FormLine{90pt}{Amount: }{\tt\$100,00}%
        \hfill
        \FormLine{150pt}{Due Date: }{\tt January 12, 1986}%
        \hskip 20pt
    }
```

generated the following output:

Amount: $100,00 Due Date: January 12, 1986

6.10.4 Another Interesting Example

Let me solve the following problem now: assume you would like to typeset a centered line, which is immediately followed by a right justified line. This "right justification" is understood with respect to the first (and centered) line. A useful macro is `\CenterRightLines`, which has the following two parameters:

- `#1`. The first line that is centered on the page.
- `#2`. The second line that is right justified with respect to the first line.

Let me show an application of this macro first. The following input was used:

```
\input inputd.tip
\InputD{crline.tip}                          % 6.10.4, p. 203.
\CenterRightLines{This is a centered line, like a quote or excerpt
        from a book.}%
           {The author's name.}
```

This generated the following output:

This is a centered line, like a quote or excerpt from a book.
The author's name.

Here is the definition of this macro:

$\mathcal{P}'$ • crline.tip •

```
\def\CenterRightLines #1#2{
```

Determine width of text to be centered.

```
    \setbox 0 = \hbox{#1}
```

Determine distance this text must have from the left margin of the page. This distance is of course identical to the distance from the end of the same text to the right margin. The length of this distance is stored in `\dimen0`.

```
17        \dimen0 = \hsize
18        \advance\dimen0 by -\wd0
19        \divide\dimen0 by 2
```

Now print the first line.

```
20        \rightline{#1\hskip\dimen0}
```

Now print the second line which has the same distance as the first line from the right margin of the text.

```
21        \rightline{#2\hskip\dimen0}
22    }
```

• End of `crline.tip` •

Note that the first line could have been printed in a variety of different ways (line 6 of the above source code), among which are:

1. `\centerline{#1}`.
2. `\leftline{\hskip\wd0 #1}`.
3. `\hbox{\hskip\wd0 #1}`.

See 40.1.3, p. IV-297, for another solution to the same problem, this time based on `\halign`.

6.11 \hidewidth

The plain format macro `\hidewidth` is defined as follows:

```
\newskip\hideskip
\hideskip = -1000pt plus 1fill
\def\hidewidth{\hskip\hideskip}
```

As the name of this macro suggests, it "hides the width of some entity," because, if necessary, the glue defined through this macro can stretch as far as necessary.

Now compare the following two hboxes:

```
\hbox to \hsize{\hidewidth XXX\hidewidth}
\hbox to \hsize{\hfil      XXX\hfil}
```

First compute the *natural* width where stretchabilities and shrinkabilities are ignored. The natural width of the *first* box is a *large negative* value because the natural width of the two `hidewidth` generated glues is −2000pt each. The width of the three characters "XXX" can be ignored in this case. On the other hand, the *natural width* of the *second box* is the widths of the three characters "XXX," because the natural widths of the `\hfil`-generated glues are zero.

The output generated by both boxes is the same: the text "XXX" centered on the line. The stretchability of glues in both boxes is infinite and the badness of both boxes is zero.

6.12 Infinite Glues and Hboxes

Infinite glues may be used in hboxes of predetermined width. Recall that in the **`\centerline`** macro, equal amount of stretchability of the infinite glues inserted to the left and to the right of the text makes the glues symmetrical causing the text to be printed centered. Here is a brief example:

```
\hbox to \hsize{%
    \hskip 0pt plus 1fil
    {\tt Sample}%
    \hskip 0pt plus 1fil
}%
```

In the following width equation, the infinite glue's natural widths are zero, their *stretchabilities* are regarded as unknowns x. Function wd is supposed to compute the width of a string.

$$\backslash\texttt{hsize} = 0 + x + \mathrm{wd}(\texttt{Sample}) + 0 + x$$

This equation solved for x becomes:

$$x = \frac{\backslash\texttt{hsize} - \mathrm{wd}(\texttt{Sample})}{2}$$

This result, of course, is exactly what we expected: both glues will stretch by half the difference between the line width and the width of the text to be centered.

Here is another example. The first glue has a natural width different from zero, and the remaining space is divided up in a 2:1 ratio.

```
\hbox to \hsize{%
    \hskip 1in plus 2fil
    {\tt Sample}%
    \hskip 0pt plus 1fil
}%
```

The resulting width equation reads (unit inch):

$$\backslash\texttt{hsize} = 1 + 2x + \mathrm{wd}(\texttt{Sample}) + 0 + x$$

This equation solved for x becomes (unit inch):

$$x = \frac{\backslash\texttt{hsize} - 1 - \mathrm{wd}(\texttt{sample})}{3}$$

In other words, the distance of the word "**`Sample`**" from the left margin of the text is $1 + 2 * x$ (unit inch again).

6.13 Token Parameters \everyhbox and \everyvbox

TeX has a token parameter **\everyhbox**, which, as its name suggests, is evaluated each time an **\hbox** command is executed. There is also a **\everyvbox** token register, which is evaluated each time a **\vbox**, **\vtop** or **\vcenter** command is executed.

So far I have not come up with any "deeply useful" applications of these token registers. But here is something you may enjoy: I used these token registers to count the number of hboxes and vboxes generated when processing this series. In particular the display verbatim mode used in this series (see 18.3.12, p. III-43) generates numerous hboxes. To do so the following TeX source file is read in at the beginning of each part of this series:

$\mathcal{P}$ • evhvbox.tip •

```
\newcount\HBoxCount
\everyhbox = {\global\advance\HBoxCount by 1 }
\newcount\VBoxCount
\everyvbox = {\global\advance\VBoxCount by 1 }
```

This TeX source file includes the definition of the following macro **\EndEveryBox**, which is invoked at the end of every part. This macro writes the number of hboxes and vboxes generated so far to the log file.

```
\def\EndEveryBox{%
     \wlog{}%
     \wlog{HBOXCOUNT \the\HBoxCount}%
     \wlog{VBOXCOUNT \the\VBoxCount}%
     \wlog{}%
}
```

• End of evhvbox.tip •

I then wrote a small command procedure that would collect these counter values from the log files of the various parts of this series and would add all these values. The result is when processing this series 175929 hboxes and 17417 vboxes are generated.

6.14 Summary

- There are two different box types, hboxes (discussed in this chapter), and vboxes (subject of the next chapter).
- All boxes have three dimensions: a height, depth and width. They also have a baseline and a reference point.
- Hboxes are built using **\hbox**. The material in an hbox is collected left to right.

- Hboxes can contain characters (and font changes), horizontal glue (and leaders), other boxes generated in a variety of ways and potentially raised and lowered, and rules generated using `vrule`. If the height and/or depth of a rule in an hbox is undetermined, the rule inherits those dimensions from the hbox it is part of.
- The height and the depth of an hbox are determined by the maximum height and depth of any item the hbox contains. The natural width of a box is determined by the sums of all widths of its components. The user can force the actual width to be different using the `\hbox to` ⟨dimen⟩ and `\hbox spread` ⟨dimen⟩ construct.
- Zero width hboxes can be used to trick TeX into not moving the current reference point despite the fact that the item being printed has a non-zero width.
- Single lines of text can be placed in a variety of different ways using one of the `\...line` type of macros.
- Tables can be built very easily using hboxes.

7 Vertical Boxes

A good comprehension of Chapter 6 for understanding this chapter is useful, because, when possible, I will explain a vertical box concept referring to the corresponding hbox concept.

7.1 Basics of Vertical Boxes

7.1.1 Primitives `\vbox`, `\vtop` and `\vcenter` for the Generation of Vboxes

Generating hboxes we discussed *one* instruction, `\hbox`. To generate vertical boxes *three* instructions exist: `\vbox`, `\vtop` and `\vcenter` exist. These three instructions will be compared later in detail; for now simply remember that the main difference between these instructions is where the reference point of the box being generated is positioned.

7.1.2 Making Vboxes Visible

Similar to the way we used the `\HboxR` macro in the preceding chapter, we will use macros `\VboxR`, `\VtopR` and `\VcenterR` in this chapter in place of `\vbox`, `\vtop` and `\vcenter` to generate visible vboxes; see 9.3.9, p. 334, for details.

7.1.3 Comparing Hboxes and Vboxes

Let me compare horizontal and vertical boxes briefly (note the concepts mentioned below are explained in further detail in the rest of this chapter; the basics of this list should be understandable now):

1. When TeX collects the material of a vbox, it is in *inner vertical mode*. TeX is in *restricted horizontal mode* when building an hbox.
2. Material in a vertical box is accumulated *top to bottom*, in a horizontal box the material is accumulated *left to right*.
3. There are three different instructions to build vboxes (`\vbox`, `\vtop` and `\vcenter`), whereas there is only one instruction (`\hbox`) to build a horizontal box.
4. Just as hboxes can be used to prevent "horizontal breaks," vboxes can be used to prevent "vertical breaks" (page breaks). For instance, a word included in an hbox will not be hyphenated inside a paragraph, a paragraph included inside a vbox will not be broken across two pages.
5. The curly braces surrounding the content of a vbox (using either of the commands `\vbox`, `\vtop` or `\vcenter`) establishes an implicit group. The same is true for the curly braces of the `\hbox` command. See 19.4.10, p. III-106, for details on implicit groups.
6. Inside a vbox inline math mode as well as display math mode can be used, whereas inside an hbox only inline math mode can be used.

7.1.4 The Vertical List of a Vbox

When the material for a vertical box is collected TeX is in *inner vertical mode*. Similar to the horizontal list of an hbox (6.2.2, p. 163) there is a *vertical list* used to collect the material of a vbox. I will now discuss the items which can go on the vertical list of a vbox.

1. *Characters* can be stored inside a vbox. Note that there is an essential difference between the treatment of characters in vboxes and hboxes. While in an hbox characters are simply collected left to right, in vboxes characters are regarded as part of paragraphs. In other words, it is more accurate to say that *paragraphs* (rather than characters) can be stored inside vboxes, and these paragraphs, of course, contain characters. A paragraph in a vbox can be terminated by any of the usual ways of terminating a paragraph (see 10.5, p. II-12). Such a paragraph is also terminated by the end of the vbox in which it is contained.

   The main difference between building a paragraph inside a vbox compared to the regular way of building a paragraph is the fact that the page breaking algorithm is not called after the paragraph has been built. Therefore a vbox that is too high ("too high" with respect to some unspecified value) is not broken up.

   All the parameters which control the shape of a paragraph are valid inside a vbox. For instance, `\hsize` controls the width of the paragraph typeset inside a vbox. `\parskip` determines the separation of paragraphs within one vbox. Note that if the first paragraph inside a vbox is not preceded by any other material TeX will *not* insert `\parskip` before this paragraph. See 10.8, p. II-25, for details on `\parskip`.

2. *Boxes.* Other boxes can be stored inside a vbox.
   (a) These boxes can be vboxes or hboxes.
   (b) A box can be retrieved from a box register with `\box`, `\copy`, `\unhbox`, `\unvbox`, `\unhcopy` and `\unvcopy` and then become part of a vbox.
   (c) A box can be moved left and right using `\moveleft` and `\moveright`. Each of these instructions must be followed by a dimension specifying the amount of movement to the right and left. This dimension in turn must be followed by the box which is being moved to the left and right.

       A box inside a vbox *cannot* be moved up and down with `\raise` or `\lower` (one would have to use vertical glue for that purpose). In a similar way one cannot use `\moveright` and `\moveleft` inside a horizontal box to move items left and right (one would have to use horizontal glue under those circumstances).
3. *Vertical glue.* Explicit vertical glue can be generated inside a vertical box using `\vskip` to skip up and down. Note that positive vertical glue causes TeX to skip downwards. Implicit vertical glue can also appear on the vertical list of a vbox. See 5.1, item 2, p. 121, for a general discussion of glue.

   Note that *vertical leaders* fall into the same category and that we can look at them as a form of vertical glue (vertical leaders are seldom used).
4. *Vertical kern.* Vertical glue and kern relate the same way horizontal glue and kern relate; see 5.4.8, p. 140, for details.
5. *Horizontal rules.* Horizontal rules can be inserted in a vbox with the `\hrule` command. See 5.7, p. 154, has details on this command and dimensions on horizontal rules. rules. This chapter also gives some additional examples.
6. *Math mode material.* Inline or display math formulas can be inserted inside `\vboxes`. Note that the fact that inline math mode equations are allowed in vboxes should not surprise you because they are really part of paragraphs, and paragraphs are legal in vboxes.
7. *Penalties.* Penalties (vertical penalties) are discussed in 5.8, p. 157, and are of interest in particular if a vertical box is unboxed and split by the page breaking algorithm or through `\vsplit`.
8. *Marks* and *insertion material* can also appear on a vertical list. They will be discussed later, and are of lesser importance here where we discuss the geometry of vboxes.

7.2 Building Simple Vboxes

We will now present some vbox examples containing paragraphs and other boxes. You will see a great variety of things you can do with vboxes. Vbox-based examples are in general more interesting than hbox-based examples, because they offer quite a large variety. Still, the examples should be easy to understand. As usual you are encouraged to enter those examples yourself and to experiment with TEX.

7.2.1 A Paragraph Inside a Vbox, Centering a Vbox

This is an example showing how two paragraphs are enclosed inside a vbox and how this vbox is centered using display math mode. Note that `\hsize` is set inside this box, and that this setting of `\hsize` only affects the two paragraphs inside the vbox, because the curly braces of a `\vbox` command establish an implicit group. Note also that the first paragraph is *not* preceded by `\parskip` glue, because this paragraph is the very first item of the vbox.

Here is the input for our example:

```
\input inputd.tip
\InputD{box-mac.tip}                     % 9.3.14, p. 343.
$$
    \VboxR{
        \hsize = 3.0in
        \parskip = 12pt
        This is just some text, so we can show that a
        vbox can be centered with display math mode.
        It's easy and straightforward.

        And here is another short paragraph. Note that this
        paragraph will appear together with the previous paragraph,
        on the same page. And because we used the {\tt\string\VboxR}
        command you can see the vbox being built here.
    }
$$
\bye
```

The output generated by the preceding TEX source code reads as follows:

This is just some text, so we can show that a vbox can be centered with display math mode. It's easy and straightforward.

And here is another short paragraph. Note that this paragraph will appear together with the previous paragraph, on the same page. And because we used the `\VboxR` command you can see the vbox being built here.

Note that in the next example (although the very first item of the vbox is glue of zero length) the first paragraph is preceded by `\parskip` glue. Here is the input used:

```
\input inputd.tip
```

```
\InputD{box-mac.tip}                        % 9.3.14, p. 343.
$$
    \VboxR{
        \hsize = 3.0in
        \parskip = 12pt
        \vskip 0pt
        This is just some text, so we can show that a
        {\tt\string\vbox} can be centered with display math mode.
        It's easy and straightforward.

        And here is another short paragraph. Note that this
        paragraph will appear together with the previous paragraph,
        on the same page. And because we used the {\tt\string\VboxR}
        command you can see the vbox being built here.
    }
$$
\bye
```

The output generated by the preceding TEX source code is as follows:

This is just some text, so we can show that a \vbox can be centered with display math mode. It's easy and straightforward.

And here is another short paragraph. Note that this paragraph will appear together with the previous paragraph, on the same page. And because we used the \VboxR command you can see the vbox being built here.

7.2.2 Vertical Glue and Other Boxes Inside Vboxes

Here is an example demonstration how vertical glue and boxes can be used inside a vbox. Note that some of the boxes are extracted from a box register. The following input was used for the example.

```
\input inputd.tip
\InputD{box-mac.tip}                        % 9.3.14, p. 343.
$$
    \VboxR{
        \setbox 0 = \hbox{Some box, from box register 0.}
        \setbox 1 = \hbox{Some box, from box register 1.}
        \copy0
        \vskip 10pt
        \copy0
        \vskip 5pt
```

```
            \box1
            \vskip 5pt
            \copy0
            \hbox{And another box.}
            \vskip 5pt
            \vbox{%
                \hsize = 2.0in
                \raggedright
                This is so wonderful. Now we show
                that it is even possible to have a vbox
                inside a vbox.
            }
        }
    $$
    \bye
```

The preceding source code generates the following output:

Some box, from box register 0.

Some box, from box register 0.

Some box, from box register 1.

Some box, from box register 0.
And another box.
This is so wonderful. Now we show that it is even possible to have a vbox inside a vbox.

7.2.3 More on Boxes Inside Vboxes, `\leavevmode`

Now we will discuss some examples with horizontal boxes inside a vbox. I will also introduce the `\leavevmode` macro.

The first character of each paragraph has a dual function: it tells TEX to start a paragraph and to print this character (see 10.4.1, p. II-11, for details).

Under certain circumstances TEX must be told explicitly to start a paragraph. This is in particular the case, if the very first item of a paragraph is an hbox. Let us discuss this using the following example (`\parindent` is non-zero so you very easily see where a paragraph is started):

```
$$
    \vbox{%
        \hsize = 2.70in
        \parskip = 12pt
        \parindent = 15pt
        \raggedright

```

```
8              \hbox{1: A box}               % 1st block.
9              \hbox{2: Another one}
10             \hbox{3: A third one}
11
12             4: A paragraph starts here. % 2nd block.
13             \hbox{5: Box A}
14             \hbox{6: Box B}
15             \hbox{7: Box C.}
16
17             \leavevmode                   % 3rd block.
18             \hbox{8: Box X}
19             \hbox{9: Box Y}
20             \hbox{10: Box Z}
21             11:~Some text here.
22         }
23     $$
```

The preceding source code generates the following output:

1: A box
2: Another one
3: A third one

4: A paragraph starts here. 5: Box A
6: Box B 7: Box C.

8: Box X 9: Box Y 10: Box Z 11: Some
text here.

Now let me discuss in more detail what happened.

1. The first three hboxes (1:, 2: and 3:) are regarded as three separate boxes that are accumulated vertically inside the vbox. TEX started the vbox in inner vertical mode, therefore these three boxes are collected top to down.
2. In the second block the "4" of "4: A paragraph starts here" begins a paragraph. The hboxes of source code lines 12, 13 and 14 are part of the paragraph. This paragraphs is ended by the empty line 15 of the above source code. The hboxes of source code lines 12, 13 and 14 are part of the paragraph. If one omitted the `\hbox{...}` around source code lines 12, 13 and 14, TEX would be able to generate a line break in the middle of one of the three text pieces of texts includes in the three hboxes.
3. The third block of examples starting with `\leavevmode` in source code line 16 shows how it is possible to begin a paragraph with an hbox by using the `\leavevmode` macro. This instruction tells TEX to begin a paragraph. Therefore the following three hboxes (source code lines 17–19) are regarded as part of a paragraph and are printed left to right and so forth, identical to 2. of this list.

Let me rewrite the input to the previous examples to resemble the resulting output more closely. Note that although the input was reformatted, no change in the output itself takes place.

```
$$
    \vbox{%
        \hsize = 2.35in
        \raggedright
        \parskip = 12pt
        \hbox{1: A box}
        \hbox{2: Another one}
        \hbox{3: A third one}

        A paragraph starts here. \hbox{4: Box A} \hbox{5: Box B}
        \hbox{6: Box C.}

        \leavevmode \hbox{7: Box X} \hbox{8: Box Y}
        \hbox{9: Box Z} Some text here.
    }
$$
```

When `\leavevmode` is used in horizontal mode, i.e., inside a paragraph, it has no effect. Look at the following input:

```
$$
    \vbox{
        \hsize = 3.0in
        This is \leavevmode fun and it does indeed \leavevmode
        work. This is just a little text and now we are done
        with this test so good luck!
    }
$$
```

This input generates the following output:

This is fun and it does indeed work. This is just a little text and now we are done with this test so good luck!

Here is another example for `\leavevmode`. For this series I needed a macro to mark TEX's primitives in the index by a small asterisk. To do so I would use the `\llap` macro (which generates an hbox), and because this appears at the beginning of a paragraph a `\leavevmode` had to be inserted. The macro `\PrimitiveMarker` generates the desired marker.

$\mathcal{P}'$ • `primmark.tip` •

```
\def\PrimitiveMarker{%
    \leavevmode
```

Start a group because of the following font size and typeface change.

```
    {%
        \footnotesize\tt
```

Finally print the marker.

```
        \llap{*}%
```

```
    }%
}
```

• End of `primmark.tip` •

7.2.4 Moving Items Inside a Vbox Horizontally, `\moveleft`, `\moveright`

Discussing hboxes you learned that it was possible to raise and lower such boxes using `\raise` and `\lower`. To move items inside an hbox to the left and right, horizontal glue is used. In the case of a vbox, material is collected vertically and can be moved up and down using vertical glue. In order to shift material left and right within a vbox `\moveleft` and `\moveright` can be used. Both instructions must be followed by a dimension which specifies the amount of the movement and a box, the item to be moved. These two instructions are obviously orthogonal to `\raise` and `\lower`.

This is a simple example using `\moveleft` and `\moveright`:

```
\input inputd.tip
\InputD{box-mac.tip}                      % 9.3.14, p. 343.
$$
    \VboxR{
        \hbox{1: This is a line.}
        \moveleft 0.5in\HboxR{2: This is another line.}
        \moveright0.5in\HboxR{3: This is the last line.}
    }
$$
\bye
```

This input generates the following output:

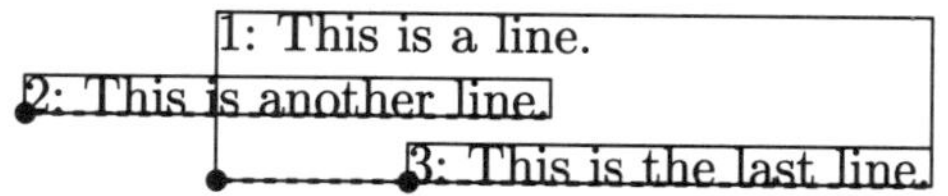

34.5, p. IV-66, contains an application of `\moveright` in the context of an output routine: a whole page is shifted to the left or to the right before being written to the `dvi` file, depending on whether it is a left-hand or a right-hand page of a document printed double sided.

7.3 Line Spacing and Interline Glue

In computing line spacing, TEX by default prints lines with equal vertical distance (equal distance between the baselines of these lines), unless there is material of *excessive height or depth* in a line. In that case the line spacing is corrected by TEX in such a way that lines do not overlap.

In general, the line spacing in TeX is controlled by the glue parameter **\baselineskip**, which determines *the distance between consecutive baselines.* **\baselineskip = 12pt** is the usual value for a single line spaced document, if the basic font size is 10 pt. More details are to follow in this Section.

The default of **\baselineskip** is zero as it is the case for any other glue parameter. Usually, of course, this parameter is set to a value such as 12 pt (as it is the case in the plain format).

Note that when we talk about line spacing then the term *lines* is not really quite accurate. It would be more accurate to say *boxes*, but for most cases these boxes are the lines of a paragraph. Such a "line" could be generated by a macro such as **\centerline** or directly (**\hbox**).

7.3.1 Overlapping of Lines Is Prevented

The following is a brief example of how TeX will not allow lines run into each other, when the default settings of the plain format are in effect. By setting **\baselineskip** to zero we in effect told TeX to print all lines on top of each other. But TeX will refuse to do so. Here is the source code of the example being used:

```
$$
    \vbox{
        \baselineskip = 0pt
        \hsize = 3.2in
        \TeX{} is much more clever than you think. A value of zero
        for {\tt\string\baselineskip} should print all lines
        on top of each other. But \TeX{} will not do that, at least
        if the default settings for line spacing are in effect.
    }
$$
```

The above source code generates the following output:

TeX is much more clever than you think. A value of zero for **\baselineskip** should print all lines on top of each other. But TeX will not do that, at least if the default settings for line spacing are in effect.

As mentioned earlier TeX accommodates lines with material of excessive height or depth. Such lines can be, for instance, generated by inline mathematical equations with fractions, superscripts or subscripts. Here is the example (actually it does not take that many superscripts to generate a formula of excessive height): $a^{b^{c^{d^{e^{f}}}}}$. Observe how the distance between the line preceding the mathematical formula and the line containing the mathematical formula was increased by TeX compared with the spacing between all other lines.

7.3.2 Changing \baselineskip

Here is another example (**\baselineskip** is set to 18 pt), resulting in a one-and-a-half line spacing. The following input was used:

```
$$
    \vbox{
        \baselineskip = 18pt
        \hsize = 3.2in
        Here is an example with a value of 18~pt for
        {\tt\string\baselineskip}. This spaces out the
        text more than usual. Of course you could set
        {\tt\string\baselineskip} to an even larger
        value.
    }
$$
```

The above source code generates the following output:

Here is an example with a value of 18 pt for **\baselineskip**. This spaces out the text more than usual. Of course you could set **\baselineskip** to an even larger value.

Let us see what happens, when **\baselineskip** is changed repeatedly in a sequence of boxes. Here is the TEX source code used (empty lines are inserted for improved readability and have no influence on the meaning of the TEX code):

```
$$
    \vbox{
        \baselineskip = 12pt
        \hbox{1: Fun}
        \hbox{2: Also fun}

        \baselineskip = 20pt

        \hbox{3: Next line}
        \hbox{4: Another one}

        \baselineskip = 12pt

        \hbox{5: There is a line}
        \hbox{6: That's it}

        \baselineskip = 20pt

        \hbox{7: Last line}
    }
$$
```

This input generates the following output. Note that when **\baselineskip** is changed it changes the interline spacing between the preceding and the following line.

1: Fun
2: Also fun

3: Next line

4: Another one
5: There is a line
6: That's it

7: Last line

Changing `\baselineskip` in the middle of a paragraph is a different story; see 12.2, p. II-110.

7.3.3 Typical Settings of `\baselineskip`

Note that `\baselineskip` is a *glue* parameter, not a *dimension* parameters as you might assume first. Therefore, `\baselineskip` can be set to a value allowing for stretching and shrinking. Normally though, and this is the assumption we will work under in general, `\baselineskip` is assumed to have no stretchability and shrinkability. Therefore one generally looks at `\baselineskip` as a dimension and not a glue.

See 15.4.3, p. II-258, for proper settings of `\baselineskip` given a specific font size.

7.3.4 Explaining `\baselineskip`, `\lineskiplimit`, and `\lineskip`

There are all together *three* parameters which control the line spacing in TeX (not only `\baselineskip`).

1. `\baselineskip` is, as mentioned before, a *glue parameter*. It specifies the *desired distance* between the baselines of two consecutive lines or boxes.

   The plain format's default of this parameter is 12 pt.
2. `\lineskiplimit` is a *dimension parameter*. Its value specifies a threshold distance: if lines were spaced out using `\baselineskip` and that would make these lines closer than `\lineskiplimit` (measured from the bottom of the preceding line to the top of the next line), then TeX will take some corrective action.

   The default for this parameter is 0 pt in the plain format. The default for `\lineskiplimit` is zero, because the default setting of `\baselineskip` would normally give the proper interline distance.

3. `\lineskip` is a *glue parameter.* The amount of glue specified through this register is inserted (instead of `\baselineskip`), if the lines printed `\baselineskip` apart would be too close.

   The default for this parameter is 1 pt in the plain format. The glue value assigned to this register (similar to `\baselineskip`), is normally glue which cannot stretch or shrink.

   By setting this parameter to 1pt (rather than 0 pt) a minimum distance of 1 pt is ensured between two lines which are regarded as too close.

7.3.5 Computing the Interline Glue

Let us now discuss precisely how the interline glue is computed. Note that the desired distance between two consecutive lines, more precisely the desired distance between the baselines of those lines, is `\baselineskip`. TEX will try to print the lines according to this specification. For the following discussion let us talk about two consecutive lines a and b. The variable d_a stands for the depth of line a, h_b stands for the height of line b.

1. First we need to define what "two lines are too close" means precisely. For that purpose TEX computes the distance $v = \texttt{\baselineskip} - d_a - h_b$ which is obviously the amount of vertical space between the two lines a and b, if these two lines are printed `\baselineskip` apart.

   There are two different cases of how v and the value of `\lineskiplimit` relate:

   (a) If $v \geq \texttt{\lineskiplimit}$, then TEX regards the two lines *as far apart enough.*

   This is the normal case if `\baselineskip` is set to a "reasonable" value and if neither line is excessively high or deep. In this case vertical glue in the amount of v is inserted between the two lines a and b. Therefore the two lines a and b will be printed `\baselineskip` apart (the distance measured between the two baselines of the two lines) because $v + d_a + h_b = \texttt{\baselineskip}$.

   Recall that the default for this threshold distance `\lineskiplimit` in the plain format is 0 pt; in other words unless printing two lines `\baselineskip` apart would lead to overlap, the lines are regarded as not being too close.

   (b) If $v < \texttt{\lineskiplimit}$, TEX regards the two lines as *too close.*

   When this is the case, vertical glue in the amount of `\lineskip` is inserted between the two lines a and b. The two baselines of a and b are therefore printed $\texttt{\lineskip} + d_a + h_b$ apart.

The following additional details (ignored in the preceding discussion) are important:

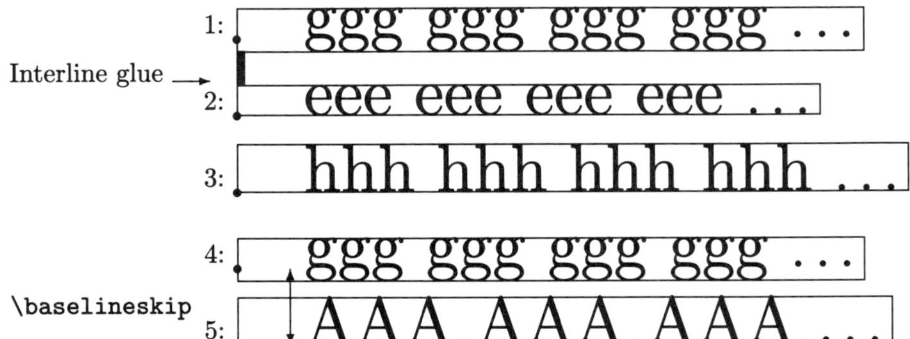

Figure 7.1. Illustration of interline glue.

1. 7.3.8, p. 226, states that any additional vertical glue between two lines *a* and *b* is ignored during the above interline computation is concerned.
2. 7.3.9, p. 227, discusses the fact that it is not really the depth of line *a* which is used to compute the interline glue but the content of the dimension parameter `\prevdepth`. This is less important for the usual workings of the interline glue computations because TEX automatically stores the depth of the preceding line in `\prevdepth`. This discussion also explains `\nointerlineskip` which prevents the insertion of interline glue completely.
3. No interline glue is inserted between a box and a rule, a rule and a box or two rules; see 7.3.14, p. 233, for a discussion of this issue.

7.3.6 An Example of Interline Glue Computations

Let us look at examples of the computation of interline glue. In Fig. 7.1 on this page the reference points of all five lines are indicated by bullets. Note that the lines have varying height and depth, and while they are spaced out equally (measuring the distance between baselines) the amount of interline glue inserted between the various lines is actually quite different. For instance, the amount of interline glue inserted between lines 3 and 4 is much larger (because of the zero depth of line 3 and the relatively small height of line 4) than the interline glue inserted between lines 4 and 5 (because of the relatively large depth of line 4 and the large height of line 5).

Fig. 7.1 on this page is somewhat misleading in that lines usually do not contain always the same character. The same character in each line was used in the figure to demonstrate that the space between the lines (measured from the bottom of a line to the top of the next line) is usually not the same when the desired effect is to keep the distance between the baselines the same.

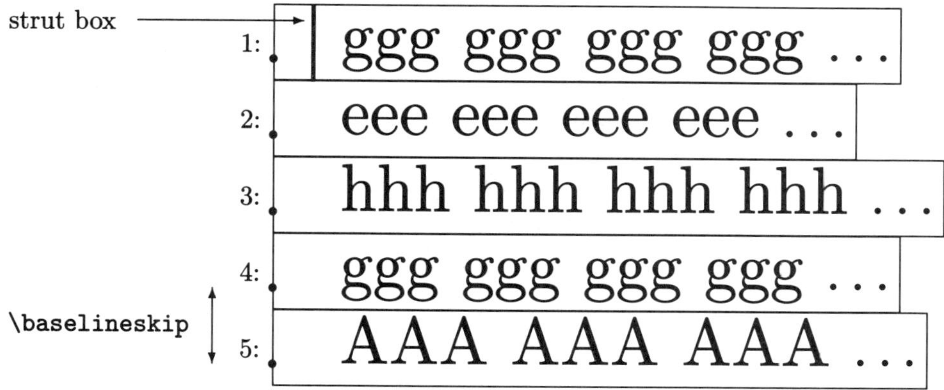

Figure 7.2. Illustration of using struts to control line spacing.

In Fig. 7.1 on the previous page we have four different cases:

line 1 / 2:	line 1: descenders	line 2: no ascenders
line 2 / 3:	line 2: no descenders	line 3: ascenders
line 3 / 4:	line 3: no descenders	line 4: no ascenders
line 4 / 5:	line 4: ascenders	line 5: descenders

In general you should note that the terminology used in the context of line spacing tends to be imprecise: one states "`\baselineskip` glue is inserted between lines," but the amount of interline glue actually inserted is less (because the depth of the preceding line and the height of the following line are subtracted); although the computation of glue is based on the value of `\baselineskip`.

Let us look at another example of the interline glue computations of TEX. The following source file is used:

• `ex-intlgl.tip` •

```
\vbox{%
    \hsize = 3in
```

Initialize all three line spacing controlling parameters.

```
    \baselineskip = 12pt        % Identical to default.
    \lineskiplimit = 0pt        % Identical to default.
    \lineskip = 15pt            % Large value, not default.
```

Load a "very big" font.

```
    \font\mybiggy = cmr17 scaled \magstep 3
    Let me write a few lines of text. Just so we have
    some sample lines. Let's look at the spacing now
    when we insert a character of excessive height
    {\mybiggy ``T''} as we just did. Suddenly there
    is a huge space between the line
    preceding the ``big~T'' and the current line.
    That's it for now.
}
```

• End of `ex-intlgl.tip` •

Let me write a few lines of text. Just so we have some sample lines. Let's look at the spacing now when we insert a character of excessive height

"T" as we just did. Suddenly there is a huge space between the line preceding the "big T" and the current line. That's it for now.

Figure 7.3. Another interline glue computation example.

This source code generates the output in Figure 7.3 on this page. Let us analyze this figure. The line with the "big T" in it is the only line in the above example regarded as "excessively high," and therefore TEX will *not* use glue based on `\baselineskip` but will insert vertical glue in the amount of `\lineskip` between the line containing the "big T" and the preceding line. Because of the large value of `\lineskip`, these two lines are spaced apart quite far (the rather large value for `\lineskip` is atypical and was chosen here simply for the example).

7.3.7 Visualizing Interline Glue Computations

Studying this TEX source code and the log file generated by this source code will illustrate TEX's interline glue computations. A paragraph is stored inside a vbox, which is assigned to a box register. The box register's content is then dumped into the log file using `\ShowBoxDepthOne`. See 4.5.15, p. 111, for a description of the `\ShowBoxDepthOne` macro.

Here is the TEX source code of the example:

• `show-base.tip` •

```
\input inputd.tip
\InputD{shboxes.tip}                    % 4.5.15, p. 111.
```

Load some large font.

```
\font\mybiggy = cmr17 scaled \magstep3
```

The plain format values are used in the experiment and repeated for clarity only.

```
\baselineskip = 12pt
\lineskip = 1pt
\lineskiplimit = 0pt
```

Now typeset one paragraph (`\hfil\break` generates explicit line breaks inside this paragraph; see 10.10.1, p. II-36) and store it in a vbox. This vbox is assigned to a box register and then dumped into the log file.

```
\setbox 0 = \vbox{%
    ggg ggg ggg ggg\hfil\break
    eee eee eee eee\hfil\break
```

```
    hhh hhh hhh hhh\hfil\break
    ggg ggg ggg ggg\hfil\break
    AAA AAA AAA AAA\hfil\break
    {\mybiggy Tg}\hfil\break
    This is just some regular text, which contains all type of
    characters, descenders, ascenders---take what you like, and
    you would find it. We need a little more text, so you can see
    that usually in every line there is a descender and an ascender
    and so this way the value of the interline glue is in effect
    always the same. We want to have some more lines in this
    paragraph---the alternative would have been to make the
    horizontal size smaller.
}
```

Dump this box into the log file.

```
\ShowBoxDepthOne{0}
\bye
```

• End of `show-base.tip` •

The preceding TeX source code generates the following log file. Compare the input closely with Fig. 7.1, p. 222. Observe that while in the log file TeX reports that `\baselineskip` was inserted between two lines, it is of course not glue in the amount of `\baselineskip` which is inserted. It simply means that the computation of the glue inserted was based on `\baselineskip`.

• `show-base.log` •

```
This is TeX, C Version 3.14 (...)
**&/usr/local/tex/lib/fmt/plain show-base.tip
(show-base.tip (inputd.tip
(namedef.tip
) (inputdl.tip
\@InputDStream=\write0
))
(shboxes.tip
)
> \box0=
\vbox(135.45796+0.0)x469.75499
.\hbox(4.30554+1.94444)x469.75499, glue set 379.75482fil []
.\penalty 150
.\glue(\baselineskip) 5.75002
.\hbox(4.30554+0.0)x469.75499, glue set 406.42169fil []
.\glue(\baselineskip) 5.05556
.\hbox(6.94444+0.0)x469.75499, glue set 393.08813fil []
.\glue(\baselineskip) 7.69446
.\hbox(4.30554+1.94444)x469.75499, glue set 399.75482fil []
.\glue(\baselineskip) 3.22224
.\hbox(6.83331+0.0)x469.75499, glue set 369.75482fil []
.\glue(\lineskip) 1.0
.\hbox(20.4+5.80798)x469.75499, glue set 436.12653fil []
.\glue(\lineskip) 1.0
.\hbox(6.94444+1.94444)x469.75499, glue set 0.1007 []
.\glue(\baselineskip) 3.11111
```

```
.\hbox(6.94444+1.94444)x469.75499, glue set 0.15697 []
.\glue(\baselineskip) 3.11111
.\hbox(6.94444+1.94444)x469.75499, glue set 0.1774 []
.\glue(\baselineskip) 3.11111
.\hbox(6.94444+1.94444)x469.75499, glue set 0.3439 []
.\penalty 150
.\glue(\baselineskip) 3.11111
.\hbox(6.94444+0.0)x469.75499, glue set 416.83826fil []

<to be read again>
}
l.23 \ShowBoxDepthOne{0}

)
No pages of output.
```

Let us briefly discuss one specific example of the interline computations in this log file. The depth of the very first line is 1.94444 pt, the height of the second line is 4.30554 pt. Subtracting both amounts from the value of `\baselineskip` (which is 12 pt) results in an interline glue value of 5.75002 pt. This is exactly the interline glue inserted by TEX between the first and second line of the paragraph.

The second observation discussing the preceding log file focuses on what is a typical value for the interline glue. Note that once the first six lines of the paragraph are completed (all of them are generated using explicit line break instructions) the amount of interline glue inserted is always the same. The reason for this is very simple: because an average line contains at least one character with an ascender and at least one character with a descender, the height and depths of most lines are all the same. And this in turn means that the interline glue computed is always the same.

It is, by the way, rather important that you appreciate using a box register to analyze TEX's processing: some material is saved in a box register, which is then dumped into the log file.

7.3.8 Interline Glue Computations and `\vskips`

Interline glue computation of two lines a and b is done *disregarding* any other vertical glue between the two lines. For example, assume there are two lines a and b for which the interline glue is computed as 4 pt (assume also that these two lines are not of excessive height and depth and therefore this interline glue computation is based on `\baselineskip`). Now assume that a `\vskip 3pt` instruction is inserted between these two lines. Even under those circumstances TEX will still compute the interline glue as 4 pt. Therefore the distance between the two baselines of those two lines will be `\baselineskip` + 3 pt when printed.

7.3.9 The Depth of the Preceding Box or Line, \prevdepth

I mentioned briefly before that it is really **\prevdepth** (and not the depth of the last box added to the current vertical list) which is taken into account when TeX computes the interline glue. This distinction is normally not important because TeX loads **\prevdepth** automatically with the depth of the preceding box. You are allowed to change **\prevdepth** although this is usually unnecessary.

Let me discuss two instances where **\prevdepth** is relevant:

1. If **\prevdepth** ≤ -1000 pt, then *no interline glue at all* is inserted by TeX. The next Subsection discusses the macro **\nointerlineskip**, which suppresses the interline glue between the current and the next following line by setting **\prevdepth** to -1000 pt. Note that no interline glue is inserted at all (rather than interline glue of zero length).
2. TeX initializes **\prevdepth** to -1000 pt at the beginning of a vertical list, i.e., at the beginning of a vbox. This is the reason why the first box of the vertical list of a vbox is *not* preceded by interline glue.

   The same remark applies to the vertical lists of a **\vadjust** and **\insert** which is currently secondary for the discussion here.

Here is an example of how interline glue can be generated for the very first line of a vbox. The first example shows that normally no interline glue is inserted. In the second example **\prevdepth** is set to 2 pt and TeX is tricked into thinking that the first box is preceded by an item which is 2 pt deep.The interline glue inserted before the first box (in the second example) is therefore computed as follows: **\baselineskip** $-$ 2 pt $-$ 6.94444 pt (the latter is the height of **\hbox{ABC}**).

Here is the source code of the example:

• **show-prevdepth.tip** •

```
\input inputd.tip
\InputD{shboxes.tip}                    % 4.5.15, p. 111.
\setbox 0 = \vbox{%                     % First example.
    \hbox{ABC}
    \hbox{DEF}
}
\ShowBoxDepthOne{0}
\setbox 1 = \vbox{%                     % Second example.
    \prevdepth = 2pt
    \hbox{ABC}
    \hbox{DEF}
}
\ShowBoxDepthOne{1}
\bye
```

• End of **show-prevdepth.tip** •

The log file generated by the above source code reads as follows:

• **show-prevdepth.log** •

```
This is TeX, C Version 3.14 (...)
**&/usr/local/tex/lib/fmt/plain show-prevdepth.tip
(show-prevdepth.tip (inputd.tip
(namedef.tip
) (inputdl.tip
\@InputDStream=\write0
)) (shboxes.tip
)
> \box0=
\vbox(18.83331+0.0)x21.8056
.\hbox(6.83331+0.0)x21.8056 []
.\glue(\baselineskip) 5.16669
.\hbox(6.83331+0.0)x20.97227 []

<to be read again>
}
l.7 \ShowBoxDepthOne{0}

> \box1=
\vbox(22.0+0.0)x21.8056
.\glue(\baselineskip) 3.16669
.\hbox(6.83331+0.0)x21.8056 []
.\glue(\baselineskip) 5.16669
.\hbox(6.83331+0.0)x20.97227 []

<to be read again>
}
l.13 \ShowBoxDepthOne{1}

)
No pages of output.
```

7.3.10 Suppressing Interline Glue Using `\nointerlineskip`

Based on the discussion of the previous Subsection it should be obvious how to suppress interline glue. Set `\prevdepth` to a value ≤ -1000 pt. The macro `\nointerlineskip` does just that:

```
\def\nointerlineskip{%
    \prevdepth = -1000pt
}
```

Note that the interline glue of any of the following lines is *not* affected, only the interline glue normally inserted between the preceding and the following box.

The workings of `\nointerlineskip` is revealed in the following example:

• `ex-noint.tip` •

```
\input inputd.tip
\InputD{shboxes.tip}                    % 4.5.15, p. 111.
```

```
\InputD{ts-fonts.tip}                    % 16.1.9, p. II-271.
\setbox 0 = \vbox{
    \hbox{\Large ABC}
    \nointerlineskip
    \hbox{\Large DEF}
    \nointerlineskip
    \hbox{\Large XXX}
    \hbox{\Large LLL}
}
\ShowBoxDepthOne{0}
\bye
```

• End of `ex-noint.tip` •

The output generated by the preceding code reads as follows:

This example generates the following log file:

• `ex-noint.log` •

```
This is TeX, C Version 3.14 (...)
**&/usr/local/tex/lib/fmt/plain ex-noint.tip
(ex-noint.tip (inputd.tip
(namedef.tip
) (inputdl.tip
\@InputDStream=\write0
))
(shboxes.tip
) (ts-fonts.tip
(lfondem.tip
) (ts-subst.tip
(substf.tip
) (newoutfr.tip
)) (fsized.tip
\CurrentFontSize=\dimen16
) (newfont.tip
(testdef.tip
))
\DefineFontSizeGroup: defining group "V" (5 pt)
\DefineFontSizeGroup: defining group "VII" (7 pt)
\DefineFontSizeGroup: defining group "VIII" (8 pt)
\DefineFontSizeGroup: defining group "IX" (9 pt)
\DefineFontSizeGroup: defining group "X" (10 pt)
\DefineFontSizeGroup: defining group "XII" (12 pt)
\DefineFontSizeGroup: defining group "XIII" (13.14 pt)
\DefineFontSizeGroup: defining group "XVII" (17.28 pt)
\DefineFontSizeGroup: defining group "XXI" (20.74 pt)
```

```
\DefineFontSizeGroup: defining group "XXV" (24.88 pt)
)
> \box0=
\vbox(38.93694+0.0)x28.9351
.\hbox(8.97899+0.0)x28.04845 []
.\hbox(8.97899+0.0)x26.97627 []
.\hbox(8.97899+0.0)x28.9351 []
.\glue(\baselineskip) 3.02098
.\hbox(8.97899+0.0)x24.11714 []

<to be read again>
}
l.12 \ShowBoxDepthOne{0}

)
No pages of output.
```

7.3.11 How to Disable and Enable Interline Glue, `\offinterlineskip`, `\normalbaselines`

Macro `\offinterlineskip` disables interline glue. The effect of macro `\offinterlineskip` can be undone by enclosing it inside a group and terminating the group (which is usually the case) or by calling macro `\normalbaselines`.

Also note a *significant difference* between `\nointerlineskip` and `\offinterlineskip` in that `\offinterlineskip` will still insert interline glue, but the length of this glue is zero (`\nointerlineskip` makes TeX to insert *no glue* at all). See 5.4.7, p. 139, for a discussion of the issue of no glue versus glue of zero length.

The definition of `\offinterlineskip` is as follows[1]:

```
\def\offinterlineskip{%
    \baselineskip = -1000pt
    \lineskip = 0pt
    \lineskiplimit = \maxdimen
}
```

How does this macro work? `\lineskiplimit` is set to the largest possible dimension in TeX which is `\maxdimen`. This tricks TeX's interline glue computations into thinking that *all* lines are "too close" in the sense previously defined. Therefore TeX will *always* insert `\lineskip` glue between all lines and none of the interline glue computations will be based on `\baselineskip`. Because `\lineskip`

---

[1] I choose to reprint the definition used in the plain format as of the printing of this series. Donald E. Knuth in a letter in September of 1990 confirmed that the change of `\baselineskip` is not necessary and must be a leftover from a time when the interline glue computation was done slightly differently. Therefore the setting of `\baselineskip` is not discussed below.

is set to zero, interline glue of length zero is inserted.

In a certain sense, the plain format macro `\normalbaselines` executes the inverse function of `\offinterlineskip`. It undoes `\offinterlineskip` by setting all values back to their defaults. The definition of this macro including some dimension and glue register definitions is as follows:

```
\newskip\normalbaselineskip      \normalbaselineskip = 12pt
\newskip\normallineskip          \normallineskip = 1pt
\newdimen\normallineskiplimit    \normallineskiplimit = 0pt

\def\normalbaselines{%
    \baselineskip = \normalbaselineskip
    \lineskip = \normallineskip
    \lineskiplimit = \normallineskiplimit
}
```

See 40.3.1, p. IV-304, for a sample application of `\normalbaselines`. The `\normalbaselines` macro is rarely needed because usually `\offinterlineskip` is enclosed in a group; when the group ends, so does the effect of the `\offinterlineskip`.

At the end of the plain format source code (typically stored in a file called `plain.tex`) `\normalbaselines` is called to initialize `\baselineskip`, `\lineskip` and `\lineskiplimit`.

7.3.12 Comparing `\offinterlineskip` and `\nointerlineskip`

Recall that calling would insert interline glue with a value of zero (rather than *no* interline glue at all). By contrast, actually prevents any interline glue from being inserted. The following example illustrates this point:

• `ex-noint-2.tip` •

```
\input inputd.tip
\InputD{shboxes.tip}                         % 4.5.15, p. 111.

\setbox 0 = \vbox{
    \hbox{ABC}
    \nointerlineskip
    \hbox{DEF}
    \nointerlineskip
    \hbox{XXX}
}
\ShowBoxDepthOne{0}

\setbox 1 = \vbox{
    \offinterlineskip
    \hbox{ABC}
    \hbox{DEF}
    \hbox{XXX}
}
```

```
\ShowBoxDepthOne{1}
\bye
```

• End of `ex-noint-2.tip` •

This example generates the following log file at which you should examine very closely (see 5.4.7, p. 139, for a discussion of the differences between no glue and glue of zero amount).

• `ex-noint-2.log` •

```
This is TeX, C Version 3.14 (...)
**&/usr/local/tex/lib/fmt/plain ex-noint-2.tip
(ex-noint-2.tip (inputd.tip
(namedef.tip
) (inputdl.tip
\@InputDStream=\write0
))
(shboxes.tip
)
> \box0=
\vbox(20.49994+0.0)x22.50005
.\hbox(6.83331+0.0)x21.8056 []
.\hbox(6.83331+0.0)x20.97227 []
.\hbox(6.83331+0.0)x22.50005 []

<to be read again>
}
l.11 \ShowBoxDepthOne{0}

> \box1=
\vbox(20.49994+0.0)x22.50005
.\hbox(6.83331+0.0)x21.8056 []
.\glue(\lineskip) 0.0
.\hbox(6.83331+0.0)x20.97227 []
.\glue(\lineskip) 0.0
.\hbox(6.83331+0.0)x22.50005 []

<to be read again>
}
l.19 \ShowBoxDepthOne{1}

)
No pages of output.
```

7.3.13 The Definition of Macro `\AlwaysBaselineskip`

Suppose you *not* want TEX to be clever, and you prefer that it space out lines with material of excessive height and depth. The macro will in a certain sense implement an opposite function of `\offinterlineskip`. `\lineskiplimit` is set to `-\maxdimen` by `\AlwaysBaselineskip` to make TEX think that *no lines* are too close. Therefore the line spacing as defined by `\baselineskip` will be preserved under all circumstances.

Here is the definition of this macro.

$\mathcal{P}'$ • `alwbase.tip` •

```
\def\AlwaysBaselineskip{%
    \lineskiplimit = -\maxdimen
}
```

• End of `alwbase.tip` •

For an an example of the application of this macro, look at the following source code:

```
\input inputd.tip
\InputD{alwbase.tip}                         % 7.3.13, p. 233.
$$
    \vbox{
        \hsize = 3.0in
        \baselineskip = 6pt
        \AlwaysBaselineskip
        In this paragraph we show that by calling the macro
        {\tt \string\AlwaysBaselineskip} we can actually get lines
        which run into each other. The paragraph is
        set with a value for {\tt\string\baselineskip} of 6~pt.
    }
$$
\bye
```

This source code generates the following output:

In this paragraph we show that by calling the macro `\AlwaysBaselineskip` we can actually get lines which run into each other. The paragraph is set with a value for `\baselineskip` of 6 pt.

7.3.14 Interline Glue and Horizontal Rules

No interline glue is inserted between horizontal rules (generated by `\hrule`), between a box and an `\hrule` and between an `\hrule` and a box. Let me demonstrate this with the following example:

• `ex-boxandrules.tip` •

```
\input inputd.tip
\InputD{shboxes.tip}                         % 4.5.15, p. 111.
\setbox 0 = \vbox{
    \hrule height 2pt depth 2pt width 2pt
    \hbox{ABC}
    \hrule height 2pt depth 2pt width 2pt
```

```
    \hrule height 2pt depth 2pt width 2pt
    \hrule height 2pt depth 2pt width 2pt
    \hbox{Something}
    \hrule height 2pt depth 2pt width 2pt
    \hbox{Nothing}
    \hbox{Everything}
}
\ShowBoxDepthOne{0}
\bye
```

• End of `ex-boxandrules.tip` •

The preceding source file generates the following log file:

• `ex-boxandrules.log` •

```
This is TeX, C Version 3.14 (...)
**&/usr/local/tex/lib/fmt/plain ex-boxandrules.tip
(ex-boxandrules.tip (inputd.tip
(namedef.tip
) (inputdl.tip
\@InputDStream=\write0
)) (shboxes.tip
)
> \box0=
\vbox(54.66664+1.94444)x48.22235
.\rule(2.0+2.0)x2.0
.\hbox(6.83331+0.0)x21.8056 []
.\rule(2.0+2.0)x2.0
.\rule(2.0+2.0)x2.0
.\rule(2.0+2.0)x2.0
.\hbox(6.94444+1.94444)x46.11124 []
.\rule(2.0+2.0)x2.0
.\hbox(6.94444+1.94444)x35.27788 []
.\glue(\baselineskip) 3.11111
.\hbox(6.94444+1.94444)x48.22235 []

<to be read again>
}
l.14 \ShowBoxDepthOne{0}

)
No pages of output.
```

7.3.15 Increasing Interline Spacing Using Macro `\openup`

The `\openup` macro of the plain format is used to increase all three parameters `\baselineskip`, `\lineskip` and `\lineskiplimit` uniformly by the same amount. A call to this macro must be followed by a dimension specifying the increase (this dimension seems to be a parameter of the macro but really is not;

the macro uses **\afterassignment** (see 23.1, p. III-235) to load the dimension into \dimen0).

```
\def\openup{%
    \afterassignment\@penup
    \dimen@ =
}
\def\@penup{%
    \advance\lineskip by \dimen@
    \advance\baselineskip by \dimen@
    \advance\lineskiplimit by \dimen@
}
```

Observe that not only **\baselineskip** is increased by the specified amount, but also **\lineskiplimit** and **\lineskip** so that the "minimum distance" between lines which is enforced by the two parameters **\lineskip** and **\lineskiplimit** is increased by the same amount **\baselineskip** is increased.

7.4 Struts

One can ensure constant line spacing through the use of interline glue where TEX does all the necessary computations or by inserting struts, where the user is responsible for constant line spacing and the automatic mechanism of TEX is disabled. A a *strut* is a vertical rule, which has the desired height and depth but zero width (which makes this vertical rule invisible, one of our requirements).

A *strut* is a vertical rule which has a specified height and depth, and a zero width.

Struts are not used for the typesetting of paragraphs, but they are used to typeset tables with vertical rules. See 39.4, p. IV-271, for more details on why struts are used in the first place. Struts are discussed here rather than in the chapters on tables because we are already dealing with line spacing computations anyway.

For the following assume that none of the lines contain any material of excessive height or depth as far as the desired line spacing is concerned. Rather than use interline glue, we will now make *each line of the same height and depth.* We then stack these lines directly on top of each other, *without* any interline glue in between them (actually there will be still interline glue between these lines but it will be zero). If the sum of the height and depth of each line adds up to **\baselineskip**, then we achieve the same effect as before because the baselines of all our lines will be **\baselineskip** apart.

The question now is how one can force lines to be of a certain height and depth (under the assumption that none of the lines contain material of excessive height and depth.) Remember that the height and depth of a line or hbox is determined by the deepest and highest item in this hbox. Thus if a strut with the proper height and depth is inserted into the hbox, the hbox will have the desired dimensions. It is here where the assumption that the hbox did not contain any material of excessive height or depth is important, because otherwise the inserted strut could not control the height or the depth of the box being generated.

To achieve a line spacing with struts corresponding to some value of **\baselineskip**, one typically makes the height of the strut 70% of **\baselineskip**, and the depth of the strut the remaining 30% of **\baselineskip**. These values are used in some generic strut generating macros (7.4.3, p. 239) and these percentages are also used in the next Subsection.

7.4.1 Different Ways to Generate Struts and Strut-Like Constructs

Let us now discuss a variety of different ways to construct struts and strutlike constructs (the next Subsection will present some specific examples). Note also that we will discuss an approach where no strut is used but the height and depth of an hbox is manipulated directly.

1. As mentioned before, a strut is a vertical rule of zero width. This is the usual way a strut is constructed. To achieve a line spacing of 12 pt using our 70% / 30% rule we might define a strut as follows: **\vrule height 8.5pt depth 3.5pt width 0pt**.

   One of the advantages of defining a strut this way is that the strut (more precisely its dimensions) can be changed easily by appending a new height or depth specification to the "old" strut definition; see 5.7.1, item 3, p. 155.

   Note that TeX enters horizontal mode at this point in time if it was not already in horizontal mode; see 10.4.1, p. II-11.

   7.4.3, p. 239, presents macros to automatize the computation of a strut.
2. Store the strut (generated the standard way that is using a zero width rule) in an hbox and then use **\unhcopy** to extract the strut. That is a little more efficient than the previous approach. The disadvantage is that the height or depth of the strut cannot be changed by appending new dimension specifications.

   Here is a strut definition along those lines as it is used in the plain format:

```
\newbox\strutbox
\setbox\strutbox = \hbox{\vrule height8.5pt depth3.5pt width 0pt}
\def\strut{%
    \relax
    \ifmmode
        \copy\strutbox
    \else
        \unhcopy\strutbox
    \fi
}
```

3. Instead of inserting a strut into an hbox it is possible to manipulate the dimensions of the hbox directly. For that purpose the hbox is assigned to a box register and then the dimensions of the box register are manipulated according to 4.5.9, p. 100. An example of this technique will be shown in

the next Subsection; this approach is mentioned in the context of struts to demonstrate a different way to solve the same problem.

4. Sometimes strut-like constructs with a height or depth of zero are needed. Here is how those can be generated (the approach presented in item 1 of this list works equally well; compare the following approach also with 6.4.4, p. 180).
   (a) To generate a "strut" of a specific height and zero depth build a vbox of the specified height using `\vbox to` as in `\vbox to 10pt{}`. This generates a 10 pt high and 0 pt deep box. See 7.5.6, p. 251, for a more detailed discussion of the `\vbox to` ⟨dimen⟩ construct.
   (b) To generate a "strut" of a specific depth and zero height build a vbox of a specific depth using the `\vtop to` construct as in `\vtop to 10pt{}`. This generates a box which is 10 pt deep and 0 pt high. See 7.5.6, p. 251, for a more detailed discussion of the `\vtop to` ⟨dimen⟩ construct.

7.4.2 Strut Examples

I will now present a series of examples using some of the constructs offered in the previous Subsection. First, some boxes are printed that have spacing controlled by `\baselineskip`. Then strut-based spacing is presented. Note the `\offinterlineskip` instruction of line 10 of the source code below; this instruction disables the automatic interline glue computation (see 7.3.11, p. 230) and is usually applied when using strut-based line spacing.

• `ex-strut.tip` •

```
1  \input inputd.tip
2  \InputD{box-mac.tip}                    % 9.3.14, p. 343.
3  $$
4      \vbox{
```

The first three boxes use spacing based on `\baselineskip`.

```
5          \HboxR{\llap{1: }AAA}
6          \HboxR{eee}
7          \HboxR{gggg gggg}
8
9          \vskip 10pt
```

There will be no interline glue for the remainder of the examples.

```
10         \offinterlineskip
```

Print three boxes, but use no struts: non-constant spacing.

```
11         \HboxR{\llap{2: }AAA}
12         \HboxR{eee}
13         \HboxR{gggg gggg}
14
15         \vskip 10pt
```

Print more boxes, now with struts inserted. Actually, we do *not* insert a standard strut of zero width. What is inserted are rules of different widths (1pt, 2pt, and 3pt). We might call these rules "visible strut." The workings of the visible struts can be seen clearly: they increase the height and depth of all boxes compared with the three preceding boxes.

```
        \HboxR{\llap{3: }%
                \vrule height 8.5pt depth 3.5pt width 1pt\ AAA}
        \HboxR{eee\vrule   height 8.5pt depth 3.5pt width 2pt}
        \HboxR{gggg \vrule height 8.5pt depth 3.5pt width 3pt\ gggg}

        \vskip 10pt
```

The next set of examples uses "real" struts and use invisible vertical rules (of zero width).

```
        \HboxR{\llap{4: }%
            \vrule height 8.5pt depth 3.5pt width 0pt AAA}
        \HboxR{\vrule height 8.5pt depth 3.5pt width 0pt eee}
        \HboxR{\vrule height 8.5pt depth 3.5pt width 0pt gggg gggg}

        \vskip 10pt
```

The preceding examples are repeated using a macro `\strut` rather than repeating the strut rule in each box. Note that the following definition of `\strut` is *different* from the definition of the `\strut` macro in the plain format.

```
        \def\strut{\vrule height 8.5pt depth 3.5pt width 0pt}
        \HboxR{\llap{5: }\strut 5: AAA}
        \HboxR{\strut eee}
        \HboxR{\strut gggg gggg}

        \vskip 10pt
```

Next is another approach (mentioned before in 7.4.1, item 3, p. 236). Rather than using struts, each box is assigned to a box register and the dimensions (height and depth) of the box register are set to the height and depth of a strut, if a strut were used.

```
        \setbox 0 = \hbox{\llap{6: }AAA}
            \ht0 = 8.5pt  \dp0 = 3.5pt  \BoxR 0
        \setbox 0 = \hbox{eee}
            \ht0 = 8.5pt  \dp0 = 3.5pt  \BoxR 0
        \setbox 0 = \hbox{ggg}
            \ht0 = 8.5pt  \dp0 = 3.5pt  \BoxR 0
```

The end of the examples is reached.

```
    }
$$
```

• End of `ex-strut.tip` •

The preceding source code generates output which is reprinted in Figure 7.4 on the next page.

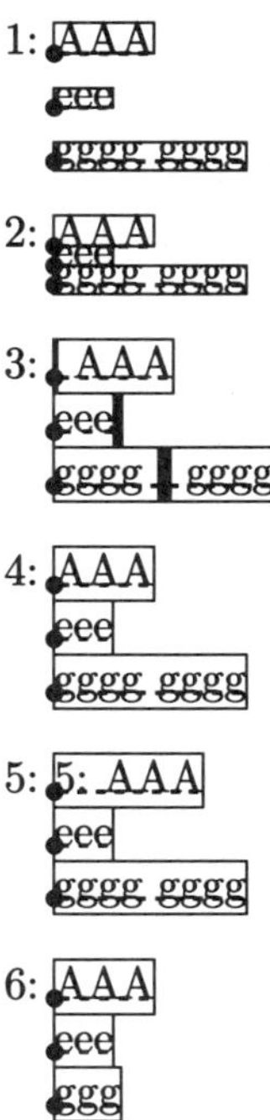

Figure 7.4. Strut example output.

7.4.3 Automatic Strut Computations, Macros `\ComputeStrut`, `\HigherStrut` and `\DeeperStrut`

Struts may be computed automatically by macros. The strut computations offered in the following macros use the current value of `\baselineskip` to compute the dimensions of the strut. As you can see from the definition of `\offinterlineskip` (7.3.11, p. 230), this macro redefines `\baselineskip`. Therefore the later following macro `\ComputeStrut` (which depends on the value of `\baselineskip`) must be called *before* invoking `\offinterlineskip`.

I also present the definitions of macros `\HigherStrut` and `\DeeperStrut`. These macros compute a strut, that is by a given amount higher or deeper than the regular strut as it is set up by `\ComputeStrut`.

7.4.3.1 The Beginning of the Macro Source File

The beginning of the source code file is next.

$\mathcal{P}'$ • **setstrut.tip** •

```
\catcode`\@ = 11
```

Save the current value of \baselineskip here (\baselineskip is redefined by \offinterlineskip).

```
\newdimen\@StrutBaseDimension
```

\@StrutSkipTemp is a temporary dimension register for some strut dimension computations.

```
\newdimen\@StrutSkipTemp
```

7.4.3.2 Macros \ComputeStrut and \MyStrut

Now define macro \ComputeStrut (without parameters). The macro saves the current value of \baselineskip so it is later available for building the strut. After \ComputeStrut was called, the strut itself can be generated using the control sequence \MyStrut. This control sequence generates a \vrule of zero width. The height of the \vrule is 70% of the value of \baselineskip when \ComputeStrut was invoked. The depth of \MyRule is 30% of \baselineskip.

```
\def\ComputeStrut{%
     \@StrutBaseDimension = \baselineskip
```

Generate an error if \baselineskip is negative. The assumption in this case is that \offinterlineskip was called before \ComputeStrut.

```
     \ifdim\baselineskip < 0pt
         \errhelp = {You probably called \string\offinterlineskip
                 before \string\ComputeStrut}
         \errmessage{\string\ComputeStrut: negative
                 \string\baselineskip (\the\baselineskip)}%
     \fi
}
```

Now define macro \MyStrut (no parameters) as a \vrule with dimensions as just explained.

```
\def\MyStrut{%
     \vrule height 0.7\@StrutBaseDimension
            depth 0.3\@StrutBaseDimension
            width 0pt
}
```

7.4.3.3 The Definition of \HigherStrut

Next define macro \HigherStrut. The one parameter, #1, of this macro is a dimension s. A strut is generated identical to \MyStrut, except that the height of the strut generated by \HigherStrut is s higher than the strut generated by \MyStrut.

```
\def\HigherStrut #1{%
```

```
    \@StrutSkipTemp = 0.7\@StrutBaseDimension
    \advance\@StrutSkipTemp by #1%
    \vrule height \@StrutSkipTemp
           depth 0.3\@StrutBaseDimension
           width 0pt
}
```

7.4.3.4 The Definition of `\DeeperStrut`

Macro `\DeeperStrut` also has one parameter, `#1`, a dimension s. This time a strut is generated that is s deeper than that generated by `\MyStrut`.

```
\def\DeeperStrut #1{%
    \@StrutSkipTemp = 0.3\@StrutBaseDimension
    \advance\@StrutSkipTemp by #1%
    \vrule height 0.7\@StrutBaseDimension
           depth \@StrutSkipTemp
           width 0pt
}
```

7.4.3.5 The End of this Macro Source File

Initialize the strut definition, just in case the user forgets it.

```
\ComputeStrut
\catcode`\@ = 12
```

• End of `setstrut.tip` •

7.4.4 Macro `\ReduceToStrut` to Generate a Strut Based on Some Arbitrary Text

Finally let me define a macro which will define a strut based on the height and depth of some material. The material itself is the only parameter, `#1`, to this macro. The material itself is not printed.

$\mathcal{P}'$ • `redtost.tip` •

```
\catcode`\@ = 11
\newbox\@ReduceToStrutBox
\def\ReduceToStrut #1{%
    \setbox\@ReduceToStrutBox = \hbox{#1}%
    \vrule height \ht\@ReduceToStrutBox
           depth  \dp\@ReduceToStrutBox
           width 0pt
}
```

```
\catcode`\@ = 12
```

• End of `redtost.tip` •

7.5 The Dimensions of Vboxes

The next task will be to determine how TeX computes the dimensions of a vertical box and how this computation differs among the three different instructions that generate vboxes: `\vbox`, `\vtop` and `\vcenter`.

7.5.1 The Width of Vboxes

The *width* of a vertical box is the same regardless of whether the vbox is generated by `\vbox`, `\vtop` or `\vcenter`. It is the maximum width of any item in the vertical list of the box. Observe that when a paragraph is enclosed inside a vbox then regardless of the width of the lines of a paragraph the assumption is that all lines are `\hsize` wide. In particular the values of `\leftskip` and `\rightskip` are irrelevant in this case; see 10.6, p. II-14. If the width of all items were to be negative the width of the resulting vbox is zero.

Since we assume all lines are `\hsize` wide, the width of the vertical box constructed by `\vbox{A}` will be `\hsize` because the box contains a "paragraph" that is one character in length only. The width of `\vbox{\hbox{A}}` would be only the width of the "A," because the width of the vbox is determined by the width of the hbox it contains, and the width of the hbox built by `\hbox{A}` is the width of character "A."

Observe that the computation to determine the width of a vbox corresponds to the computations of height and depth of an hbox: the dimension is the maximum value of that dimension of any item contained in the box. The widest item within a vbox determines the width of a vbox the same way the highest and deepest items within an hbox determine the height and depth of an hbox.

Note also that this analogy is valid when it comes to the computation of the dimensions of rules. If the width of an `\hrule` inside a vbox is not specified, then it inherits the width from the vbox it is enclosed in. A similar argument is true for hboxes: in an hbox the height and depth of the hbox determine the height and depth of a `\vrule` unless those parameters are specified explicitly.

The primitive `\vcenter` can only be used in math mode and also is a little more restricted than `\vbox` or `\vtop`; see 7.5.5, p. 248, for a discussion. Otherwise, as far as the width computation is concerned, `\vcenter` is treated as just another type of a vbox.

7.5.2 The Height and Depth Computations of Vboxes

In discussing height and depth computations of vboxes distinguishing among the three vbox generating instructions is necessary.

Let me first address the problem of the reference point of the vbox being generated with any of the three commands. For this purpose the following example is used:

• ex-vb-1.tip •

```
\input inputd.tip
\InputD{box-mac.tip}                          % 9.3.14, p. 343.
```

First define macro \FourHBoxes. This macro has two parameters:

- #1. One of \vbox, \vtop or \vcenter.
- #2. The corresponding macro \VboxR, \VtopR or \VcenterR.

```
\def\FourHBoxes #1#2{
    #2{%
        \hbox{1: Top line ({\tt \string#1})}
        \hbox{2: Second line}
        \hbox{3: Third line}
        \hbox{4: Last line, what else?}
    }%
}
```

Now generate three vboxes, using each of the instructions \vbox, \vcenter and \vtop once.

```
$$
    \hbox{%
        \FourHBoxes{\vbox}{\VboxR}
        \hskip 13pt
        $\FourHBoxes{\vcenter}{\vcenter}$%
        \hskip 13pt
        \FourHBoxes{\vtop}{\VtopR}
    }
$$
\bye
```

• End of ex-vb-1.tip •

The preceding source code's output can be found in Figure 7.5 on the next page.

Let us quickly discuss how the various boxes are built. From the diagram we conclude that the sum of height and depth of all three boxes is the same. The only thing that is different is *where* the reference point is located and therefore how the height and depth are distributed.

The reference point is placed by TeX as follows:

1. In case of a \vbox make the reference point of the vbox to be generated the

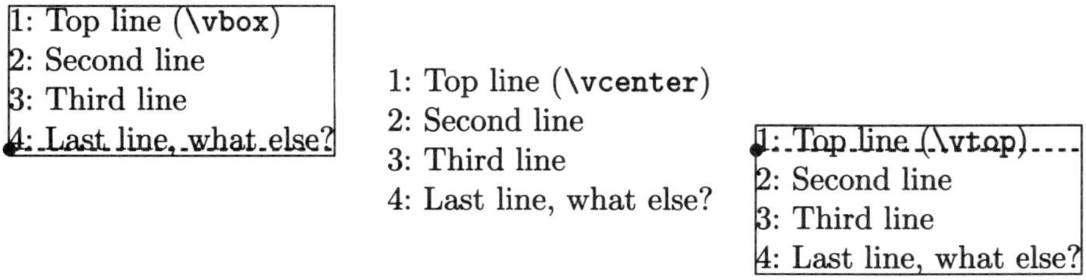

1: Top line (\vbox)
2: Second line
3: Third line
4: Last line, what else?

1: Top line (\vcenter)
2: Second line
3: Third line
4: Last line, what else?

1: Top line (\vtop)
2: Second line
3: Third line
4: Last line, what else?

Figure 7.5. Comparing `\vbox`, `\vtop` and `\vcenter`.

reference point of the *last* item on the vertical list. In our example above this is the reference point of the first `\hbox` ("4: Last line, what else?").

Therefore vboxes generated by `\vbox` have a tendency to be rather deep, because all items after the first item are placed below the reference point (discarding any "strange" `\vskip`s right now).

2. In case of a `\vtop` make the reference point of the `\vtop` the reference point of the *first* item on the vertical list. In our example above this is the reference point of the last `\hbox` ("1: Top line").

   Therefore vboxes generated by `\vtop` have a tendency to be rather high, because all items except for the last item are placed above the reference point (discarding any "strange" `\vskip`s right now).

3. In case of a `\vcenter` use a reference point exactly between the two reference points for the same box built with `\vbox` and `\vtop`.

   Obviously, vboxes generated by `\vcenter` tend to have identical or at least almost identical heights and depths.

7.5.3 Some More Examples of Vbox Dimension Computations

Let me repeat the preceding examples with some glue as the first and last item to show how vertical glue influences the output and in particular what this glue does to the positioning of the reference point of the vbox being generated. The following source code is used:

• `ex-vb-2.tip` •

```
\input inputd.tip
\InputD{box-mac.tip}                    % 9.3.14, p. 343.
```

First define macro `\FourHBoxesX` to generates four hboxes and two glues. This macro is very similar to the definition of `\FourHboxes` given previously.

```
\def\FourHBoxesX #1#2{
    #2{
        \vskip 30pt                        % ADDED
        \hbox{1: Top line ({\tt \string#1})}
        \hbox{2: Second line}
```

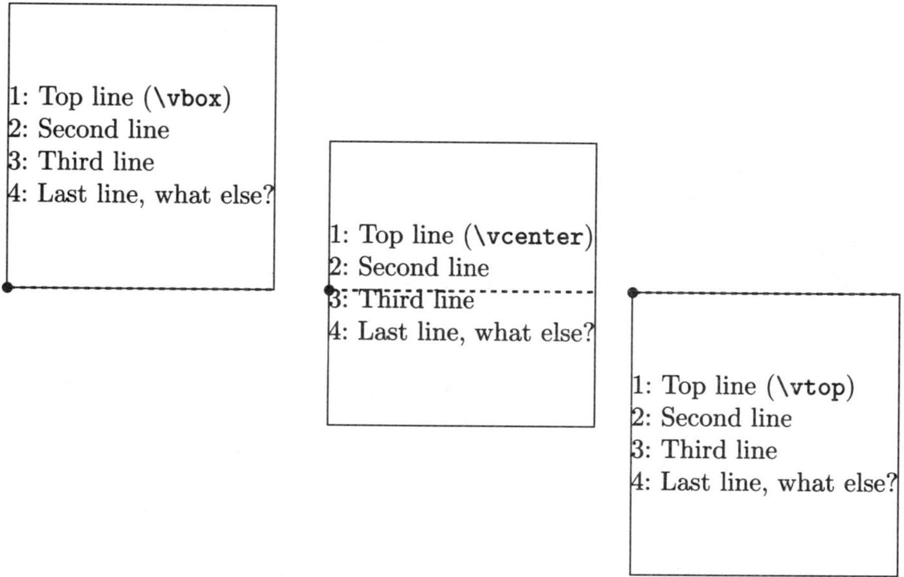

Figure 7.6. Another comparison between `\vbox`, `\vtop` and `\vcenter`.

```
        \hbox{3: Third line}
        \hbox{4: Last line, what else?}
        \vskip 30pt                          % ADDED
    }
}
```

Now generate three vboxes, using each of the instructions `\vbox`, `\vcenter` and `\vtop`.

```
$$
    \hbox{%
        \FourHBoxesX{\vbox}{\VboxR}
        \hskip 14pt
        $\FourHBoxesX{\vcenter}{\VcenterXR}$%
        \hskip 14pt
        \FourHBoxesX{\vtop}{\VtopR}
    }
$$
\bye
```

• End of `ex-vb-2.tip` •

The preceding source code's output can be found in Figure 7.6 on this page.

Now we will see an example where rules are the first and last items of the vboxes being generated. Here is the input used.

• `ex-vb-3.tip` •

```
\input inputd.tip
```

```
\InputD{box-mac.tip}                     % 9.3.14, p. 343.
```

First define a macro that generates four hboxes conveniently.

```
\def\FourHBoxesY #1#2{
    #2{%
        \hrule height 5pt depth 3pt width 30pt
        \hbox{1: Top line}
        \hbox{2: Second line}
        \hbox{3: Third line}
        \hbox{4: Last line, what else?}
        \hrule height 6pt depth 6pt width 40pt
    }%
}
```

Now generate three vboxes, using each of the instructions `\vbox`, `\vcenter` and `\vtop`.

```
$$
    \hbox{%
        \FourHBoxesY{\vbox}{\VboxR}
        \hskip 15pt
        $\FourHBoxesY{\vcenter}{\vcenter}$%
        \hskip 15pt
        \FourHBoxesY{\vtop}{\VtopR}
    }
$$
\bye
```

• End of ex-vb-3.tip •

The preceding source code generates the following output:

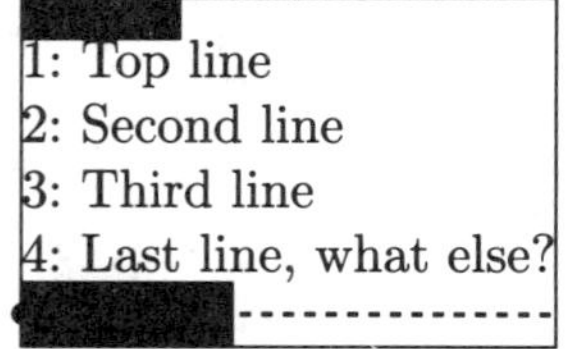

1: Top line
2: Second line
3: Third line
4: Last line, what else?

1: Top line
2: Second line
3: Third line
4: Last line, what else?

7.5.4 Limiting the Depth of a Vbox, \boxmaxdepth

The `\boxmaxdepth` parameter, a dimension parameter, determines the maximum depth of a vertical box being built. If the depth of a box computed according to the rules of the preceding subsections exceeds `\boxmaxdepth`, the following computation is performed by TEX:

1. The depth of the box is reduced to `\boxmaxdepth`.
2. The amount by which the depth was reduced in the preceding step is added to the height of the vbox.

In other words, the reference point is moved down (from the original location) so that the depth of the resulting box is `\boxmaxdepth`.

Let us study an example of limiting the depth of a vbox now:

• `ex-bm.tip` •

```
\input inputd.tip
\InputD{box-mac.tip}                          % 9.3.14, p. 343.
```

Define a macro `\BoxMaxDepthEx` which generates a sample vbox. The depth of this vbox (because it is generated by `\vbox`) is determined by the depth of the *last* item in it. The last item is an `\hbox` that, due to the `\vrule`, contains, is 15 pt deep. This macro has one parameter (`#1`), a dimension assigned to `\boxmaxdepth`.

```
\def\BoxMaxDepthEx #1{%
    \VboxR{
        \boxmaxdepth = #1
        \hbox{First line ({\tt\string\boxmaxdepth} is
                        \the\boxmaxdepth)}
        \hbox{Second line}
        \hbox{Last line \vrule height 0pt depth 15pt width 2pt}
    }
}
```

Now show three examples. Note that the second and third examples show the influence of `\boxmaxdepth`. The depth of the second box is 10 pt, and the depth of the third box is 0 pt.

```
\vbox{%
    \openup 3pt
    \centerline{\BoxMaxDepthEx{\maxdimen}}
    \centerline{\BoxMaxDepthEx{10pt}}
    \centerline{\BoxMaxDepthEx{0pt}}
}
\bye
```

• End of `ex-bm.tip` •

The preceding source generates Figure 7.7 on the next page.

The default of `\boxmaxdepth` in the plain format is `\maxdimen`. In other words, a vertical box can have any depth in the plain format and therefore `\boxmaxdepth` has no influence in the plain format.

Note that there is another very similar dimension parameter, `\maxdepth`, that determines the maximum depth *of the current page* being built in box register 255 and handed to the output routine. See item 2 in 32.6.1, p. IV-28, for details.

Another very similar dimension parameter is `\splitmaxdepth`. See 8.2.11, p. 293, for details.

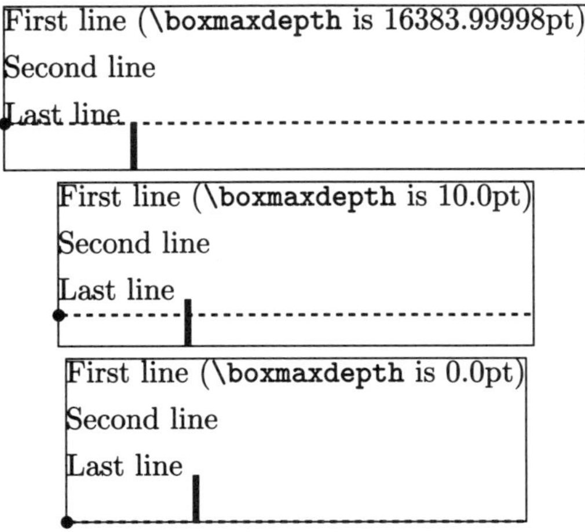

Figure 7.7. A **\boxmaxdepth** related example.

7.5.5 A Discussion of `\vcenter` and Its Restrictions, Macro `\VcenterX`

In the following discussing of `\vcenter` be aware of the following two restrictions, when it comes to the application of `\vcenter`:

1. `\vcenter` can only be used in math mode.
2. `\vcenter` cannot be used to generate a vbox that can be assigned to a box register.

For example, the fact that `\vcenter` can *only* be used in math mode implies that the following TeX source is illegal (this does not mean that you may not want to write this code, in fact there are cases where you would like to write code exactly along the lines below):

```
This is some text. \vcenter{\hbox{top}\hbox{bottom}}. More text.
```

Instead you must use the following trick: enclose the whole construct inside an hbox inside which you use math mode.

```
This is some text. $\vcenter{\hbox{top}\hbox{bottom}}$. More text..
```

Note that TeX inserts **\mathsurround** glue around the "inline math equation" which really only contains the `\vcenter`. This glue should be set to zero, because otherwise the resulting hbox becomes a little wider than the `\vcenter`-generated vbox it encloses. The default of **\mathsurround** is 0 pt, and this horizontal glue is inserted before and after the "mathematical equation."

```
This is some text. \hbox{\mathsurround = 0pt
    $\vcenter{\hbox{top}\hbox{bottom}}$}. More text.
```

The preceding discussion naturally leads to the definition of a `\VcenterX` macro which is largely identical to `\vcenter`, except that it can be used in any mode, not only math mode. This macro could be defined as follows:

```
\def\VcenterX #1{%
    \hbox{%
        \mathsurround = 0pt
        $\vcenter{#1}$%
    }%
}
```

This definition has the disadvantage that the following construct would be illegal: `\VcenterX\bgroup ...\egroup` (but the corresponding construct based on `\vcenter` would be legal).

The following definition of `\VcenterX` is finally chosen. Note that the macro definition is quite complicated, because this macro definition *also* allows you to use a `\VcenterX to` ⟨dimen⟩ or `\VcenterX spread` ⟨dimen⟩ type of call.

$\mathcal{P}'$ • `vcentx.tip` •

```
\catcode`\@ = 11
```

We need to reserve a box in which the `\vcenter`-related box is collected.

```
\newbox\@VcenterXBox
```

In the dimension register declared below save the dimension of a `\VcenterX to` ⟨dimen⟩ or `\VcenterX spread` ⟨dimen⟩ type of call.

```
\newdimen\@VcenterDimen
```

The macro definition of `\VcenterX` begins here. An hbox is started immediately so that `\VcenterX` can be used with `\setbox`.

```
\def\VcenterX{%
    \hbox\bgroup
        \mathsurround = 0pt
```

Next you need to discriminate between three different types of calls. For that purpose execute `\futurelet` and let macro `\@VCenterXA` decide which of the three cases applies.

```
    \futurelet\@VCenterXToken\@VCenterXA
}
```

Now define macro `\@VCenterXA`. This macro determines which type of call was used:

1. `\VcenterX {...}`
2. `\VcenterX to ... {...}`
3. `\VcenterX spread ... {...}`

```
\def\@VCenterXA{%
    \ifx\@VCenterXToken\bgroup
        \let\@VcenterXNext = \@VcenterXOrdinary
    \else
        \ifx\@VCenterXToken t%
            \let\@VcenterXNext = \@VcenterXTo
```

```
        \else
            \let\@VcenterXNext = \@VcenterXSpread
        \fi
    \fi
    \@VcenterXNext
}
```

The following macro is called if it was an ordinary `\VcenterX` type of call, without any dimension specifications using `to` or `spread`.

```
\def\@VcenterXOrdinary{%
    \def\@VcenterCommand{\vcenter}%
```

The purpose of the following two instructions is to drop the opening curly brace (or `\bgroup`) following a call to macro `\VcenterX`.

```
    \afterassignment\@VcenterXB
    \let\@VcenterDrop =
}
```

The following macro is called in the case of a `\VcenterX to` ⟨dimen⟩ type of call. This macro causes the dimension to be absorbed next.

```
\def\@VcenterXTo to{%
    \def\@VcenterCommand{to}%
    \afterassignment\@VcenterXToSpread
    \@VcenterDimen =
}
```

The same deal for `\VcenterX spread` ⟨dimen⟩.

```
\def\@VcenterXSpread spread{%
    \def\@VcenterCommand{spread}%
    \afterassignment\@VcenterXToSpread
    \@VcenterDimen =
}
```

Now build the `\vcenter` command you will eventually apply, and then drop the following opening curly brace (or `\bgroup`).

```
\def\@VcenterXToSpread{%
    \edef\@VcenterCommand{%
        \vcenter\@VcenterCommand \the\@VcenterDimen
    }%
    \afterassignment\@VcenterXB
    \let\@VcenterDrop =
}
```

Finally `\vcenter` is executed. The resulting box is stored in box register `\@VcenterXBox`.

```
\def\@VcenterXB{%
    \setbox\@VcenterXBox = \hbox\bgroup
        $%
        \@VcenterCommand\bgroup
    \aftergroup\@VcenterXC
}
```

The following macro's execution is triggered by the `\aftergroup` of the preceding macro.

```
\def\@VcenterXC{%
```

Terminate the math mode and the `\hbox` started in the preceding macro. Then produce the box.

```
      $%
      \egroup
      \box\@VcenterXBox
```

Terminate the `\hbox` started at the beginning of the `\VcenterX` execution.

```
      \egroup
}
\catcode`\@ = 12
```

• End of `vcentx.tip` •

And here is an application of this macro. The following input was used:

```
\input inputd.tip
\InputD{vcentx.tip}                    % 7.5.5, p. 249.
Here is a little {\tt \string\VcenterX} example:
\VcenterX{\hbox{ABC}\hbox{DEF}} and
\VcenterX\bgroup\hbox{XXX}\hbox{Y}\egroup
```

The output generated by the preceding input reads as follows:

Here is a little `\VcenterX` example: ABC DEF and XXX Y

The second point made at the beginning of this Subsection was that `\vcenter` cannot be used to generate a vbox that is assigned to a box register. The following input in TEX is *illegal*:

```
\setbox 0 = \vcenter{...}
```

as well as the following:

```
$\setbox 0 = \vcenter{...}$
```

Note though that the following input is legal using the preceding macro, which proves its usefulness also in this case (see also 9.3.9.2, p. 336.):

```
\setbox 0 = \VcenterX{...}
```

7.5.6 Predefined Heights or Depths in Vboxes: `\vbox`, `\vtop` and `\vcenter` `to` or `spread` ⟨dimen⟩

We will now discuss the following six constructs:

1.

   (a) `\vbox to` ⟨dimen⟩
   (b) `\vbox spread` ⟨dimen⟩

2.
   (a) `\vtop to` ⟨dimen⟩
   (b) `\vtop spread` ⟨dimen⟩

3.
   (a) `\vcenter to` ⟨dimen⟩
   (b) `\vcenter spread` ⟨dimen⟩

These six constructs were grouped into three pairs, and within each pair the two constructs are equivalent in the same sense that `\hbox to` ⟨dimen⟩ and `\hbox spread` ⟨dimen'⟩ are equivalent; 6.4.1, item 1.c, p. 177. Therefore I will only discuss the `\v... to` ⟨dimen⟩ type of instructions.

The interpretation of those instructions is fairly easy.

1. `\vbox to` ⟨dimen⟩ generates a vbox of the specified height (stretching and shrinking any glue of the vertical list of the box if necessary).
2. `\vtop to` ⟨dimen⟩ generates a vbox of the specified depth (stretching and shrinking any glue of the vertical list of the box if necessary).
3. `\vcenter to` ⟨dimen⟩ generates a vbox of the specified half height and half depth (stretching and shrinking any glue of the box if necessary).

Note the following special applications of `\vbox to` and `\vtop to` (compare this with `\hbox to` ⟨dimen⟩ `{}`; see 6.4.4, p. 180):

1. `\vbox to` ⟨dimen⟩ `{}` generates an empty box whose height is determined by ⟨dimen⟩. Depth and width of the box are zero.
2. `\vtop to` ⟨dimen⟩ `{}` generates an empty box whose depth is determined by ⟨dimen⟩. Height and width of the box are zero.

Instead of lengthy explanations we will present some examples now. The box used to demonstrate the instructions contains three lines and three `\vfil` glues that will all stretch equally.

• `ex-vboxto.tip` •

```
\input inputd.tip
\InputD{box-mac.tip}                    % 9.3.14, p. 343.
```

The following macro has three arguments:

- `#1`: one of `\vbox`, `\vtop` or `\vcenter`.
- `#2`: the corresponding `\V...R` command.
- `#3`: any additional specification for the vbox generating command `#1` such as "`to 1.0in`."

```
\def\MasterBox #1#2#3{%
    #2#3{%
        \hbox{1: {\tt\string#1 #3}}
```

```
            \vfil
            \hbox{2: DEF}
            \vfil
            \hbox{3: XXX}
            \vfil
        }
}
```

First some examples based on `\vbox` first.

```
\centerline{%
    \MasterBox{\vbox}{\VboxR}{}
    \hskip 15pt
    \MasterBox{\vbox}{\VboxR}{to 1.0in}
    \hskip 15pt
    \MasterBox{\vbox}{\VboxR}{to 1.5in}
}
```

Then some examples based on `\vtop`.

```
\centerline{%
    \MasterBox{\vtop}{\VtopR}{}
    \hskip 15pt
    \MasterBox{\vtop}{\VtopR}{to 1.0in}
    \hskip 15pt
    \MasterBox{\vtop}{\VtopR}{to 1.5in}
}
```

Finally some examples based on `\vcenter`.

```
\endinput
\centerline{%
    \MasterBox{\VcenterX}{\VcenterXR}{}%
    \hskip 15pt
    \MasterBox{\VcenterX}{\VcenterXR}{to 1.0in}%
    \hskip 15pt
    \MasterBox{\VcenterX}{\VcenterXR}{to 1.5in}%
}
```

• End of `ex-vboxto.tip` •

The preceding source code generates the following output:

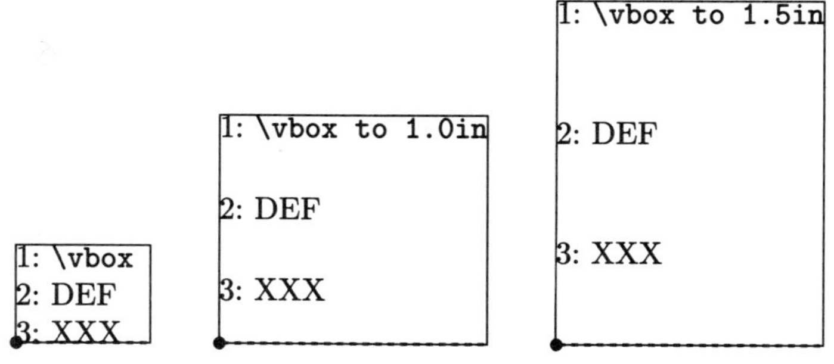

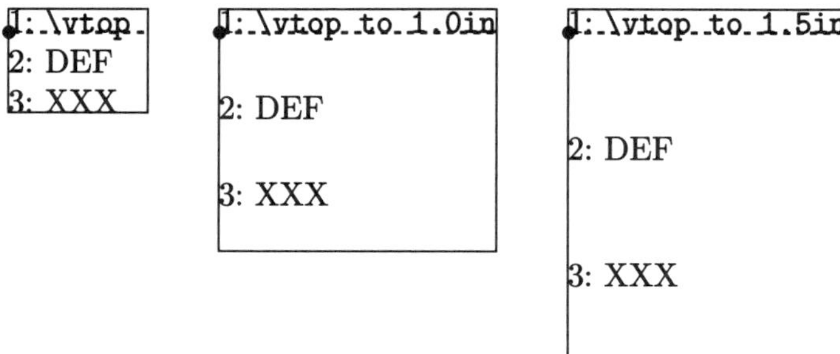

7.5.7 A Macro to Shift the Reference Point of a Box Up or Down, `\ShiftRefPointUpOrDown`

Now let me present macro `\ShiftRefPointUpOrDown`. This macro will take a vbox (the macro also allows work with an hbox, although this application occurs only rarely) and shifts the reference point up or down by a specified dimension. The resulting box will "look the same as the original box": the box content is not affected, in particular all items within the box are still positioned identically with respect to each other. The resulting box's height and depth will be changed though reflecting the change in the reference point. The original box may have a height of 10 pt and a depth of 20 pt while the resulting box may have a height of 25 pt and a depth of 5 pt. Note that the sum of height and depth stays the same.

The macro `\ShiftRefPointUpOrDown` has two parameters:

- `#1`. A box register index of a box register containing the box of which the reference point is shifted up or down. This box therefore must be stored in a box register.
- `#2`. A dimension s which determines the change in height and depth of the box stored in the box register. The change is as follows (note that for $s > 0$ the reference point is shifted *down* by s and for $s < 0$ the reference point is shifted *up* by $-s$):

  1. s is added to the height of the box contained in this box register.
  2. s is subtracted from the depth of this box register.

  As stated before, the sum of height and depth stays the same with the following exception: if the height and/or depth as computed in the preceding step is negative, it will be set to zero.

Here is the definition of this macro:

$\mathcal{P}'$ • **`shiftudb.tip`** •

```
\InputD{chboxd.tip}                        % 4.5.10, p. 102.
\InputD{box-mac.tip}                       % 9.3.14, p. 343.
```

```
\def\ShiftRefPointUpOrDown #1#2{%
    \AdvanceBoxDimension{\ht#1}{#2}%
    \ifdim\ht#1 < 0pt
        \ht#1 = 0pt
    \fi
    \AdvanceBoxDimension{\dp#1}{-#2}%
    \ifdim\dp#1 < 0pt
        \dp#1 = 0pt
    \fi
}
```

• End of **shiftudb.tip** •

Here is an application of this macro. Assume the following TEX source file is given:

• **ex-shud.tip** •

```
\input inputd.tip
\InputD{shiftudb.tip}                           % 7.5.7, p. 254.
```

Load box register 0 with some sample text.

```
\setbox 0 = \vbox{%
    \hsize = 2.0in
    \raggedright
    This is a lot of fun, and as we go on, let me have
    a little more text, so everything wraps around a little
    bit, at least.
}
```

Make three copies of the vbox just generated.

```
\setbox1 = \copy0
\setbox2 = \copy0
\setbox3 = \copy0
```

Shift the various boxes.

```
\ShiftRefPointUpOrDown{1}{24pt}
\ShiftRefPointUpOrDown{2}{-24pt}
\ShiftRefPointUpOrDown{3}{-36pt}
```

Now print the original boxes and the three shifted copies.

```
$$
    \vbox{
        \hbox{%
            \BoxR 0
            \hskip 30pt
            \BoxR 1
        }
        \bigskip
        \hbox{%
            \BoxR 2
            \hskip 30pt
            \BoxR 3
        }
```

```
        }
$$
\bye
```

• End of ex-shud.tip •

The preceding source file generates the following text:

This is a lot of fun, and as we go on, let me have a little more text, so everything wraps around a little bit, at least.

This is a lot of fun, and as we go on, let me have a little more text, so everything wraps around a little bit, at least.

This is a lot of fun, and as we go on, let me have a little more text, so everything wraps around a little bit, at least.

This is a lot of fun, and as we go on, let me have a little more text, so everything wraps around a little bit, at least.

7.5.8 Alignment Problems in Vboxes

The following explanation requires a good understanding of `\valign`; see 41.5, p. IV-355. Assume you wish to align two vertical boxes, side by side, both boxes shifted upwards as far as possible (in other words, top flush). This may be trivial but nevertheless is a very useful application of `\valign`. You might use the following approach:

• ex-vflush.tip •

```
\input inputd.tip
\InputD{box-mac.tip}                          % 9.3.14, p. 343.
\centerline{%
    \tabskip = 5pt
    \valign{%
        #\vfil
    \cr
        \VboxR{%
            \hbox{eeee}
            \hbox{FFFF}
            \hbox{bbbb}
        }\cr
        \VboxR{%
            \hbox{FFFF}
            \hbox{gggg}
            \hbox{XXXX}
            \hbox{XXXX}
```

```
            \hbox{XXXX}
        }\cr
    }
}
\bye
```

• End of `ex-vflush.tip` •

The above source file generates the following output:

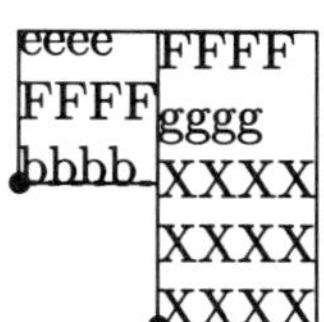

You immediately can see that the baselines of the individual lines do not line up, which has to do with the fact that the very first lines of each of the two outermost boxes are of different height. Here is how it can be corrected: one enables TEX's line spacing mechanism so it is also applied to the very first line. This can be done very easily adding a `\prevdepth = 2pt` to the beginning of each of the outermost vboxes. I choose a value of 2 pt because this means that the baseline of the first box within each outermost vbox will be 10 pt from the top edge of the box. The value of 10 pt corresponds to the default setting of `\topskip`, a parameter that also applied line spacing to the first line (`\topskip` forms a kind of `\baselineskip` for the very first line of a page); see 32.4.2, p. IV-12, for details. Here is the corrected example:

• `ex-vflush-2.tip` •

```
\input inputd.tip
\InputD{box-mac.tip}                          % 9.3.14, p. 343.
\centerline{%
    \tabskip = 5pt
    \valign{%
        #\vfil
    \cr
        \VboxR{%
            \prevdepth = 2pt
            \hbox{eeee}
            \hbox{FFFF}
            \hbox{bbbb}
        }\cr
        \VboxR{%
            \prevdepth = 2pt
            \hbox{FFFF}
            \hbox{gggg}
            \hbox{XXXX}
            \hbox{XXXX}
            \hbox{XXXX}
        }\cr
    }
}
```

```
\bye
```

• End of ex-vflush-2.tip •

The preceding source code generates the following output:

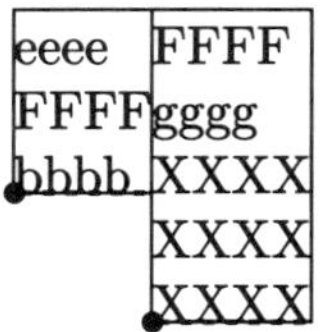

Another solution of the previous problem would have been to insert a strut with a height of 10 pt into the first box.

7.6 Summary

In this chapter we learned the following:

- There are three different instructions to generate vboxes: `\vbox`, `\vtop` or `\vcenter`. The main difference between these three instructions is where the reference point of the resulting series is located and therefore how the height and depth of the box is distributed. In the case of a vbox generated by `\vbox` the reference point of the vbox is identical with the reference point of the first item on the vertical list of the vbox. Therefore a vbox generated by `\vbox` is usually rather deep. For vboxes generated by `\vtop` the last item on the vertical list defines the reference point. Therefore vboxes generated by `\vtop` have a tendency of being rather high. Vboxes generated by `\vcenter` fall in between; note that `\vcenter` can only be used in math mode.
- The vertical list of a vbox can be compared with the horizontal list of an hbox. The main difference is that on a vertical list the material is collected top to bottom. Note also that a vertical list can contain lines of a paragraph and equations in display math mode.
- The `\leavevmode` macro allow one to instruct TeX to enter horizontal mode (the mode which processes a paragraph). This instruction is needed if an hbox is the very first item of a paragraph, because hboxes do not start paragraphs.
- Items can be moved left and right on a vertical list using `\moveleft` and `\moveright`.
- The line spacing in TeX is controlled by three parameters: `\baselineskip` (the ideal and normal distance between baselines of two consecutive boxes), `\lineskiplimit` (defining a threshold dimension and informing TeX when two lines are regarded as being too close) and `\lineskip` (glue inserted between two consecutive lines if TeX determined that two lines are too close).
- `\prevdepth` (depth of the previous line) is another dimension parameter used in line spacing computations. It is normally automatically loaded with the depth of the preceding box, but it can be set to a specific value by the user. If

set to −1000 pt (as it is done by the `\nointerlineskip` macro) no interline glue at all is inserted.

- `\offinterlineskip` causes TeX to insert zero interline glue between all boxes; `\normalbaselines` or grouping can be used to undo the effect of `\offinterlineskip`. If `\offinterlineskip` is in effect, typically struts are used to increase the height and depth of consecutive lines artificially so that these consecutive lines are spaced out equally (measured between the baselines of those boxes). Note that struts are normally generated by vertical rules of zero width. Other methods of manipulating the dimensions of boxes exist, like direct manipulation of the dimensions of a box stored in a box register. This chapter presented some macros for the automatic computation of struts.
- TeX does not insert any interline glue before and after horizontal rules.
- The width of a vbox is determined by the widest item on the vertical list of the vbox. Similar to `\hbox to` and `\hbox spread` type of constructs the same instructions exist for vertical boxes, as, for instance, `\vbox to` ⟨dimen⟩. The latter constructs a vbox of the specified height. Note that this usually implies stretching or shrinking glues on the vertical list of the vbox.
- The depth of a vbox can be limited by setting `\boxmaxdepth` to the desired maximum. By default this parameter is set to `\maxdimen` and therefore, if set to the default, has no effect.

8
More on Vertical Boxes

This chapter continues the discussion of vboxes. We will see how to unwrap and split vboxes. We will present more complicated vbox examples and discuss how to take boxes apart using `\last...` type of instructions. We will also discuss general macros for vertical spacing instructions.

8.1 Unwrapping Boxes Using `\un...` Primitives

Sometimes it is useful to "unbox" previously built boxes with the purpose of gaining direct access to the horizontal list of an hbox or the vertical list of a vbox. The primitives `\unhbox`, `\unvbox`, `\unhcopy` and `\unvcopy` do exactly that. All these primitives work on boxes stored in box registers. Therefore each of these instructions must be followed by a box register's number.

The difference between `\unhbox` and `\unhcopy` (and between `\unvbox` and `\unvcopy`) is the same as between `\box` and `\copy`. `\unhcopy` and `\unvcopy` do *not* destroy the contents of the box registers they extract information from whereas `\unhbox` and `\unvbox` do.

Remember that `\box` and `\copy` simply extract the content of a box register, i.e., they generate a duplicate of the box stored in the box register. `\unhbox`, on the other hand, generates a copy of *the horizontal list of an hbox* stored in the box register. This hbox is therefore completely "unpacked" and its horizontal list is generated (rather than the whole box). One of the most important aspects of this is that all glues of the generated list regain their shrinkability and stretchability.

The corresponding `\unvbox` command generates the copy of the vertical list of the original vbox. Similar to `\unhbox` all glues on the horizontal list of the box being unwrapped regain their stretchability and shrinkability.

Note that `\unhbox` and `\unhcopy` should really have been discussed in the preceding chapter, but because of the very advanced nature of these instructions it seemed to be more natural to discuss these instructions here.

The `\un...` instructions just mentioned will be discussed now. You might also want to look at the application of `\unvbox` in 8.2.8, p. 285.

8.1.1 Showing the Workings of `\unhbox`, etc.

The following series of examples should explain the workings of these instructions very easily. The examples will use `\unhcopy` exclusively which is sufficient demonstrating the workings of these instructions.

```
    \setbox 1 = \hbox to 2.0in{$|$\hfil XXX\hfil$|$}
    \setbox 2 = \hbox to 1.0in{$|$\hfill TTT\hfill$|$}
    \def\vr{\vrule height 4pt depth 2pt width 6pt}
1:  \hbox {\copy1 \vr \copy2}
```
XXX TTT
```
2:  \hbox {\copy1 \vr \unhcopy2}
```
XXX TTT
```
3:  \hbox spread 1in {\copy1 \vr \unhcopy2}
```
XXX TTT
```
4:  \hbox {\unhcopy1 \vr \copy2}
```
XXX TTT
```
5:  \hbox spread 1in {\unhcopy1 \vr \copy2}
```
XXX TTT
```
6:  \hbox {\unhcopy1 \vr \unhcopy2}
```
XXX TTT
```
7:  \hbox spread 1in {\unhcopy1 \vr \unhcopy2}
```
XXX TTT

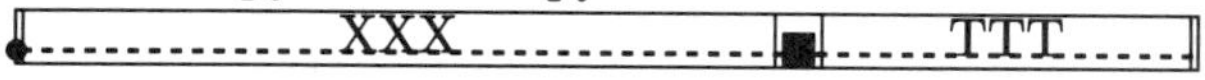

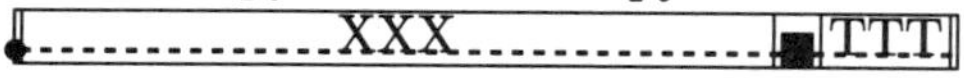

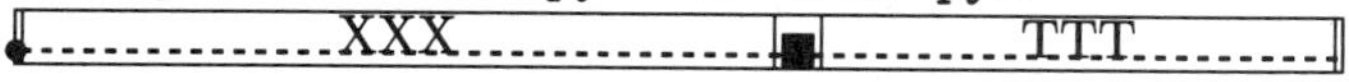

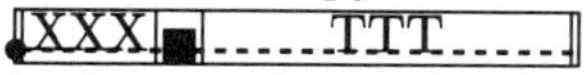

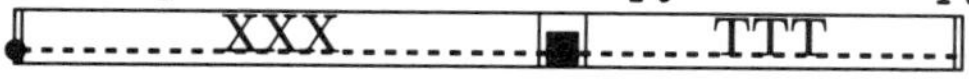

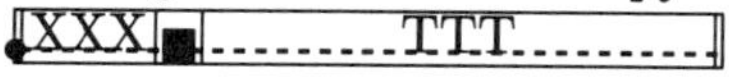

- *Example 1.* Copies of box registers 1 and 2 are placed side by side. The new box is 3 in wide, the sum of the widths of the two original boxes.
- *Example 2.* A copy of the first box is put together with an "unwrapped copy" of the second box. This example is therefore equivalent to the following TEX instructions: `\hbox{\hbox to 2.0in{...}\vr\vrule\hfill TTT\hfill}`. The two `\hfill` glues resulting from `\unhcopy2` will *not* stretch (their natural width is zero), because the outermost hbox is not "enticing" any glue to stretch using `\hbox to` or `\hbox spread`.
- *Example 3.* This example is almost identical to the preceding example but now the `\hfill`s generated by the `\unhcopy2` will stretch. They are the only source of stretchability in the box being built. The box generated by `\copy 1` stays rigid.
- *Example 4.* This example is almost identical to Example 2, but now the roles of the first and second box (box register 1 and 2) contained in the outer box are reversed. The `\hfil`s from box register 1 do not stretch.
- *Example 5.* This example is the same as Example 3, but again the roles of the first and second box are reversed. Now the `\hfil`s stretch.

- *Example 6.* This example is equivalent to the following TeX source:
  `\hbox{$|$\hfil XXX\hfil $|$\vr$|$\hfill TTT\hfill$|$}`
  Because the outermost box is not stretched, the `\hfil` and `\hfill` glues do not stretch.
- *Example 7.* This example is almost identical to the preceding example except that now the `\hfill` glues stretch. Note that because of the lower rank of the `\hfil` glues in the glue hierarchy the `\hfil` glues do *not* stretch; see 5.4.4, p. 137.

8.1.2 Interline Glue and \unvbox

An important detail about using `\unvbox` and `\unvcopy` is that no interline glue (`\baselineskip` or `\lineskip`) is inserted *before* the vertical list which is extracted.

For example look at the following input:

• ex-unvng.tip •

```
\input inputd.tip
\InputD{shboxes.tip}                        % 4.5.15, p. 111.
\setbox 0 = \vbox{\hbox{Something}}
\setbox 1 = \vbox{
      \copy 0
      \copy 0
      \unvcopy 0
      \unvcopy 0
      \copy 0
}
\ShowBoxDepthOne{1}
\bye
```

• End of ex-unvng.tip •

This source code generates the following log file:

• ex-unvng.log •

```
This is TeX, C Version 3.14 (...)
**&/usr/local/tex/lib/fmt/plain ex-unvng.tip
(ex-unvng.tip (inputd.tip
(namedef.tip
) (inputdl.tip
\@InputDStream=\write0
))
(shboxes.tip
)
> \box1=
\vbox(48.72221+1.94444)x46.11124
.\vbox(6.94444+1.94444)x46.11124 []
.\glue(\baselineskip) 3.11111
.\vbox(6.94444+1.94444)x46.11124 []
```

```
.\hbox(6.94444+1.94444)x46.11124 []
.\hbox(6.94444+1.94444)x46.11124 []
.\glue(\baselineskip) 3.11111
.\vbox(6.94444+1.94444)x46.11124 []

<to be read again>
}
l.11 \ShowBoxDepthOne{1}

)
No pages of output.
```

8.1.3 Determining the Natural Height or Depth of a Vbox, \NaturalHeight, \NaturalDepth

One application of \unvbox is in the definition of macro \NaturalHeight which computes the natural height of a vbox. This macro loads a dimension register with the natural height of a box. It has two parameters:

- #1. The dimension register which will be loaded with the height.
- #2. A box register containing a vbox from which the natural height will be extracted.

The macro \NaturalDepth is almost identical but this time the natural *depth* of a vbox is computed and returned in #1.

$\mathcal{P}'$ • nathd.tip •

```
\catcode`\@ = 11
\newbox\@NBox
\def\NaturalHeight #1#2{%
    \setbox\@NBox = \vbox{\unvcopy #2}
    #1 = \ht\@NBox
}
\def\NaturalDepth #1#2{%
    \setbox\@NBox = \vbox{\unvcopy #2}
    #1 = \dp\@NBox
}
\catcode`\@ = 12
```

• End of nathd.tip •

8.1.4 The Macro \Vtbox to Move the Reference Point of a Vbox

The macro \Vtbox converts a vertical box generated using \vbox to an "equivalent" vertical box generated by \vtop (the term equivalent means that the vertical list of the original and the derived box are equivalent; therefore the sums of height and depth are identical). The only difference between the boxes is that the application of `\Vtbox` moves the reference point such that the box generated looks like it had been generated using `\vtop` originally, instead of `\vbox`. Note that this problem cannot be solved using the macro `\ShiftRefPointUpOrDown` (7.5.7, p. 254) because this macro requires one to know the amount of shifting to be done.

$\mathcal{P}'$ • `vtbox.tip` •

The `\Vtbox` macro has the following two parameters:

- `#1`. The box register number containing the original vbox generated by `\vbox`. Note that this vbox must be stored in a box register, and that the result is stored in the same box register, thus losing the original box.
- `#2`. For this parameter specify `\global` if the execution of this macro is supposed to have a global effect on the box register. Provide an empty parameter if the change of the box register should be not global only.

Note that the macro `\Vtbox` is equivalent to the much simpler TeX instruction "`\setbox #1 = \vtop{\unvbox #1}`," if none of the glues of the vertical list of the vbox stored in box register `#1` are stretched or pushed together. Our macro here is able to deal with boxes which contain stretched or pushed together glue.

```
\catcode`\@ = 11
```

A temporary dimension register and a temporary box register are allocated now.

```
\newdimen\@VtboxDim
\newbox\@VtboxBox
```

Now the macro definition of `\Vtbox` begins.

```
\def\Vtbox #1#2{%
```

First compute the sum of the height and depth of the original box.

```
        \@VtboxDim = \ht#1%
        \advance\@VtboxDim by \dp#1%
```

Now get the height and depth of the unstretched box (the box may have been stretched or pushed together and this stretching or shrinking must be restored later).

```
        \setbox\@VtboxBox = \vbox{\unvcopy #1}%
```

Compute the net loss (or gain) in the sum of height and depth when the box was allowed to unstretch (if `\@VtboxDim` is zero after the two computations, then this means that the original box was neither stretched nor pushed together).

```
        \advance\@VtboxDim by -\ht\@VtboxBox
        \advance\@VtboxDim by -\dp\@VtboxBox
```

Now use the vertical list of the original box and build the box using `\vtop` instead of `\vbox`. The sum of the height and depth of the box being built now will be the same as the sum of the height and depth of the original box because the box generated by `\vtop` is stretched or pushed together (if necessary) by the proper amount.

```
        #2\setbox #1 = \vtop spread \@VtboxDim {\unvbox #1}%
```

We reached the end of this macro.

```
}
\catcode`\@ = 12
```

• End of `vtbox.tip` •

Here is an application of the `\Vtbox` macro. First we will build a vertical box using `\vbox`. Then we will print this box and call the above macro to make it a vertical box based on `\vtop`. This is the source code of the input:

```
\input inputd.tip
\InputD{vtbox.tip}                          % 8.1.4, p. 265.
\InputD{box-mac.tip}                        % 9.3.14, p. 343.
\setbox 0 = \vbox to 1.5in{%
    \baselineskip = 12pt plus 100pt
    \hbox{First line}
    \hbox{Second line}
    \hbox{Third line}
    \hbox{Last line}
}
\setbox1 = \copy0
\Vtbox{1}{}%
$$
    \hbox{\CopyR 0 \hskip 30pt \CopyR 1}
$$
```

The preceding source code generates the following output:

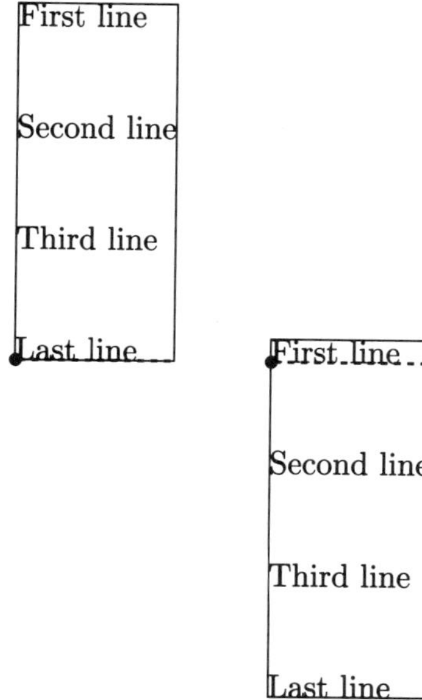

8.2 Splitting Vboxes, \vsplit

The command `\vsplit` is a little more complicated primitive, that is much easier to understand once you have seen a sufficient number of examples and also once you have a clear idea of the geometry of vboxes that are split by this instruction. The `\vsplit` instruction is used to vertically split the vertical list of a vbox into two parts.

Some applications of `\vsplit` are:

1. `\vsplit` can be used to *split off the header of a table* built with `\halign`. This header can then be replicated for a table continuing over multiple pages; see 41.3, p. IV-344. See the same reference for an example where `\vsplit` is used to split tables which would otherwise be longer than one page.
2. `\vsplit` can be used to "take a paragraph apart" by breaking it up into single lines. It it then possible to add line numbers to each line of the paragraph; see 8.2.12, p. 296.
3. One way to generate *double column text* is to double `\vsize` (the page length). TeX will now generate the left and right-hand column of one page together (resulting in one long narrow page). This double long column is then split into two properly sized columns which are then printed side by side. The splitting operation by which the long narrow page is split up into two columns uses `\vsplit`. See 37.2, p. IV-166, for an example.

8.2.1 The Syntax of \vsplit

The `\vsplit` instruction requires the vbox that will be split to be stored in a box register ⟨source⟩ (⟨source⟩ obviously stands for the box register index of that box). This box register will be called the *source box register.* Frequently we only talk about the *source box* and mean by that the box stored in the source box register.

Furthermore a dimension ⟨dimen⟩ must be given which specifies the height of the material to be split off by `\vsplit` from the source box. This material is removed from the source box forming what will be called the *destination box.*

Here is the syntax of the `\vsplit` instruction:

`\vsplit` ⟨source⟩ `to` ⟨dimen⟩

Frequently as a practical matter, and in particular for the following examples, the destination box is stored in a box register itself (we do this mainly to be able to inspect the generated destination box in detail using `\showbox` or macros related to `\showbox`). Including the assignment of the destination box to a box register, the syntax of the `\vsplit` command reads as follows (⟨dest⟩ is obviously the box register index of the box register that is used to hold the destination box):

`\setbox` ⟨dest⟩ `=` `\vsplit` ⟨source⟩ `to` ⟨dimen⟩

Please note that the discussion of `\vsplit` below does *not* contain a discussion of how marks ("mark" is a TeX term discuss in 34.7, p. IV-81) are handled in `\vsplit`; see 34.7.3.1, p. IV-83, for details.

8.2.2 The First \vsplit Example

Here is the source code of the first `\vsplit` example (this is followed by the printout of the log file generated by this source code. Ignore the setting of `\splittopskip` right now):

• ex-vsplit.tip •

```
\input inputd.tip
\InputD{emptybox.tip}                     % 4.5.12, p. 103.
\InputD{shboxes.tip}                      % 4.5.15, p. 111.
\vfuzz = 0pt
\splittopskip = 0pt
```

Declare the source and destination box registers.

```
\newbox\SourceBox
\newbox\DestinationBox
```

Load the source box register with a vbox that contains two other boxes. The widths of the two boxes contained in the source box are irrelevant. Because of `\offinterlineskip`, zero glue is inserted between the two boxes.

```
\setbox\SourceBox = \vbox{
     \offinterlineskip
     \EmptyBox{3pt}{2pt}{30pt}
     \EmptyBox{6pt}{4pt}{40pt}
}
```

Show the source box.

```
\message{(1) Source box (initially):}
\ShowBoxDepthOne{\SourceBox}
```

Split off the first box contained in the source box. A dimension of 3 pt is chosen because this is the height of the material that is supposed to be split off (and therefore it is the height of the first box contained inside the source box).

```
\setbox\DestinationBox = \vsplit\SourceBox to 3pt
```

Show the contents of the source as well as the destination box after this `\vsplit` operation is completed.

```
\message{(2) After first \string\vsplit:}
\message{Source box:}         \ShowBoxDepthOne{\SourceBox}
\message{Destination box:}  \ShowBoxDepthOne{\DestinationBox}
```

Split off the second box from the original source box leaving the source box empty. A `\vsplit`-related dimension of 6 pt is chosen because this is the height of the material that we try to split off this time (this material is, with the exception of \splittopskip, really the only material left inside the source box).

```
\setbox\DestinationBox = \vsplit\SourceBox to 6pt
```

Show source and destination boxes again. Note that the source box register is empty now.

```
\message{(3): After second \string\vsplit:}
\message{Source box:}       \ShowBoxDepthOne{\SourceBox}
\message{Destination box:}  \ShowBoxDepthOne{\DestinationBox}
```

End of example.

```
\bye
```

• End of ex-vsplit.tip •

The log file generated from the preceding input reads as follows:

• ex-vsplit.log •

```
This is TeX, C Version 3.14 (...)
**&/usr/local/tex/lib/fmt/plain ex-vsplit.tip
(ex-vsplit.tip (inputd.tip
(namedef.tip
) (inputdl.tip
\@InputDStream=\write0
))
(emptybox.tip
) (shboxes.tip
)
\SourceBox=\box16
\DestinationBox=\box17
(1) Source box (initially):
> \box16=
\vbox(11.0+4.0)x40.0
.\hbox(3.0+2.0)x30.0 []
.\glue(\lineskip) 0.0
.\hbox(6.0+4.0)x40.0 []

<argument> \SourceBox

}
l.14 ...oxDepthOne{\SourceBox}

(2) After first \vsplit: Source box:
> \box16=
\vbox(6.0+4.0)x40.0
.\glue(\splittopskip) 0.0
.\hbox(6.0+4.0)x40.0 []

<argument> \SourceBox

}
l.17 ...oxDepthOne{\SourceBox}
```

```
Destination box:
> \box17=
\vbox(3.0+2.0)x30.0
.\hbox(3.0+2.0)x30.0 []

<argument> \DestinationBox

}
l.18 ...thOne{\DestinationBox}

(3): After second \vsplit: Source box:
> \box16=void

<argument> \SourceBox

}
l.21 ...oxDepthOne{\SourceBox}

Destination box:
> \box17=
\vbox(6.0+4.0)x40.0
.\glue(\splittopskip) 0.0
.\hbox(6.0+4.0)x40.0 []

<argument> \DestinationBox

}
l.22 ...thOne{\DestinationBox}

)
No pages of output.
```

This was just a first and very simple example; the interpretation of many details will not be discussed in the following subsections.

8.2.3 Glue Is Removed at a Break Point

Observe that when the original source box was built in the previous example TEX inserted vertical glue between the two boxes contained in the source box. This glue was `\lineskip` glue in the amount of 0 pt because `\offinterlineskip` was in effect.

Note that this glue was removed during the first split operation. 5.4.6, p. 139, discusses the fact that glue is a discardable item that is *removed* when the break point occurs at it; in our example here, the 0 pt `\lineskip` glue forms the break point for the first `\vsplit` application. TEX *requires* the presence of such glue to break up a vertical list in the first place as we will see shortly.

Our next example is along the same lines as the preceding example. This time *multiple* vertical glues are inserted between the two internal boxes of the source box. *All* these glues disappear and are removed because the `\vsplit` operation splits the vertical list of the source box at this point. The first glue is removed because it forms the break point. The second, third and fourth glues follow the first glue immediately and therefore are removed too. See 10.10.5, p. II-42, for another example where multiple horizontal glues are removed at a break point.

• `ex-vsplit-2.tip` •

The initial part of this example resembles the preceding example.

```
\input inputd.tip
\InputD{emptybox.tip}                        % 4.5.12, p. 103.
\InputD{shboxes.tip}                         % 4.5.15, p. 111.
\vfuzz = 0pt
\splittopskip = 0pt
\newbox\SourceBox
\newbox\DestinationBox
```

Now initialize the source box as just explained. Three glues (all `\vskip 1.0in`) are inserted between the two boxes (a fourth glue, `\lineskip` in the amount of 0 pt, is inserted by TeX).

```
\setbox\SourceBox = \vbox{
    \offinterlineskip
    \EmptyBox{3pt}{2pt}{30pt}
    \vskip 1.0in \vskip 1.0in \vskip 1.0in
    \EmptyBox{6pt}{4pt}{40pt}
}
```

Show the initial box.

```
\message{(1) Source box (initial):}
\ShowBoxDepthOne{\SourceBox}
```

Split the first box contained in the source box off and show the resulting boxes. The dimension chosen here to remove the first box within the source box is again 3 pt, the height of the first box within the source box.

```
\setbox\DestinationBox = \vsplit\SourceBox to 3pt

\message{(2) After \string\vsplit:}
\message{Source box:}
\ShowBoxDepthOne{\SourceBox}
\message{Result box:}
\ShowBoxDepthOne{\DestinationBox}
\bye
```

• End of `ex-vsplit-2.tip` •

The preceding source code generated the following log file. Note that all three `\vskip`s and the `\lineskip` glue cannot be found in either the source box or destination box after the `\vsplit` was performed.

• ex-vsplit-2.log •

```
This is TeX, C Version 3.14 (...)
**&/usr/local/tex/lib/fmt/plain ex-vsplit-2.tip
(ex-vsplit-2.tip (inputd.tip
(namedef.tip
) (inputdl.tip
\@InputDStream=\write0
))
(emptybox.tip
) (shboxes.tip
)
\SourceBox=\box16
\DestinationBox=\box17
(1) Source box (initial):
> \box16=
\vbox(227.80997+4.0)x40.0
.\hbox(3.0+2.0)x30.0 []
.\glue 72.26999
.\glue 72.26999
.\glue 72.26999
.\glue(\lineskip) 0.0
.\hbox(6.0+4.0)x40.0 []

<argument> \SourceBox

}
l.15 ...oxDepthOne{\SourceBox}

(2) After \vsplit: Source box:
> \box16=
\vbox(6.0+4.0)x40.0
.\glue(\splittopskip) 0.0
.\hbox(6.0+4.0)x40.0 []

<argument> \SourceBox

}
l.20 ...oxDepthOne{\SourceBox}

Result box:
> \box17=
\vbox(3.0+2.0)x30.0
.\hbox(3.0+2.0)x30.0 []

<argument> \DestinationBox

}
l.22 ...thOne{\DestinationBox}

)
No pages of output.
```

8.2.4 Protecting Glue at a Break Point

Let us study a slight variant of the preceding example. If, for example, a penalty of 10,000 is inserted before all four glues, the penalty will tell TeX to avoid a break under all circumstances (see 5.8.1, p. 158). This penalty is not only in effect for the first but also for the immediately following three more glues and therefore no break will take place. It is important to notice that the penalty is *not* solely applied to the glue immediately following it.

Here is the source code of the example:

• `ex-vsplit-3.tip` •

```
\input inputd.tip
\InputD{emptybox.tip}                          % 4.5.12, p. 103.
\InputD{shboxes.tip}                           % 4.5.15, p. 111.
\vfuzz = 0pt
\splittopskip = 0pt
\newbox\SourceBox
\newbox\DestinationBox
\setbox\SourceBox = \vbox{
    \offinterlineskip
    \EmptyBox{3pt}{2pt}{30pt}
```

The following `\penalty 10000` was added compared to the preceding example.

```
    \penalty 10000
    \vskip 1.0in
    \vskip 1.0in
    \vskip 1.0in
    \EmptyBox{6pt}{4pt}{40pt}
}
```

Show the initial source box now.

```
\message{(1) Source box (initial):} \ShowBoxDepthOne{\SourceBox}
```

Perform a `\vsplit`.

```
\setbox\DestinationBox = \vsplit\SourceBox to 3pt
\message{(2) After \string\vsplit:}
\message{Source box:} \ShowBoxDepthOne{\SourceBox}
\message{Result box:} \ShowBoxDepthOne{\DestinationBox}
\bye
```

• End of `ex-vsplit-3.tip` •

The preceding source code generated the following log file. Note that the penalty of 10000 and all the following four glue items stayed intact.

• `ex-vsplit-3.log` •

```
This is TeX, C Version 3.14 (...)
**&/usr/local/tex/lib/fmt/plain ex-vsplit-3.tip
(ex-vsplit-3.tip (inputd.tip
(namedef.tip
) (inputdl.tip
```

```
\@InputDStream=\write0
))
(emptybox.tip
) (shboxes.tip
)
\SourceBox=\box16
\DestinationBox=\box17
(1) Source box (initial):
> \box16=
\vbox(227.80997+4.0)x40.0
.\hbox(3.0+2.0)x30.0 []
.\penalty 10000
.\glue 72.26999
.\glue 72.26999
.\glue 72.26999
.\glue(\lineskip) 0.0
.\hbox(6.0+4.0)x40.0 []

<argument> \SourceBox

}
l.17 ...oxDepthOne{\SourceBox}

Overfull \vbox (224.80997pt too high) detected at line 18

\vbox(3.0+4.0)x40.0
.\hbox(3.0+2.0)x30.0
..\hbox(3.0+2.0)x30.0
.\penalty 10000
.\glue 72.26999
.\glue 72.26999
.\glue 72.26999
.etc.

(2) After \vsplit: Source box:
> \box16=void

<argument> \SourceBox

}
l.20 ...oxDepthOne{\SourceBox}

Result box:
> \box17=
\vbox(3.0+4.0)x40.0
.\hbox(3.0+2.0)x30.0 []
.\penalty 10000
.\glue 72.26999
.\glue 72.26999
.\glue 72.26999
.\glue(\lineskip) 0.0
.\hbox(6.0+4.0)x40.0 []
```

```
<argument> \DestinationBox
}
l.21 ...thOne{\DestinationBox}
)
No pages of output.
```

Recall that the penalty must precede all four glues. For instance, assume `\SourceBox` is initialized as follows:

```
\setbox\SourceBox = \vbox{
    \offinterlineskip
    \EmptyBox{3pt}{2pt}{30pt}
    \vskip 1.0in
    \penalty 10000
    \vskip 1.0in
    \vskip 1.0in
    \EmptyBox{6pt}{4pt}{40pt}
}
```

Then the first glue would form a legal break point.

8.2.5 Protecting Glue at a Break Point, Exceptions

There is another interesting variant of the previous example (that initially looks more academic than anything else, but which bit me once) and that is the following. Take the preceding example but add a `\write` instruction between the first and the second glue: the preceding penalty suddenly no more protects the second and third glue.

Here is the example (it is identical to the preceding example except for the addition of a `\write` and a removal of the `\ShowBoxDepthOne` call of the initial version of the source box):

• `ex-vsplit-4.tip` •

```
\input inputd.tip
\InputD{emptybox.tip}                          % 4.5.12, p. 103.
\InputD{shboxes.tip}                           % 4.5.15, p. 111.
\vfuzz = 0pt
\splittopskip = 0pt
\newbox\SourceBox
\newbox\DestinationBox
\setbox\SourceBox = \vbox{
    \offinterlineskip
    \EmptyBox{3pt}{2pt}{30pt}
    \penalty 10000
    \vskip 1.0in
```

The following `\write` was added compared to the previous example.

```
    \write1{Something to write}
    \vskip 1.0in
    \vskip 1.0in
    \EmptyBox{6pt}{4pt}{40pt}
}
\setbox\DestinationBox = \vsplit\SourceBox to 3pt
\message{(2) After \string\vsplit:}
\message{Source box:} \ShowBoxDepthOne{\SourceBox}
\message{Result box:} \ShowBoxDepthOne{\DestinationBox}
\bye
```

• End of `ex-vsplit-4.tip` •

The log file produced by this example reads as follows (compare in particular the content of `\SourceBox` and `\DestinationBox` with the contents of the same registers in the preceding example):

• `ex-vsplit-4.log` •

```
This is TeX, C Version 3.14 (...)
**&/usr/local/tex/lib/fmt/plain ex-vsplit-4.tip
(ex-vsplit-4.tip (inputd.tip
(namedef.tip
) (inputdl.tip
\@InputDStream=\write0
))
(emptybox.tip
) (shboxes.tip
)
\SourceBox=\box16
\DestinationBox=\box17
Overfull \vbox (74.26999pt too high) detected at line 18
\vbox(3.0+0.0)x30.0
.\hbox(3.0+2.0)x30.0
..\hbox(3.0+2.0)x30.0
.\penalty 10000
.\glue 72.26999
.\write1{Something to write}
(2) After \vsplit: Source box:
> \box16=
\vbox(6.0+4.0)x40.0
.\glue(\splittopskip) 0.0
.\hbox(6.0+4.0)x40.0 []
<argument> \SourceBox
}
l.20 ...oxDepthOne{\SourceBox}
Result box:
> \box17=
```

```
\vbox(3.0+0.0)x30.0
.\hbox(3.0+2.0)x30.0 []
.\penalty 10000
.\glue 72.26999
.\write1{Something to write}

<argument> \DestinationBox

}
l.21 ...thOne{\DestinationBox}

)
No pages of output.
```

The same problems occurs when `\write` is replaced by `\mark`. Here is the example source code:

• `ex-vsplit-5.tip` •

```
\input inputd.tip
\InputD{emptybox.tip}                          % 4.5.12, p. 103.
\InputD{shboxes.tip}                           % 4.5.15, p. 111.
\vfuzz = 0pt
\splittopskip = 0pt
\newbox\SourceBox
\newbox\DestinationBox
\setbox\SourceBox = \vbox{
    \offinterlineskip
    \EmptyBox{3pt}{2pt}{30pt}
    \penalty 10000
    \vskip 1.0in
```

In the preceding example the following instruction is a `\write`.

```
    \mark{I have a lot of fun.}
    \vskip 1.0in
    \vskip 1.0in
    \EmptyBox{6pt}{4pt}{40pt}
}
\setbox\DestinationBox = \vsplit\SourceBox to 3pt
\message{(2) After \string\vsplit:}
\message{Source box:} \ShowBoxDepthOne{\SourceBox}
\message{Result box:} \ShowBoxDepthOne{\DestinationBox}
\bye
```

• End of `ex-vsplit-5.tip` •

The log file produced by this example reads as follows (it is essentially identical to the log file of the immediately preceding example):

• `ex-vsplit-5.log` •

```
This is TeX, C Version 3.14 (...)
**&/usr/local/tex/lib/fmt/plain ex-vsplit-5.tip
(ex-vsplit-5.tip (inputd.tip
(namedef.tip
```

```
) (inputdl.tip
\@InputDStream=\write0
))
(emptybox.tip
) (shboxes.tip
)
\SourceBox=\box16
\DestinationBox=\box17

Overfull \vbox (74.26999pt too high) detected at line 18

\vbox(3.0+0.0)x30.0
.\hbox(3.0+2.0)x30.0
..\hbox(3.0+2.0)x30.0
.\penalty 10000
.\glue 72.26999
.\mark{I have a lot of fun.}

(2) After \vsplit: Source box:
> \box16=
\vbox(6.0+4.0)x40.0
.\glue(\splittopskip) 0.0
.\hbox(6.0+4.0)x40.0 []

<argument> \SourceBox

}
l.20 ...oxDepthOne{\SourceBox}

Result box:
> \box17=
\vbox(3.0+0.0)x30.0
.\hbox(3.0+2.0)x30.0 []
.\penalty 10000
.\glue 72.26999
.\mark{I have a lot of fun.}

<argument> \DestinationBox

}
l.21 ...thOne{\DestinationBox}

)
No pages of output.
```

Finally, the same problem occurs when a `\special` is inserted. Here is the example source code:

• `ex-vsplit-6.tip` •

```
\input inputd.tip
\InputD{emptybox.tip}                     % 4.5.12, p. 103.
\InputD{shboxes.tip}                      % 4.5.15, p. 111.
```

```
\vfuzz = 0pt
\splittopskip = 0pt
\newbox\SourceBox
\newbox\DestinationBox
\setbox\SourceBox = \vbox{
    \offinterlineskip
    \EmptyBox{3pt}{2pt}{30pt}
    \penalty 10000
    \vskip 1.0in
```

In the preceding example the following instruction is a `\write`.

```
    \special{Something special}
    \vskip 1.0in
    \vskip 1.0in
    \EmptyBox{6pt}{4pt}{40pt}
}
\setbox\DestinationBox = \vsplit\SourceBox to 3pt
\message{(2) After \string\vsplit:}
\message{Source box:} \ShowBoxDepthOne{\SourceBox}
\message{Result box:} \ShowBoxDepthOne{\DestinationBox}
\bye
```

• End of `ex-vsplit-6.tip` •

The log file produced by this example reads as follows (it is essentially identical to the log file of the immediately preceding example):

• `ex-vsplit-6.log` •

```
This is TeX, C Version 3.14 (...)
**&/usr/local/tex/lib/fmt/plain ex-vsplit-6.tip
(ex-vsplit-6.tip (inputd.tip
(namedef.tip
) (inputdl.tip
\@InputDStream=\write0
))
(emptybox.tip
) (shboxes.tip
)
\SourceBox=\box16
\DestinationBox=\box17

Overfull \vbox (74.26999pt too high) detected at line 18

\vbox(3.0+0.0)x30.0
.\hbox(3.0+2.0)x30.0
..\hbox(3.0+2.0)x30.0
.\penalty 10000
.\glue 72.26999
.\special{Something special}

(2) After \vsplit: Source box:
> \box16=
\vbox(6.0+4.0)x40.0
```

```
.\glue(\splittopskip) 0.0
.\hbox(6.0+4.0)x40.0 []

<argument> \SourceBox

}
l.20 ...oxDepthOne{\SourceBox}

Result box:
> \box17=
\vbox(3.0+0.0)x30.0
.\hbox(3.0+2.0)x30.0 []
.\penalty 10000
.\glue 72.26999
.\special{Something special}

<argument> \DestinationBox

}
l.21 ...thOne{\DestinationBox}

)
No pages of output.
```

8.2.6 Leaders Are Removed at a Break Point

Leaders and glue are almost identical, as we discussed in 5.6, p. 145. It is only natural therefore for TEX to also remove a leader at a break point of a `\vsplit` operation (or for that matter any combination of leaders and glue). Here is a variant of the example at the beginning of the preceding Subsection (8.2.5, p. 275) using leaders instead of glue.

• `ex-vsplit-7.tip` •

```
\input inputd.tip
\InputD{emptybox.tip}                        % 4.5.12, p. 103.
\InputD{shboxes.tip}                         % 4.5.15, p. 111.
\vfuzz = 0pt
\splittopskip = 0pt
\newbox\SourceBox
\newbox\DestinationBox
\setbox\SourceBox = \vbox{
    \offinterlineskip
    \EmptyBox{3pt}{2pt}{30pt}
    \leaders\hrule\vskip 1.0in
    \leaders\hrule\vskip 1.0in
    \leaders\hrule\vskip 1.0in
    \EmptyBox{6pt}{4pt}{40pt}
}
```

Show the source box, execute `\vsplit`, and show source and destination boxes. The dimension of the `\vsplit` is chosen the way it was explained before.

```
\message{(1) Source box (initial):} \ShowBoxDepthOne{\SourceBox}
\setbox\DestinationBox = \vsplit\SourceBox to 3pt
\message{(2) After \string\vsplit:}
\message{Source box:} \ShowBoxDepthOne{\SourceBox}
\message{Result box:} \ShowBoxDepthOne{\DestinationBox}
\bye
```

• End of `ex-vsplit-7.tip` •

The above source file code generates the following log file (at this time in our experiment source and destination boxes *after* the `\vsplit` are identical to the source and destination boxes of the first example in the preceding Subsection).

• `ex-vsplit-7.log` •

```
This is TeX, C Version 3.14 (...)
**&/usr/local/tex/lib/fmt/plain ex-vsplit-7.tip
(ex-vsplit-7.tip (inputd.tip
(namedef.tip
) (inputdl.tip
\@InputDStream=\write0
))
(emptybox.tip
) (shboxes.tip
)
\SourceBox=\box16
\DestinationBox=\box17
(1) Source box (initial):
> \box16=
\vbox(227.80997+4.0)x40.0
.\hbox(3.0+2.0)x30.0 []
.\leaders 72.26999 []
.\leaders 72.26999 []
.\leaders 72.26999 []
.\glue(\lineskip) 0.0
.\hbox(6.0+4.0)x40.0 []

<argument> \SourceBox

}
l.16 ...oxDepthOne{\SourceBox}

(2) After \vsplit: Source box:
> \box16=
\vbox(6.0+4.0)x40.0
.\glue(\splittopskip) 0.0
.\hbox(6.0+4.0)x40.0 []

<argument> \SourceBox

}
```

```
l.19 ...oxDepthOne{\SourceBox}

Result box:
> \box17=
\vbox(3.0+2.0)x30.0
.\hbox(3.0+2.0)x30.0 []

<argument> \DestinationBox

}
l.20 ...thOne{\DestinationBox}

)
No pages of output.
```

8.2.7 The Insertion of `\splittopskip` Glue by TEX

If you have analyzed the preceding examples carefully then you have probably assumed that `\splittopskip` glue is inserted by TEX into the source box after a split operator. This glue (minus the height of the first item) is inserted *after* the material which is split off has been removed. If the glue value computed comes out negative, a glue in the amount of zero is inserted. In other words the glue inserted is never negative.

This glue is very similar to the function of `\topskip`. The explanation for `\topskip` given in 32.4.2, p. IV-12, applies also to `\splittopskip`. The `\splittopskip` glue is nothing else than a special glue (similar to `\baselineskip`) for the very first item of the vertical list of the new and reduced source box. The `\splittopskip` glue allows you to ensure that the baseline of the first line of some text stored in the source box is always at a fixed position after the `\vsplit` operation was executed (assuming this line is not of excessive height).

Before we discuss an example showing the effect of `\splittopskip`, note that this glue is also used in case insertions are split; see 35.4.1.4, p. IV-99, for details.

Here is the next example to show the workings of `\splittopskip`. The following source code is used:

• `ex-vsplit-8.tip` •

```
\input inputd.tip
\InputD{shboxes.tip}                        % 4.5.15, p. 111.
\InputD{emptybox.tip}                       % 4.5.12, p. 103.
\vfuzz = 0pt
\baselineskip = 12pt
\splittopskip = 12pt
\newbox\SourceBox
\newbox\DestinationBox
```

Initialize the source box and show the source box's content.

```
\setbox\SourceBox = \vbox{
    \hbox{First Line}
    \hbox{Second Line}
    \hbox{Third Line}
    \hbox{Fourth Line}
}
\message{(1) Initial source box:}
\ShowBoxDepthOne{\SourceBox}
```

Actually print the source box.

```
\leftline{\bf Initial source box:}
    \nobreak \vskip 3pt
    \moveright 1.0in \copy\SourceBox
```

Split two lines (the first two boxes) off the source box. The `\vsplit` dimension of 20 pt that will be used is computed as follows: 8 pt + `\baselineskip`.

```
\setbox\DestinationBox = \vsplit\SourceBox to 20pt
```

Now show the source box and the destination box in the log file.

```
\message{(2) After \string\vsplit:}
\message{Source box:} \ShowBoxDepthOne{\SourceBox}
\message{Result box:} \ShowBoxDepthOne{\DestinationBox}
```

Now actually print both boxes.

```
\bigskip
\leftline{{\bf Source box after {\tt\string\vsplit}:}}
    \moveright 1.0in\copy\SourceBox
\smallskip
\leftline{{\bf Destination box after {\tt\string\vsplit}:}}
    \moveright 1.0in\copy\DestinationBox
```

Now print the two boxes side by side.

```
\bigskip
\leftline{\bf Now show both boxes side by side:}
\leftline{%
    \hskip 1.0in
    \box\DestinationBox
    \hskip 0.2in
    \box\SourceBox
}
\bye
```

• End of `ex-vsplit-8.tip` •

The log file generated by the above example reads as follows:

• `ex-vsplit-8.log` •

```
This is TeX, C Version 3.14 (...)
**&/usr/local/tex/lib/fmt/plain ex-vsplit-8.tip
(ex-vsplit-8.tip (inputd.tip
(namedef.tip
) (inputdl.tip
\@InputDStream=\write0
```

```
))
(shboxes.tip
) (emptybox.tip
)
\SourceBox=\box16
\DestinationBox=\box17
(1) Initial source box:
> \box16=
\vbox(42.83331+0.0)x52.91676
.\hbox(6.83331+0.0)x43.41675 []
.\glue(\baselineskip) 5.05556
.\hbox(6.94444+0.0)x52.91676 []
.\glue(\baselineskip) 5.05556
.\hbox(6.94444+0.0)x47.38898 []
.\glue(\baselineskip) 5.05556
.\hbox(6.94444+0.0)x51.97234 []

<argument> \SourceBox

}
l.16 ...oxDepthOne{\SourceBox}

Underfull \vbox (badness 10000) detected at line 20

\vbox(20.0+0.0)x52.91676
.\hbox(6.83331+0.0)x43.41675
..\tenrm F
..\tenrm i
..\tenrm r
..\tenrm s
..\tenrm t
..etc.
.\glue(\baselineskip) 5.05556
.\hbox(6.94444+0.0)x52.91676
..\tenrm S
..\tenrm e
..\tenrm c
..\tenrm o
..\tenrm n
..etc.

(2) After \vsplit: Source box:
> \box16=
\vbox(24.0+0.0)x51.97234
.\glue(\splittopskip) 5.05556
.\hbox(6.94444+0.0)x47.38898 []
.\glue(\baselineskip) 5.05556
.\hbox(6.94444+0.0)x51.97234 []

<argument> \SourceBox

}
```

```
l.22 ...oxDepthOne{\SourceBox}

Result box:
> \box17=
\vbox(20.0+0.0)x52.91676
.\hbox(6.83331+0.0)x43.41675 []
.\glue(\baselineskip) 5.05556
.\hbox(6.94444+0.0)x52.91676 []

<argument> \DestinationBox

}
l.23 ...thOne{\DestinationBox}

[1] )
Output written on ex-vsplit-8.dvi (1 page, 784 bytes).
```

The above source code generates the following output:

Initial source box:

First Line
Second Line
Third Line
Fourth Line

Source box after \vsplit:

Third Line
Fourth Line

Destination box after \vsplit:

First Line
Second Line

Now show both boxes side by side:

First Line   Third Line
Second Line   Fourth Line

8.2.8 Using a Penalty in \vsplit

One item you had to know on all the preceding examples was the height of the material to be split off. While this height can frequently be computed, there are other cases where you would like to instruct TEX to "split here" without specifying any dimension. Here is how this can be done in TEX: a penalty of -10000 is inserted at the break point. This will force `\vsplit` to break at this point later provided ⟨dimen⟩ of `\vsplit` is set to a sufficiently large value.

A penalty of $-10,000$ can be inserted directly using the `\penalty` primitive or by using macros `\break` or `\eject`.

Here is the source code of an example showing this technique.

• ex-vsplit-pen.tip •

```
\input inputd.tip
\InputD{shboxes.tip}                          % 4.5.15, p. 111.
\InputD{emptybox.tip}                         % 4.5.12, p. 103.
\vfuzz = 0pt
\splittopskip = 0pt
\offinterlineskip
\newbox\SourceBox
\newbox\SourceBoxCopy
\newbox\DestinationBox
```

Initialize the source box register and show its content.

```
\setbox\SourceBox = \vbox{
    \EmptyBox{3pt}{2pt}{30pt}
    \penalty -10000          % or \break
    \EmptyBox{6pt}{4pt}{40pt}
}
\setbox\SourceBoxCopy = \copy\SourceBox
\message{(1) Source box:}
\ShowBoxDepthOne{\SourceBox}
```

Split off the first box contained in the source box. Because of the $-10,000$ penalty any splitoff dimension greater than the height of the desired break point can be used.

```
\setbox\DestinationBox = \vsplit\SourceBox to 1000pt
\message{(2) After first \string\vsplit:}
\ShowBoxDepthOne{\SourceBox}
\ShowBoxDepthOne{\DestinationBox}
```

Fix up the destination box now. This is an important step to correct the excessive height of the destination box which was caused by a totally "out of order" ⟨dimen⟩ specification.

```
\setbox\DestinationBox = \vbox{\unvbox\DestinationBox}
\message{(3) Fixed up \string\DestinationBox}
\ShowBoxDepthOne{\DestinationBox}
```

Now repeat the preceding experiment. Let me show now how you can avoid a message about an underfull vbox by setting `\vbadness` temporarily to 10,000. Note that no message to such effect will be printed now.

```
\message{(4) Reload source box}
\setbox\SourceBox = \box\SourceBoxCopy
```

Repeat `\vsplit` now. Then fix up the destination box as before.

```
{%
    \vbadness = 10000
    \global\setbox\DestinationBox = \vsplit\SourceBox to 1000pt
}
\setbox\DestinationBox = \vbox{\unvbox\DestinationBox}
\bye
```

• End of ex-vsplit-pen.tip •

The above source code generated the following log file:

• ex-vsplit-pen.log •

```
This is TeX, C Version 3.14 (...)
**&/usr/local/tex/lib/fmt/plain ex-vsplit-pen.tip
(ex-vsplit-pen.tip (inputd.tip
(namedef.tip
) (inputdl.tip
\@InputDStream=\write0
))
(shboxes.tip
) (emptybox.tip
)
\SourceBox=\box16
\SourceBoxCopy=\box17
\DestinationBox=\box18
(1) Source box:
> \box16=
\vbox(11.0+4.0)x40.0
.\hbox(3.0+2.0)x30.0 []
.\penalty -10000
.\glue(\lineskip) 0.0
.\hbox(6.0+4.0)x40.0 []

<argument> \SourceBox

}
l.17 ...oxDepthOne{\SourceBox}

Underfull \vbox (badness 10000) detected at line 18

\vbox(1000.0+2.0)x30.0
.\hbox(3.0+2.0)x30.0
..\hbox(3.0+2.0)x30.0

(2) After first \vsplit:
> \box16=
\vbox(6.0+4.0)x40.0
.\glue(\splittopskip) 0.0
.\hbox(6.0+4.0)x40.0 []

<argument> \SourceBox

}
l.20 ...oxDepthOne{\SourceBox}

> \box18=
\vbox(1000.0+2.0)x30.0
.\hbox(3.0+2.0)x30.0 []

<argument> \DestinationBox

```

```
50 }
51 l.21 ...thOne{\DestinationBox}
52
53 (3) Fixed up \DestinationBox
54 > \box18=
55 \vbox(3.0+2.0)x30.0
56 .\hbox(3.0+2.0)x30.0 []
57
58 <argument> \DestinationBox
59
60 }
61 l.24 ...thOne{\DestinationBox}
62
63 (4) Reload source box )
64 No pages of output.
```

An important aspect of this example is line 23 where we use as proposed a dimension for `\vsplit` which certainly exceeds the height of what we want to split up. We end up with the proper material in box register 1, but the height of this material is 1000 pt. This is corrected in line 31 where we unwrap the content of box register 1 to put it back immediately. "Unwrapping" means to get the original list of a box back instead of the box as a whole. This way we end up with a box which has its natural height and depth as its dimensions.

8.2.9 The ⟨dimen⟩ of `\vsplit` ⟨dimen⟩

There are several factors involved in specifying the value of the dimension when you apply `\vsplit`:

1. First of all, if you can use the approach presented in the previous Subsection then everything is very easy, because you do not really need to compute any dimension. By giving a logical description of where the break should be executed, you will have given TEX enough information for the desired brake point.
2. Next note that `\splittopskip` should be set properly so that the dimensions of your source box, after some material is split off, are set properly.
3. The ⟨dimen⟩ you specify with a `\vsplit` will be forced as the height on the destination box. TEX will stretch or shrink any glues if this should be necessary, but even if there are no such glue available, ⟨dimen⟩ will become the height of the destination box. Look, for instance, at the output of `\ShowBoxDepthOne{\SourceBox}` (source code line 20) of the preceding example, i.e., after the first `\vsplit` was executed.
4. Finally note that `\vsplit` in general "prefers" material which is too short over material which is too long.

To prove the last point look at the following example. First load the source box.

• ex-vsplit-d.tip •

```
\input inputd.tip
\InputD{shboxes.tip}                    % 4.5.15, p. 111.
\InputD{emptybox.tip}                   % 4.5.12, p. 103.
\setbox 0 = \vbox{
    \offinterlineskip
    \EmptyBox{10pt}{4pt}{20pt}
    \EmptyBox{10pt}{4pt}{20pt}
    \EmptyBox{10pt}{4pt}{20pt}
}
\ShowBoxDepthOne{0}
```

For the following `\vsplit` operation to split up the first two boxes contained in the master vbox we would choose 24 pt as the dimension (the sum of the height and the depth of the first box and the height of the second box). Now let me use a dimension that is only slightly smaller and you will see that TeX will *not* split up the first and second box contained in the source box but the first box only.

```
\setbox 1 = \vsplit 0 to 23.99pt
\message{Source box:}       \ShowBoxDepthOne{0}
\message{Destination box:}  \ShowBoxDepthOne{1}
\bye
```

• End of ex-vsplit-d.tip •

The log file generated by the preceding source file reads as follows:

• ex-vsplit-d.log •

```
This is TeX, C Version 3.14 (...)
**&/usr/local/tex/lib/fmt/plain ex-vsplit-d.tip
(ex-vsplit-d.tip (inputd.tip
(namedef.tip
) (inputdl.tip
\@InputDStream=\write0
))
(shboxes.tip
) (emptybox.tip
)
> \box0=
\vbox(38.0+4.0)x20.0
.\hbox(10.0+4.0)x20.0 []
.\glue(\lineskip) 0.0
.\hbox(10.0+4.0)x20.0 []
.\glue(\lineskip) 0.0
.\hbox(10.0+4.0)x20.0 []

<to be read again>
}
l.10 \ShowBoxDepthOne{0}

Underfull \vbox (badness 10000) detected at line 11

\vbox(23.99+4.0)x20.0
```

```
.\hbox(10.0+4.0)x20.0
..\hbox(10.0+4.0)x20.0

Source box:
> \box0=
\vbox(24.0+4.0)x20.0
.\glue(\splittopskip) 0.0
.\hbox(10.0+4.0)x20.0 []
.\glue(\lineskip) 0.0
.\hbox(10.0+4.0)x20.0 []

<to be read again>
}
l.12 ...^^I\ShowBoxDepthOne{0}

Destination box:
> \box1=
\vbox(23.99+4.0)x20.0
.\hbox(10.0+4.0)x20.0 []

<to be read again>
}
l.13 ...^^I\ShowBoxDepthOne{1}

)
No pages of output.
```

8.2.10 Splitting Requires Glue or Penalty (or Both)

For TEX to split a box either a glue or a penalty (or both) must be present. This is demonstrated in the next example where I built a source box containing two boxes (with no interline glue between the two boxes through the use of `\nointerlineskip`). When we try to use `\vsplit` to split off the first box within the source box, we will not succeed.

Here is the source of our example:

• `ex-vsplit-noglue.tip` •

```
\input inputd.tip
\InputD{shboxes.tip}                    % 4.5.15, p. 111.
\InputD{emptybox.tip}                   % 4.5.12, p. 103.
\vfuzz = 0pt
\splittopskip = 0pt
\newbox\SourceBox
\newbox\DestinationBox
```

Now construct a vertical box (`\SourceBox`) from two other vertical boxes (initially stored in `\SourceBoxTwo` and `\SourceBoxThree`) with *no* interline glue between these two boxes (not even glue of zero length).

```
\setbox\SourceBox = \vbox{
    \EmptyBox{6pt}{2pt}{4pt}
    \nointerlineskip
    \EmptyBox{6pt}{2pt}{4pt}
}
```

Now show the initial source box.

```
\message{(1) Initial box:}
\ShowBoxDepthOne{\SourceBox}
```

Try to split off the first box from the source box. It fails, despite a perfect dimension used by \vsplit! Show the destination box.

```
\setbox\DestinationBox = \vsplit\SourceBox to 6pt
\message{(2) After \string\vsplit:}
\ShowBoxDepthOne{\DestinationBox}
\ShowBoxDepthOne{\SourceBox}
```

Try again. Now insert a penalty between the two boxes of the main source box. Show the source box in the log file.

```
\setbox\SourceBox = \vbox{
    \EmptyBox{6pt}{2pt}{4pt}
    \nointerlineskip
    \penalty 0
    \EmptyBox{6pt}{2pt}{4pt}
}
\message{(3) Initial box, second run:}
\ShowBoxDepthOne{\SourceBox}
```

Try to split up the first box from the source box now. It does work now.

```
\setbox\DestinationBox = \vsplit\SourceBox to 6pt
\message{(4) After \string\vsplit, second run:}
\ShowBoxDepthOne{\DestinationBox}
\ShowBoxDepthOne{\SourceBox}

\bye
```

• End of ex-vsplit-noglue.tip •

Here is the log file generated by the above source code.

• ex-vsplit-noglue.log •

```
This is TeX, C Version 3.14 (...)
**&/usr/local/tex/lib/fmt/plain ex-vsplit-noglue.tip
(ex-vsplit-noglue.tip (inputd.tip
(namedef.tip
)
(inputdl.tip
\@InputDStream=\write0
)) (shboxes.tip
) (emptybox.tip
)
\SourceBox=\box16
\DestinationBox=\box17
```

```

(1) Initial box:
> \box16=
\vbox(14.0+2.0)x4.0
.\hbox(6.0+2.0)x4.0 []
.\hbox(6.0+2.0)x4.0 []

<argument> \SourceBox

}
l.14 ...oxDepthOne{\SourceBox}

Overfull \vbox (8.0pt too high) detected at line 15

\vbox(6.0+2.0)x4.0
.\hbox(6.0+2.0)x4.0
..\hbox(6.0+2.0)x4.0
.\hbox(6.0+2.0)x4.0
..\hbox(6.0+2.0)x4.0

(2) After \vsplit:
> \box17=
\vbox(6.0+2.0)x4.0
.\hbox(6.0+2.0)x4.0 []
.\hbox(6.0+2.0)x4.0 []

<argument> \DestinationBox

}
l.17 ...thOne{\DestinationBox}

> \box16=void

<argument> \SourceBox

}
l.18 ...oxDepthOne{\SourceBox}

(3) Initial box, second run:
> \box16=
\vbox(14.0+2.0)x4.0
.\hbox(6.0+2.0)x4.0 []
.\penalty 0
.\hbox(6.0+2.0)x4.0 []

<argument> \SourceBox

}
l.26 ...oxDepthOne{\SourceBox}

(4) After \vsplit, second run:
> \box17=
```

```
\vbox(6.0+2.0)x4.0
.\hbox(6.0+2.0)x4.0 []

<argument> \DestinationBox

}
l.29 ...thOne{\DestinationBox}

> \box16=
\vbox(6.0+2.0)x4.0
.\glue(\splittopskip) 0.0
.\hbox(6.0+2.0)x4.0 []

<argument> \SourceBox

}
l.30 ...oxDepthOne{\SourceBox}

)
No pages of output.
```

8.2.11 The Dimension Parameter \splitmaxdepth

TeX has a dimension parameter **\splitmaxdepth** that limits the depth of the *destination box* generated by an application of **\vplit** operation. This parameter is very similar to the **\boxmaxdepth** parameter (see 7.5.4, p. 246), and its default is also **\maxdimen**, which is the reason why you have never seen any influence of this parameter in any of the preceding examples.

Note that the value of this parameter is also used in the splitting of insertions. See 35.4.1.4, p. IV-99, for details.

Here is an example which shows the use of **\splitmaxdepth**.

• ex-vsplit-max.tip •

```
\input inputd.tip
\InputD{shboxes.tip}                    % 4.5.15, p. 111.
\InputD{emptybox.tip}                   % 4.5.12, p. 103.
\vfuzz = 0pt
\splittopskip = 0pt

\newbox\SourceBox
\newbox\SourceBoxCopy
\newbox\DestinationBox
```

Initialize the source box register and show its content.

```
\setbox\SourceBox = \vbox{
    \EmptyBox{3pt}{2pt}{30pt}
    \EmptyBox{6pt}{4pt}{40pt}
}
```

```
\setbox\SourceBoxCopy = \copy\SourceBox
\message{(1) Source box:}
\ShowBoxDepthOne{\SourceBox}
```

Make a copy of this box.

```
\setbox\SourceBoxCopy = \copy\SourceBox
```

Split off the first box contained in the source box. `\splitmaxdepth` is set to its default.

```
\splitmaxdepth = \maxdimen
\setbox\DestinationBox = \vsplit\SourceBox to 3pt
\message{(2) After first \string\vsplit:}
\ShowBoxDepthOne{\SourceBox}
\ShowBoxDepthOne{\DestinationBox}
```

Repeat the operation, this time setting `\splitmaxdepth` to zero.

```
\splitmaxdepth = 0pt
\setbox\DestinationBox = \vsplit\SourceBoxCopy to 3pt

\message{(3) After second \string\vsplit:}
\ShowBoxDepthOne{\SourceBoxCopy}
```

Now compare the following result stored in the destination box with the destination box previously generated.

```
\ShowBoxDepthOne{\DestinationBox}
\bye
```

• End of `ex-vsplit-max.tip` •

The preceding output generates the following log file:

• `ex-vsplit-max.log` •

```
This is TeX, C Version 3.14 (...)
**&/usr/local/tex/lib/fmt/plain ex-vsplit-max.tip
(ex-vsplit-max.tip (inputd.tip
(namedef.tip
) (inputdl.tip
\@InputDStream=\write0
))
(shboxes.tip
) (emptybox.tip
)
\SourceBox=\box16
\SourceBoxCopy=\box17
\DestinationBox=\box18
(1) Source box:
> \box16=
\vbox(15.0+4.0)x40.0
.\hbox(3.0+2.0)x30.0 []
.\glue(\baselineskip) 4.0
.\hbox(6.0+4.0)x40.0 []

<argument> \SourceBox
```

```

}
l.16 ...oxDepthOne{\SourceBox}

(2) After first \vsplit:
> \box16=
\vbox(6.0+4.0)x40.0
.\glue(\splittopskip) 0.0
.\hbox(6.0+4.0)x40.0 []

<argument> \SourceBox

}
l.21 ...oxDepthOne{\SourceBox}

> \box18=
\vbox(3.0+2.0)x30.0
.\hbox(3.0+2.0)x30.0 []

<argument> \DestinationBox

}
l.22 ...thOne{\DestinationBox}

Overfull \vbox (2.0pt too high) detected at line 24

\vbox(3.0+0.0)x30.0
.\hbox(3.0+2.0)x30.0
..\hbox(3.0+2.0)x30.0

(3) After second \vsplit:
> \box17=
\vbox(6.0+4.0)x40.0
.\glue(\splittopskip) 0.0
.\hbox(6.0+4.0)x40.0 []

<argument> \SourceBoxCopy

}
l.27 ...pthOne{\SourceBoxCopy}

> \box18=
\vbox(3.0+0.0)x30.0
.\hbox(3.0+2.0)x30.0 []

<argument> \DestinationBox

}
l.28 ...thOne{\DestinationBox}

)
No pages of output.
```

8.2.12 Applying \vsplit: Adding Line Numbers to the Beginning of Every Line of a Paragraph

I will now show an application of `\vsplit` where line numbers are added to each line of the paragraph. For instance, in some legal documents such as patent applications line numbers of the typeset text are customary. First the paragraph is typeset, then the paragraph is taken apart again using `\vsplit` and then line numbers are added.

$\mathcal{P}'$ • splitpar.tip •

Let us define a macro `\PrintParWithLineNumbers` that has one parameter, `#1`, the paragraph to typeset. Because of the additional space occupied by the line numbers the paragraph normally starts with an instruction that reduces `\hsize`.

```
\catcode`\@ = 11
```

Declare a counter for the line numbers.

```
\newcount\@PPLineNumber
```

Store the whole paragraph initially in the first box register. The second box register is a temporary box register that will be loaded with the current line which was split off using `\vsplit`.

```
\newbox\@PrintParWithLinesBox
\newbox\@PrintParWithLinesTemp
```

The definition of `\PrintParWithLineNumbers` begins here.

```
\def\PrintParWithLineNumbers #1{%
      \par
```

Initialize the line counter and set up `\splittopskip`.

```
      \@PPLineNumber = 1
      \splittopskip = 0.6666\baselineskip
```

Typeset the paragraph and store it in a box register.

```
      \setbox\@PrintParWithLinesBox = \vbox{#1}
```

Start the recursion now.

```
      \@PrintParWithLineNumbers
}
```

Macro `\@PrintParWithLineNumbers` will in a recursive way split off one line at a time from the paragraph as the line was saved in a box register, add a line number and print the line.

```
\def\@PrintParWithLineNumbers{
```

End the recursion if the source box of the `\vsplit` operation (initially containing the whole paragraph) is empty.

```
      \ifvoid\@PrintParWithLinesBox
          \let\@PPNext = \relax
```

```
    \else
```

The source box register is not empty. Split off a line.

```
        \setbox\@PrintParWithLinesTemp =
            \vsplit\@PrintParWithLinesBox to 0.666\baselineskip
```

Now print the line just split off together with a line number. The `\hskip 10pt` determines the distance between the line number being printed and the beginning of the line.

```
        \hbox{%
            \llap{%
                \the\@PPLineNumber:%
                \hskip 10pt
            }%
            \box \@PrintParWithLinesTemp
        }%
```

Increment the line number. Restart recursion (see 27.1, p. III-397, for details on recursion).

```
        \advance\@PPLineNumber by 1
        \wlog{Line \the\@PPLineNumber}%
        \let\@PPNext = \@PrintParWithLineNumbers
    \fi
```

Recursion, if at all, happens here.

```
    \@PPNext
}
\catcode`\@ = 12
```

• End of `splitpar.tip` •

For a sample application of the previous macro the following input was used:

```
\input inputd.tip
\InputD{splitpar.tip}                    % 8.2.12, p. 296.
$$
    \vbox{
        \PrintParWithLineNumbers{%
            \hsize = 3.0in
            This is our sample paragraph. It has some lines and it
            has lines. Yes, it has many lines, all lines which we
            call sample paragraph simplistic lines. This is
            clearly a paragraph with many silly sample lines.
            This is still our sample paragraph. It has some
            lines and it has lines. Yes, it has many lines,
            all lines which we call sample paragraph
            simplistic lines. This is undoubtedly
            paragraph with many silly sample lines.
            This is our sample paragraph. It has some lines
            and it has lines. Yes, it has many lines,
            all lines which we call sample paragraph
            simplistic lines. This is unfortunately
            a paragraph with many silly sample lines.
```

```
            }
        }
$$
\bye
```

This text generates the following output:

1: This is our sample paragraph. It has some
2: lines and it has lines. Yes, it has many lines, all
3: lines which we call sample paragraph simplistic
4: lines. This is clearly a paragraph with many silly
5: sample lines. This is still our sample paragraph. It
6: has some lines and it has lines. Yes, it has many
7: lines, all lines which we call sample paragraph sim-
8: plistic lines. This is undoubtedly paragraph with
9: many silly sample lines. This is our sample para-
10: graph. It has some lines and it has lines. Yes,
11: it has many lines, all lines which we call sample
12: paragraph simplistic lines. This is unfortunately a
13: paragraph with many silly sample lines.

8.3 Making a Box Larger, `\BoxLarger`

The knowledge you have gained so far by studying this and the preceding Chapter allows us to solve the following problem: define macro `\BoxLarger` which has two parameters `#1` and `#2`:

- `#1`. This parameter is any type of box which can be also a `\box` or `\copy` instruction to extract a box from a box register.
- `#2`. A dimension. This dimension specifies the width of an imaginary "white band" that is placed around the box specified as the first parameter. The name of this macro `\BoxLarger` suggests exactly that.

$\mathcal{P}'$ • `box-larg.tip` •

```
\def\BoxLarger #1#2{%
```

Combine everything into one new box.

```
    \vbox{%
```

The following generates white space of the specified dimension above the box `#1`.

```
        \vskip #2
        \hbox{%
```

The following `\hskip` moves the whole box to the right by `#2`.

```
                    \hskip #2%
```

Print the box.

```
                    \hbox{#1}%
```

Some additional horizontal space at the end.

```
                    \hskip #2%
                }%
```

White space on the bottom is generated here.

```
            \vskip #2
        }%
    }
```

• End of box-larg.tip •

8.4 Another More Complicated Vbox Example

In this Section I will introduce a more complicated vbox example that was derived in order to typeset the chapter headings of this series. The specifications for chapter headings read as follows (these specifications can be found in Guidelines (1990)):

1. The chapter number is to be set in a 20 pt font (a 21 pt font is actually used), where the top of the chapter number *touches* the top of the text area of the page.
2. The chapter title is set to be leftflush using the same font. The vertical location of the *first* line of the chapter heading is supposed to be 3 pc below the top of the text area of the page.
3. Lines within the heading are typeset tight, that is line spacing and font size are identical.
4. The distance from the top of the text area to the first line of the chapter's *text* should be 14 pc. (This means that regardless of the number of lines of the chapter heading itself the chapter *text* always begins at the same vertical position).

Note that `\baselineskip` is 12 pt for the most in this document and therefore has to be set to the appropriate value inside the following macro definition.

Macro `\ChapterHeadingTeXIP` implements such a chapter heading and has the following two parameters:

- `#1`. The chapter's number.
- `#2`. The text of the heading of the chapter.

The source code containing the macro definition is next. This macro is one of the macros in this series which you might not be able to use directly but only after you adjusted it to your own needs.

$\mathcal{P}'$ • ts-chhe.tip •

```
\InputD{parin.tip}                    % 10.9.4, p. II-35.
\InputD{shboxes.tip}                  % 4.5.15, p. 111.
\InputD{alwbase.tip}                  % 7.3.13, p. 233.
```

The macro definition begins here.

```
\def\ChapterHeadingTeXIP #1#2{%
```

Build a vbox which includes the whole heading. This vbox is assigned to a box register so later the dimensions of this box can be written to the log file ensuring proper dimensions.

```
      \setbox 1 =
```

The box being built here is 13 pc high. This value is computed from the desired distance of the first line of text after the chapter heading (14 pc according to the employed style file rules) minus 1 pc, the value of `\baselineskip` which will be inserted by TeX between the chapter heading box printed here and the first line of ordinary text. Note also that the vbox being built here has a depth of zero.

```
      \vbox to 13pc{
```

No paragraph indentation is needed inside the heading. A boldface font of 21 pt is used; see 16.1.9.4, p. II-274, for the information that `\huge` represents a 21 pt font in this series. The same dimension is used also as value for `\baselineskip`.

```
            \hyphenpenalty = 10000
            \parindent = 0pt
            \huge
            \bf
            \baselineskip = 21pt
            \AlwaysBaselineskip
```

The chapter number is next, enclosed in an hbox. Because this chapter number hbox comes first within the vbox being built here, no preceding interline glue is inserted which positions the chapter number top flush. Use `\copy` instead of `\box` so the dimensions of the chapter number box are not lost.

```
            \setbox 0 = \hbox{#1}%
            \copy0
```

Now position the baseline of the first line of the chapter's heading such that it is 3 pc below the top of the text area of the page. This is achieved by computing `\parskip` as the requested distance of 3pc minus the height and depth of the chapter's number box (in box register 0) minus `\baselineskip` (inserted by TeX automatically between the chapter number box and the first line of the chapter heading). The value of `\parskip` as computed here is also written to the log file.

```
            \parskip = 3pc
            \advance\parskip by -\dp0
            \advance\parskip by -\ht0
            \advance\parskip by -\baselineskip
```

```
        \wlog{\string\ChapterHeadingTeXIP: computed value
            of \noexpand\parskip is \the\parskip.}%
```

Now set up printing the chapter heading text ragged right.

```
        \spaceskip = 0.3333em
        \xspaceskip = \spaceskip
        \rightskip = 0pt plus 4em
```

Finally actually print the chapter heading text.

```
        #2
```

Done with the heading's text.

```
        \par
```

Add white space on the bottom of the vbox just built.

```
        \vfil
    }
```

Print the chapter heading now including the chapter number now. See above for an explanation why the vertical spacing works out correctly.

```
    \box 1
```

No indentation of the following text.

```
    \SuppressNextParIndent
}
```

• End of `ts-chhe.tip` •

8.5 Removing Items from a Box Related List

The discussion of this Section explains how the last item in a list of a box can be accessed. TeX defines the following primitives to do so (all primitives somehow always relate to the *last* item of the list of a box):

- `\lastbox`. Remove the last item of a box which should be another box. If the last item is not a box, a void box is produced. See 8.5.1 on the next page for details.
- `\lastpenalty`. Produce the penalty value of the last item of a box which should be a penalty. If it is not a penalty, a zero value is produced.
- `\lastskip`. Similar to `\lastpenalty` relating to glue instead.
- `\lastkern`. Similar to `\lastpenalty` and `\lastskip` relating to kern instead.
- `\unpenalty`. Remove the last item of a box, a penalty. Nothing happens, if the last item is not a penalty.
- `\unskip`. Similar to `\unpenalty` relating to glue though.
- `\unkern`. Similar to `\unpenalty` and `\unskip`, relating to kern though.

We now will present some examples relating to the list of primitives just offered.

8.5.1 The `\lastbox` Primitive

The function of the primitive `\lastbox` can be described as follows:

1. If the last item stored on the list of the current "master box" is a box, then this last box is *produced and removed* from the "master box."
2. If the last item stored on the list of the current "master box" is *not* a box, then a void box is constructed.
3. `\lastbox` always produces a void box when used in math mode.
4. `\lastbox` cannot be used to remove a box already contributed to the main vertical list.

8.5.1.1 An Example of Applying `\lastbox`

Let me give you an example. For this example the following source code is used:

• `ex-lastbox.tip` •

```
\input inputd.tip
\InputD{shboxes.tip}                          % 4.5.15, p. 111.
\setbox 0 = \vbox{%
    \hbox{ABC}
    \hbox{DEF}
}
\message{Original content of box register 0}
\ShowBoxDepthOne{0}
```

Now remove the last item (the second hbox) from this box as follows:

```
\setbox 0 = \vbox{
    \unvbox 0
    \global\setbox 1 = \lastbox
}
\message{Content of box register 0 after \noexpand\lastbox
            was executed.}
\ShowBoxDepthOne{0}
\message{The box removed is the following.}
\ShowBoxDepthOne{1}
\bye
```

• End of `ex-lastbox.tip` •

The log file generated by the preceding source reads as follows:

• `ex-lastbox.log` •

```
This is TeX, C Version 3.14 (...)
```

```
**&/usr/local/tex/lib/fmt/plain ex-lastbox.tip
(ex-lastbox.tip (inputd.tip
(namedef.tip
) (inputdl.tip
\@InputDStream=\write0
))
(shboxes.tip
) Original content of box register 0
> \box0=
\vbox(18.83331+0.0)x21.8056
.\hbox(6.83331+0.0)x21.8056 []
.\glue(\baselineskip) 5.16669
.\hbox(6.83331+0.0)x20.97227 []

<to be read again>
}
l.8 \ShowBoxDepthOne{0}

Content of box register 0 after \lastbox was executed.
> \box0=
\vbox(12.0+0.0)x21.8056
.\hbox(6.83331+0.0)x21.8056 []
.\glue(\baselineskip) 5.16669

<to be read again>
}
l.15 \ShowBoxDepthOne{0}

The box removed is the following.
> \box1=
\hbox(6.83331+0.0)x20.97227
.\tenrm D
.\tenrm E
.\tenrm F

<to be read again>
}
l.17 \ShowBoxDepthOne{1}

)
No pages of output.
```

8.5.1.2 `\lastbox` and Shifted Boxes

The following example shows how information is actually lost in a `\lastbox` application. This example differs from the previous example only in that now the second box within the master box is shifted to the right. However, the *amount* by which the box is shifted to the right is lost during the `\lastbox` operation. There is *no* parameter like `\lastshift` that would be set as side effect of `\lastbox`.

Here is the example:

• ex-lastbox-2.tip •

```
\input inputd.tip
\InputD{shboxes.tip}                         % 4.5.15, p. 111.
\setbox 0 = \vbox{
    \hbox{ABC}
    \moveright 2in\hbox{DEF}
}
\message{Original content of box register 0.}
\ShowBoxDepthOne{0}
```

Now remove the last item (the second hbox) from this box as follows:

```
\setbox 0 = \vbox{
    \unvbox 0
    \global\setbox 1 = \lastbox
}
\message{Content of box register 0 after \noexpand\lastbox
            was executed.}
\ShowBoxDepthOne{0}
\message{The box removed is the following.}
\ShowBoxDepthOne{1}
\bye
```

• End of ex-lastbox-2.tip •

The log file generated by the preceding example reads as follows:

• ex-lastbox-2.log •

```
This is TeX, C Version 3.14 (...)
**&/usr/local/tex/lib/fmt/plain ex-lastbox-2.tip
(ex-lastbox-2.tip (inputd.tip
(namedef.tip
) (inputdl.tip
\@InputDStream=\write0
))
(shboxes.tip
) Original content of box register 0.
> \box0=
\vbox(18.83331+0.0)x165.51227
.\hbox(6.83331+0.0)x21.8056 []
.\glue(\baselineskip) 5.16669
.\hbox(6.83331+0.0)x20.97227, shifted 144.54 []

<to be read again>
}
l.8 \ShowBoxDepthOne{0}

Content of box register 0 after \lastbox was executed.
> \box0=
\vbox(12.0+0.0)x21.8056
.\hbox(6.83331+0.0)x21.8056 []
.\glue(\baselineskip) 5.16669
```

```

<to be read again>
}
l.15 \ShowBoxDepthOne{0}

The box removed is the following.
> \box1=
\hbox(6.83331+0.0)x20.97227
.\tenrm D
.\tenrm E
.\tenrm F

<to be read again>
}
l.17 \ShowBoxDepthOne{1}

)
No pages of output.
```

8.5.1.3 `\lastbox` When the Last Item Is Not a Box

When `\lastbox` is applied when the last item on the current list is *not* a box, a void box is produced by `\lastbox`. *No error* is generated.

• `ex-lastbox-3.tip` •

```
\input inputd.tip
\InputD{shboxes.tip}                          % 4.5.15, p. 111.
\setbox 0 = \vbox{
    \hbox{ABC}
    \vskip 1.0in
}
\message{Original content of box register 0}
\ShowBoxDepthOne{0}
```

The last item on the current vertical list is not a box anymore.

```
\setbox 0 = \vbox{
    \unvbox 0
    \global\setbox 1 = \lastbox
}
\message{Content of box register 0 after \noexpand\lastbox
            was executed.}
\ShowBoxDepthOne{0}
\message{The box "removed" is the following.}
\ShowBoxDepthOne{1}
\bye
```

• End of `ex-lastbox-3.tip` •

The log file generated by the preceding example reads as follows:

• `ex-lastbox-3.log` •

```
This is TeX, C Version 3.14 (...)
**&/usr/local/tex/lib/fmt/plain ex-lastbox-3.tip
(ex-lastbox-3.tip (inputd.tip
(namedef.tip
) (inputdl.tip
\@InputDStream=\write0
))
(shboxes.tip
) Original content of box register 0
> \box0=
\vbox(79.1033+0.0)x21.8056
.\hbox(6.83331+0.0)x21.8056 []
.\glue 72.26999

<to be read again>
}
l.8 \ShowBoxDepthOne{0}

Content of box register 0 after \lastbox was executed.
> \box0=
\vbox(79.1033+0.0)x21.8056
.\hbox(6.83331+0.0)x21.8056 []
.\glue 72.26999

<to be read again>
}
l.15 \ShowBoxDepthOne{0}

The box "removed" is the following.
> \box1=void

<to be read again>
}
l.17 \ShowBoxDepthOne{1}

)
No pages of output.
```

8.5.2 Examples of `\lastskip`, `\lastkern`, `\lastpenalty`

The three primitives `\lastskip`, `\lastkern` and `\lastpenalty` all work according to very similar rules. We will begin with an explanation of `\lastskip`.

As in the case of `\lastbox` we have to make a distinction between two cases:

1. If the last item on the current list is a glue, the amount of this glue can be retrieved using `\lastskip`. For instance, `\the\lastskip` will print the amount of the last glue on the last list.

Note that contrary to `\lastbox` the glue item is *not* removed from the vertical list of the box being taken apart. If the glue item should also be removed use `\unskip`. `\unskip` will not work on the main vertical list though.

2. If the last item on the current list is *not* a glue, then `\lastskip` evaluates to zero. For instance, `\the\lastskip` will print `0pt` in this case.

   Note that due to this fact it is *impossible* to find out whether the last item on the list of a box is no glue or a glue in the amount of zero.

Here is a brief `\lastskip` example (`\lastkern` and `\lastpenalty` are so similar that no example will be offered):

• `ex-lastskip.tip` •

```
\input inputd.tip
\InputD{shboxes.tip}                          % 4.5.15, p. 111.
\newskip\askip
\newskip\bskip
\setbox 0 = \vbox{
    \hbox{ABC}
    \vskip 1.0in
```

Execute `\the\lastskip` after a vertical glue now.

```
    \global\askip = \the\lastskip
```

Another round immediately after a box.

```
    \hbox{DEF}
    \global\bskip = \the\lastskip
}
```

Print out both values saved `\lastskip` values.

```
\wlog{1. The first \noexpand\lastskip is \the\askip}%
\wlog{2. The second \noexpand\lastskip is \the\bskip}%
```

Now show the list of the box that was just produced. Note that `\lastskip` did not remove the glue item.

```
\message{Show box register 0}
\ShowBoxDepthOne{0}
```

The last item on the vertical list of the box is a glue item that can be removed using `\unskip`.

```
\setbox 0 = \vbox{
    \unvbox 0
    \unskip
}
\message{Content of box register 0 after \noexpand\unskip
    was executed.}
\ShowBoxDepthOne{0}
\bye
```

• End of `ex-lastskip.tip` •

The log file generated by the preceding source reads as follows:

• ex-lastskip.log •

```
This is TeX, C Version 3.14 (...)
**&/usr/local/tex/lib/fmt/plain ex-lastskip.tip
(ex-lastskip.tip (inputd.tip
(namedef.tip
) (inputdl.tip
\@InputDStream=\write0
))
(shboxes.tip
)
\askip=\skip18
\bskip=\skip19
1. The first \lastskip is 72.26999pt
2. The second \lastskip is 0.0pt
Show box register 0
> \box0=
\vbox(91.1033+0.0)x21.8056
.\hbox(6.83331+0.0)x21.8056 []
.\glue 72.26999
.\glue(\baselineskip) 5.16669
.\hbox(6.83331+0.0)x20.97227 []

<to be read again>
}
l.15 \ShowBoxDepthOne{0}

Content of box register 0 after \unskip was executed.
> \box0=
\vbox(91.1033+0.0)x21.8056
.\hbox(6.83331+0.0)x21.8056 []
.\glue 72.26999
.\glue(\baselineskip) 5.16669
.\hbox(6.83331+0.0)x20.97227 []

<to be read again>
}
l.22 \ShowBoxDepthOne{0}

)
No pages of output.
```

8.5.3 An Example of Using \unskip

Here is an example showing an application of \unskip.

• ex-unskip.tip •

Define a macro printing the TEX logo *followed by a space.*

```
\def\TeXX{\TeX\space}
```

Now use this macro in some text. It's nice, you don't have to write `\TeX\space` anymore, simply write `\TeXX`.

```
\TeXX is a fantastic product.
```

On the other hand sometimes the space automatically inserted by `\TeXX` can be a problem. On the other hand it can be eliminated very easily using `\unskip`.

```
I like \TeXX\unskip.
\bye
```

• End of `ex-unskip.tip` •

The preceding source code generates the following output:

TeX is a fantastic product. I like TeX.

8.6 Vertical Spacing Macros

The macros presented in this Section were developed to solve the following problem that occurs in format design. Let's say you would like to specify a vertical skip between an item you just finished (like the header of a section) and the following text. But because you don't know precisely what this following text will be, you are not able to specify the precise skip amount. For instance, you might want to insert a vertical skip of 10 pt after the header. Let us assume that this header is immediately followed by a numbered list and that the numbered list macros insert an additional 3 pt before the first item of the numbered list. If this numbered list occurs in the middle of some text, then this 3 pt of additional vertical space are exactly what you want to slightly offset the numbered list from the text preceding it. On the other hand in the case of the numbered list preceded by a header, you would like to insert only the maximum of the two skip values (that is 10 pt) and *not* the sum of 13 pt of the two values. The problem is, of course, that at the time of generating the vertical skip of 10 pt you don't know "what is coming," a list or something else. Similarly the list macros should be kept simple without having to test all sorts of flags which would allow the list macros to determine what the preceding text was to adjust the vertical skip amount appropriately.

I will therefore now define macro `\MaxVskip` which has one parameter, `#1`, a glue value (which can also be stored in a glue or dimension register). If there is already glue of *at least the amount specified by* `#1` on the vertical list, then the macro does nothing. If there is glue some glue g *of less than the specified amount* `#1` on the vertical list, the glue g is removed and replaced by glue `#1`. The word remove is not quite correct here: vertical glue of the amount $-g$ is inserted (which in effect eliminates the present glue g) before glue in the amount of `#1` is inserted.

The net effect is that the current vertical list contains the larger of the current vertical glue and **#1**.

$\mathcal{P}'$ • vsmax.tip •

```
\catcode`\@ = 11
```

Allocate a private glue register.

```
\newskip\@MaxVskipGlue
```

The macro definition begins here.

```
\def\MaxVskip #1{%
```

Force vertical mode, just to be sure.

```
    \par
```

Load the requested skip amount into a glue register (see 4.4, p. 94, for an explanation why **#1** is not used directly).

```
    \@MaxVskipGlue = #1\relax
    \ifdim\lastskip < \@MaxVskipGlue
```

We determined that either the last item on the current vertical list is no glue (`\lastskip` is zero in that case) or not the required amount (`\lastskip` is nonzero in that case).

```
        \ifdim\lastskip = 0pt
        \else
```

There is already glue on the vertical list which is insufficient in length. Its effect is undone.

```
            \vskip -\lastskip
        \fi
```

The glue as specified by **#1** is inserted.

```
        \vskip\@MaxVskipGlue
    \fi
}
\catcode`\@ = 12
```

• End of vsmax.tip •

Following is an example of the application of this macro.

• ex-vsmax.tip •

```
\input inputd.tip
\InputD{vsmax.tip}                          % 8.6, p. 310.
\InputD{shboxes.tip}                        % 4.5.15, p. 111.
\setbox 0 = \vbox{
    \hbox{First line}
    \vskip 3pt
    \MaxVskip{6pt plus 1pt minus 3pt}
    \hbox{Second line}
    \vskip 6pt
    \MaxVskip{3pt plus 1pt minus 3pt}
```

```
    \hbox{Third line}
    \vskip 6pt
    \MaxVskip{3pt plus 1pt minus 3pt}
    \MaxVskip{12pt plus 1pt minus 3pt}
    \MaxVskip{3pt plus 1pt minus 3pt}
    \MaxVskip{15pt plus 1pt minus 3pt}
    \MaxVskip{3pt plus 1pt minus 3pt}
    \hbox{Third line}
}
\ShowBoxDepthOne{0}
\bye
```

• End of `ex-vsmax.tip` •

The preceding source code generates the following log file

• `ex-vsmax.log` •

```
This is TeX, C Version 3.14 (...)
**&/usr/local/tex/lib/fmt/plain ex-vsmax.tip
(ex-vsmax.tip (inputd.tip
(namedef.tip
) (inputdl.tip
\@InputDStream=\write0
))
(vsmax.tip
\@MaxVskipGlue=\skip18
) (shboxes.tip
)
> \box0=
\vbox(69.94444+0.0)x49.44453
.\hbox(6.94444+0.0)x39.94452 []
.\glue 3.0
.\glue -3.0
.\glue 6.0 plus 1.0 minus 3.0
.\glue(\baselineskip) 5.05556
.\hbox(6.94444+0.0)x49.44453 []
.\glue 6.0
.\glue(\baselineskip) 5.05556
.\hbox(6.94444+0.0)x43.91675 []
.\glue 6.0
.\glue -6.0
.\glue 12.0 plus 1.0 minus 3.0
.\glue -12.0 plus -1.0 minus -3.0
.\glue 15.0 plus 1.0 minus 3.0
.\glue(\baselineskip) 5.05556
.\hbox(6.94444+0.0)x43.91675 []

<to be read again>
}
l.20 \ShowBoxDepthOne{0}

)
No pages of output.
```

8.7 Summary

In this chapter we learned the following:

- `\unhbox` and `\unvbox` can be used to regenerate the horizontal or vertical list of a box that is stored in a box register. These instructions destroy the content of the box register (use `\unhcopy` or `\unvcopy` if you would like to avoid this). Note that any glue on the horizontal or vertical list generated this way regains its stretchability or shrinkability.

  The preceding primitives allow one to write macros that compute the natural height or depth of a vbox. One may also write macros that transform a vbox generated using `\vbox` into a vbox as would have been generated by `\vtop`.
- A macro to shift up or down the reference point of a box (which is normally a vbox) was presented. Also a macro to enlarge a box was shown. Additional more complicated vbox related examples were demonstrated.
- `\vsplit` splits the vertical list of a vbox. In order to do so glue and/or penalties must be present at the split point and this glue and/or penalties is removed when the split takes place.

  `\splittopskip` glue is inserted as the first item of the vertical list of the source box immediately after the material which is split off was removed.

  Leaders and glue are identical when it comes to `\vsplit`. `\vsplit` can be used in double column page layout and to split a paragraph into single lines to add line numbers to it.
- A vertical spacing macro computing the maximum of a specified value and the last glue on the current vertical list was discussed.
- `\lastbox`, `\lastskip`, `\lastkern` and `\lastpenalty` can be used to take the list of any box apart. `\lastbox` actually removes the last item of the current box if this last item is a box itself. To remove other items from the list of a box you must use `\unskip`, `\unkern` and `\unpenalty` (the corresponding `\un...` instructions do not remove the items from the list of the current box).

9
Boxes and Rules

This chapter contains special examples concerning the application of boxes. TEX can draw simple graphs draw rules around boxes. The macros presented in this chapter are quite useful in the development of TEX code involving complicated boxes.

9.1 Rule Placement and Borderline of Boxes

We need to discuss next the placement of rules (non-zero thickness) representing a borderline with respect to the actual *borderline* (of zero thickness) of a box. This borderline can be represented by four *rules* as in ▭ on the top, one on the bottom, one on the left and one on the right of the box. There are three alternatives defined in this chapter how these non-zero thickness borderline rules are placed with respect to the borderline of a box:

1. Placement M: the borderline rules are placed in the *middle* of the invisible borderline; the borderline divides the borderline rules into two halves.
2. Placement O: the borderline rules surround the invisible borderline so that the borderline *touches the inside of the borderline rules.* The rules are placed on the *outside* of the box.
3. Placement I: the borderline rules surround the box, so that the rules' outsides touch the borderline. The borderline rules are *inside* the borderline of the box.

9.2 Macros to Draw Simple Graphs

Several macros allow to manipulate horizontal and vertical lines to draw simple graphs. Remember that any box (regardless of its content) can be printed without moving the current reference point, if all dimensions of that box are zero (if not zero initially, then the dimensions are simply set to zero). Details follow shortly.

Note the following macros are not as complete and powerful as, for instance, the macros of LaTeX's picture environment. But the main purpose here is *not* to offer sophisticated macros for the generation of graphs but to show examples of using boxes, box registers and glues.

The following macros are defined below:

1. `\SetScale`. This macro defines the scaling. It is assumed that the user defines some scale, then all coordinates and other dimensions are given with respect to that scale. The macro has one parameter, `#1`, a length (a TeX dimension) that represents one user unit.
2. `\SetLineThickness`. This macro is called to set the thickness (`#1`) of any lines drawn with macros `\DrawHLine` and `\DrawVLine`.
3. `\SetGraphDataBox`. This macro loads the contents of a box register with a black square; this square is printed to represent a data point. The size of this square, a dimension, is the only parameter (`#1`) to this macro.
4. `\DrawDataBox`. Given a pair of x and y coordinates, this macro prints the data box at the specified point. The parameters of this macro follow below.
5. `\DrawHLine`. This macro draws a *horizontal line*, starting at a specified point, of a specified length.
6. `\DrawVLine`. This macro is similar to `\DrawHLine`, but it draws a *vertical* line.

The last three macros introduced in the preceding list will be discussed in more detail below.

9.2.1 The Macro Source Code

Following is the source code of the graph macros.

$\mathcal{P}'$ • graphmac.tip •

```
\InputD{box-zero.tip}                    % 4.5.13, p. 104.
\catcode`\@ = 11
```

`\@ScaleLength` is a dimension, the distance, that corresponds to one user unit.

```
\newdimen\@ScaleLength
```

Define the macro `\SetScale`, which sets `\@ScaleLength`. This macro has one parameter, `#1`, the real length of one user unit.

```
\def\SetScale #1{%
    \@ScaleLength = #1
}
```

By default 1 mm per user unit is used (I realize that using the unit Millimeters is somewhat inconsistent with the rest of the series).

```
\SetScale{1mm}
```

`\@LineThickness` is a dimension register that holds the thickness (obviously a dimension) of horizontal and vertical lines drawn by any of the following macros.

```
\newdimen\@LineThickness
```

Recall that macro `\SetLineThickness` establishes the thickness of horizontal and vertical lines. It has one parameter, `#1`, a dimension, which determines the thickness of all horizontal and vertical lines drawn by `\DrawHLine` and `\DrawVLine`.

```
\def\SetLineThickness #1{%
    \@LineThickness = #1
}
```

The default line thickness is 0.3 mm.

```
\SetLineThickness{0.3mm}
```

The following box register is loaded later with an hbox of zero height, width, and depth. This hbox contains a square rule, that is centered with respect to the reference point of the box. This box is used to "print" a data point. The following macro `\SetGraphDataBox` loads this register.

```
\newbox\@GraphDataBox
```

A call to `\SetGraphDataBox` initializes the graph data box register. A call to this macro determines the size of the square drawn when a data point is printed. Recall that this macro has one parameter (`#1`) that is a dimension, the width and height of the square used to draw the data point. The `\hskip` below and the dimensions of the `\vrule` are chosen in such a way that the reference point of the box being constructed is exactly in the middle of the square rule.

```
\def\SetGraphDataBox #1{%
    \dimen0 = #1%
    \setbox\@GraphDataBox =
        \hbox{%
            \hskip -0.5\dimen0
            \vrule height 0.5\dimen0
                   depth  0.5\dimen0
                   width  1.0\dimen0
        }%
    \ZeroBox{\@GraphDataBox}%
}
```

By default "data boxes" have a height and width of 2 mm.

```
\SetGraphDataBox{2mm}
```

Now define `\DrawDataBox`, a macro to "paint" a data point using a copy of the data point box (the construction of the data point box was just explained). The macro has two parameters, the x and y coordinates of the data point (enclosed in parentheses and separated by a comma from each other). The data point is indicated by a black box where the center of this black box has the same coordinates as the data point. The purpose of the `\hskip` and the `\raise` instructions is to move the current position to the desired location. Then the data point is painted by making a copy of the box stored in box register \@GraphDataBox.

```
\def\DrawDataBox (#1,#2){%
    {%
        \setbox0 = \hbox{%
            \hskip #1\@ScaleLength
            \raise #2\@ScaleLength\copy\@GraphDataBox
        }%
        \ZeroBoxOut{0}%
    }%
}
```

The macro \DrawHLine draws a horizontal line. The starting point of the horizontal lines is determined by the first two parameters of the macro, which are enclosed in parentheses and separated by a comma. The third parameter, #3, defines the length of the rule drawn to the right. All parameters are specified in the user's coordinate system. The placement of this rule is a "placement M" (see 9.1, p. 313). The length, #3, cannot be negative. For example, one cannot draw a rule to the left of the starting point (#1,#2).

```
\def\DrawHLine (#1,#2)#3{%
    {%
        \setbox0 = \hbox{%
            \hskip #1\@ScaleLength
            \raise #2\@ScaleLength
                \hbox{%
                    \vrule height 0.5\@LineThickness
                           depth  0.5\@LineThickness
                           width  #3\@ScaleLength
                }%
        }%
        \ZeroBoxOut{0}%
    }%
}
```

The macro \DrawVLine is almost identical to the preceding macro, but this time a vertical line is drawn. This vertical line extends above the initial point (#1,#2) and is as long as specified by #3. As before the length (#3) cannot be negative. Thus one could not draw a rule extending below (#1,#2).

```
\def\DrawVLine (#1,#2)#3{%
    {%
        \setbox0 = \hbox{%
            \hskip #1\@ScaleLength
            \hskip -0.5\@LineThickness
            \raise #2\@ScaleLength
                \hbox{%
                    \vrule height #3\@ScaleLength
                           depth  0pt
                           width  \@LineThickness
                }%
        }%
```

```
          \ZeroBoxOut{0}%
      }%
}
\catcode`\@ = 12
```

• End of **graphmac.tip** •

9.2.2 An Example Applying the Presented Macros

An example of the application of the previous macros can be found in Fig. 9.1 on the next page that was generated using the following source code.

• **ex-f-graph.tip** •

```
\input inputd.tip
\InputD{graphmac.tip}                        % 9.2.1, p. 314.
\InputD{doloop.tip}                          % 27.1.8, p. III-412.
```

Get a box register in which the graph is built.

```
\newbox\GraphExampleBox
\setbox\GraphExampleBox = \hbox{%
```

The first \DrawDataBox marks the origin of the coordinate system used in the example. Don't forget a percent sign after each drawing instruction to prevent spaces from sneaking in.

```
      \DrawDataBox(0,0)%
```

Put in an x-axis.

```
      \DrawHLine(-5,0){80}%
```

Marks are printed every 10 millimeters using the \DoLoop macro.

```
      \DoLoop{\count9}{0}{10}{70}{%
          \DrawVLine(\the\count9,0){2}%
      }%
```

Put in a y-axis.

```
      \DrawVLine(0,-5){80}%
```

Marks every 10 millimeters using the \DoLoop macro.

```
      \DoLoop{\count9}{0}{10}{70}{%
          \DrawHLine(0,\the\count9){2}%
      }%
```

Some data boxes.

```
      \DrawDataBox(10,10)%
      \DrawDataBox(20,20)%
      \DrawDataBox(30,10)%
```

Some rules.

```
      \DrawHLine(25,25){60}%
```

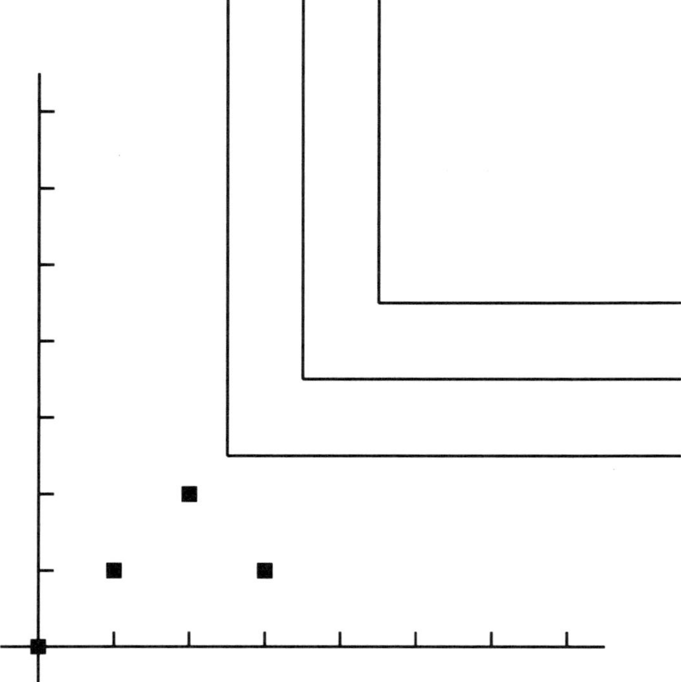

Figure 9.1. Graph macro example.

```
        \DrawHLine(35,35){50}%
        \DrawHLine(45,45){40}%

        \DrawVLine(25,25){60}%
        \DrawVLine(35,35){50}%
        \DrawVLine(45,45){40}%
}
```

Done with generating a graph. Adjust the dimensions of the box just built (that box has a height, depth and width of zero) to the maximum dimensions used in drawing the diagram.

```
\dp\GraphExampleBox = 5mm
\ht\GraphExampleBox = 85mm
\wd\GraphExampleBox = 85mm
```

• End of `ex-f-graph.tip` •

9.3 Drawing Rules Around a Box

There are various approaches to drawing rules around boxes. The macros used to solve this illustrate various approaches and are listed in order of increasing complexity and power. The last set of macros (`\HboxR`, `\VboxR`, etc.) are in particular useful.

Here is a brief overview of the macros:

1. `\BoxingA` draws rules around a box. See 9.3.1 on this page.
2. `\BoxingB` is the same as `\BoxingA`, but the thickness of the rules around the box can be changed by the user. See 9.3.3, p. 321.
3. `\BoxingC` is the same as `\BoxingB`, additionally the reference point of the box is marked by a bullet (•). See 9.3.4.2, p. 323.
4. `\BoxingD` is the same as `\BoxingC`, additionally also the baseline of the box is marked with a dashed line. See 9.3.4.3, p. 324.
5. `\BoxingE` generates a ruled box which is almost identical to the unruled box. All preceding macros generate boxes with rules that have quite different dimensions and reference points compared to the unruled boxes. The `\BoxingE` macro eliminates this problem to a large extent. See 9.3.7, p. 332, for details.
6. `\HboxR`, `\VboxR`, `\VtopR`, `\BoxR` and `\CopyR` are the champions of the "draw rules around boxes macros." These macros are almost identical to `\hbox`, `\vbox`, `\vtop`, `\box` and `\copy`. Rules are drawn around those boxes, the reference point is marked with a bullet (•), and the baseline is marked with a dashed line. This is all done by generating a new box (with rules and marking of baseline and basepoint) with dimensions and reference point the *same* as those of the original box. See 9.3.9, p. 334, for the definitions of these macros.

9.3.1 A Simple Macro to Draw Rules Around a Box (`\BoxingA`)

The following macro `\BoxingA` draws rules around a box. It makes use of the fact that horizontal rules (`\hrule`s) inside a vbox stretch to the width of the box, and that vertical rules (`\vrule`s) inside an hbox stretch to the height and depth of that box (if no dimensions for those rules are specified). This macro has one parameter, `#1`, which is a box; around this box rules are drawn (placement O). This argument can be an `\hbox`, `\vbox` or `\vtop`-generated box; the box can also be extracted from a box register using `\box` or `\copy`.

Here is the definition of this macro.

$\mathcal{P}'$ • boxing1.tip •

```
\def\BoxingA #1{%
    \vbox{%
        \hrule
        \hbox{%
            \vrule
            #1%
            \vrule
        }%
        \hrule
```

```
    }%
}
```

• End of boxing1.tip •

Here is an example application of this macro. It uses the following source code:

```
\input inputd.tip
\InputD{boxing1.tip}                      % 9.3.1, p. 319.

\medskip

\centerline{%
    \BoxingA{\hbox{This is fun}}%
    \hskip 20pt
    \BoxingA{\hbox{AA gg TT}}%
}
```

The preceding source code generates the following output:

This is fun   AA gg TT

9.3.2 An Example Application of \BoxingA: Reserving Space for a Figure, \FigureBox

One application of the preceding macros is to mark some space for a figure in a document, where the figure is to be glued-in later. For this purpose we will use the \FigureBox macro. Its two parameters are the following (the depth of the box printed is set to zero by the macro):

- #1. The height.
- #2. The depth.

The definition of the \FigureBox macro follows:

$\mathcal{P}'$ • figbox.tip •

```
\InputD{emptybox.tip}                     % 4.5.12, p. 103.
\def\FigureBox #1#2{%
    \BoxingA{%
        \EmptyBox{#1}{0pt}{#2}%
    }%
}
```

• End of figbox.tip •

For instance, \FigureBox{2.0in}{4.0in} prints the following box with rules:

9.3.3 A Macro for Drawing Rules Around Boxes with User-Controlled Thickness of those Rules, `\BoxingB`

The macro `\BoxingB` is identical to the preceding macro `\BoxingA` with the exception that the thickness of the rules is determined by the dimension stored in dimension register `\BoxRuleThickness` (placement O). This dimension can be changed by the user at any point.

$\mathcal{P}'$ • `box-thck.tip` •

`\BoxRuleThickness` is a dimension register which holds the thickness (a dimension) of the rules, when using the `\BoxingB` and following macros. It is initialized to 0.4 pt. A separate source code file is used for this because this dimension register is also used later by other macros.

```
\newdimen\BoxRuleThickness
\BoxRuleThickness = 0.4pt
```

• End of `box-thck.tip` •

The source code containing the definition of macro `\BoxingB` starts now. This macro has one parameter (`#1`) the box around which rules are drawn. The definition is very similar to the definition of `\BoxingA`.

$\mathcal{P}'$ • `boxing2.tip` •

```
\InputD{box-thck.tip}                         % 9.3.3, p. 321.

\def\BoxingB #1{%
    \vbox{%
        \hrule height \BoxRuleThickness
        \hbox{%
            \vrule width \BoxRuleThickness
            #1%
            \vrule width \BoxRuleThickness
        }%
```

```
            \hrule height \BoxRuleThickness
        }%
}
```

• End of `boxing2.tip` •

An example of the application of the preceding macro follows. The input

```
\input inputd.tip
\InputD{boxing2.tip}                            % 9.3.3, p. 321.

\medskip
\centerline{%
    \BoxRuleThickness = 1.0pt   \BoxingB{\hbox{short example}}%
    \hskip 20pt
    \BoxRuleThickness = 2.0pt   \BoxingB{\hbox{another one ggTT}}%
}
```

generates the following output:

short example   another one ggTT

9.3.4 Macros Including the Marking of Reference Points of Boxes, `\BoxingC`, and Baseline, `\BoxingD`

The following macros mark the reference point of a box by a bullet, •, and the baseline by a dashed line. They do so with the help of a box of zero dimensions which contains a centered bullet. This "bullet box" is printed immediately before the box to be marked. Therefore, the reference point of the box coincides with the center of the bullet, exactly as intended.

9.3.4.1 Two Auxiliary Macro Source Files

The TEX source code that follows requires a box register containing a centered bullet. Because this centered bullet is needed again later, a separate source code file for its definition is used.

$\mathcal{P}'$ • `box-bul.tip` •

```
\InputD{box-zero.tip}                          % 4.5.13, p. 104.
\catcode`\@ = 11
```

Get a box register to hold the box containing the bullet.

```
\newbox\@BulletBox
```

The following instruction centers the bullet with respect to the reference point of the box that is being constructed. The dimensions of the `\hskip` and the `\lower` were found by trial and error.

```
\setbox\@BulletBox =
```

```
        \hbox{%
            \hskip -2.3pt
            \lower 2.5pt \hbox{$\bullet$}%
        }
```

Set all dimensions of this box to zero.

```
\ZeroBox{\@BulletBox}
\catcode`\@ = 12
```

• End of `box-bul.tip` •

Now let us define some additional box registers which are used throughout the following macros. Again, a separate macro source file is used.

$\mathcal{P}'$ • `box-bb.tip` •

```
\catcode`\@ = 11
```

The *user's box* will be saved later in box register `\@BoxingBox`.

```
\newbox\@BoxingBox
```

The *leaders* for *marking the baseline* of a box will later be saved in the following box register.

```
\newbox\@BaseLineLeaders
\catcode`\@ = 12
```

• End of `box-bb.tip` •

9.3.4.2 The Definition of `\BoxingC`

The following source file contains the definition of `\BoxingC`.

$\mathcal{P}'$ • `boxing3.tip` •

```
\InputD{box-bul.tip}                    % 9.3.4.1, p. 322.
\InputD{box-thck.tip}                   % 9.3.3, p. 321.
\catcode`\@ = 11
```

The `\BoxingC` macro draws rules around a box. The macro has one parameter, `#1`, a box around which rules are drawn. The thickness of the rules can be varied changing `\BoxRuleThickness`, the same way this could be done in `\BoxingB`. The reference point of this box is indicated by a bullet (which is the new feature of `\BoxingC` compared with `\BoxingB`).

```
\def\BoxingC #1{%
    \vbox{%
        \hrule height \BoxRuleThickness
        \hbox{%
            \vrule width \BoxRuleThickness
```

The reference point is marked by a bullet just before the box itself is printed.

```
            \copy\@BulletBox
            #1%
```

```
                \vrule width \BoxRuleThickness
            }%
            \hrule height \BoxRuleThickness
        }%
}
\catcode`\@ = 12
```

• End of `boxing3.tip` •

9.3.4.3 The Definition of Macro `\BoxingD`

Macro `\BoxingD` is identical to the preceding macro `\BoxingC` except that *additionally* the *baseline* of the box being printed is marked by a *dashed line.* This dashed line is generated using leaders (see 5.6, p. 145). In order to print this dashed line, its length (that is the width) of the user box, must be determined. The user's box is saved in box register `\@BoxingBox` so that the width can be accessed very easily (`\wd\@BoxingBox`). The part of the code of the preceding macro `\BoxingC`, which deals with marking the reference point by a •, is repeated below, because `\BoxingD` has the same feature.

Here is the macro source file which contains the definition of `\BoxingD`.

$\mathcal{P}'$ • `boxing4.tip` •

```
\InputD{box-zero.tip}                    % 4.5.13, p. 104.
\InputD{box-bul.tip}                     % 9.3.4.1, p. 322.
\InputD{box-bb.tip}                      % 9.3.4.1, p. 323.
\InputD{box-thck.tip}                    % 9.3.3, p. 321.
\catcode`\@ = 11
```

The macro `\BoxingD` draws rules around a box. The macro's one parameter (`#1`) is a box. To summarize, macro `\BoxingD` has the following properties:

1. It draws rules around a box.
2. The thickness of these rules is under the control of the user.
3. The reference point of the box is indicated by a bullet.
4. The baseline of the box is indicated by a dashed line.

```
\def\BoxingD #1{%
```

Start with a box. The type of box doesn't really matter. It is of importance for the way the rules around the box are added though.

```
        \vbox{%
```

Save the user's box.

```
            \setbox\@BoxingBox = #1%
```

Generate a visible representation of the baseline from leaders.

```
            \setbox\@BaseLineLeaders = \hbox to \wd\@BoxingBox{%
                \xleaders\hbox to 4pt{%
```

```
                \hskip 1pt
                \vrule depth 0.4pt height 0.4pt width 2pt
                \hfil
                }%
            \hfil
        }%
```

Set all dimensions of the box, which contains the dashed line to indicate the baseline, to zero.

```
        \ZeroBox{\@BaseLineLeaders}%
```

Draw the top horizontal rule.

```
        \hrule height \BoxRuleThickness
```

Draw the box with vertical rules to the left and right.

```
        \hbox{%
            \vrule width \BoxRuleThickness
```

Mark the reference point.

```
            \copy\@BulletBox
```

Draw the baseline.

```
            \box\@BaseLineLeaders
```

Print the box itself.

```
            \box\@BoxingBox
```

Draw the vertical rule on the right hand side.

```
            \vrule width \BoxRuleThickness
        }%
```

Draw the bottom horizontal rule.

```
        \hrule height \BoxRuleThickness
```

That's it.

```
    }%
}
\catcode`\@ = 12
```

• End of `boxing4.tip` •

Let me now present an example of the application of `\BoxingD`. Here is the source code of this example:

```
\input inputd.tip
\InputD{boxing4.tip}                    % 9.3.4.3, p. 324.
\centerline{%
    \BoxingD{\hbox{ABgh\raise4pt\hbox{DE}}}
}
```

The output generated by the example reads as follows:

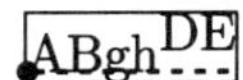

9.3.5 Correcting Reference Point and Dimensions

If you analyzed the previous examples carefully, you discovered the following problems with *all* the macros presented so far:

1. The width, height, and depth of the *boxes with rules* are *different* than the dimensions of the *original box*, the one without rules.
2. The *reference point* of the *original* box and that of the *box with rules* are also *different.*

To give you a specific example, look at the following input:

```
\centerline{%
     \hbox{example}%
     \hskip 15pt
     \BoxingD{\hbox{example}}%
}
```

The output generated by this input reads as follows. Note that the baselines of the two printings of the word "example" do not line up. The baseline of the second printing of example coincides with the bottom rule, and is *not* where the dashed lines seems to suggest (if that were the case the two "example"s would line up horizontally).

example example

The macros that will be developed now are supposed to correct these deficiencies. Therefore, they need to fulfill the following requirements:

1. All dimensions of the ruled box must be exactly the same as the dimensions of the original box; they will be accurate down to the scaled point.
2. The reference point of the box with rules and the reference point of the original box must be identical.
3. The rules around the boxes are positioned according to placement M (9.1, p. 313).

These macros are developed in two steps. First we present macros that generate boxes, which contain *nothing but rules.* One could think of these boxes as containing rules around an empty box. When the dimensions of these "rule only boxes" are set to zero, then these boxes can overlay the user's box. This superimposition leads to the desired marking of boxes by rules, baseline, and bullet. The second step is to integrate these macros with macros that not only print rules but also the user's box.

9.3.6 Rule Macros for Marking Boxes

This Subsection presents macros to print rules around empty boxes. Three different macros are presented below where each macro corresponds to one of the three placements discussed before: one macro places the borderline rules according to placement O, one places them according to placement M, and one according to placement I (9.1, p. 313).

Note that for the following macros you need to understand rules with negative dimensions; see 5.7.1, item 5, p. 156.

Also note that these macros `\RulesOnSide`, `\RulesInSide` and `\RulesOutSide` mark the reference point of the empty reference box by a bullet. However these macros do *not* include the marking of the baseline with a dashed line.

Below you may read "a horizontal rule is drawn now" (meaning a horizontal rule as far as you and I are concerned), but that the actual command to draw this rule may be `\vrule` ("vertical rule"), because TEX is in horizontal mode. The reverse is also true: you may read that a vertical rule is being drawn with the `\hrule` primitive, because TEX is in vertical mode. See 5.7, p. 154, for a discussion of this issue.

9.3.6.1 The Beginning of the Definitions of `\Rules...Side` Macros

The source code of the "rules around empty boxes macros" begins here.

$\mathcal{P}'$ • `boxing5.tip` •

```
\InputD{box-zero.tip}                          % 4.5.13, p. 104.
\InputD{box-bul.tip}                           % 9.3.4.1, p. 322.
\InputD{box-bb.tip}                            % 9.3.4.1, p. 323.
\InputD{box-thck.tip}                          % 9.3.3, p. 321.
\catcode`\@ = 11
```

Sometimes it is useful to disable the bullet printing for the reference point and to disable the marking of the baseline with a dashed line. The default is to draw the bullet and to draw the baseline. Enter `\BulletAndBaseLinefalse` to disable both.

The following conditional suggests that the macros below also deal with drawing the base line as a dashed line. This is not true, but other macros (which do both, mark the base point and the base line) also refer to this conditional; therefore its name.

```
\newif\ifBulletAndBaseLine
\BulletAndBaseLinetrue
```

9.3.6.2 The Definition of Macro `\RulesOutSide`

Given the dimensions of a box macro `\RulesOutSide` draws rules around a box. The thickness of the rules are determined by `\BoxRuleThickness`. The placement of these borderline rules is a placement O.

The `\RulesOutSide` macro has three parameters which are all dimensions, the dimensions of an empty box.

- #1. A height.
- #2. A depth.
- #3. A width.

```
\def\RulesOutSide #1#2#3{%
```

Start a group (all the `\Rules...Side` macros do, because they change box register 0).

```
        {%
                \setbox 0 = \hbox{%
```

Mark the reference point of the box (if enabled).

```
                        \ifBulletAndBaseLine
                                \copy\@BulletBox
                        \fi
```

Go left and draw the left vertical rule.

```
                        \hskip -\BoxRuleThickness
                        \vrule width \BoxRuleThickness height #1 depth #2%
```

Go right and draw the right vertical rule.

```
                        \hskip #3%
                        \vrule width \BoxRuleThickness height #1 depth #2%
```

Compute in `\dimen0` the length of the horizontal rules on top and bottom. This value is also the distance that must be traveled to the left before drawing the vertical rules.

```
                        \dimen0 = #3%
                        \advance \dimen0 by 2\BoxRuleThickness
```

Travel to the left as computed.

```
                        \hskip -\dimen0
```

Draw the top horizontal rule. Compute in `\dimen2` the height of this rule. Note that the rule is to be drawn outside the boundaries of the box (placement O).

```
                        \dimen2 = #1%
                        \advance\dimen2 by \BoxRuleThickness
                        \vrule width \dimen0 height \dimen2 depth -#1%
```

Return to the left after this rule is drawn. Compute in `\dimen2` the depth of this rule (like all others this rule is to be drawn outside the boundaries of the box).

```
                        \hskip -\dimen0
                        \dimen2 = #2%
                        \advance\dimen2 by \BoxRuleThickness
```

Now draw the bottom horizontal rule.

```
                        \vrule width \dimen0 height -#2 depth \dimen2
                }%
```

Finally print the box that was just constructed, but set the dimensions of this box to zero, before you print it.

```
            \ZeroBoxOut{0}%
        }%
    }
```

9.3.6.3 The Definition of Macro \RulesInSide

The macro \RulesInSide is identical to \RulesOutSide, except that the *outside* of the rules touch the boundaries of the box (placement I).

This macro has the same three parameters as the preceding macro, three dimensions of an empty box:

- #1. The height.
- #2. The depth.
- #3. The width.

```
\def\RulesInSide #1#2#3{%
    {%
        \setbox 0 = \hbox{%
```

Mark the reference point of the box (if enabled).

```
            \ifBulletAndBaseLine
                \copy\@BulletBox
            \fi
```

Draw the left vertical rule.

```
            \vrule width \BoxRuleThickness height #1 depth #2%
            \hskip #3%
            \hskip -\BoxRuleThickness
            \hskip -\BoxRuleThickness
```

Draw the right vertical rule.

```
            \vrule width \BoxRuleThickness height #1 depth #2%
            \hskip -#3%
```

Load \dimen2 with the depth of the top horizontal rule.

```
            \dimen2 = #1%
            \advance\dimen2 by -\BoxRuleThickness
```

Draw the top horizontal rule.

```
            \vrule width #3 height #1 depth -\dimen2
```

Return to the starting point of the preceding horizontal rule.

```
            \hskip -#3%
```

Load \dimen2 with the height of the bottom horizontal rule.

```
            \dimen2 = #2%
```

```
                \advance\dimen2 by -\BoxRuleThickness
```

Draw this rule now.

```
                \vrule width #3 height -\dimen2 depth #2%
            }%
```

Set all dimensions of the box just constructed (with rules) to zero and print the box.

```
            \ZeroBoxOut{0}%
        }%
}
```

9.3.6.4 The Definition of Macro \RulesOnSide

The macro \RulesOnSide generates rules that are *centered* on the borderline of the box (placement M). This macro is by far the most important one (in relation to the preceding two macros), because it is essential in the definition of the later following macros \HboxR, \VboxR, \VtopR, \BoxR, and so forth.

This macro has the same three parameters as the preceding two macros, three dimensions of an empty box:

- #1. The height.
- #2. The depth.
- #3. The width.

```
\def\RulesOnSide #1#2#3{%
    {%
        \setbox 0 = \hbox{%
```

Mark the reference point of the box (if enabled).

```
            \ifBulletAndBaseLine
                \copy\@BulletBox
            \fi
```

Draw the left vertical rule. Note that the rule is halfway inside the box and halfway outside.

```
            \hskip -0.5\BoxRuleThickness
            \vrule width \BoxRuleThickness height #1 depth #2%
```

Skip to the start of the right vertical rule.

```
            \hskip #3%
            \hskip -\BoxRuleThickness
```

Draw the right vertical rule.

```
            \vrule width \BoxRuleThickness height #1 depth #2%
```

Move back so that the current horizontal position becomes that of the reference point (the current vertical position is that of the reference point, from the beginning of the execution of this macro).

```
                \hskip -#3%
                \hskip -\BoxRuleThickness
```

Compute, in \dimen0, the length (width as far as TEX is concerned) of both horizontal rules.

```
                \dimen0 = #3%
                \advance\dimen0 by \BoxRuleThickness
```

Compute dimensions of the top horizontal rule: \dimen2 is the height, \dimen4 is the depth.

```
                \dimen2 = #1%
                \advance\dimen2 by 0.5\BoxRuleThickness
                \dimen4 = #1%
                \advance\dimen4 by -0.5\BoxRuleThickness
                \dimen4 = -\dimen4
                \vrule width \dimen0 height \dimen2 depth \dimen4
```

Undo the effect of moving to the right after drawing this rule.

```
                \hskip -\dimen0
```

Draw the bottom horizontal rule: \dimen2: height, \dimen4: depth.

```
                \dimen2 = #2%
                \advance\dimen2 by -0.5\BoxRuleThickness
                \dimen2 = -\dimen2
                \dimen4 = #2%
                \advance\dimen4 by 0.5\BoxRuleThickness
                \vrule width \dimen0 height \dimen2 depth \dimen4
            }%
```

Set all dimensions of the box to zero and then print the box.

```
        \ZeroBoxOut{0}%
    }%
}
\catcode`\@ = 12
```

• End of boxing5.tip •

9.3.6.5 Examples Using \RulesOutSide, \RulesInSide and \RulesOnSide

The preceding macros all generate boxes of zero dimensions. Following is the source code of an example so you can actually see this and an application of these macros in general.

• ex-boxing5.tip •

```
\input inputd.tip
\InputD{boxing5.tip}                    % 9.3.6.1, p. 327.
```

Set the thickness of all rules to 6 pt.

```
\BoxRuleThickness = 6pt
```

In the following, all `\Rules...` macro-calls generate boxes of zero dimensions, in particular zero width. Therefore, `\hskip`s had to be inserted to space the boxes out horizontally.

```
\line{%
     \hskip 5pt
     {\tt\string\RulesOutSide:} \RulesOutSide{10pt}{10pt}{30pt}%
     \hskip 40pt
     {\tt\string\RulesOnSide:}  \RulesOnSide{10pt}{10pt}{30pt}%
     \hskip 40pt
     {\tt\string\RulesInSide:}  \RulesInSide{10pt}{10pt}{30pt}%
     \hfil
}
```

• End of `ex-boxing5.tip` •

The output generated reads as follows:

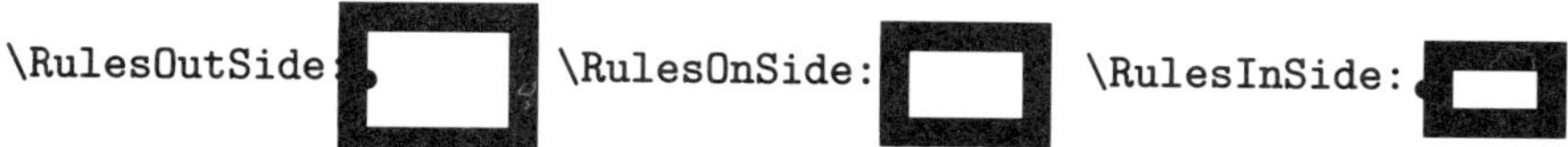

Here you can clearly see where the rules are drawn. For instance, because `\RulesInSide` draws the rules *inside* the borderline of a box, a relatively small amount of white space of 4 pt is drawn (this value can be computed by adding the height and depth of this box and subtracting twice the thickness of the rules). By contrast, if `\RulesOutSide` is used, the white area surrounded by rules is 20 pt high and 30 pt deep ("high" is used to refer to the sum of height and depth, of course).

9.3.7 The Definition of Macro `\BoxingE`

Having presented `\RulesOnSide` in the preceding Subsection, we can discuss a new boxing macro `\BoxingE` which fulfills the requirement for the "next generation of box-drawing macros." The source code containing the definition of this macro begins here.

$\mathcal{P}'$ • `boxing6.tip` •

```
\InputD{box-zero.tip}                    % 4.5.13, p. 104.
\InputD{boxing5.tip}                     % 9.3.6.1, p. 327.
\catcode`\@ = 11
```

The `\BoxingE` macro draws rules around a box, marking the reference point by a bullet and the baseline by a dashed line. In addition to that and contrary to the preceding `\Boxing...` macros, this is all done without a change in the dimensions or reference point of the box being generated. This macro has one parameter (`#1`), the box being drawn with rules around it.

Here is the definition of this macro.

```
\def\BoxingE #1{%
    \hbox{%
```

Save the user's box in a box register.

```
        \setbox\@BoxingBox = #1%
```

Draw the baseline using a dashed line computed from leaders.

```
        \setbox\@BaseLineLeaders = \hbox to \wd\@BoxingBox{%
            \xleaders\hbox to 4pt{%
                \hskip 1pt
                \vrule depth 0.4pt height 0.4pt width 2pt
                \hfil
            }%
            \hfil
        }%
```

Set all dimensions of the baseline box to zero.

```
        \ZeroBox{\@BaseLineLeaders}%
```

The following three items will be generated in the given order (nothing has been printed so far):

1. The baseline, with the help of leaders, is printed. A box with zero dimensions is generated; this feature is disabled if `\ifBulletAndBaseLine` evaluates to false.
2. The rules around the box (the macro used for that purpose will also mark the reference point by a bullet, if `\ifBulletAndBaseLine` evaluates to true). This feature can be disabled, see above.
3. The user's box itself.

```
        \ifBulletAndBaseLine
            \box\@BaseLineLeaders
        \fi
        \RulesOnSide
            {\ht\@BoxingBox}%
            {\dp\@BoxingBox}%
            {\wd\@BoxingBox}%
        \box\@BoxingBox
    }%
}
\catcode`\@ = 12
```

• End of `boxing6.tip` •

9.3.8 An Example of Using `\BoxingE`

The following TeX source code is used for an example with `\BoxingE`. This example also shows that `\BoxingE` calls can be nested inside each other.

```
\input inputd.tip
\InputD{boxing6.tip}                          % 9.3.7, p. 332.
$$
    \vbox{
        \BoxingE{\hbox{ABg}}
        \medskip
        \BoxingE{%
            \hbox{%
                \hbox{AB}%
                \raise 15pt \BoxingE{%
                    \hbox{DE}%
                }%
                \raise 25pt \BoxingE{%
                    \hbox{gg}%
                }%
            }%
        }%
    }
$$
```

This source code generates the following output:

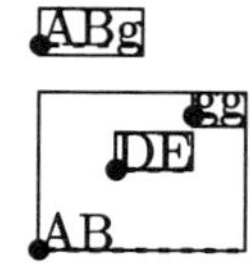

9.3.9 Replacing `\hbox` by `\HboxR`, `\vbox` by `\VboxR`, etc.

To push the idea discussed in the preceding Subsection even further, I designed macros `\HboxR`, `\VboxR`, `\VtopR`, `\BoxR` and `\CopyR`, which correspond to `\hbox`, `\vbox`, `\vtop`, `\box` and `\copy` respectively. These macros are equivalent to the extent that they allow the use of `spread` ⟨dimen⟩ and `to` ⟨dimen⟩ to modify their dimensions in the same way that `spread` ⟨dimen⟩ and `to` ⟨dimen⟩ can be used with commands `\hbox`, `\vbox` or `\vtop`. Henceforth `\xbox` will stand for one of these three primitives.

The main difference between the macros defined below and the original primitives is that here the boxes are printed with rules around them, the reference point is marked with a bullet, and the baseline is indicated by a dashed line.

Once you load these macros, `\XboxR` can be used instead of `\xbox` while debugging some TEX source code. The rules, reference point and base rule provide a clear indication of the placement and dimensions of boxes.

To disable the printing of rules and baselines later, enter `\let\XboxR = \xbox`; all boxes `\XboxR` commands are then interpreted as `\xbox` commands.

In my experience, these macros are *extremely* useful. For instance, they allow you to test output routines very easily because they provide a clear indication of the dimensions of a box. Compare, for instance, the output in Fig. 34.3, p. IV-68, with the output of Fig. 34.4, p. IV-69.

The following macros have also been designed in such a way that they can be used with `\bgroup` and `\egroup` to delimit the contents of a box. In other words, even in `\xbox\bgroup ABC\egroup` you can replace `\xbox` by `\XboxR`!

Furthermore, the macros can be used in a nested fashion (as you can have `\xbox` calls inside other `\xbox` calls, so also you can nest `\XboxR` calls). Calls of `\XboxR` can also be used in a `\setbox` type of setup; therefore `\setbox0 = \XboxR{...}` would be perfectly legal.

9.3.9.1 Initial Definitions for These Macros

Let us now define the macros that we just discussed.

$\mathcal{P}'$ • `boxing7.tip` •

```
\InputD{boxing6.tip}                        % 9.3.7, p. 332.
\InputD{vcentx.tip}                         % 7.5.5, p. 249.
\catcode`\@ = 11
```

`\@BoxRDimen` is a dimension register that is used to save ⟨dimen⟩ of an `\xbox spread` ⟨dimen⟩ or `\xbox to` ⟨dimen⟩ type of command.

```
\newdimen\@BoxRDimen
```

Save the user's box here in box register `\@BoxRBox` and the user's box register number in `\@BoxRNumber`.

```
\newbox\@BoxRBox
\newcount\@BoxRNumber
```

Now define macros `\HboxR`, `\VboxR`, `\VtopR`, and `\VcenterXR` which are identical to `\hbox`, `\vbox`, `\vtop`, or `\VcenterX` with rules around the box. The dimensions of the boxes with rules are identical (to the scaled point). Placement M is used for the placement of rules to mark the borderline of a box.

Note that there is *no* macro `\VcenterR` defined that would relate to `\vcenter` the same way `\xbox` and `\XboxR` relate. See 7.5.5, p. 248, for a brief comparison of `\vcenter` with `\vbox` and `\vtop`. The macros below do contain the definition of a macro `\VcenterXR`, which is a "ruled version" of `\VcenterX` (see the same reference).

9.3.9.2 Definitions of \HboxR, \VboxR, etc.

In the following definitions a box is started *immediately* allowing a `\XboxR` command to be used with `\setbox`.

The `\def\@WhichBox{\xbox}` definitions below are used to save the type of box requested by the user. The `\@WhichBoxDimen` macro's definition is either empty or expands to something like `to 1.4in` or `spread 20pt`.

Define `\HboxR` now.

```
\def\HboxR{%
```

```
      \hbox\bgroup
      \def\@WhichBox{\hbox}%
      \def\@WhichBoxDimen{}%
      \@BoxRaa
}
```

Next define \VboxR.

```
\def\VboxR{%
      \vbox\bgroup
      \def\@WhichBox{\vbox}%
      \def\@WhichBoxDimen{}%
      \@BoxRaa
}
```

Next define \VtopR.

```
\def\VtopR{%
      \vtop\bgroup
      \def\@WhichBox{\vtop}%
      \def\@WhichBoxDimen{}%
      \@BoxRaa
}
```

Next is the definition of macro \VcenterXR. This macro is special in the sense that \vcenter can only be applied in math mode, but that restriction does not apply to \VcenterXR. The macro \VcenterXR relates to \VcenterX, *not* \vcenter.

```
\def\VcenterXR{%
      \hbox\bgroup
      \def\@WhichBox{\VcenterX}%
      \def\@WhichBoxDimen{}%
      \@BoxRaa
}
```

Now define the macro \BoxR, which is identical to \box, except for its rules, reference point and baseline markings. Also define a macro \CopyR, the counterpart of \copy. Note that \BoxR and \CopyR start with an immediate creation of a box. The number of the box register to be printed is saved using \afterassignment.

Ultimately, a \BoxR or \CopyR call is simply converted to an \HboxR call, and the "real work" of drawing rules around the box contained in the box register is done by \HboxR. For the \BoxR command it doesn't really matter which box type is saved in \@WhichBox.

```
\def\BoxR{%
      \hbox\bgroup
      \def\@WhichBox{\hbox}%
      \def\@WhichBoxDimen{}%
```

Absorb the box register number and then continue execution by expanding macro \@BoxRB.

```
      \afterassignment\@BoxRB
      \@BoxRNumber =
```

```
}
```

This macro is called once the box register's number was collected.

```
\def\@BoxRB{%
    \HboxR{\box\@BoxRNumber}%
    \egroup
}
```

The code of \CopyR is almost identical to the code of \BoxR.

```
\def\CopyR{%
    \hbox\bgroup
    \def\@WhichBox{\hbox}%
    \def\@WhichBoxDimen{}%
    \afterassignment\@CopyRbb
    \@BoxRNumber =
}
\def\@CopyRbb{%
    \HboxR{\copy\@BoxRNumber}%
    \egroup
}
```

9.3.9.3 The Definition of Macro \@BoxRaa

Now define the macro \@BoxRaa. This macro's purpose is to determine in which of the following three ways \XboxR macro was called:

1. \XboxR {...}
2. \XboxR to ⟨dimen⟩ {...}
3. \XboxR spread ⟨dimen⟩ {...}

As before, \XboxR stands for one of \HboxR, \VboxR, \VtopR or \VcenterXR. The \futurelet primitive is used to look ahead to determine which of the cases of the preceding list applies. If case 1 applies, \@BoxRb is expanded, if case 2 applies, \@BoxRbTo is expanded, and if case 3 applies, \@BoxRbSpread is expanded.

```
\def\@BoxRaa{%
    \futurelet\@BoxRSymbol\@BoxRA
}
```

\@BoxRA branches by evaluating the \futurelet of the preceding macro.

```
\def\@BoxRA{%
    \ifx\@BoxRSymbol\bgroup
```

Case \XboxR {...} (case 1) applies.

```
        \let\@BoxitNext = \@BoxRb
    \else
        \if\@BoxRSymbol t%
```

Case \XboxR to ⟨dimen⟩ {...} (case 2) applies.

```
                \let\@BoxitNext = \@BoxRbTo
            \else
```

Case \XboxR spread ⟨dimen⟩ {...} (case 3) applies.

```
                \let\@BoxitNext = \@BoxRbSpread
            \fi
        \fi
        \@BoxitNext
}
```

9.3.9.4 The Definition of Macro \@BoxRb

The macro \@BoxRb drops the opening curly brace (or \bgroup) and assigns the user's box to box register \@BoxRBox, and then uses \BoxingE to draw rules around the box, mark the reference point, and mark the baseline.

```
\def\@BoxRb{%
    \afterassignment\@BoxRbTwo
    \let\@BoxDrop =
}
```

The following macro is called immediately after the opening curly brace (or \bgroup) is dropped. Now the user's box is assigned to box register \@BoxRBox. Because of the \aftergroup command macro \@BoxRbThree is executed.

The purpose of the following \expandafter below is to force the expansion of macro \@WhichBoxDimen *before* the expansion of \@WhichBox. This order of expansion is necessary, if \@WhichBox expands to \VcenterX.

```
\def\@BoxRbTwo{%
    \setbox\@BoxRBox = \expandafter\@WhichBox\@WhichBoxDimen\bgroup
    \aftergroup\@BoxRbThree
}
```

The following macro is called *after* the user's box was collected in box register \@BoxRBox. The box can be printed next and the group started at the beginning of \XboxR is terminated.

```
\def\@BoxRbThree{%
    \BoxingE{\box\@BoxRBox}%
    \egroup
}
```

9.3.9.5 The Definitions of \@BoxRbTo, \@BoxRbSpread, and \@BoxRbMoreSpreadTo

Macro \@BoxRbTo removes the "to" from the main token list, reads the dimension following "to" by using \afterassignment and then calls \@BoxRbMore-

SpreadTo.

```
\def\@BoxRbTo to{%
    \def\@WhichBoxDimen{to}%
    \afterassignment\@BoxRbMoreSpreadTo
    \@BoxRDimen =
}
```

The following macro does the same thing for the \XboxR spread type of call.

```
\def\@BoxRbSpread spread{%
    \def\@WhichBoxDimen{spread}%
    \afterassignment\@BoxRbMoreSpreadTo
    \@BoxRDimen =
}
```

The \@BoxRbMoreSpreadTo does the final work by building the user's box and assigning it to a box register (using \@BoxRbTwo defined above). Then the work continues as if it were a case 1 type of box (referring to the list of 9.3.9.3, p. 337). The purpose of the following \let is to drop the following opening curly brace or \bgroup.

```
\def\@BoxRbMoreSpreadTo{%
    \edef\@WhichBoxDimen{\@WhichBoxDimen \the\@BoxRDimen}%
    \afterassignment\@BoxRbTwo
    \let\@BoxDrop =
}
\catcode`\@ = 12
```

• End of boxing7.tip •

9.3.10 Examples

Examples of the \XboxR macros just discussed are next, printed side by side comparing \xbox and \XboxR type of macro calls.

9.3.10.1 First Example

Here is the input used in the first example:

```
\input inputd.tip
\InputD{boxing7.tip}                      % 9.3.9.1, p. 335.

\centerline{%
    \hbox{This is fun}%
    \hskip 20pt
    \HboxR{This is fun}%
}

\bigskip
```

```
\centerline{%
    \hbox{ABC \raise 10pt \hbox{XXX} KK}%
    \hskip 20pt
    \HboxR{ABC \raise 10pt\hbox{XXX} KK}%
    \hskip 20pt
    \hbox{ABC \raise 10pt \HboxR{XXX} KK}%
}
```

The input generates the following output:

This is fun This is fun

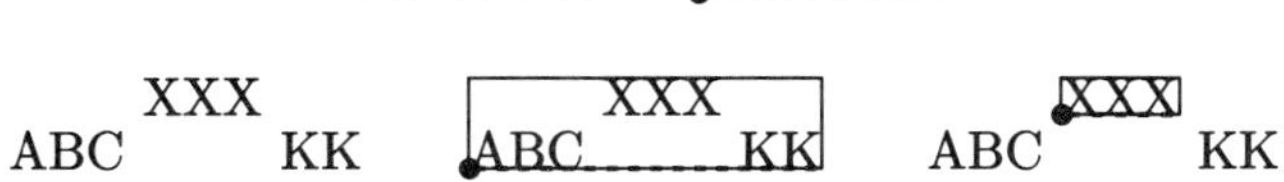

9.3.10.2 Second Example

The curly braces following an `\hbox` and an `\HboxR` can be replaced by `\bgroup` and `\egroup` as indicated in the second example. The input to this example reads as follows:

```
\input inputd.tip
\InputD{boxing7.tip}                    % 9.3.9.1, p. 335.
\centerline{%
    \hbox\bgroup This is fun.\egroup
    \hskip 20pt
    \HboxR\bgroup This is fun.\egroup
}
```

The output generated is the following:

This is fun. This is fun.

9.3.10.3 Third Example

Here is another `\HboxR to` example using the following source code (rather than writing `\HboxR to \hsize` you can use the macros of 9.3.13, p. 343).

```
\input inputd.tip
\InputD{boxing7.tip}                    % 9.3.9.1, p. 335.
\vbox{%
    \hbox  to \hsize{\hfil 1: This is fun.\hfil}
    \HboxR to \hsize{\hfil 2: This is fun.\hfil}
}
```

This example generates the following output:

1: This is fun.

2: This is fun.

9.3.10.4 The Fourth Example

Next I would like to include an example application of `\VcenterX` and `\VcenterXR`. Here is the source code used for the example.

```
\input inputd.tip
\InputD{boxing7.tip}                           % 9.3.9.1, p. 335.
\InputD{vcentx.tip}                            % 7.5.5, p. 249.
\centerline{\VcenterX{\hbox{This is fun.}\hbox{This too.}}}
\bigskip
\centerline{\VcenterXR{\hbox{This is fun.}\hbox{This too.}}}
```

This input generates the following output:

This is fun.
This too.

This is fun.
This too.

9.3.10.5 Dimensions and the \XboxR Macros

The dimensions of a box generated using `\hbox` and one generated using `\HboxR` are absolutely identical, as illustrated by the following example (these examples also show that the box resulting from an `\XboxR` call can be assigned to a box register using `\setbox`).

```
\setbox 0 = \hbox{%
    AB
    \raise 4pt \hbox{XX}
    \lower 20pt \hbox{XX}%
}
\setbox 1 = \HboxR{%
    AB
    \raise 4pt \hbox{XX}
    \lower 20pt \hbox{XX}%
}

The dimensions of box register~0 are (\the\ht0 \space +
\the\dp0 \space $*$ \the\wd0).

The dimensions of box register~1 are (\the\ht1 \space +
\the\dp1 \space $*$ \the\wd1).
```

The output generated by this example reads as follows:

The dimensions of box register 0 are (10.83331pt + 20.0pt ∗ 51.25009pt).

The dimensions of box register 1 are (10.83331pt + 20.0pt ∗ 51.25009pt).

9.3.11 Empty Ruled Boxes, \EmptyRuledBox

The following macro generates an empty ruled boxes and has the following three parameters:

- #1. Height.
- #2. Depth.
- #3. Width.

The definition of this macro begins here:

$\mathcal{P}'$ • emprubox.tip •

```
\catcode`\@ = 11
\newbox\@EmptyRuledBox
\def\EmptyRuledBox #1#2#3{%
    \setbox\@EmptyRuledBox = \hbox{}%
    \ht\@EmptyRuledBox = #1\relax
    \dp\@EmptyRuledBox = #2\relax
    \wd\@EmptyRuledBox = #3\relax
    \HboxR{\box\@EmptyRuledBox}%
}
\catcode`\@ = 12
```

• End of emprubox.tip •

9.3.12 Eliminating Ruled Boxes, \EliminateRuledBoxes

To *eliminate* all rules, marked baselines and so on call the following macro \EliminateRuledBoxes. Calling this macro is easier than editing your text and replacing every instance of \XboxR by \xbox. Also, once you have removed all \XboxR calls reinserting them back into the text is a pain, should you want to do so.

Macro \EliminateRuledBoxes is trivial: it uses \let to redefine all the \XboxR macros.

$\mathcal{P}'$ • boxrelim.tip •

```
\InputD{vcentx.tip}                       % 7.5.5, p. 249.
\def\EliminateRuledBoxes{%
    \let\HboxR = \hbox
    \let\VboxR = \vbox
    \let\VtopR = \vtop
    \let\VcenterXR = \VcenterX
    \let\BoxR = \box
    \let\CopyR = \copy
}
```

• End of boxrelim.tip •

9.3.13 `\LineR`, `\LeftLineR`, `\RightLineR` and `\CenterLineR`

I have found it very useful to use the following additional macro definitions. These macros closely resemble the `\line`, `\centerline`, ..., macros of 6.6, p. 185 (see the reference for an explanation of these macros and their arguments).

$\mathcal{P}'$ • `linesr.tip` •

```
\InputD{boxing7.tip}                          % 9.3.9.1, p. 335.
\def\LineR{\HboxR to \hsize}
\def\LeftlineR   #1{\LineR{#1\hss}}
\def\RightlineR  #1{\LineR{\hss#1}}
\def\CenterlineR #1{\LineR{\hss#1\hss}}
```

• End of `linesr.tip` •

9.3.14 The Combined Loading of the Most Important Box-Related Macros

This short macro source file loads all box and rule-related macros that are frequently used. I usually load this macro source file and do not bother with loading individual macro source files presented in this Chapter.

$\mathcal{P}'$ • `box-mac.tip` •

```
\InputD{boxing7.tip}                          % 9.3.9.1, p. 335.
\InputD{box-larg.tip}                         % 8.3, p. 298.
\InputD{emptybox.tip}                         % 4.5.12, p. 103.
\InputD{emprubox.tip}                         % 9.3.11, p. 342.
\InputD{boxrelim.tip}                         % 9.3.12, p. 342.
\InputD{linesr.tip}                           % 9.3.13, p. 343.
```

• End of `box-mac.tip` •

9.4 Summary

In this Chapter we learned:

- Simple graphs consisting of horizontal and vertical lines and square points can be easily drawn using the macros presented in this Chapter. These macros make use of the fact that when a box of zero dimensions is printed, the current reference point of TeX does not move (if this printing happens in vertical mode, interline glue must be disabled first, by calling `\offinterlineskip`).

- Macros drawing rules around boxes can be developed in such a way that these rules (and the marking of the reference point and the baseline) do *not* change the dimensions and the reference point of the resulting macros. Consequently one can define macros `\HboxR`, `\VboxR`, `\VtopR`, and `\VcenterXR`, which are essentially interchangeable with `\hbox`, `\vbox`, `\vtop`, and `\VcenterX`.
- The macros just discussed are extremely useful in any "box-intensive" TeX design. Enabling and disabling the "visible printing of boxes" is also quite straightforward.

Bibliography

Let me begin this bibliography with some general remarks about books relating to TeX and typesetting.

For books which may improve your knowledge with respect to typesetting and design, I would give the following recommendations: Tufte (1983) is a very interesting book concerning the design of tables. In Chicago (1982) you find a very valuable source concerning styles and any other information pertaining to writing books and many other types of documents. This book provides information about how to do indices, whether or not to capitalize a figure caption, what words to capitalize in a chapter or other title, and so forth. I have tried to follow the standards of this book.

In Lee (1979) you find an excellent book about bookmaking. Strunk (1979) is an old time classic. Concerning typesetting terminology, I find Craig (1978) extremely useful. The explanations in this book are very straightforward and to the point. This book's dedication reads, "Dedicated to the designer who uses phototypesetting without really understanding it." I found this to be true.

Note that Knuth (1986a) is frequently referred to as the TeXbook in this series.

If a reference below contains "`WEB` program," then this means that the documentation is part of a `WEB` program (which by definition contains its own documentation). All of the `WEB` programs cited below belong to a standard TeX distribution. There is now a very nice book you can read about `WEB` which I can highly recommend, because it very eloquently makes the case for "literate programming." See Knuth (1992).

In case you are looking for one of the file format definitions (such as the `pk` file type) be sure to use the references listed below, because some of the file types (for instance, the `dvi` file type) were redefined during the history of TeX.

As far as PostScript is concerned note that there are three books listed below. I added the specification "the red book," the "blue book" or the "green book" to it, because all three books carry distinctive colors and in particular in the early days when there were no alternative PostScript books available one usually referred to these books by their color. The former red PostScript book is now red and white (I personally don't like the new design that much) and that took away some from the colored references to these books.

Anyway, it is time for the bibliography itself now.

Bechtolsheim S (1988) Using the Emacs Editor to Safely Edit TEX Sources, Conference Proceedings, TEX Users Group, Ninth Annual Meeting, Montreal, August 24–24, 1988, TEXniques, Publications for the TEX Community, Number 7.

Bechtolsheim S (1989) A `dvi` File Processing Program, TUGBOAT, 10:3, pp. 329–332.

Bechtolsheim S (1990a) A TEX Font Catalogue, Integrated Computer Software, Inc., West Lafayette, IN.

Bechtolsheim S (1990b) TEXPS, A TEX POSTSCRIPT Software Package, Integrated Computer Software, Inc., West Lafayette, IN.

Bechtolsheim S (1990c) A Universal TEX Preprocessor and `make` Related Utility, Integrated Computer Software, Inc., West Lafayette.

Chicago Manual of Style (1982), Thirteenth Edition, The University of Chicago Press, Chicago

Craig J (1978) Phototypesetting: A Design Manual, Watson-Guptill Publications, New York.

Victor Eijkhout (1992) TEX by Topic, a TEXnician's Reference, Addison-Wesley Publishing Company, Inc., Reading, MA.

Fuchs DR (1981) The Format of `PXL` Files, TUGBOAT 2:3, pp. 8–12.

Fuchs DR (1982) The Format of TEX's `dvi` Files, TUGBOAT 3:2, pp. 14–19.

Guidelines (1990) Guidelines for the Preparation of a Typeset Camera-Ready Manuscript, Springer-Verlag, New York.

Herwijnen Eric van (1990) Practical SGML, Kluwer Academic Publishers, Dordrecht, Netherlands.

Kabelschacht A (1987) `\expandafter` vs. `\let` and `\def` in Conditionals and a Generalization of PLAIN's `\loop`, TUGBOAT 8:2, pp. 184–185.

Knuth DE (1983) The `PROFILE` Processor, Version 1.1, November 1983, `WEB` program.

Knuth DE (1986a) The TEX Book, Addison-Wesley Publishing Company, Inc., Reading, MA.

Knuth DE (1986b) TEX: The Program, Addison-Wesley Publishing Company, Inc., Reading, MA.

Knuth DE (1986c) The METAFONT Book, Addison-Wesley Publishing Company, Inc., Reading, MA.

Knuth DE (1986d) The Metafont Program, Addison-Wesley Publishing Company, Inc., Reading, MA.

Knuth DE (1986e) Computer Modern Fonts, Addison-Wesley Publishing Company, Inc., Reading, MA.

Knuth DE (1988) The `WEB` System of Structured Documentation, `WEB` program (`tangle`, `weave`) (documentation is part of the software).

Knuth DE (1989) The `GFtoDVI` Processor, Version 3.0, a `WEB` program.

Knuth DE (1990) The New Versions of TEX and METAFONT, TUGBOAT, 10:3, pp. 325–328.

Lamport L (1985) The LATEX Manual, Addison-Wesley Publishing Company, Inc., Reading, MA.

Lamport L (1987) *Makeindex*: an Index Processor for LATEX. Source code of document comes with the `makeindex` software.

Lee M (1979) Bookmaking: the illustrated guide to the design/production/editing, R. R. Bowker, New York.

Patashnik O (1985), BibTeXing, Version of May 23, 1985 (this documentation comes with the BibTeX software).

Platt C (1985) Macros for Two-Column Format, TUGboat 6:1, pp. 29–30.

PostScript (1985a) PostScript Language, Tutorial and Cookbook, Adobe Systems, Inc., Addison-Wesley Publishing Company, Inc., Reading, MA. The *blue* book.

PostScript (1985b) PostScript Language, Reference Manual, 2nd Edition, Adobe Systems, Inc., Addison-Wesley Publishing Company, Inc., Reading, MA. The *red* book.

PostScript (1988) PostScript Language, Language Program Design, Adobe Systems, Inc., Addison-Wesley Publishing Company, Inc., Reading, MA. The *green* book.

Rokicki T (1985) Packed (PK) Font File Format, TUGboat 6:1, pp. 115–120.

Rokicki T (1988) The `GFread` Processor, Version 1.1, July 11, 1988, `WEB` program.

Sewell W (1989) Weaving a Program, Literate Programming in `WEB`, Van Nostrand Reinhold, New York.

Shakespeare W (1605) King Lear, Edited by Alfred Harbage, Penguin Books, New York, revised edition 1970.

Solomon D (1990a) Output Routines: Examples and Techniques. Part I: Introduction and Examples, TUGboat 11:1, pp. 69–84.

Solomon D (1990b) Output Routines: Examples and Techniques. Part II: OTR Techniques, TUGboat 11:2, pp. 212–249.

Spivak M (1986) The Joy of TeX, American Mathematical Society, Providence, RI.

Spivak M (1989) LAMS-TeX The Synthesis, TeXplorators Corporation, Houston, TX.

Stallmann R (1986) GNU Emacs Manual, Free Software Foundation, Cambridge, MA.

Strunk W, Jr. and White EB (1979) The Elements of Style, Macmillan Publishing Co., Inc., New York, NY.

Tufte ER (1983) The Visual Display of Quantitative Information, Graphics Press, Cheshire, CT.

Webster (1985) Webster's Standard American Style Manual, Merriam-Webster, Inc., Springfield, MA.

Index

Each volume contains a comprehensive index. The index is followed by a separate index of all published source code files. Primitives in the index are marked by an asterisk, e.g., *\par.

Source Code File Index

This index is an index of all the *published* source code files in this series. Most macro source code files belong to the `texip` format (defined in 31.3, p. III-612). If you use this format no special action is necessary to use most of the published macro source files of this series. Those files which do *not* belong to the `texip` format are marked by an asterisk (*).